A HISTORY OF APOLOGETICS

THEOLOGICAL RESOURCES is a series of books taking its impulse from the striking renewal of interest in theology to-day. That renewal is unique in theological history, because its impetus derives from all the churches and because evidence for it abounds in all countries. The contributors to the series have been chosen, therefore, for their suitability to particular subjects rather than for denominational uniformity. There are two General Editors, John P. Whalen, formerly acting head of the Catholic University of America, and Jaroslav Pelikan, a prominent Lutheran Pastor, at present the Titus Street Professor of Ecclesiastical History at Yale University.

In commenting on the current theological revival, the General Editors write—'this interest, vital though it is, stands in danger of being lost in superficiality and trivialized into a fad. The answer to this danger is greater depth. *THEOLOGICAL RESOURCES* is intended to supply that depth.'

AVERY Robert *DULLES*

A HISTORY OF
APOLOGETICS

HUTCHINSON OF LONDON

CORPUS OF NEW YORK

HUTCHINSON & CO *(Publishers)* LTD
178–202 Great Portland Street, London W1

London Melbourne Sydney
Auckland Johannesburg Cape Town
and agencies throughout the world

First published 1971

*This book has been set in Times type, printed in Great Britain
on antique wove paper by Anchor Press, and
bound by Wm. Brendon, both of Tiptree, Essex*

ISBN 0 09 105150 9

Contents

Abbreviations

ActApS	*Acta apostolicae sedis.* Rome, 1909–.
AmEcclRev	*American Ecclesiastical Review.* Washington, 1889–.
AncChrWr	*Ancient Christian Writers.* Westminster, Md., and London, 1946–.
ANF	*Ante-Nicene Fathers.* Translations of the Writings of the Fathers down to A.D. 325. American rev. ed., 10 vols. New York, 1893–99; reprinted Grand Rapids, 1951–56.
AnalGreg	*Analecta gregoriana.* Rome, 1930–.
AnnalPhilChr	*Annales de philosophie chrétienne.* Paris, 1830–1913.
ArchFrPraed	*Archivum fratrum praedicatorum.* Rome, 1931–.
CDh	Anselm of Canterbury. *Cur Deus homo.*
C. gent.	Thomas Aquinas. *Summa contra gentiles.*
CorpRef	*Corpus reformatorum.* Halle, 1834–52; Braunschweig, 1852–96; Berlin, 1900–06; Leipzig, 1906–.
CSEL	*Corpus scriptorum ecclesiasticorum latinorum.* Vienna, 1866–.

DBSuppl — *Dictionnaire de la bible. Supplément*, edited by L. Pirot et al. Paris, 1928–.

Denz — H. Denzinger. *Enchiridion symbolorum, definitionum et declarationum de rebus fidei et morum.* 32d ed., rev. by A. Schönmetzer. Freiburg i. Br., 1963.

De ver. — Thomas Aquinas. *Quaestiones disputatae de veritate.*

DictApolFoiCath — *Dictionnaire apologétique de la foi catholique.* 4th ed. Edited by A. d'Alès. 4 vols. Paris, 1909–28; table analytique, 1931.

DivThomF — *Divus Thomas.* Fribourg, 1914–54.

DTC — *Dictionnaire de théologie catholique.* Edited by A. Vacant et al. 15 vols. Paris, 1903–50; indexes, 1951–.

EphemThLov — *Ephemerides theologicae lovanienses.* Bruges, 1924–.

FathCh — *The Fathers of the Church.* A New Translation. Edited by R. J. Deferrari et al. New York, 1947–60; Washington, 1961–.

Greg — *Gregorianum.* Rome, 1920–.

Hist. eccl. — Eusebius of Caesarea. *Historia ecclesiastica.*

JRelig — *Journal of Religion.* Chicago, 1921–.

LCC — *Library of Christian Classics.* Philadelphia, 1953–.

LexThK² — *Lexikon für Theologie und Kirche.* Rev. ed., by J. Höfer and K. Rahner. 11 vols. Freiburg i.Br., 1957–.

LoebClLib — *Loeb Classical Library.* London, New York, and Cambridge, Mass., 1912–.

LXX — Septuagint version.

MedRenSt — *Mediaeval and Renaissance Studies.* London, 1949–.

MelSciRel — *Mélanges de science religieuse.* Lille, 1944–.

NCE — *New Catholic Encyclopedia.* 15 vols. New York, 1967.

NicPNicChFath — *A Select Library of the Nicene and Post-Nicene Fathers.* Edited by P. Schaff. 14 vols. New York, 1886–1900. Second series, edited by P. Schaff and H. Wace, 1890–1900.

NouvRevTh	*Nouvelle revue théologique.* Tournai, Louvain, and Paris, 1869–.
PG	*Patrologia graeca.* Edited by J. P. Migne. 161 vols. Paris, 1857–66.
PL	*Patrologia latina.* Ed. J. P. Migne. 217 vols.; indexes, 4 vols. Paris, 1878–90.
Quasten Patr	J. Quasten. *Patrology.* 3 vols. Westminster, Md., 1950–. In progress.
ReallexAntChr	*Reallexikon für Antike und Christentum.* Edited by T. Klausner. Stuttgart, 1941–.
RechScRel	*Recherches de science religieuse.* Paris, 1910–.
RevScRel	*Revue des sciences religieuses.* Strasbourg, 1921–.
RHE	*Revue d'histoire ecclésiastique.* Louvain, 1900–.
SourcesChr	*Sources chrétiennes.* Edited by H. de Lubac et al. Paris, 1941–.
ST	Thomas Aquinas. *Summa theologiae.*
ThSt	*Theological Studies.* Woodstock, Md., 1940–.
VigChr	*Vigiliae christianae.* Amsterdam, 1947–.
Vulg	Vulgate.

Editors' Foreword

From the conflicts of the early church with Judaism and paganism to the modern 'warfare of science with theology,' no enterprise has more consistently dominated theological controversy than the defense of the claim that God has revealed himself definitively in the events and the message of the gospel. That claim has had to assert itself against alternative systems of absolute and final revelation (e.g., Judaism and Islam), against theories of general and universal revelation (e.g., syncretism, ancient and modern), against the denial of the possibility of revelation at all (e.g., rationalism and naturalism). Since the Enlightenment, the apologetic task has acquired a new centrality in theology. The questions raised by Descartes and Kant have pushed the epistemological issue to the fore, obliging theology, too, to give an account of its ways of knowing. The discoveries of modern science have rendered questionable the form and the content of many traditional doctrines purportedly based on revelation, such as creation *ex nihilo* in six days. The renewal of contact between Christendom and the world religions, brought on by the voyages of exploration and the expansion of Christian missions, has prompted the critics and even the defenders of the faith to raise the question of the uniqueness of Christianity with a new poignancy.

There is, then, no need to justify the inclusion of *A History of Apologetics* in such a series as this. But conventional apologetics is in the embarrassing position of answering questions that no one is asking any more. If the 'Gentiles' against whom Thomas Aquinas wrote his *Summa Contra Gentiles* were interested even then in the arguments he formulates, their modern descendants are not; and therefore his modern descendants dare not repeat his arguments as though they still spoke to the condition of our contemporaries. What is needed is an apologetic that will start with the *Sitz im Leben* of twentieth-century thought, listen to its criticisms, and put forth the truth-claims of the gospel both forcefully and modestly. This monograph lays the foundation for such an apologetic.

Traditionally, the partner of theology in the apologetic dialogue has been philosophy, often some form of idealism. But to assert the Christian understanding of revelation today, it is necessary to draw upon many other areas of human experience and reflection as well, and that is what the historical narrative of this monograph seeks to do. At least as distinctive is its appreciation of other perspectives than its own. The God who has revealed himself in Jesus Christ is the God of the whole world and of all men. Significantly, the history of Christian apologetics began with a similar openness, in the address of the apostle Paul on the Areopagus, and only rarely has this openness been matched in mainline theology. Christian theology still stands or falls with the claim to revelation. Whether one accepts that claim or rejects it, he will find here an instructive account of how the major systems of theology have formulated the case for Christianity.

J.P.W.

J.P.

Preface

In the minds of many Christians today the term apologetics carries unpleasant connotations. The apologist is regarded as an aggressive, opportunistic person who tries, by fair means or foul, to argue people into joining the Church. Numerous charges are laid at the door of apologetics: its neglect of grace, of prayer, and of the life-giving power of the word of God; its tendency to oversimplify and syllogize the approach to faith; its dilution of the scandal of the Christian message; and its implied presupposition that God's word should be judged by the norm of fallible, not to say fallen, human reason.

Some Christian apologists have no doubt been guilty on each of these counts. But it might pay to ask: when such charges are made, do the accusers have in mind the great masters of apologetics or rather the quacks, the shysters, the second-rate practitioners? Before passing judgment on apologetics as a whole, one ought to study the tradition at its best. Let us therefore look again at Clement and Origen, Eusebius and Augustine, Aquinas and Ficino, Pascal and Butler, Newman and Blondel. A closer look will reveal that many of the apologists were sincere and courageous men who viewed the relationship between faith and reason in many different ways. Men of prayer, some of them struggled for decades to know God's will for themselves. Learned men, they spared no pains to make sure that their religious commitment was intellectually honest. Men of talent, even of genius, they incisively probed both the dynamism of the human spirit in its quest for God and the dynamism of God's word as it encounters the spirit of man. Men of eloquence, some of them set down their reflections in immortal classics.

The present volume is not intended as an apology for Christianity, still less an apology for apologetics. It aims simply to tell the story of the various ways in which thoughtful Christians, in different ages and cultures, have striven to 'give a reason for the hope that was in them' (cf. 1 Pt 3.15). The goals and methods of apologetics have frequently shifted. The earliest apologists were primarily concerned with obtaining civil toleration for the Christian community—to prove that Christians were not malefactors deserving the death penalty. Gradually through the early centuries the apologies for Christianity became less defensive. Assuming the counteroffensive, they aimed to win converts from other groups. Some were addressed to pagans, others to Jews. Subsequently apologetics turned its attention to Moslems, then to atheists, agnostics, and religious indifferentists. Finally apologists came to recognize that every Christian harbors within himself a secret infidel. At this point apologetics became, to some extent, a dialogue between the believer and the unbeliever in the heart of the Christian himself. In speaking to his unregenerate self the apologist assumed—quite correctly—that he would best be able to reach others similarly situated.

Like other efforts to find the *logos* in the Christian *mythos,* or to give rational expression to the deepest movements of the human spirit, apologetics has been only partly successful. It has accounted for some things but has left others unexplained. Granted the inevitable disparity between motivation and reflection, between reflection and conceptualization, and between conceptualization and language, it is not surprising that apologists have often stammered in their attempts to give their real reasons for believing. If the human spirit is always a mystery to itself, it is still more mysterious when it wrestles with God, when the divine Spirit groans within it.

Besides encountering these general obstacles that face apologetics as such, individual apologists have been beset by a multitude of particular difficulties. They have suffered from the relatively undeveloped state of exegesis, historiography, or the natural sciences at the time they were writing. They have been subject to the *Zeitgeist* of their age and harried by the pressing practical problems confronting the Church at various historical junctures. They have also, of course, been humanly limited in their intellectual and other endowments. Quite properly, too, most apologists have sought to speak meaningfully to their contemporaries rather than to later generations. Not surprisingly, therefore, no apologist from previous centuries or generations precisely fills the prescription that might be written for a present-day apologetic. But a careful reading of the old masters in the field reveals that the same basic problems continually recur and that it is almost impossible to say anything substantially new. In such a time as our own, when many Christians find it especially difficult to articulate the reasonableness of their faith, it can be particularly profitable to review the record of the past.

In writing the history of apologetics I have had to make some difficult decisions regarding the authors to be included and the relative emphasis to be given to each. To avoid misunderstanding it may be helpful to mention some of the principles by which I have been guided.

On the supposition that Christian apologetics presupposes a commitment to Christianity as God's definitive revelation to mankind, I have generally excluded or mentioned only as background religious thinkers who did not look upon Christianity as their own religion or who did not accept it as a revelation. For this reason I have passed over Bergson and referred only briefly to Kant.

Seeking to limit myself to what may be called Christian apologetics, I have also omitted or mentioned only in passing controversialists whose primary concern was to prove that a certain form of Christianity—e.g., Anglicanism—was the true one. On this ground I have omitted authors such as John Jewel and William Chillingworth. If I have included some denominational apologists, such as Balmes and Harnack, it is generally on the ground that their arguments for their denominational affiliation practically coincided with their arguments for Christianity.

For similar reasons I have excluded thinkers whose primary contribution was to defend the credibility of certain particular doctrines, such as the inerrancy of the Bible, the virginity of Mary, the Real Presence, or whatever. Apologists of the 'question box' variety, numerous though they have been, fall outside the scope of a study such as this.

Because I am concerned here with the general credibility of Christianity, I have given attention—and, I hope, due attention—to Protestant as well as Catholic authors. It is fitting that tribute should be given to the great Protestant defenders of Christianity: since the 16th century Protestant and Catholic apologists have incessantly influenced and imitated each other.

In my selection of authors and comparisons between their works I have not sought to exclude all value-judgments, but I have tried to keep my subjective views from obscuring the materials themselves. For the most part I have been content to summarize objectively the writings of the apologists of the past. Such objective reporting would seem to be most in keeping with the nature and purposes of a 'resource' volume for this series.

Finally, I should explain that I make no effort in these pages to urge any particular theory about what apologetics ought to be. I am intending to follow up this volume with a companion piece on the theory of apologetics, in which I shall deal with the task, methods, and prospects of apologetics, especially in terms of the needs of the Church today. The present volume, however, should be able to stand on its own as an independent piece. Presumably it should fill a need, since no substantial history of apologetics, to my knowledge, has been recently published. The only complete historical surveys—those of Karl Werner, Otto Zöckler, and Jules Martin—were all composed more than 60 years ago; they were never translated into English and can be found only in a few well-stocked libraries.

The paucity of recent histories of apologetics is partly due to the fact that apologetics itself has for some time been under a cloud. The reputation of apologetics reached its nadir when Barth's influence was at its height—that is to say, from about 1920 to 1950. Since the 1950s, particularly among the younger Protestant theologians, there have been some indications that apologetics may be experiencing a revival. Schubert Ogden, an acute observer and participant in current theology, has recently said as much. 'The safest generalization about Protestant theology since World War II is that it has evidenced a growing concern with its inescapable apologetic task.'[1] In the minds of many Catholics apologetics still connotes the jejune rationalism of the manuals and tracts of the past century, but the recent revival of interest in Blondel and the efforts to answer objections such as those expressed by Charles Davis will perhaps pave the way for an apologetic renewal.[2]

If the theologians of the coming generation are to take full responsibility for the truth-claims that seem to be inseparable from Christianity itself, the apologetical task will have to be carried on. In view of all that has been learned from depth psychology about the unconscious, from sociology about ideologies and plausibility structures, from comparative religion about the faiths of other peoples, and from linguistic analysis about the hazards of metaphysical discourse, the contemporary believer can scarcely stave off the real difficulties by an easy appeal to 'blind faith.' Every Christian must somehow come to terms with the current objections to religious faith and weigh the legitimacy and rationality of his own commitment. As this effort is made, there will surely be a renewal of interest in the great apologists of the past. The present volume, I trust, will help to arouse and will to some degree satisfy such an interest.

It remains for me to express my gratitude to the many friends and advisers who have assisted me with this work. I am particularly indebted to Rev. John P. Whalen, to Rev. Earl A. Weis, S.J., and to the other members of the editorial board and staff of Catholic Theological Encyclopedia for their unfailing cooperation. I am likewise grateful to the late Dr. Martin R. P. McGuire of Corpus Instrumentorum, who read the first draft of this manuscript a few weeks before his regretted death on March 15, 1969, and to Professor Jaroslav Pelikan of Yale University, who gave me many valuable suggestions, especially concerning the patristic period and the Protestant theologians. I have also received helpful criticisms from the Rev. Christian P. Ceroke, O. Carm., of The Catholic University of America, and from the Rev. Joseph A. Fitzmyer, S.J., of the University of Chicago, both of whom read, in an earlier draft, the section on the New Testament. My colleagues at Woodstock College, the Rev. Walter J. Burghardt, S.J., and the Rev. Robert E. Carter, S.J., both supplied me with additional suggestions regarding the treatment of the Fathers of the Church. In a work such as this, one is necessarily dependent on more persons than one can name.

Woodstock, Md. AVERY DULLES, S.J.

CHAPTER ONE

Apologetics in the New Testament

The New Testament is primarily concerned with telling the story of Jesus and with drawing the consequences of that story for belief, for worship, and for the practical conduct of human life. On the surface the Gospels and Epistles, the Acts, and the Apocalypse appear to be addressed to convinced Christians. Unlike the apologists of the next centuries, the NT writers do not engage in arguments with unbelievers or vacillating believers as to why one should be a Christian. Reserving for later discussion the extent to which the authors of the NT may have been directly motivated by apologetical concerns, it is sufficient to affirm at the outset that a careful study of the NT throws considerable indirect evidence on the way in which the infant Church carried out its apologetical encounter with Judaism, with paganism, and with deviant tendencies that arose within the Christian community. This is apparent from the apologetically significant themes that are present, in a diffused way, throughout the NT.

APOLOGETICAL MOTIFS IN THE EARLY TRADITION

Before being an apologetic, Christianity was of course a message. It began as a conviction that Jesus was Messiah and Lord, and this conviction seems to have drawn its overpowering force from the event of the Resurrection. As the message concerning Jesus as risen Lord was proclaimed, it gave rise to certain questions and objections from inquirers, from believers, and from adversaries. In answer to such objections, and possibly also in anticipation of foreseen objections, the Christian preachers spoke about the signs and evidences they had found convincing. They insisted, for instance, that Jesus spoke with unique power, that He performed wondrous deeds, that He fulfilled the OT messianic prophecies, and that He had undoubtedly risen from the dead. Factual memories, dogmatic reflections, and apologetical arguments became so intertwined in the apostolic preaching that it would be artificial to try to draw a line between them. To the minds of believing Christians, the events themselves bore witness to the divine mission of Jesus, interpreted the meaning of His career, and served to clear up the doubts and difficulties that might arise in the minds of those called to believe. To some degree, therefore, apologetics was intrinsic to the presentation of the kerygma.

The Earliest Preaching

An unquestionably early statement, which stands close to the primitive Christian kerygma, may be found in the opening verses of 1 Corinthians, chapter 15. Here Paul, seeking to meet an objection concerning the general resurrection, adduces a standard series of testimonies to the Resurrection of Jesus and adds a personal recollection regarding his own encounter with the risen Lord. A similar mixture of proclamation and apologetic may be found in the so-called kerygmatic sermons of Acts (2.14–40, 3.12–26, 4.8–12, 5.29–32, 10.34–43, 13.13–41). C. H. Dodd and others have shown that these sermons contain statements that for the most part can be paralleled from the Epistles of Paul and that may therefore be presumed to stand close to the earliest proclamation.[1] From both sources one may infer that Christianity began as a proclamation that Jesus, being raised from the dead, had entered into His messianic lordship and was seated at God's right hand. Both Acts and Paul, moreover, view Jesus' humiliations, suffering and death as a divinely willed prelude to His glorious exaltation.

These Christian claims were of course contestable and had to be backed up by some kind of reasoned defense. The Christians appealed in the first instance to passages in the Psalms and the Prophets that were, they maintained, fulfilled by the Resurrection. This event, as understood by Christians, was the literal realization of what had been prophesied, for example, by Ps 2.7–8: 'I will tell of the decree of the Lord: He said to me, "You are my son, today I have begotten you. Ask of me and I will make the nations your heritage, and the ends of the earth your possession"' (cf. Acts 2.26, 13.33; Heb 1.5, 5.5).*

---

* Scripture will be quoted according to the Revised Standard Version (Oxford Annotated Bible; New York, 1965) unless special reasons demand a personal translation in an individual case. Psalms will be cited according to the Hebrew enumeration.

So too the exaltation of Jesus could be interpreted by reference to Ps 110.1, 'The Lord says to my lord: "Sit at my right hand till I make your enemies your footstool"' (cf. Mt 22.44 and parallels; Acts 2.34–35; Heb 1.13, 8.1, 10.12–13).

The Church also interpreted the Resurrection in terms of the Servant Songs of Isaiah (especially 42.1) and the Son of Man texts in Daniel (e.g., 7.13). Psalm 118 contained many verses that could be applied both to the Passion and to the Resurrection. Verse 22, 'The stone which the builders rejected has become the head of the corner,' as shall be seen, had many applications in controversy with the Jews. Psalm 16.9–10 was frequently quoted in the Septuagint version: 'Moreover my flesh will dwell in hope. For thou wilt not abandon my soul to Hades, nor let thy Holy One see corruption.' According to the argument that Luke places on the lips of Peter and Paul in Acts 2.25–28 and 13.35, this text was not literally verified in the case of David ('His tomb is with us to this day,' Acts 2.29; and he 'saw corruption,' Acts 13.36) but only in the case of Jesus, whom God raised to life.

In several NT texts the point is made that Jesus' Resurrection 'on the third day' fulfilled the Scriptures (1 Cor 15.4; cf. Lk 24.46). The insistence on the third day is not easy to explain by reference to OT prophecy, though perhaps an allusion to Hos 6.2 is intended. In answer to this difficulty some have suggested that Jesus Himself, in predicting His Passion and Resurrection, had called attention to the third day as the time of His revival (see, e.g., Mk 8.31, 9.31, 10.34). This suggestion, of course, is not certainly correct, since we cannot know the exact words used by Jesus.

The positive redemptive value of the Passion and death of Jesus would presumably have been an ingredient in the primitive preaching itself and cannot therefore be written off as an afterthought introduced for apologetical reasons. The earliest preaching appears to have viewed the Passion in the light of certain OT texts, such as Isaiah, chapter 53, and Zechariah, chapters 11 and 12, although these texts were not understood messianically by the Jews. In so utilizing the texts the Church may have been guided by Jesus' own understanding of His mission as servant, as He would have proposed it to His disciples.[2]

Apologetic Development

Once the Church had set forth its view of the death and Resurrection of Jesus, interpreted in the light of the Hebrew Scriptures, certain objections would naturally have arisen, thus prompting developments that were simultaneously dogmatic and apologetic.

The Ascension

It would have been asked, for example, where is the Messiah now and what difference has His alleged triumph made? In response to questions such as these, the Church would have adduced and perhaps amplified its conviction that Jesus was presently in heaven, reigning at the right hand of the Father (Ps 16.11, 110.1). In Acts 3.21 Luke portrays Peter as telling the Israelites that heaven must keep Jesus 'until the time for establishing all that God spoke by the mouth of his holy prophets from of old.' Paul in 1 Cor 15.25 teaches that Jesus must reign 'until he has put all his enemies under his feet' (cf. Ps 110.1). Other texts stress that it is He who will return in power as judge of the living and of the dead.

In the interim, Christ exercises His dominion on earth through the outpouring of the Holy Spirit. The early community called attention to its charismatic gifts as evidence that Jesus, having received the Holy Spirit, had poured it out in the manner foretold of the messianic era. Peter in his Pentecost sermon (Acts 2.16–21) quotes Joel 3.1–5 to this effect. Other New Testament authors allude to texts such as Ezek 36.27–28, in which the Lord promises to put His own spirit in the heart of the new Israel. The gift of prophecy is, in Paul's eyes, a particularly striking sign that God is among the Christian people (1 Cor 14.25).

The Passion

The humiliations and death of Jesus gave rise to a number of serious objections that had to be met by the Church's apologetic. The fact that Jesus was rejected by the leading authorities of the synagogue and was convicted of blasphemy was hard enough to explain. In addition, the very manner of His death was such as to call down upon Him the curse of Dt 21.23: 'a hanged man is accursed by God.'

To these difficulties the Christians replied that the humiliations and sufferings of Jesus were part of the redemptive plan of God set forth in the Fourth Servant Song (Is ch. 52–53): 'He was wounded for our transgressions, he was bruised for our iniquities; upon him was the chastisement that made us whole, and with his stripes we are healed' (Is 53.5). The objection regarding the curse incurred by Jesus is met by Paul with a somewhat complicated exegetical argument, the style of which would have been familiar to the rabbis of the time.

All who seek justification through the Law, he maintains, are under a curse, for it is impossible to keep the Law in its entirety. To them applies the text, 'Cursed be every one who does not abide by all things written in the book of the Law, and do them' (Gal 3.10, quoting Dt 27.26). To break the power of this curse, according to Paul, Jesus was made subject to the other curse mentioned in Dt 21.23. Having been cursed for man's sake, Jesus liberates man to seek justice not through the works of the Law but through faith in Him (cf. Gal 3:10–14).

The widespread failure of the Jews to recognize Jesus as Messiah presumably constituted a major obstacle to the evangelization of Israel. In answer to this difficulty, a number of OT quotations would seem to have been adduced. In addition to the Fourth Servant Song, mentioned above, the Christians appealed frequently to Is 6.9–10, which describes God's blinding of those who were to hear the preaching of Isaiah. This text, cited in all four Gospels and in Acts 28.26–27, was doubtless one of the pillars of the primitive apologetic.[3]

Not content with alleging the mere fact that God foresaw and intended the blindness of the Jews, Paul in Romans elaborates a theological explanation of their present situation—a problem that seems to have tormented Paul personally. In Romans, ch. 9 to 11, he argues that this does not mean that God has broken His promises to Israel or ceases to love His people, but simply that a provisional failure of the Jews as a group to recognize Christ is necessary to further God's total plan of salvation, which extends likewise to the Gentiles. Paul predicts that after the evangelization of the Gentiles is complete the Jews will claim their rightful inheritance and enrich both themselves and the Church by their acceptance of Christ.

A particular difficulty regarding the Passion that seems to have troubled the early Christians was the treachery of Judas. How could Jesus have miscalculated so seriously as to choose a traitor as one of the Twelve? This objection, like the others, was met in the first instance by Scriptural quotations. Jn 13.18 cites Ps 41.9: 'Even my bosom friend in whom I trusted, who ate of my bread, has lifted up his heel against me.' Mk 14.18 seems to contain an allusion to the same text and likewise insists that Jesus Himself was fully aware of what Judas was about to do. The Judas-apologetic was then extended to include the subsequent actions of Judas in selling his master, in buying the potter's field, and in hanging himself (or in suffering some kind of violent death, if one follows the popular account in Acts 1.18 rather than that in Mt 27.5). All these incidents are explained as fulfillments of OT predictions, as one may see, for example, from

Mt 27.3–10. Needless to say, there is legendary material in these passages.

A comparative study of the Passion narratives in the four Gospels reveals an increasing preponderance of apologetical motifs. This is apparent, first, in the growing insistence that every detail unfolds 'as it was written' in the OT. Also the Apostles are excused more and more for their cowardice, until, in the Fourth Gospel, Jesus Himself is portrayed as granting them leave to depart (Jn 18.8). Finally, the later traditions, especially in Luke and John, tend to exculpate the Romans, whereas there is a corresponding tendency to inculpate the Jews.[4]

Origins of Jesus

A further apologetical problem centered about the origins of Jesus. The early Church seems to have looked upon Him as having come from Galilee, without inquiring more closely into His descent and birthplace. Yet there was a tradition, supported by Scriptural texts (e.g., 2 Sm 7.12–13; Ps 89.3–4, 132.11–12; Dn 9.25), to the effect that the Messiah would be a royal scion of David's line and not an obscure villager from Galilee (cf. Jn 1.45–46). In response to this point of view, the Church seems to have taught at a relatively early period that Jesus was, in His human ancestry, a direct descendant of David (Rom 1.3; cf. Acts 13.17–23).

There was even an expectation that the Messiah was to be born in Bethlehem, the city of David (Mic 5.1; cf. Mt 2.5, Jn 7.42). The infancy gospels of Matthew and Luke explain that Jesus, although conceived in Nazareth, was born in Bethlehem. The manner in which the birth stories are told, especially in Matthew, indicates a strongly apologetic concern. This is evident, for example, from the way in which the term *Nazōraios* (which is subject to a variety of possible interpretations) is taken by Matthew as a reference to the town in which Jesus was to be conceived (Mt 2.23).[5]

The Public Life

Once it was claimed that Jesus was eligible as the Messiah thanks to His Davidic descent and that the very town of His birth was a fulfillment of prophecy, a host of problems arose concerning His public life. At what time, if at all, did Jesus claim to be the Messiah, and why did He not succeed in winning general recognition for His claims in His public ministry?

As regards Jesus' messianic claims, the early apologetic showed no interest in establishing, as many modern writers wish to do, the messianic consciousness of Jesus and its development. Rather, stress was placed on the fact that God pointed to Jesus as His beloved Son. Texts such as Ps 2.7 and Is 42.1, which originally had been taken to refer to the manifestation of Jesus at the Resurrection, were gradually transferred to the baptism of Jesus and even to His Transfiguration (Lk 3.22, 9.35; Acts 10.38; 2 Pt 1.17). According to some scholars the time of Jesus' manifestation as Messiah, originally viewed as the Resurrection, was gradually advanced in date until at length His birth was identified as the moment of revelation.[6]

As a means of reconciling the fact that Jesus really was the Son of God with the recollections concerning His actual ministry, which had not been conspicuously messianic, Mark uses the device known as the messianic secret. The manifestations of Jesus' messiahship in Mark usually occur only in the presence of a relatively small group of disciples, and Jesus on these occasions frequently commands the witnesses to be silent about what they have seen and heard until after He has risen from the dead (e.g., Mk 1.34, 44; 3.12; 5.42; 7.36; 8.30; 9.9). The messianic secret, of course, may have been something more than an apologetic device. In Mark's theology it brings out the hidden and mysterious character of the dawning of the kingdom, which is not intended to be revealed except to a small band of elite until the time for its general diffusion has arrived. Moreover, it is entirely possible that Jesus Himself may have wished to keep His identity secret from the majority of the Jews, since they would not have been capable of grasping His messiahship in accordance with Jesus' own conceptions.

The other synoptic Evangelists, while they do not stress the messianic secret except in passages borrowed from Mark, record Jesus' ambivalent attitude toward messianic appellations. On the one hand Jesus does not deny that He is the Messiah, thus giving an indication that He really is such; but on the other hand He never uses the term of Himself, and when others use it of Him He generally replies by substituting the term Son of Man. This term, which has its roots in Dn 7.13 and in the expectations of sectarian apocalyptic (Enoch, ch. 46 to 71; 2 Esdras 13.25–26, 29–32, 52), was perhaps more congenial to the self-understanding of Jesus than crudely messianic terms such as Messiah and Son of David.[7]

In order to account for the fact that Jesus' teaching became the property of a small band of disciples, the early Church made much of the mysterious and veiled manner of His public proclamation. He was said to have spoken for the most part in parables, the meaning of which eluded the majority of His hearers, whose minds were blinded.

In this connection the Evangelists make use of the text previously mentioned, Is 6.9–10, which is now placed upon the lips of Jesus Himself (Mk 4.12 and parallels). This quotation would seem to imply that Jesus, according to the early apologetic, deliberately used parables to prevent His doctrine from being understood by the generality of His hearers. Thus a point that the early community insisted upon for apologetic reasons ironically became an embarrassment to the apologetics of later centuries, which seeks to explain away the apparent harshness of Jesus' exclusivism!

Yet even the Twelve, as portrayed by Mark, are far from successful in penetrating the secret of the kingdom of God. The Evangelist keeps repeating that 'their hearts were hardened' (6.52; cf. 3.5, 8.17). On one occasion Jesus, alluding to the OT, puts to them the question, 'Having eyes do you not see, and having ears do you not hear?' (Mk 8.17; cf. Jer 5.21; Ezek 12.2). Even Peter thinks in a human rather than a divine way (Mt 8.33). Consequently none of the disciples understands the Passion predictions (8.32). The risen Jesus has to rebuke them roundly for their unbelief (Lk 24.25, 45; cf. Mk 16.14).

This obtuseness of the disciples, while it doubtless rests upon authentic recollections, serves the purposes of apologetic insofar as it explains why the disciples, during Jesus' lifetime, understood so little of His person and mission. It also makes more impressive the conversion that they underwent under the impact of the Easter events.

The Miracles of Jesus

Just as the preaching of Jesus is presented as intelligible only to a few and as very imperfectly understood even by them, so too, according to the Evangelists, the miracles were of limited evidential value. They furnished sufficient indications of Jesus' mission but were not so overwhelming as to convince all who saw them. Thus the early Church could point to the miracles as signs truly marking Jesus out as one 'approved by God' (Acts 2.22) and yet could explain why, in spite of these signs, Jesus' contemporaries did not recognize Him as Son of God until after His Resurrection.

While all the Gospels present the miracles as aids to faith, a difference of emphasis may be noted between the Synoptic Gospels and John. The Synoptic Gospels portray the miracles as works of divine power, evoking wonder and amazement. They are seen predominantly as acts by which Satan is overthrown and the kingdom of God is inaugurated, and only in connection with this efficacy does their sign value become apparent. In the Fourth Gospel, however, the miracles are studied more reflectively from the point of view of their symbolic or didactic significance. The number of miracles is sharply reduced; only seven are narrated in the public ministry. The significance of these seven is brought out by long interpretative discourses, and in these discourses the miracles are related to the person of Jesus rather than primarily, as in the Synoptics, to the dawning of the kingdom of God.[8]

Notwithstanding this difference of emphasis, all four Gospels recognize the miracles as providing motives of credibility. Jesus does not indeed consent to perform miracles merely in order to display His supernatural power, as if to overwhelm and compel the assent of others. Ordinarily speaking, some measure or degree of faith is pre-required on the part of those who ask for miracles.[9] Jesus rebukes those who demand extraordinary signs as a condition for faith in Him, and praises those who believe in simple reliance on His word. Yet He insists also that the signs He works are such as to increase the culpability of those who, having seen His works, still refuse to believe (cf. Mt 11.20–24; Jn 15. 24). If the miracles authenticate the message of Jesus, this is in great part because they blend harmoniously with the good news of salvation that He brings into the world, in accordance with the promises and expectations that stem from the OT.[10]

CHANGING CONTEXTS: ACTS, PAUL, AND HEBREWS

In order to disentangle the various strands of New Testament apologetics, it will be helpful to keep in mind the contrasting situations in which the Church found itself at various stages in the 2d half of the 1st century.

Acts

Some good indications concerning this development, especially in the early period, are furnished by the book of Acts.[11] The original proclamation of the kerygma and the polemical encounters that this provoked between the young Church and normative Judaism have already been commented on here. In successive chapters of Acts, Luke has given miniature sketches of the Church's apologetic in various situations. Stephen's defense, in chapter 7, is in fact a counterattack on Palestinian Judaism from the point of view of the Greek-speaking, or Hellenist, wing of the early Church. Stephen proclaims in the boldest terms that God does not dwell in manmade temples but is to be sought through the Prophets and especially through Christ, whom Stephen identifies as the prophet like himself predicted by Moses (Dt 18.15–18). The Jews of the 1st century are in Stephen's eyes—like their ancestors—a stubborn people 'uncircumcised in heart and ears' who never cease resisting the Holy Spirit and who have persecuted all the true Prophets of God (7.51–52). Some of the same arguments urged by Stephen in his own defense will be taken up again in the Epistle to the Hebrews.

In chapter 10 Luke briefly indicates the manner in which Christianity was proclaimed to the uncircumcised on Palestinian soil. The address of Peter to the household of Cornelius in verses 36–43 reads like an expanded version of the Christological sections of the Pentecost speech in chapter 2. As some have noted, the theology is characteristically Lucan—especially the idea that Jesus was anointed with the Holy Spirit and with power (v. 37). Considerable stress is laid on the healings and exorcisms of Jesus and on the testimony of those who were privileged to eat and drink with Jesus in His risen life.

Beginning with chapter 11 the focus of interest in Acts shifts to the Gentile world. In chapter 14 Luke begins to show the shape that Christian proclamation took when confronted by paganism. The population of Lystra, amazed at the healing of the cripple, addresses Barnabas and Paul respectively by the titles of Zeus and Hermes. The Apostles take the occasion to launch a vigorous attack on polytheism.

> We also are men, of like nature with you, and bring you good news, that you should turn from these vain things to a living God who made the heaven and the earth and the sea and all that is in them. In past generations he allowed all the nations to walk in their own ways; yet he did not leave himself without witness, for he did good and gave you from heaven rains and fruitful seasons, satisfying your hearts with food and gladness. [14.15–17]

This popular type of natural theology prepares for Paul's apologetic to the cultured Greeks at Athens.

Acts 17 gives Luke's account of Paul's address to the Council of the Areopagus. Opening with a tactful *captatio benevolentiae* Paul is presented as complimenting the Athenians on their religiousness and as calling attention to one of the altars dedicated 'to an unknown god'; this affords him grounds for declaring that he is not preaching any strange and outlandish deity. 'What therefore you worship as unknown, this I proclaim to you' (v. 23). He then declares firmly to the Athenians that God is the creator of all things, that He does not dwell in manmade shrines, and that He in no way depends upon

His creatures for any benefit to Himself. All mankind is one, and all nations are intended by God to seek and find Him. That God is intimately near to each man Paul proves by quotations from two Greek poets, Epimenides and Aratus. Then, reiterating a point already made at Lystra, Paul adds that in times past God mercifully overlooked the idolatry of the pagans. Now, however, all men are called upon to turn to the true God, who has drawn near in Christ. In conclusion Paul warns his hearers that God will judge the whole world through this man, whom He has raised from the dead.

The doctrine of the Resurrection provoked scorn and incredulity among Paul's philosophically minded auditors at Athens. Even among Christian converts—as one learns from 1 Corinthians—this doctrine was to meet with misunderstanding and resistance. Paul's apologetic to the Athenians, while it seems to have met with success as long as he was talking about God and religion in general terms, was rejected at the point where he introduced Christology.

For the purposes here it is not necessary to settle the long-standing controversy as to how accurately Luke summarizes what Paul actually said on this or indeed on any occasion. Dibelius, Pohlenz, and others have maintained that the speech, shot through with Stoic natural theology, could not possibly represent the authentic thinking of Paul.[12] But in his widely noticed doctoral dissertation, *The Areopagus Speech and Natural Revelation*, Bertil Gärtner plausibly contends that the leading ideas of the Areopagus speech are not those of pagan philosophical theology but of Jewish monotheistic propaganda, which had already, even before the time of Paul, taken up some Stoic themes and inserted them into the Israelite religious tradition.[13]

Paul

In the earliest of his letters (A.D. 50–51), Paul writes from Corinth to his converts at Thessalonica which he visited shortly before he visited Athens on his second missionary journey. He shows somewhat the same mentality that is reflected in the Areopagus sermon. Others tell us, he states in his congratulatory preface, 'how you turned to God from idols, to serve a living and true God, and to wait for his Son from heaven, whom he raised from the dead, Jesus, who delivers us from the wrath to come' (1.9–10).

In his first letter to the Corinthians, whom Paul had evangelized shortly after his stay at Athens, he again exhibits his distrust of Greek wisdom and his well-founded fear that philosophy, which for the Greeks always involves commitment to a determinate way of life, could corrupt the faith of his new converts. In the early chapters of this letter Paul draws a sharp contrast between two modes of religious knowledge, the one consisting of human wisdom, the other of obedience to divine revelation. For Paul, the first leads only to pride and delusion. In order to put an end to the boastfulness of philosophy, God has chosen to save the world by what the unspiritual regard as foolishness, especially by the crowning foolishness of the cross. Paul does not wish to support his preaching by any philosophical argumentation but solely by the power of the Holy Spirit, who gives fecundity to the preaching of the revealed word (1 Cor 3.6). Paul's discussion of the relationship between faith and reason in the opening chapters of 1 Corinthians was to provide eloquent texts for all those theologians who in subsequent centuries were to glory in the contrast between the two.

As already mentioned, Greek philosophy seems to have led the Corinthians into difficulties regarding the resurrection of the body. Paul replied that if bodily resurrection were not possible, it would follow that Christ had not risen and hence that the cornerstone of the apostolic preaching was a falsehood. Lest anyone should entertain such a suspicion, Paul reiterated the grounds of the Church's Resurrection faith. He founded this exclusively on the testimonies of those to whom the risen Christ appeared, and his list of primitive testimonies still constitutes one of the strongest apologetic arguments for the actual occurrence of Jesus' Resurrection.

In his letter to the Romans Paul gives the fullest statement of his case against idolatry, which he regards as the ultimate source of all the moral degradation in the pagan world. This idolatry is in Paul's view an inexcusable defection from the original worship of the one true God. 'For although they knew God they did not honor him as God or give thanks to him, but they became futile in their thinking and their senseless minds were darkened. Claiming to be wise, they became fools, and exchanged the glory of the immortal God for images resembling mortal man or birds or animals or reptiles' (Rom 1.21–23). Although Paul's primary intention here is to confirm his readers in their worship of the true God and to account for the depravity of their pagan contemporaries, he is probably aware of the apologetical implications of his remarks. To worship the true God is the only reliable safeguard against falling into the vices here described.

In a full treatment of Paul's apologetic it would be necessary to consider also his answer to various heretical tendencies that he seeks to crush. Especially in his letters to the Galatians and Colossians he argues against a servile reliance on the prescriptions of the Mosaic Law and a superstitious worship of angels. He shows how these deviations are basically incompatible with Christian faith and with the freedom of the Christian man.

Hebrews

While it is not genuinely Pauline in its authorship, the Epistle to the Hebrews may conveniently be mentioned here. In the subtitle of his respected commentary on this letter,[14] Alexander B. Bruce called it 'the first apology for Christianity.' In correspondence with a community of Christian converts from Judaism who were in danger of slipping away from their faith, the writer set out to commend Christianity as the perfect religion. He faced, in particular, three stumbling blocks: first, that the divinely appointed religion of Israel should have been eclipsed; second, that Jesus should have had to undergo suffering and humiliation; and third, that Christianity lacked a sacrificial ritual comparable to that of Judaism. In his reply the author showed that Christ fulfilled and surpassed everything for which men formerly looked to angels, to Moses, to Aaron, and to the priests and Prophets of the Old Law. The detailed and systematic theology of mediation contained in this Epistle is of great dogmatic significance, but it also has, as Bruce contends, an apologetic aspect. In the latter half of the 20th century, when the Christian churches are witnessing the collapse of many time-honored beliefs and practices, it is encouraging to read again the message of Hebrews, which calls for a dynamic and forward-looking faith similar to that of Abraham when he set forth from Ur 'not knowing where he was to go' (11.8).

THE FOUR EVANGELISTS AS APOLOGISTS

Before concluding this analysis of the NT one must ask to what extent the four Gospels (and Acts, which is the second part of Luke's Gospel) fit into the category of apologetic documents. As is obvious at a glance, they bear little resemblance to modern apologetical treatises. They are narrative in form and contain little sustained argumentation. They purport to tell a story rather than to prove a case. Yet the question may still be asked to what degree they are motivated by the intention of persuading unbelievers to accept Christianity or of helping believers to overcome their doubts and hesitations. If one defines apologetics in terms of this general inten-

B

tion, one will find at least an apologetical ingredient in all these writings.

Mark

Of the four Evangelists, Mark stands closest to the primitive kerygma. He is content to do little more than present the figure of Jesus as the Church remembers Him in faith and to watch Him in action as He struggles against the demonic forces that hold mankind in weakness, ignorance, and fear. Mark presents an unforgettable portrait of the Son of God at war with the Satanic powers arrayed against Him. With divine power Jesus casts out demons, cures illnesses, forgives sins. Even the unruly elements are subject to His mighty word. When unjustly accused by the Scribes and Pharisees, Jesus majestically silences their objections. When the disciples begin to doubt or to weaken, Jesus confirms their wavering faith with a word of comfort, rebuke, or explanation. The event of the Resurrection, toward which the whole Gospel ineluctably moves, signifies the triumph of Jesus' power over all the forces of evil—sin, sickness, death, blindness, and unbelief.

In narrating this sublime history Mark furnishes abundant materials for the defense of the Christian faith. He explains why the disciples were first drawn to Jesus and strongly held to Him and why Jesus in spite of His sovereign power was rejected and put to death. He makes much of the enthusiasm of the crowds who followed Jesus in Galilee and Jerusalem and shows how the very popularity of Jesus aroused the jealousy of the chief priests. He quite frankly exposes the doubts, confusion, and discouragement of the disciples, which prevented them from fully understanding what Jesus was saying until He had risen from the dead.

Much of the apologetical material in Mark is simply taken over from the pre-Markan tradition. But Mark adds, as has been noted, his own special emphasis on the messianic secret and on the explicitness with which Jesus predicted the events of the Passion.

Summarizing Mark's intentions, Bishop Rawlinson remarked that this Gospel was written 'partly to edify converts, and to satisfy a natural curiosity about how Christianity began, and partly to supply Christian preachers with materials for missionary preaching, and partly also to furnish a kind of armoury of apologetical arguments for use in controversy with opponents, whether Jewish or heathen.'[15] Far from excluding one another, these various motives would have been mutually supportive.

Matthew

Matthew's Gospel, like Mark's, is undoubtedly written for a community of believing Christians, not for outsiders. Yet it has considerable apologetical significance, for it contains materials developed for the use of converts from Judaism. In all probability the Evangelist was writing for a group that 'was still beset by antagonistic Jews at close quarters and therefore required both directly apologetical material and also the narrative of "how it all began" which is indirectly of great apologetical importance.'[16] Although some have called Matthew the Gospel for the Jews, Moule remarks that it might more correctly be called the 'Gospel against the Jews,' for it contains an abundance of ammunition for Christians under attack from non-Christian Jews.[17] Matthew's pervasive use of prophetic texts with assertions of their fulfillment in the life of Jesus is obviously designed to prove to rabbinic readers that Jesus is, as the Church claims, the divinely promised Messiah. As a subsidiary purpose, Matthew aims to explain to Jewish-Christian readers why the Gentiles are taking over the kingdom of God, and this too pertains to his apologetic.[18]

In the narrative sections peculiar to Matthew, apologetical concerns are evident. For example, the Matthean infancy narrative is built around five scriptural quotations with solemn assertions regarding their fulfillment in particular incidents. Later, to account for the humble and unobtrusive character of Jesus' public ministry, Matthew introduces a long quotation from Is 14.1–4, which may be taken as Matthew's summary of Jesus' career, ending with the prediction that the beloved Servant will bring 'justice to victory; and in his name will the Gentiles hope' (Mt 12.21). In the central section of his Gospel, Matthew introduces a number of important pericopes regarding the Church and Peter's position in it. These texts, the most famous of which deals with Peter's reception of the keys to the kingdom of heaven (Mt 16.19), have provided materials for ecclesiastical apologetics in subsequent centuries. The long series of woes against the Scribes and Pharisees in chapter 23 is presumably designed to combat the claims of rabbinic Judaism in the Evangelist's own time. The story of the Passion and Resurrection, as Matthew presents it, has a great number of legendary features evidently introduced for apologetical motives. Among these one may signalize the suicide of Judas (27.3–6), Pilate's wife's dream (27.19), and the stationing and the bribery of the guards at the tomb of Jesus (27.62–66, 28.11–15).[19]

Luke-Acts

Luke and Acts constitute a two-volume work, the purpose of which is stated in the preface to the Gospel, Lk 1.1–4, the operative words of which are: 'It seemed good to me also, having followed all things closely for some time past, to write an orderly account for you, most excellent Theophilus, that you may know the truth concerning the things of which you have been informed.'

There has been much speculation as to the identity of Theophilus, a name that is literally translated God-loving (or possibly, loved by God). Some have supposed that he was the lawyer who undertook Paul's defense at Rome and that Luke was supplying materials for use at the trial, but this scarcely seems likely in view of the abundance of material in Luke and Acts that would not be useful for forensic purposes. Others have suggested that Theophilus was the secret name by which Flavius Clemens, the first cousin of the Emperor Domitian, was known in the Roman Church.[20] Clemens's wife, Domitilla, is known to have been a Christian, and he himself was at least an inquirer. In support of this theory is the fact that the title *Your Excellency* implies a high position in Roman society. If Luke wrote for Clemens, the work would have been written about A.D. 95 and its purpose would presumably have been, in part, to win civil toleration for the Christian religion.

Whoever Theophilus may have been, there are good grounds for thinking that Luke hopes through his history to win favor for Christianity on the part of Roman authorities. He gives a generally flattering portrait of the Romans who enter his story. In the Gospel he is at pains to show that Pilate was not responsible for the death of Jesus—three times over he declares him innocent (23.4, 14, 22)—but that the guilt rested upon the Jewish priests and the mob incited by them. At the moment of Jesus' death the Roman centurion loudly proclaims His innocence (23.47). Throughout the book of Acts Luke shows esteem for Roman justice. Sergius Paulus (Acts 13.7, 12), the magistrates at Philippi (Acts 16.37–39), Gallio at Corinth (18.12–17), the Asiarchs and other officers at Ephesus (19.31, 35–41), Felix, Festus, and others in Palestine (Acts, ch. 24 to 26) exemplify the positive value of the imperial law in protecting Paul from the unjust allegations of hostile Jews, even though Felix at one point hopes for a bribe (24.26) and Festus seeks to win favor from the Jews (24.27). All of this fits in well with the theory that Luke-Acts might have been a kind of political apologetic.

This intention, however, by no means accounts for everything in Luke's work. By his own declaration, he is writing for the sake of grounding more securely in the tradition someone who has already been instructed in Christianity. The most salient characteristic of Luke's work, as Conzelmann points out,[21] is its original theology of redemptive history, which meets a theological need of the Church in the closing decades of the 1st century. As the years rolled on, it became apparent to the early Christians that the end of the world could no longer be regarded as imminent.[22] Luke was one of those who undertook to recast the Christian message in a way that would allow for a continuation of life in this world notwithstanding the fact that the 'last age' had come with the Christ-event. In this connection he developed a new theology of the Church and of the Holy Spirit. He depicted the Church as the messianic society of mutual charity and peace. This larger theologico-apologetical purpose is connected with the political apologetic. Because Christianity was a continuing fact of history, 'it was necessary to establish a harmonious working relationship between the Church and the supreme secular powers.'

John

The Fourth Gospel, like the third, contains an explicit declaration of the author's purpose: 'these [signs] are written so that you may believe that Jesus is the Christ, the Son of God, and that believing this you may have life in his name' (20.31). Exegetes, however, do not agree as to whether the author here has in mind the leading of unbelievers to Christian faith or the fostering of the life of faith in those who already believe in Christ.

From an analysis of the contents of the Gospel, in the light of what is known about the religious situation at the time in a locality such as Ephesus, one can think of various groups that the Evangelist might have been addressing. The constant insistence throughout the early chapters on the superiority of Jesus to John the Baptist (cf. 1.8–9, 1.20, 3.30, 3.38) suggests the possibility that one purpose of the Gospel may have been the refutation of the claims of some of the sectarian followers of the Baptist, who apparently flourished in and about Ephesus (Acts 19.1–7).

One of the most striking features of the Fourth Gospel is its recurrent use of the term 'the Jews' as a technical term for the religious authorities hostile to Jesus (as contrasted with the term Israel, which for John is a title of honor). Jesus Himself, as portrayed by John, resorts to rabbinic techniques of argumentation in order to defend His right to be called the Son of God (10.34–36, cf. 8.44–47, 54–55).

These disputes give the impression of reflecting the struggle going on in the Church in John's own time rather than during the life of Jesus, when a term such as 'the Jews' would not have had this restricted application. John's Gospel, moreover, is studded with formula quotations from the Jewish Scriptures, somewhat similar to those of Matthew. He introduces such quotations to explain, for example, the unbelief of the Jews (12.38), the treachery of Judas (13.18), the parting of Jesus' garments and the casting of lots for His seamless robe (19.24), and His limbs being unbroken (19.36).

Features such as these have suggested to some modern authors (van Unnik, J. A. T. Robinson) that the primary intent of the Gospel may have been to serve as a missionary handbook to help convert diaspora Jews. But Raymond E. Brown seems to be on safer ground when he emphasizes rather the defensive purpose of the Gospel, to sustain the faith of Christians who were under attack from Jewish propaganda. Yet Brown concedes that there was one group that John may have been addressing with a certain missionary hopefulness— Judeo-Christians in the diaspora synagogues who accepted Christ but had not yet broken with Judaism. Chapter 9, as Brown points out, lends itself easily to being interpreted as an invitation to such Judeo-Christians to imitate the courage of the man born blind and to accept excommunication for their faith in Jesus.[23]

But John's horizons are far wider. He records the Christian witness in a way calculated to appeal to men looking for light in the Hellenistic world at the close of the 1st century. The universal significance of Christ as the light and savior of the world is clearly brought out. The Word who enlightens every man (1.9) becomes flesh to save the world (3.17, 4.42) and is raised up in order to draw all men to Himself (12.32). His redemptive purposes extend not only to the Jewish nation but to all the scattered children of God (11.52), including the other sheep not of Israel's fold (10.16). In his use of cosmic imagery (e.g., light, life, word) John draws upon a vocabulary that would have been familiar not only to Hellenistic Jews but to the cosmopolitan population of a city such as Ephesus, where Oriental faiths, entering into contact with Greek philosophy, were issuing in mystery religions and Gnostic speculations such as have survived in the *Corpus hermeticum*. While one has no proof of direct contact between John and the Hermetic literature, the two may easily be understood as coming out of a similar background; C. H. Dodd and C. K. Barrett have shown this.

Although various Church Fathers report that John's Gospel was directed against heretics such as Cerinthus (Irenaeus), Ebion (Jerome), and Valentinus (Victorinus of Pettau), a careful study of the Gospel, as Brown points out, gives little support for the view that the refutation of Christian heresy was a major concern of the author.

All things considered, it seems likely that John had chiefly in mind as probable readers the Christians living in a city such as Ephesus. Barrett correctly observes that 'it seems very doubtful whether anyone, however intelligent, who had not a good grounding in the gospel tradition and elementary Christian theology would appreciate it.'[24] The subtle liturgical and sacramental allusions throughout the Gospel would surely pass over the heads of even highly educated pagans. Thus it would be an error to look upon this work, any more than any other of the NT writings, as primarily addressed to those who did not yet profess the Christian faith. John's Gospel is undoubtedly aimed at sustaining and intensifying the life of faith of all its readers, and in this sense has affinities with apologetical literature.

CONCLUSION

While none of the NT writings is directly and professedly apologetical, nearly all of them contain reflections of the Church's efforts to exhibit the credibility of its message and to answer the obvious objections that would have arisen in the minds of adversaries, prospective converts, and candid believers. Parts of the NT—such as the major Pauline letters, Hebrews, the four Gospels, and Acts—reveal an apologetical preoccupation in the minds of the authors themselves.

A critical sifting of the NT materials makes it indubitable that the Resurrection of Jesus held a place of unique importance in the earliest Christian apologetic. This event, interpreted in the light of Biblical prophecy, was seen as the great sign that Jesus had been divinely constituted as Messiah and Lord. The charismatic phenomena in the early community, especially the gifts of prophecy and miracle-working, were viewed as evidences that the risen Lord had sent forth His Spirit upon the Christian community and was at work through it, establishing His messianic reign. The last age of the world, therefore, had already begun in the Church.

In addition to these arguments, which presumably belonged to the stock in trade of the entire community, Paul makes use of other arguments against the pagans. In particular he contends that those who fall away from the worship of the living and true God, who has now revealed Himself in Jesus, inevitably fall into idolatry, cruelty, mutual hatred, and all manner of perversion.

The letter to the Hebrews, the best example of the early Christian apologetic to the Jews, shows how Christianity, thanks to the perfect mediatorship of Jesus, surpassingly fulfills all the authentic values of the OT.

The four Evangelists have each their own distinctive slant on the way Jesus manifests Himself as the divine redeemer. Mark conveys this realization by evoking numinous sentiments of awe and fascination. He vividly portrays the impact made by the Son of God upon the Apostles as He walked among men. They are dazzled and stupefied, as if by a brilliance too great for them to take in. Matthew, addressing Christians not as yet fully weaned from Judaism, depicts Jesus as the new Moses, teaching a new and higher justice. Luke— both in his Gospel and in his 'second volume,' Acts—describes the insertion of the Church as a Spirit-filled community into the midst of world history and shows its links with Jerusalem and Rome. John, finally, proposes the image of Jesus as the Light who has come into the world to shine upon the children of God in every nation and to give them a more abundant life of freedom, truth and mutual love.

The primary commendation of the good news as set forth in the Gospels would seem to be the attractiveness of the message itself—or rather of the reality that Christ brought into the world. But not all are drawn to the faith. The Evangelists, particularly John, teach that no one can sincerely accept the Christian message unless he experiences the inner attraction of grace and is willing to live up to the moral demands of the gospel. To those who are called and are willing to sacrifice all else for the following of Christ, the Gospel gives a joy and peace that are not of this world.

The primary sign of credibility, to judge from the Gospels, would seem to be the person of Jesus, with His vitality, determination, and compassion, and His uniquely authoritative manner of teaching and acting. As secondary signs, not wholly separable from the person and work of Jesus, the Gospels call attention to the miracles. Jesus Himself, according to the accounts, invokes His miracles as external confirmations of His divine mission.

Just as the Apostles explained the Resurrection of Jesus 'according to the Scriptures,' so too Jesus, according to the Evangelists, interprets His miracles according to what 'was written' of Him in the Hebrew Scriptures. Thus in the NT the miracles, the Resurrection, and the messianic prophecies coalesce into a single argument made up of many converging elements.

The NT addresses itself primarily to persons who are familiar with and who fully accept the Jewish Scriptures. The Christian fulfillment is presented as the key to the proper interpretation of the ancient texts. New forms of apologetic would become necessary when the Church, primarily based on Hellenistic soil, was forced to deal continually with men born and bred in a very different intellectual world.

CHAPTER TWO

The Patristic Era

Like the NT writings, most of the noncanonical Christian literature until about A.D. 125 was concerned with establishing the faith and discipline of the Christian community rather than with attempting to demonstrate the credibility of the Christian faith. The writings of the Apostolic Fathers (Clement of Rome, Ignatius of Antioch, Polycarp, and others), while affording valuable materials that could be exploited by the apologetics of later centuries, did not themselves engage in what one should call apologetics. After the 1st quarter of the 2nd century, however, apologetics became the most characteristic form of Christian writing. This shift from a purely intra-Church literature to documents addressed to the outside world can be attributed for the most part to four groups:

1. *Converts.* Scientifically educated men were entering the Church —men who felt the ability, the need, and the urge to come to grips with the pagan philosophy they had once espoused, to justify the radical change in their manner of life, to give a reason for the faith that was in them. This urge to speak out was admirably phrased by Justin: 'Whoever can speak out the truth and fails to do so shall be condemned by God.'[1]

2. *Philosophers.* Attacks on Christianity were no longer a mere matter of mob ignorance. Empty rumors of atheism, immorality, and Thyestean banquets began to yield to more serious and sophisticated charges. From the 2d through the 4th centuries the assault became increasingly intellectual, and Christians in response felt the need to give a more carefully reasoned justification for their faith.

3. *Emperors.* Under the Antonines, from Trajan to Commodus, the Church continued to experience severe persecutions the legal basis

22

for which was not entirely clear. The emperors, who had ultimate responsibility for the treatment of Christians, were in some cases fair-minded persons, prepared to listen to rational argument. This gave the Christians reason to hope that by presenting their case in the best light they might win civil tolerance and perhaps even persuade their secular rulers to embrace the faith. Many of the apologies were therefore addressed to emperors and other civil magistrates.

4. *Jews.* Some of the Jews outside the Church were eager to slander Christians and to denounce them to the civil authorities. The Christians sought to refute these charges and in some cases to respond in kind. As in New Testament times, they wished to persuade the Jews that Jesus Christ was the fulfillment of the hopes of ancient Israel. To those Judeo-Christians who attempted to combine faith in Christ with observance of the Mosaic Law, including the Levitical worship in the Temple, the Christians sought to demonstrate that Christ had set His faithful free from the obligations of the old covenant.

Schematically, the works of the Apologists can be divided into two main categories: political apologies, designed to win civil tolerance, and religious apologies, intended to win new converts to the faith. The religious apologies can in turn be divided into those aimed at paganism and those aimed at Judaism. While a few of the apologies fall clearly into one or another of these categories, many cut across all such schematic divisions.

From a literary point of view the controversial literature of the Christians naturally followed the patterns previously worked out on Hellenistic soil in encounters between Platonists and Aristotelians, between Stoics and Epicureans, and between Jews and pagans. Apologies and exhortations, dialogues and diatribes had been in use since the time of Plato and Aristotle.[2] Of special value as models for Christian apologetic were the assaults by the philosophers on polytheism and idolatry, and the efforts by Hellenistic Jews to establish the superiority of the Mosaic revelation over pagan wisdom.

Among the pagan opponents of superstitious religion particular mention should be made of the Stoics Zeno (late 3d century B.C.) and Apollodorus of Athens (2d century B.C.), the Academic philosopher Carneades (2d century B.C.), and the Epicurean Philodemus (1st century B.C.). The Wisdom of Solomon, composed by a Hellenistic Jew, probably in Alexandria during the 2d half of the 1st century B.C., takes over some of the same arguments to expose the folly of idolatry (see especially chapter 14).

It was at Alexandria in the 2d and 1st centuries B.C. that the Jews effected the richest synthesis between Mosaic religion and Hellenistic philosophy. Philo, who wrote at Alexandria in the 1st half of the 1st century A.D., tried to show in his voluminous commentaries on the Pentateuch that Moses had received by divine revelation a wisdom more certain and sublime than the highest speculations of the philosophers. By allegorical methods of exegesis he sought to harmonize the Jewish Scriptures with the fruits of Hellenistic speculation.

The Alexandrian Jews, like the Christians of the next few centuries, had to face the problem how the pagan sages had achieved such high insights without apparent dependence on divine revelation. To this they gave, as Professor Wolfson[3] has shown, three characteristic answers. Sometimes they said that the Greek philosophers actually depended upon Moses. This contention, which seems to go back to the Jewish Peripatetic Aristobulus (2d century B.C.), recurs in certain passages in which Philo accuses Heraclitus of having snatched his theory of the opposites from Moses 'like a thief' and maintains that the Greek legislators 'copied' the laws of Moses. In a similar vein, the fourth book of Maccabees asserts that Eleazer and his brothers were fortified by the law of reason, which was derived from the Mosaic Law.

In other passages the Jewish apologists, without insisting on actual derivation, are content to argue that Hebrew wisdom is at least more ancient than that of the Gentiles. Thus Philo, according to Wolfson,[4] sometimes says merely that Moses anticipated the discoveries of the Greek philosophers. Josephus, in his apologetic work *Against Apion* (about A.D. 93–95), insists strongly on the antiquity of the institutions of the Jews.

Third, the Jewish apologists occasionally argue that philosophy was a special gift of God to the Greeks, enabling them to discover by reason what was made known to the Jews by revelation. 'It is heaven,' writes Philo, 'which has showered philosophy upon us; it is the human mind which has received it, but it is sight which as guide has brought the two together.'[5] Some Jewish apologists, such as Josephus, argued from prophecies allegedly uttered by pagan sibyls.

These three solutions regarding the relation between revelation and philosophy will reappear in the apologetics of the Greek Fathers.

APOLOGISTS OF THE SECOND CENTURY

Two of the earliest Christian apologies are unfortunately known to scholars only from fragments quoted by other authors. One of these, the apocryphal *Preaching of Peter*, exalts Biblical monotheism and ridicules idolatry in much the same style as do the pagan philosophers and the Jewish polemicists already mentioned.[6] The other, the apology addressed by Quadratus to the Emperor Hadrian in A.D. 125, survives, it would appear, only in a single sentence quoted in Eusebius's *History of the Church* (4.3.1–2).[7] This fragment speaks of Jesus' miracles and mentions that some of the persons cured by Him or raised by Him from the dead are still alive. This point is of interest because, generally speaking, the miracles of Jesus occupy a very subordinate place in the apologetics of the first 3 centuries. The Christians did not want their faith confused with pagan thaumaturgy.

The most important Apologist prior to Justin is unquestionably the Athenian philosopher Aristides, whose brief *Apology*,[8] like that of Quadratus, was addressed to the Emperor Hadrian about 125. An early excursion into comparative religion, this work divides all mankind into five categories: barbarians, Greeks, Egyptians, Jews, and Christians. The barbarians, says the author, are in error because they adore the inanimate elements and images made in honor of these, even though it is evident to reason that the elements are moved by forces that rule over them, and thus cannot be divine. The Greeks introduce imaginary and fictitious gods, whose immoral conduct deprives them of any title to worship. The Egyptians, being more stupid than other men, adore plants, herbs, reptiles, and quadrupeds. Some of them even worship dumb idols. The Jews are superior to all previously mentioned because they adore the one God and imitate His magnanimity by practicing works of mercy, but their high principles are belied by their superstitious observances, which seem to rest on the assumption that God stands in need of gifts and sacrifices. The Christians, finally, surpass all others because they worship the one true God in uprightness, as is attested by the purity and modesty of their lives. In conformity with their faith, Christians tell the truth, show mutual love, and have compassion even for their enemies.

Notwithstanding its brevity, Aristides' *Apology* deserves high respect for its clarity and firmness of argument. By placing primary emphasis on the good moral lives of Christians, including their purity and charity, rather than the Biblical miracles, this work lays the basis for some of the most successful apologetics of the next few centuries.

The two *Apologies*[9] composed at Rome by Justin Martyr, the first about A.D. 150, the other between 155 and 160, are primarily concerned with winning civil toleration for Christians. The *First*

Apology, addressed to the Emperors Antoninus Pius and Lucius Commodus, argues in the name of fair play that Christians should not be condemned on the basis of their name alone. Just as Hadrian in his Rescript to the Proconsul of Asia (about A.D. 125) had urged that the charges against Christians should be impartially investigated, so now, Justin argues, civil authorities should take pains to see whether in fact the Christian faith is destructive of civic loyalty. After setting forth in some detail the beliefs and practices of the Christians, Justin draws the conclusion that even if the Christians should be judged foolish and misguided, at least they have done nothing worthy of the death penalty.

In his *Second Apology* Justin takes up again many of the same themes, seeking to defend his fellow religionists against a new wave of unjust condemnations. In some important sections of this work Justin attempts to relate Christianity to pagan philosophy, arguing that the philosophers achieved by reason many valid insights that Christians believe on the strength of divine revelation; but the philosophers, having only partial knowledge, fell into many errors and contradictions. In both *Apologies* Justin propounds his famous thesis that the philosophers, being enlightened by the divine Logos, were in some sense Christians without knowing it.[10]

From Justin comes the only extant 2d-century apology addressed to the Jews. His *Dialogue with Trypho the Jew*[11] was composed some time after the *First Apology*, and perhaps after the second. The first 8 chapters of this *Dialogue* are precious for their account of Justin's own conversion from paganism to Christianity, largely as a result of his study of the OT Prophets. In later chapters Justin attempts to prove from numerous scriptural prophecies the messiahship and divinity of Jesus Christ. He also answers various Jewish objections against Christianity. To the charge that the Christians are unfaithful to the Mosaic Law, Justin replies that the old law has been abrogated by the New Testament and that only the Christians are in a position to interpret the Hebrew Scriptures correctly. In the final chapters of the *Dialogue* Justin develops the idea that the Church is the new Israel and urges the Jews to repent of their obstinacy. Notwithstanding the apparent harshness of some of his statements, Justin avoids the rude anti-Semitism of some later apologists. At the end of the *Dialogue* he and Trypho take leave of each other with a friendly exchange of farewells.

If for no other reason than the sheer bulk of his achievement, Justin is the most important 2d-century Apologist. A man of noble and sincere character, he commands respect for his frank and open esteem for pagan philosophers and Jewish theologians. His style of writing is unfortunately disorderly and prolix. Many of his historical and exegetical arguments, moreover, fail to stand up under critical scrutiny.

Sometimes included in the corpus of Justin's works are several apologetical pieces written by others. The most notable of these, the *Cohortatio ad graecos (Exhortation to the Greeks)*,[12] is an eloquent appeal for conversion, probably composed in the 3d century. Unlike Justin, the author finds nothing commendable in the religion or philosophy of the Greeks. After considering in outline the religious views of the philosophers, he concludes that their sole utility is to have pointed out one another's errors. Whatever traits of authentic monotheism are to be found in Plato and others should be attributed, according to this apologist, to the influence of Moses, whose revelations were transmitted to the Greeks through the Egyptians. For fear of hemlock, he contends, Plato did not dare admit the true source of his ideas. Likewise immoderately hostile to Greek religion and philosophy is the pseudo-Justinian *Oratio ad graecos (Discourse to the Greeks)*,[13] a pamphlet written by some zealous convert probably in the period between 150 and 225.

Something of the same rigorism penetrates the work of Justin's disciple Tatian, who composed, around the time that he joined the sect of the Encratites (about 170), a bitter polemic against Greek culture[14] resembling the later works of Tertullian. After excoriating the immoralities of the Olympian gods, the absurdities of Greek mythology, the indecency of public religious festivals, and the vices and contradictions of the philosophers, Tatian briefly recounts how he himself in his search for truth came to accept the simple and sublime teaching of the Prophets, notwithstanding their despised barbarism. In the customary apologetical style Tatian attempts to prove that Moses is more ancient than Homer and all other writers. Violent and crude as he is, Tatian is not lacking in originality, intelligence, and moral character.

It is with relief that one turns from these narrow diatribes to the moderate and courteous work of Athenagoras of Athens, whom Johannes Quasten calls 'unquestionably the most eloquent of the early Christian apologists.'[15] His *Embassy* (or *Supplication*) *for the Christians*,[16] dedicated to the two Emperors Lucius Aurelius Commodus and Marcus Aurelius (reigned 176–180), is essentially a plea for civil toleration. After an introduction pointing out the great variety of religious doctrines tolerated within the Empire, and appealing to the Emperors' sense of justice, Athenagoras takes up, first, the charge that the Christians are atheists and, next, the accusation that they practice immorality.

Athenagoras demonstrates that Christians are not atheists by showing that their idea of God is more exalted and consequently more divine than anything the pagans are able to attain to. Even the polytheists, he adds, are atheists with regard to one another's gods. On philosophical grounds, moreover, it is evident that there cannot be a plurality of gods. As regards the charges of cannibalism and promiscuity that have been malignantly laid at the door of Christians, he replies that Christians are bound by their religion to very strict standards of chastity and to a respect for human life that extends even to unborn infants, thus forbidding abortion. It is quite evident, he concludes, that Christians obey the laws of the Empire and pray for its peace and prosperity.

Also of apologetical interest is Athenagoras's *On the Resurrection of the Dead*,[17] but since it deals only with this one doctrine rather than with Christianity in general it may be omitted from this survey.

More akin to Tatian in spirit, but less skillful in argument, was the Syrian bishop of Antioch, Theophilus, who composed shortly after 180 an appeal to his friend Autolycus to become a Christian.[18] Like many philosopher-converts of his time Theophilus was much impressed by the wisdom of Moses and especially by the Genesis account of the creation, which he takes to be the only reliable guide to the origins of the universe. His insistence on the extreme antiquity of the Mosaic revelation and on the supposedly prophetic oracles of the Sybils shows the extent to which he was a victim of the illusions of his day. If the *Ad Autolycum* has any value for the modern reader, this is to be found in its appeal to what a later age would call the logic of the heart. God, says Theophilus, is seen by those whose souls are open to the light of the Spirit; He is hidden to those who dwell in the darkness of sin. 'Show me what manner of man you are, and I will show you my God' (ch. 2).

In the opinion of many critics the pearl of early Christian apologetics is the brief *Letter to Diognetus*,[19] a work of much debated authorship and date. Today most scholars agree that it belongs to the period from 120 to 210. A few, influenced by Paulus Andriessen, identify it with the lost apology of Quadratus (about 125),[20] but it seems hardly likely that Quadratus would address Hadrian under the pseudonym of Diognetus; nor does the sentence quoted by Eusebius appear in the extant text of the *Letter to Diognetus*. In his edition of the *Diognetus*[21] Henri-Irénée Marrou suggests hesitantly that the author may have been Pantaenus, the Sicilian convert to

Christianity who was head of the catechetical school of Alexandria from 180 to about 199. If so, the addressee might well be the equestrian procurator, Claudius Diognetus.

The letter aims to respond to three questions put to the author by Diognetus. What sort of cult is Christianity to enable its adherents to spurn pagan gods and Jewish superstitions? What is the secret of the Christians' affectionate love for one another? And why did the new religion come into existence so late in the world's history? After a somewhat stereotyped exposure of the folly of idol worship and the formalism of Jewish observance, the author presents a striking description of the Christians as a new race of men, everywhere at home and everywhere strangers. Christians are to the world, says the author, what the soul is to the body—and this comparison he develops in a justly famous paragraph. Then he goes on to consider the source of the exceptional serenity and courage of Christians, namely the surpassing goodness of God, who has given His own Son, the guiltless one, in order that the guilty might be freed from condemnation. The final two chapters (11–12) are somewhat different in thought and style. Presumably they come from another hand.

More the preacher than the apologist, the author of the *Diognetus* was a brilliant rhetorician who painted an appealing picture of Christian faith and life. His portrait, even if idealized, undoubtedly had a basis in the Church as he and his contemporaries experienced it. Although some modern critics look upon this epistle as showy and artificial, it remains one of the most stirring presentations of the Christian ideal.

The work of the 2d-century Apologists, surveyed in the preceding pages, reflects the vigor and the inconsistencies of youth. The writers, none of them fully master of his subject, are alternately defensive and aggressive toward adversaries. In most cases they make out a strong case for religious tolerance. This they do, in the first place, by showing that Christians, far from being atheists, propose a more exalted notion of God than the other religions tolerated in the Empire. Second, they convincingly refute the charges that Christians are guilty of cannibalism and sexual promiscuity. Finally, they are on solid ground in contending that, even though one should insist that Christian teaching is absurd, the new religion contains nothing criminal or detrimental to the State.

As arguments for conversion from paganism, these authors generally show the weaknesses in pagan mythological theology and tellingly expose the immoralities fostered by paganism. They go on to demonstrate how the more elevated concept of God in the Bible inspires remarkable continence, charity, and courage on the part of the faithful. They are able to point triumphantly to the unity of Christians as a living sign of the cohesive power of the gospel. In autobiographical passages authors such as Justin and Tatian movingly indicate the motives that led to their own conversion. These personal testimonies are still impressive.

But when these authors seek to demonstrate the authenticity of the Biblical revelation, they fall into certain excesses, which are scarcely surprising since they wrote before the dawn of critical history. Relying too blindly on the claims of late Jewish apologetic, as found, for example, in Philo and Josephus, they exaggerate the antiquity of the Bible. When they insist on the perfect accord among the Biblical authors, they gloss over important differences between mutually opposed traditions. They speak of Scripture as though it were totally written by Prophets and interpret prophetic inspiration too much on the model of mantic possession, as described, for example, in the *Meno* of Plato.

These early Apologists, moreover, lack any consistent view of the value of classical culture, as found at its best in their favorite author, Plato. Too often they approach this question with the tactics of debaters. Their first wall of defense is to ridicule the Greek heritage, but their second wall is to claim for Biblical religion all the genuine value that is to be found in classicism. This they do by gratuitously postulating—again under influence of the Jewish apologists—that the Greeks had secretly pillaged from the writings of Moses. Another convenient device is to allege that God has raised up prophets among the Gentiles—a hypothesis that seemed to be confirmed by the supposed prophecies of the Sibyls (although subsequent scholarship has made it clear that the Sibylline oracles on which Jewish and Christian apologists depended were in fact interpolations). Finally, they sometimes have recourse, as does Justin, to the idea that even the pagan philosophers were enlightened by the divine Logos. This allows Justin, for instance, to claim the authentic wisdom in these writers for Christianity, while he attributes their errors to the lack of a full presence of the Logos in their midst. Justin's doctrine of the universal Logos was to have an important future in helping theologians from Clement and Origen to Tillich and K. Rahner to relate Christianity to the other religions, but in Justin's hands it is as yet little more than a defensive apologetical maneuver.

In their arguments against the Jews the Apologists rely chiefly on the alleged OT prophecies of Christ. The modern reader, accustomed to more rigorous norms of exegesis, is likely to be put off by the Apologists' neglect of the primary literal meaning of these texts. Sometimes their argument hinges on translations such as the Septuagint. When the Hebrew text does not agree, they accuse the rabbis of having mutilated the text out of hostility toward Christians.

In contending that the Jews are superstitious in their observance of the works of the Law, the Apologists may have a valid point. But they move too rapidly from this to a rejection of Judaism, without sufficiently considering whether the Hebrew faith might be capable of being corrected.

The contemporary Christian can scarcely avoid surprise at the extent to which the 2d-century Apologists rely on Moses and the Prophets as the source of their own faith. This is perhaps due to their indebtedness to Jewish apologetics against the pagans. From a modern point of view, it seems that these authors make too little of the personal character of Jesus. The moral ideals of the Sermon on the Mount are occasionally mentioned, but otherwise there is little emphasis on the doctrine, miracles, and sanctity of Jesus, or even on His Resurrection.

As might be expected at this early period, the Apologists do not have any clear theory of the relations between reason and revelation, or between Christianity and the other religions. They compare religions with a view to ascertaining which is better than the others, but they do not seek to prove the validity of religion itself or ask to what extent the diverse religions might all be bearers of divine truth. But to expect an adequate treatment of such subtle and profound questions at a time when the Church has not yet emerged from the catacombs would show a lack of historical sense. One should rather be grateful that writers such as Aristides and Justin move as far as they do toward the threshold of these questions.

THE ALEXANDRIANS OF THE THIRD CENTURY

Just as Alexandria was the city where Judaism became at home in the Hellenistic world, so it was providentially destined to be the place where Christian theology achieved maturity by entering into full communion with the heritage of Greek philosophy. The first head of the catechetical school, according to some scholars, was Athenagoras of Athens, whose irenic apologetics have already been mentioned. Pantaenus the Sicilian, who has been mentioned also, added prestige to the school. With his successors, Clement and Origen, it became the most brilliant theological center of the Christian world in the 3d century.

Clement of Alexandria (*c*. 150–*c*. 214), probably an Athenian by birth, was converted to Christianity and travelled to many lands in search of religious instruction.[22] At length he settled at Alexandria, where he put himself at the feet of Pantaenus, whom he succeeded as head of the school about 200. His principal works comprise the trilogy, the *Protrepticus (Converter)*, the *Paedagogus (Tutor)*, and the *Stromata (Miscellanies*, or, literally, *Carpets)*. The last of these probably consists of fragments of a projected work, the *Didascalus (Instructor)*. These works deal with Christ in His threefold relationship to the believer. First Christ converts, then He disciplines, and finally He imparts wisdom.

For Clement's apologetic one must look mainly to the *Protrepticus*, his exhortation to conversion.[23] Its literary form resembles that of Aristotle's *Protrepticus* and of other Greek and Roman productions, including the lost *Hortensius* of Cicero—a work which Clement himself would probably not have known. While his arguments do not greatly differ from those of Justin and other 2d-century Apologists, Clement writes in a far more polished and graceful style, calculated to attract his readers and make them enthusiastic for the following of Christ. Having himself experienced the appeal of Greek mythology, philosophy, and mystery cults, Clement is able to show how all these values are surpassingly fulfilled in Christ, the true mystagogue and the supreme master of wisdom.

In an introductory chapter Clement, capitalizing on the high regard for music in the Greek tradition, praises the wonderful power of music to give peace and strength to the human spirit. Christ, he maintains, is the minstrel who imparts harmony to the universe and makes music to God. As the new Orpheus He tames the souls of men, far more savage than those of the wildest beasts. He is the new song, which, like the canticles of David before Saul, drives out evil spirits and restores health to those disturbed in mind.

In several entertaining chapters Clement then describes the various mystery cults of the Hellenistic world, the mythical stories of the gods, and the excesses of idol worship. From this he concludes that the true atheists are not the Christians, as charged, but rather pagans, who worship under the name of God objects that are not divine. Let those in quest of truth learn not to deify the universe but to search for its creator.

Turning then to Hellenic philosophy and poetry, Clement shows that while the Greeks were involved in numerous errors they did receive some glimmerings of truth, which are to be attributed to divine inspiration. But he adds, as Justin did, that not knowing the

Word Himself, the Greeks had no sure foothold and were therefore unable to follow through on their best insights.

In two brief chapters Clement goes on to summarize the witness of the Old and New Testaments. These chapters are happily free from the wearisome and unconvincing arguments from fulfilled prophecy that encumber so many of the apologetical treatises so far examined. Clement's OT quotations emphasize the majesty of God and His love for man. In his references to the NT he makes fruitful use of Paul and the Epistle to the Hebrews to illustrate the transcendent power of the divine Word as it comes to man in Christ. This Word, according to Clement, speaks to all men:

> The Word was not hidden from any; He is a universal light; He shines upon all men. No one is a Cimmerian in respect to the Word [cf. *Odyssey* 11.13–16]. Let us hasten to salvation, to the new birth. Let us, who are many, hasten to be gathered together into one love corresponding to the union of the One Being.[24]

At this point Clement interjects some reflections on the claims of custom and shows how a false conservatism often holds men captive and prevents them from adopting what is new and better. To pass from custom to truth, he argues, is like passing from childhood to maturity. These observations were obviously relevant at a time when the most powerful opposition to Christianity, as shall be seen, was coming from the advocates of antiquity and tradition.

In a climactic chapter Clement then portrays the divine Word as the Sun of Righteousness (Mal 4.2 [=Vg Mal 3.20]) enlightening the whole world. This chapter introduces a final exhortation in which the sincere inquirer is bidden to resist the siren call of pleasure: 'Only resolve, and thou hast vanquished destruction; bound to the wood of the cross [cf. *Odyssey* 12.178], thou shalt live freed of all corruption.'[25] In a passage replete with echoes from the Dionysiac rites Clement then depicts the Logos as the true hierophant inviting mankind to share in His mysteries.

With Clement, Christian apologetics finds the first of its great masters. No longer does one feel obliged to make allowance for the inevitable crudities and blunders of an uncouth childhood. Clement is at home with his materials and by his genius infuses fresh life into the dry bones of arguments already trite. His work is well ordered, yet not wooden; he combines variety with symmetry. For the modern taste his work may be overloaded with literary allusions and rhetorical conceits, but Clement's discretion and sincerity prevent him from degenerating into aimless artificiality. He is above all a Christian humanist who moves easily amid the arts and letters of classical civilization, combining Christian piety with the highest values of ancient culture.

If his formal argumentation adds little to what has already been seen in the 2d-century Apologists, Clement contributes a new and better technique of persuasion. By means of a clearer presentation of the Christian fact, viewed in relation to the Hellenistic and Hebrew background, he illustrates how Christianity is able to fulfill and at the same time correct the religious aspirations and insights at work in human history. Unlike many of his 2d-century predecessors, Clement focuses on Christ the Incarnate Word, whom he sees at work in the depths of all human souls, leading each and all toward the moment when they can encounter His personal presence and benefit to the full from His divinizing influence.

The Alexandrian school of apologetics, brought to such great heights by Clement, was to reach its climax with Origen, who succeeded Clement as head of the catechetical school. Origen was born in Alexandria about 184. While he was still a boy he lost his father to martyrdom. His chief work in life was the study and exposition of Holy Scripture—an occupation that took him deep into textual criticism and exegesis, both literal and spiritual. To equip himself yet better he studied philosophy under Ammonius Saccas, the father of Neoplatonism. About 246, about seven years before his death, he wrote, at the request of a friend and benefactor, a detailed reply to the anti-Christian polemic of Celsus, which had been written about 178.

Before Origen's reply the work of Celsus himself should be briefly considered. Entitled the *True Doctrine (Alēthēs Logos)*, it was the most important tract against the Christian faith prior to the time of Porphyry and continued to furnish materials for tracts against Christianity until the 19th century.[26] Celsus himself was not a deep thinker but rather an ardent champion of Hellenistic culture in all its aspects as an ideal to be kept alive. An eclectic Platonist, Celsus believed in one supreme god and a multitude of local deities as his subordinates. This belief enabled him to accept all the rituals of national religion without repudiating the monotheism of the philosophers. By the true doctrine he meant that ancient tradition on which the institutions of Hellenistic society had been built. The Jews, and even more, in his opinion, the Christians, were corrupting the venerable traditions and thereby undermining the structures of society.

From the abundant quotations in Origen's reply one can reconstruct a good portion of Celsus' work, which has unfortunately perished. The book falls into two main parts, in the first of which Celsus objects to Christianity in the person of an imaginary Jew. He alleges that Jesus was born of an adulterous union, that He learned magical arts in Egypt, and that He invented the story of His own virginal conception. The Resurrection of Jesus is held to be either an imposture or a delusion suffered by the Apostles. The fact that Jesus was betrayed by one of His own disciples and suffered death is taken as proof that He could not have been divine. If Jesus had foreseen His own death, Celsus argues, He would have been able to prevent it.

In Part 2 Celsus objects in his own person. The Christians, he argues, demand a faith not based on examination, and this can only be an irrational commitment. Further, they shun open debate with the learned. They operate as a secret society and, despising wisdom, seduce the ignorant and the credulous. The Bible is full of childish legends and falls far below the finest achievements of classical history. It falsely teaches that God changes His mind, that He chooses favorites among the human race, and that He manages the whole of creation for the benefit of man alone. The acceptable doctrines of Christianity, such as its ethical teaching and its doctrine of future rewards and punishments, are also professed by the better pagan philosophers. Worship of the one supreme God should not prevent the peoples of the various nations from also propitiating the lesser deities who are particularly charged with their protection. Instead of separating themselves from the rest of men, Christians should worship the local deities, live according to the customs of their country, and do their part in military and political service.

Origen's reply, known by the title *Contra Celsum*,[27] is lengthy (more than 500 pages in most editions) and somewhat disordered. After an early section in which he takes up some of the more important questions, he begins to follow the argument of Celsus point by point. Since his answers are meticulously detailed, here no more than a few of his main contentions can be indicated.

In his preface Origen explains that faith is not based on philosophical demonstrations but, as Paul expresses it, on 'demonstration of the Spirit and of power' (1 Cor 2.4). By this Origen understands the influence of God as it comes to men through prophecies and miracles. Consequently no true believer can allow his faith to be shaken by plausible human arguments. Although there is a risk that some will be weakened in their faith by a refutation of Celsus—as if faith could really rest on human reasons—still this risk must be taken in order to help those who have little or no experience of true faith and who would consequently be misled if Celsus went unanswered.

Taking up the objections in Part 1, Origen begins by asserting that the evident nobility of Jesus' character makes it incredible that He would have invented the story of His own virginal conception in order to avoid the disgrace of illegitimacy. Equally baseless is the idea that Jesus and the Apostles, who laid down their lives for their doctrine, were fraudulent magicians.

In his effort to undermine the historicity of the Bible, Origen continues, Celsus inconsistently selects certain facts to provide a basis for his objections and dismisses others as fictions. He uses no principle of selection other than his own prejudices. In asking Christians to demonstrate the historicity of certain incidents, he makes an impossible demand, since there can be no strict proof of the reality of numerous past events—e.g., the Trojan War—that are universally admitted to have occurred. If Celsus were really the Jew in whose name he was objecting, he would admit the historical truth of the stories about Moses, and it would then be easy to convince him about Jesus, who is far more easily known.

To prove to the imaginary Jew that Jesus is the Christ, Origen argues first from the messianic prophecies, then from the miracles of Jesus, and finally from the traces of miraculous power still to be found among Christians, especially when the minds of those who accept the gospel are marvelously filled with peace and joy.

The fact that Jesus suffered and died does not prove that He did not foresee His own betrayal. Even some of the Greek heroes, such as Socrates and Leonides (the Spartan general who gave his life at Thermopylae), submitted to a death that they foresaw and could have escaped. The Resurrection of Jesus could not have been an invention because the disciples devoted themselves to preaching it at the risk of their own lives. Nor was it a fantasy, for daytime hallucinations such as the Resurrection appearances never occur among sane persons. This greatest of miracles was, moreover, predicted in prophecy.

Turning his attention now to Celsus' own objections (Part 2), Origen protests that the Christian faith is free from all obscurantism. In principle it would be desirable for all believers to be able to make a personal study of the grounds of faith, but those who have not the leisure to do so must, like the adherents of philosophical schools, rely at least initially on the authority of their teachers. Jesus, who laid down His life for the flock, is a far more trustworthy guide than the founders of the philosophical sects who enjoy so much authority among the pagans. The Christian, while he may be simple and uneducated, does not despise true wisdom. The wisdom against which Paul vituperates is a false, worldly wisdom leading to blindness.

The Mosaic history, according to Origen, far from being childish legend, is more ancient and reliable than the history of the Greeks, who gladly learned from nations older than their own. Celsus misunderstands the Bible in a slavishly literal way when he takes its anthropomorphic statements about God at face value. Unlike the Greeks whom Celsus so admires, Moses does not tell immoral and incredible tales about the gods. Nowhere does the Bible teach that, for all the favors granted to the Jews, they alone are loved by God. Christians teach that Christ came to save all sinners everywhere. As for the Biblical doctrine that all things are made for man, it agrees with sound philosophy, which places man higher in the scale of being than irrational creatures.

The fact that certain Christian doctrines are taught by Greek philosophers is no reason for denying that they are revealed. Plato, among others, was able to discern the 'invisible things of God' (cf. Rom 1.20), but neither he nor his followers avoided polytheistic worship. To worship lesser divinities is offensive to God, for He commands all things by His personal providence. The fact that angels may have some share in the government of the universe does not permit man to adore them with divine honors.

Celsus errs, finally, in imagining that it would be a disaster if the whole Empire were converted to Christianity. In answer to the true worship and prayer being offered to Him, God would surround the Empire with greater protection and blessings. As it is, Christians do no harm to the state. While refusing to bear arms and to accept certain political offices, they benefit the state by their prayers and by teaching men to live upright lives.

Origen's reply to Celsus indicates, first of all, how he would meet the objections put to him; but incidentally, in the course of his reply, Origen gives certain indications of the grounds of credibility supporting his own faith. In one important passage he asserts that '. . . the evidences of Jesus' divinity are the Churches of people who have been helped, the prophecies spoken about him, the cures which are done in his name, the knowledge and wisdom in Christ, and reason which is to be found in those who know how to advance beyond mere faith, and how to search out the meaning of the divine scriptures' (3.33). In addition, Origen often speaks of the moral stature of Christ and of the wonderful moral renewal that takes place in the lives of those who live up to their Christian faith. He alludes also to the rapid propagation of the Christian religion, which Providence has made stronger than all the worldly powers that have sought to destroy it. ·

The *Contra Celsum* ranks high among the classics of apologetics. Adopting a direct and logical style Origen pursues each argument to its ultimate conclusion. His reflections take him into profound disquisitions on subjects such as the problem of evil, the resurrection of the body, the senses of Scripture, and the functions of angels and demons. He is perhaps the first apologist who seems prepared to take on any objection that can be urged against the Christian faith, whether from the standpoint of history, of philosophy, or of the natural sciences.

For all its erudition and solidity, the *Contra Celsum* has never been popular reading. Unlike the *Protrepticus* of Clement, it is not a polished literary achievement. Following no clear outline of his own, Origen allows the order and emphasis to be chiefly dictated by Celsus' diatribe. Once Celsus' work was lost, Origen's reply became hard to follow. To some extent, also, the objections of Celsus became dated as Middle Platonism gave way to Neoplatonism in the latter part of the 3d century. Many of Origen's arguments are too much *ad hominem* to be serviceable against objections raised from other quarters.

Clement and Origen between them mark the decisive epoch when Christian apologetics achieves maturity. No longer pleading for mere toleration, whether political or intellectual, they launch a vigorous counteroffensive. Having mastered the full range of pagan philosophy and letters, they can speak as authorities in their own right. While continuing to make use of certain arguments borrowed from Platonic and Stoic philosophers, Jewish controversialists, and earlier Christian apologists, they assimilate what they borrow and make it a part of their own system. The most impressive feature of their apologetic is not so much what they have to say about any particular problem, nor even the sum total of their individual assertions, but rather the example of what they do. By their mighty syntheses they inspire faith that the gospel can engender a wisdom more comprehensive and profound than any rival religion or any philosophy that does not rest on revelation.

LATIN APOLOGISTS OF THE THIRD CENTURY

All the works analyzed thus far were composed in Greek, but at the end of the 2d century Christian apologists in the West, both in Italy and Africa, begin to write in Latin. Their works increasingly reflect the practical, Latin cast of mind, perhaps especially because so many of the apologists of this period were convert lawyers.

Remarkably placid and urbane in spirit is the dialogue *Octavius*,[28] composed about the end of the 2d century by the distinguished Roman advocate, Marcus Minucius Felix, who had become a convert to Christianity. The work is an imaginary conversation among three characters: the pagan Caecilius, the Christian Octavius, and the author, Minucius, who is supposed to be still a pagan. The author takes the role of chairman and judge.

Caecilius, in this dialogue, combines the skepticism of the Academy with religious traditionalism. The universe, he contends, is so great a riddle that human speculation can achieve no certain knowledge regarding the existence or nature of the gods. It is most prudent therefore to adhere to the religion of one's ancestors, which has brought abundant blessings to the Empire. To become a Christian, according to Caecilius, would be to join a secret society that undermines the national religion, teaches absurd doctrines, and practices moral infamies.

Octavius, in reply, readily concedes that man should begin with the effort to understand himself rather than the whole universe. But since man is not an isolated individual, he is bound to reflect on his position in the world. Contemplating the harmony of nature and the beauty of man himself, one cannot but feel the creative power of God. The best philosophers, such as Plato, hold with the Christians that God is incomprehensible, invisible, and unique. Popular imagination, however, fell away from the sound insights of philosophy and devised immoral tales about the gods. As for the greatness of Rome, it does not derive, as Caecilius imagines, from the protection of these fictitious gods, many of whom were violently captured from Rome's vanquished foes. Finally, Christians are manifestly innocent of the gross crimes imputed to them, such as ritual sacrifice and promiscuity, for their doctrine clearly inculcates reverence for life and chastity. At the conclusion of the dialogue Octavius declares himself convinced of the main points, and the three friends part on cordial terms.

As a literary composition, the *Octavius* is clear, graceful, and elegant.[29] Minucius Felix shows himself well versed in classical philosophy and letters, and expresses himself in a pleasing Ciceronian style. His argument is persuasive so far as it goes, but the exposition of Christianity, as many critics have noted, is very rudimentary. He never once quotes the Bible nor does he penetrate beyond the threshold of theology. In the author's defense it may be said that his aim is simply to write a winning introduction to Christianity for the benefit of cultivated Romans who know nothing of the Bible and have no special interest in Judeo-Christian speculation. This modest aim Minucius Felix attains with eminent success.

Because of certain correspondences with Tertullian's *To the Pagans* and *Apology*, some critics have maintained that the *Octavius* must be dependent on these works. Others contend that Tertullian, on the contrary, relies on Minucius Felix.[30] However this question may be resolved, it remains true that the two authors are vastly different in spirit and in style. Minucius Felix displays a noble reserve and consistently avoids all suggestions of polemical invective, whereas Tertullian is intense and aggressive. One can hardly imagine Tertullian writing, as Minucius Felix does in chapter 20, that the philosophers of old were truly Christians and that the Christians of today are the true philosophers. Minucius Felix writes for the dying age of Roman religion, but Tertullian represents a Church ready to challenge and defy the pagan world.

From Rome one may now turn to Carthage, which became the principal theological center for the Latin-speaking world in the 3d century. The most prominent speaker for the Carthaginian Church at the beginning of the century was Tertullian,[31] who was converted about 193 and wrote voluminously in defense of Catholicism until his lapse into Montanism about 207. He died, apparently still a Montanist, sometime after 220. A lawyer skilled in the practice of the Roman courts, he applied his extraordinary forensic talents with great success to the Christian cause. Many of his early works are primarily apologetical, whereas his later works tend toward controversy with other Christian groups.

Tertullian's *Apology* (197),[32] probably the finest of his writings, is a brilliant application of Roman juridical principles to the defense of Christianity. In the opening chapters he demonstrates with irresistible logic how repugnant the persecutions are to the traditions of Roman jurisprudence. Among all criminals, he asks, why are Christians alone convicted for their name with no investigation of their deeds? By what logic does Trajan's Rescript authorize the conviction of Christians while at the same time forbidding the state to seek them out? 'If you condemn them why not also search for them? If you do not search for them, why not also acquit them?' (ch. 2). In subsequent chapters Tertullian goes on to expose with wit and sarcasm the absurdity of the standard charges against Christians—infanticide, sexual promiscuity, and atheism. In chapter 17 he points out that the Christian conception of God as all-seeing, all-powerful, and all-perfect is that which springs spontaneously into the minds of pagans so that even they, in their unguarded moments, give testimony to the Christian God. They cry out, 'good God,' 'God almighty,' 'God grant it,' and the like. 'O testimony of the soul,' Tertullian comments, 'which is by natural instinct Christian!'

But Tertullian, unlike Justin and Minucius Felix, does not conclude that the pagans are capable of true religion apart from positive revelation. He goes on in the *Apology* to point out that God has had to raise up Prophets in order for them to accept in deliberate faith what nature already prompts them to believe. He shows how God's witnesses, the Prophets of the OT, spoke of Christ and of the punishments that would be visited on the Jewish people for their infidelity. These prophecies, Tertullian asserts, are being fulfilled as the Jews wander homeless.

Reverting to the Roman policies, Tertullian then attacks the practice of forcing the Christians to worship the gods of the Empire. 'No one, not even a man, will be willing to receive the worship of an unwilling client.' If the Egyptians were permitted by Roman law to deify birds and beasts and to condemn to death anyone who killed these 'gods,' why are the Christians forbidden to worship the one God of all? Any religion seems to be lawful except the worship of the one God to whom all men belong! (ch. 24).

The Romans have no right to argue that failure to worship their gods will undermine the Empire, since these gods cannot be shown to exist. Rome achieved its greatness before the present deities were worshipped, and most of them were violently stolen by the Romans from nations vanquished by them—a theme also developed, as we have seen, by Minucius Felix.

Having refuted the charges that Christian practices are evil, Tertullian goes on to demonstrate that they are good. He shows how Christians pray for the emperor and perform the service of pointing out to him that he too is a man. In chapter 39 he gives a moving description of the Christian way of life, reminiscent of that in Justin's *First Apology*. 'We form one body because of our religious convictions, and because of the divine origin of our way of life and the bond of a common hope.' The mutual charity of Christians is such that even their enemies exclaim, 'see how they love one another.' Everything is held in common among Christians—except, again in contrast to paganism, their wives.

In the closing chapters Tertullian sets forth his reflections upon martyrdom, for him a favorite theme. In going to their death, Christians show their supreme freedom. No one can put them to death, for they are Christians only because they will to be. Christians

do not will to suffer, but they accept suffering willingly. The vicious-
ness of the Roman officials is proof of the innocence of Christians,
whose virtue shines forth most splendidly in their destruction.
'We become more numerous every time we are hewn down by you:
the blood of Christians is seed' (ch. 50).

Tertullian's *Apology* is the most powerful and moving of its kind
in the patristic era. While it lacks the urbanity of Minucius Felix and
the philosophic depth of Clement and Origen, it throbs with a fierce
love of truth and virtue. The iron logic of Tertullian's argument
glows with passionate intensity, so that his arguments sear even as
they cut. The fervent African raises the rhetoric of the Roman courtroom to a new pitch of eloquence.

Most of Tertullian's other apologetical works are best seen in
relation to the *Apology*. His early work, *Against the Jews*, in which he
demonstrates that Christ fulfills the prophecies of the Old Testament
and supersedes its Law, may be found more briefly in chapter 20 of
the *Apology*. *To the Pagans* (early 197) may be viewed almost as a
first draft of the *Apology*. His brief treatise, *The Testimony of the Soul*
(late 197), is simply an expansion of the argument already noted in the
Apology, chapter 17. *To Scapula*, a plea for toleration in time of
persecution (about 212), recapitulates many arguments already given
in the *Apology*, felicitously developing the doctrine of religious
freedom.

Although no effort has been made to include in this survey polemical works against Christian heresies—which would involve a detailed
discussion of particular doctrines of the faith—an exception may here
be made in favor of Tertullian's *Prescription of Heretics*,[33] since this
work deals with the case against heresy in general. Like the *Apology*
it reveals the author's forensic talents at their height. Using the plea
known technically in the courts as *praescriptio*, Tertullian seeks to
bar the heretics from even entering their suit. He argues, essentially,
that Christ handed over His revelation to the Church, to be taught
by its authorized spokesmen. There is no other way of getting at
Christian revelation than by listening to those Churches that can
claim continuity with the Apostles. The heresies are new, or at least
they depart from the apostolic faith, and therefore have no right to be
heard as authentic Christianity. The heretics are not entitled to appeal
to the Scriptures, which belong to the Church alone. Their case should
therefore be dismissed out of hand rather than debated on its merits.

Tertullian's argument here is plausible and has deservedly made its
mark on subsequent theology. But he obviously does not meet all
possible objections. Might it not be, for instance, that Catholicism

has fallen away from its pristine purity and is in need of reformation? If so, can one exclude the possibility that persons lacking in juridical status might have a keener insight than the authorized officials of the legitimate Church?

In point of fact, purely formal arguments from authority do not suffice to bring conviction. That Tertullian himself saw the necessity of discussing individual heresies on their merits is proved by the fact that he wrote special treatises against Marcion, Hermogenes, Praxeas, the Valentinians, and others. Tertullian's own lapse into Montanism, moreover, is a practical denial of the principles on which his reasoning in the *Prescription* is based.

For all his cleverness Tertullian is an unreliable guide. His arguments are more adapted to the atmosphere of the courtroom than to the scholarly reflection of the schools. Although influenced by Stoicism and familiar with other schools of thought, Tertullian had little liking for dispassionate speculation. Unlike Clement and Origen, Justin and Minucius Felix, he had little respect for Socrates, Plato, and the philosophers. 'What has Jerusalem to do with Athens, the Church with the Academy, the Christian with the heretic? Our principles come from the Porch of Solomon, who had himself taught that the Lord is to be sought in simplicity of heart. I have no use for a Stoic or a Platonic or a dialectic Christianity. After Jesus Christ we have no need of speculation, after the Gospel no need of research.'[34]

To the demonstrations of philosophy Tertullian prefers the glitter of paradox. He wishes to bring out the distinctiveness of faith as it towers above all human reasoning and leaves man's intellect prostrate in adoration before the unfathomable mystery of God. 'The Son of God was crucified; I am not ashamed because man must needs be ashamed of it. And the Son of God died; it is by all means to be believed, because it is absurd [*ineptum*].'[35] Tertullian, even more than Tatian, became the master of all those Christian thinkers, including Kierkegaard and the dialectical theologians, who wished to liberate Christian faith from the straitjacket of metaphysical systems. Tertullian gloried in Christianity as an affront to reason, and whenever God's revelation is in danger of being imprisoned by human speculation, his defiant supernaturalism will again win a hearing.

Latin apologetics in the century after Tertullian produced few works of real importance. Cyprian, bishop of Carthage from 249 to 258, deserves at least a brief mention. Shortly after his conversion in 246 he wrote a lengthy letter[36] to his friend Donatus describing the firmness of conviction and serenity of spirit that he experienced following his Baptism. In this letter he deplores in conventional and rather stilted terms the vices, miseries, and dangers of the present life and concludes with an exhortation to raise one's eyes above the distractions of this world and to seek only the joys of heaven. While apologetical considerations are not absent from this letter, it belongs rather to the category of spiritual edification.

Several of Cyprian's shorter treatises are apologetical in character. His polemic *On the Vanity of Idols* (written in 247)[37] seeks to demonstrate, by arguments already seen here in Minucius Felix and Tertullian, that the idols are not divine and that there is but one God. Likewise apologetical is Cyprian's reply to Demetrianus, the proconsul of Africa (written in 252).[38] Responding to the charge that Christians are responsible for the recent plagues and famines, Cyprian attributes these evils to the senescence of the world. In vindicating the innocence of Christians and the guilt of the heathen, Cyprian repeats various arguments already used by Minucius and Tertullian.

Cyprian's principal treatise, *On the Unity of the Catholic Church* (about 251),[39] is pastoral rather than apologetical in intent; it is directed against schism rather than unbelief. But in his inspiring description of the spectacle of Catholic unity—reminiscent of certain passages in Irenaeus and Tertullian—Cyprian hints at what modern theologians often call the moral miracle of the Church—especially its universality, its inner cohesion, and its marvelous fecundity. In Cyprian's view there can be no life in Christ and hence no salvation for those who depart from the one true Church.

Cyprian also composed three books of *Testimonies*,[40] a compilation of Scripture texts, for the use of his convert friend Quirinus. The first two books, introduced by a common preface, are written in part against the Jews. Book 1, according to the prefatory letter, aims 'to show that the Jews, according to what had been foretold, had departed from God, and had lost God's favor, which had been given them in past time, and had been promised for the future; while the Christians had succeeded to their place, deserving well of the Lord by faith, and coming out of all nations from the whole world.'[41] This book consists of 24 theses on the relations between the Jews and the Gentiles. Each of these theses is backed up by a series of supporting quotations from both Testaments, intended to exhibit the harmony between the prophecy and the fulfillment.

Book 2 of the *Testimonies* deals, according to the Preface, with 'the Sacrament of Christ, that He has come who was announced according to the Scriptures, and has done and perfected all those things whereby He was foretold as being able to be perceived and known.'[42] It consists of 30 theses, all having to do with the person and the functions of Christ. These too are supported by numerous scriptural quotations.

Book 3 of the *Testimonies,* which was separately composed and apparently combined with the other two by a later editor, is also introduced by a preface to Quirinus. It contains 120 precepts for the moral guidance of the Christian, with supporting quotations from both Testaments, especially the New.

Cyprian's *Testimonies* are the best surviving example of a type of literature that must have been widespread in the early Church. Works such as Irenaeus's *Proof of the Apostolic Preaching* seem to rest upon compilations of Biblical quotations such as Cyprian's. Some scholars have conjectured that similar lists of prooftexts from the Jewish Scriptures antedated the NT itself.[43]

The Latin apologists of the 3d century are writers of exceptional energy and talent; but while they plead for the Christian cause with eloquence and skill, they cannot be compared with the Alexandrians for philosophical sophistication, comprehensive vision, and synthetic power. Their genius is practical rather than speculative. Both by natural disposition and by force of circumstance they are concerned with urgent political and pastoral issues and have little taste or leisure for broader and more philosophical questions. Unlike their counterparts in the East, they fail to set forth the case for Christianity in its full range and depth.

LATIN APOLOGISTS OF THE FOURTH CENTURY

Toward the beginning of this century, both in the East and in the West, the atmosphere changes. In spite of the sincere efforts of noble-minded men to restore ancient paganism, it becomes generally clear that paganism as a vital religious option is fast receding. While Christians continue to attack the old religions, they do so with increasing boldness and extravagance, as if they had no fear of being seriously challenged. They analyze the superstitions of their ancestors with a combination of wonder and disgust. When the triumph of Christianity is ratified by the conversion of Constantine, it becomes incumbent upon Christians to build a new religious synthesis. Even in the West the apologists feel obliged to offer their readers a global vision of life, which they generally construct by borrowing materials from the Stoic and Platonic philosophers and reshaping these in the light of the gospel.

Typical of the times is *The Case Against the Pagans* by Arnobius of Sicca.[44] The author, a layman and a new convert, shows little

C

knowledge of Christian theology, but he has a certain familiarity
with Stoic philosophy and a mass of information about ancient
religion. The first two books of his treatise are concerned with the
defense of Christianity against pagan objections and were written,
according to the best estimate, about 297. The remaining five books,
which carry the war into enemy territory by a counterattack on paganism, were presumably written sometime after 303.

Book 1 revolves about two main objections. First, it is charged
that Christians are to blame for the recent wars, famines, and pesti-
lences. Arnobius answers in his diffuse way, by a series of arguments.
He finds no evidence that these calamities have increased since
Christianity began or that, even if they have increased, they are to be
attributed to the anger of the gods rather than to merely natural
causes. In any case the charges are unfounded since they are made
by pagan priests, angry that their shrines and temples are being
deserted.

The second main objection is that Christians worship a mere man
who died upon a cross. Arnobius replies that Christ, since He
brought divine teaching, is rightly regarded as God. He proved His
divinity by many miracles attested by reliable witnesses. The divinity
of Christ is, moreover, corroborated by the rapid expansion of the
Christian faith and by the unshakable loyalty of its adherents, who are
ready to face death rather than recant. As for the crucifixion,
Arnobius answers the objections by arguments that sound Docetistic.
'That death of which you speak was of the human form assumed,
not His own; of the thing borne, not of the bearer.'[45]

In Book 2 Arnobius takes on the heathen philosophers. He objects
vehemently to Plato's doctrine that the soul is naturally immortal
and insists that it is naturally mortal though capable of receiving
immortality as a gift. In his refutation of Plato's doctrine of remin-
iscence he argues at length that the mind of man is, at birth, a
tabula rasa. Then he defends Christianity against those who attack it
on the ground of its novelty. Everything good, he says, was once
new; in fact, many aspects of Roman religion as currently practiced
are also of recent origin.

In these two opening books Arnobius shows an almost skeptical
awareness of the limitations of the human mind. He chides the
philosophers for their pride in seeking answers to curious questions.
After stating very forcefully the problem of evil (Hume could hardly
have improved on the statement), Arnobius freely admits that he has
no solution. Nor does he know why the Incarnation did not occur
earlier. To this last question he is content to retort by asking the pagan

why Hercules was not born earlier than he was. Regarding the life to come, Arnobius concedes that there is no way of strictly proving the reality of a future event. But he says that of two alternatives that are both uncertain 'we should believe the one which affords some hopes rather than the one which affords none at all.'[46] As some commentators remark, one has here an interesting anticipation of Pascal's wager argument.[47]

In the remaining five books Arnobius gives an interesting critique of the pagan religions of the Empire. He goes over some of the same ground as Clement of Alexandria but with vastly more detail concerning the myths and mysteries of various sects. Unlike Clement, who was at pains to show that the valid concerns of paganism are fulfilled in Christianity, Arnobius takes a strongly negative attitude. Influenced perhaps by Stoicism, he says that the gods are incapable of anger or other emotions; they have no sex or bodily functions. Nor are they of such a nature that they could be placated by bloody sacrifices, burnt offerings, or the games and dances with which their feasts are celebrated.

Surprisingly enough, Arnobius does not clearly deny the existence of the pagan gods. If a multiplicity of gods exist, he maintains, they are subordinate to the one supreme God and are sufficiently honored by the adoration paid to Him.

Arnobius scores a number of points against his pagan adversaries, but most of his work would be equally useful as an apology for deism. While he turns aside some illegitimate objections against Christianity, he furnishes very few positive arguments for accepting the Christian faith. In fact, it is doubtful that he knew his own religion very well. He never quotes from the OT and seems to have been largely ignorant of its contents. His references to the NT are few and generally vague. He has nothing to say about the doctrine of the Trinity and does not so much as mention the Holy Spirit. He is silent concerning the birth and Resurrection of Christ, never speaks of the Sacraments, and engages in no discussion of Church order or polity.

Lactantius, a younger contemporary and one-time pupil of Arnobius, was likewise a rhetorician by profession. From Numidia, his birthplace, he went to Nicomedia in Bithynia, where he was appointed a teacher by order of Diocletian. About 300 he became a Christian. Several years later, during the persecution of Diocletian, he was removed from his chair. After the conversion of Constantine he was returned to favor and summoned to Trèves in Gaul about 316. He spent his last years as a tutor to the emperor's son, Crispus.

Lactantius' claim to fame as an apologist rests on his principal work, the *Divine Institutes*,[48] which was probably written about 304–314 and was dedicated to Constantine. As he himself remarks, his aim, unlike that of Tertullian in the *Apology*, is not simply to answer the accusations against Christianity but to give instruction to educated pagans who might be inclined to embrace the new religion. For this reason he aims to give a positive exposition of the principal doctrines of the faith.

Few Christians before his time, Lactantius observes, wrote eloquently in defense of the faith. Tertullian, though highly learned, wrote in a rude, unpolished style, and was quite obscure. While Cyprian was a master of rhetoric, he was too much the theologian to be a good apologist. He had recourse to arguments from Scripture and to deeply mystical insights, thus going beyond the depth of his non-Christian readers. The *Octavius* of Minucius Felix succeeded admirably, but unfortunately its author did not produce other works of the same character. Like Minucius Felix, Lactantius is careful to express himself in a pure Ciceronian style and to quote almost exclusively from Greek and Latin authors. He makes extensive use of Plato, Cicero, Vergil, and Lucretius.

The first few books of the *Divine Institutes* are strongly apologetical in tone and content. Book 1 is largely devoted to establishing from reason and authority that there can be but one God and that He is all-provident. In the remainder of this book Lactantius engages in the familiar game of exposing the contradictions and absurdities in the pagan myths regarding the nature of the gods and the origins of the universe.

Book 2 surveys primeval history according to the main lines of Genesis, without, however, citing Scripture. It concludes with a polemic against images, which are presented as diabolical deceptions. In Book 3 Lactantius exposes the limitations of philosophy; while philosophy purports to be the pursuit of wisdom, he looks upon it as a futile effort to acquire wisdom by purely human powers, which are insufficient for the task. Book 4 is concerned with the divinity of Christ. Although he cites miracles as manifestations of Christ's divine power, Lactantius adds, '. . . He is believed a God by us, not for this reason, that He performed miracles (as Apollonius, for instance, is said to have done), but that we have seen that in Him were fulfilled all the things that were foretold to us by the preaching of the prophets.'[49]

Lactantius' arguments from the prophecies, however, suffer from the same defects noted in most of the apologists of the ancient

Church. He relies on doubtful readings, slanted translations, forced exegesis. He draws from apocryphal works such as the Psalms of Solomon and from forgeries such as the Sibylline Oracles, which he, like other apologists, accepts as genuine.

Books 5 and 6 of the *Divine Institutes* depart somewhat from apologetics in order to set forth the fundamental precepts of moral theology—a field in which Lactantius is at his best. But he does not neglect to score some apologetic points. In his chapter on justice he has occasion to discuss the persecutions. The fact that Christians of both sexes and of every age, tribe, and region exhibit the same contempt of death suggests that their attitude must have a basis in reason, which the heathen would do well to consider. They should ask themselves also why the Christian religion, far from being weakened and diminished by persecutions, is strengthened and increased.

Book 7, treating of eschatology, contains an interesting discussion of death and a defense of the immortality of the soul. A strong chiliast, Lactantius engages in many curious speculations about the final phase of universal history. His weaknesses as a dogmatic theologian are nowhere more apparent than in these chapters.

The *Divine Institutes* undoubtedly served to facilitate the conversion of many educated Romans to the Christian faith. Lactantius writes as a Christian thoroughly at home in the world of classical thought and deeply attached to the best interests of the Empire. His apologetic, splendid in architecture and graceful in style, contains very few original arguments. As a theologian he falls far below the standards set by Tertullian and the great Alexandrians. Nor does he have the independence of mind that gives interest to Arnobius. For all his talents he cannot be said to have made a notable contribution to the progress of apologetics.

As the 4th century progressed, the Latin apologists became more interested in enlisting state support for the new religion of the Empire than in seeking to give arguments for the truth of Christianity. A typical exhortation is *The Error of the Pagan Religions*,[50] addressed to the Christian Emperors Constantius and Constans about 346–350 by Julius Firmicus Maternus, a Sicilian-born aristocrat who had been a lawyer and then an astrologer before his conversion to Christianity. Of chief interest in this volume is a detailed but highly unflattering description of Roman paganism. The mystery cults in particular are pilloried as an obscene and diabolically inspired mockery of the true mystery of man's Redemption. In his conclusion Firmicus appeals to the legislation of Exodus and Deuteronomy as grounds for ruthlessly extirpating the worship of false gods and idols. While he lacks neither zeal nor eloquence, Firmicus scarcely breathes the true spirit of the gospel (as expressed, for instance, in Lk 9.55–56). Since he makes no effort to defend Christianity in terms that would make sense to a prospective convert, he should not actually be categorized as a Christian apologist. He is rather a polemicist against paganism.

Ambrose, who served as bishop of Milan from 374 till his death in 397, was likewise more concerned with the suppression of paganism than with giving reasons in support of Christianity. He had little respect for reason as an instrument of religious knowledge.[51] 'You are commanded to believe,' he wrote, 'not permitted to inquire.'[52] 'To Abraham it was counted righteousness that he sought not reasons but believed with most ready faith. It is good that faith should go before reason, lest we seem to exact a reason from our Lord God as from a man.'[53] 'By faith we come to knowledge, and by knowledge to discipline.'[54]

With his exorbitant exaltation of faith at the expense of reason, Ambrose quite naturally opposed any concessions to the non-Christian religions. When Symmachus, as Prefect of the City of Rome, pleaded for toleration on the ground that no one road, such as Christianity, could lead men to so great a mystery as the divine, Ambrose wrote to Valentinian II (383) arguing that every road discovered by man would be inadequate but that in Christ the very Word of God had spoken.[55] Quite characteristically, too, Ambrose in 388 used ecclesiastical sanctions to prevent Theodosius from making the Christians pay restitution to the Jews for having maliciously burned down the synagogue at Callinicum.

The controversy between Symmachus and Ambrose formed the subject of an apologetical poem, *Contra Symmachum*,[56] composed at Rome by Prudentius about 401–403. Book 1 of this poem is a polemic against pagan polytheism, reminiscent of Minucius Felix and Arnobius. In Book 2 Prudentius summarizes the arguments of Symmachus's memorial and rebuts them point by point as Ambrose had done in his letter to Valentinian II. The poem concludes with a plea to the emperor to abolish gladiatorial contests, in which human beings are made to die for the amusement of the crowds, just as formerly animals were sacrificed to the gods.

Christian apologetics in the West underwent a continuous decline in the course of the 4th century and was not to rise again until it had felt the intellectual stimulus of a new philosophical challenge. Neoplatonism was to provide this challenge, first for the Greek-speaking Church, then for the Latin.

GREEK APOLOGISTS OF THE FOURTH AND FIFTH CENTURIES

The founder of Neoplatonism, Plotinus (205–270), after studying at Alexandria under Ammonius Saccas, came to Rome in 245 and taught there until his death. His leading disciple, Porphyry (234–301), who had been an acquaintance of Origen as a youth, came from Caesarea to Athens and then, in 263, travelled to Rome to put himself at the feet of Plotinus. Plotinus and Porphyry, inspired in part by the example of the Christian theologians, erected a kind of systematic theology for late paganism and in so doing succeeded in providing a respectable intellectual alternative to Christianity.

While in Sicily in 268–270, Porphyry wrote *Against the Christians*,[57] comprising 15 books. The treatise has perished, but some excerpts have been preserved for modern times by Eusebius and other Christian writers. It seems certain that Porphyry assailed the Church partly on philosophical and partly on historical grounds. In philosophy he would have objected to the Christian doctrines that the world had a beginning and has an end in time, that evil is real, and that the dead would rise in body. His historical objections were based on a detailed critique of Scripture not unlike that set forth by Celsus' Jew. In particular Porphyry attacked the historicity of the NT accounts of the ancestry of Jesus, His miracles, and His Resurrection.

The Christian apologist who most effectively answered Porphyry was Eusebius of Caesarea. Although famed chiefly as a Church historian, Eusebius deserves high praise for his apologetical works, which make him, in the opinion of some authorities, the leading apologist of the ancient Church. Born in Caesarea about 263, he was educated there. He had to flee from his native city during the persecution of Diocletian, but he returned and in 313 was elected bishop of that city. From that time until his death about 339 he was a close theological adviser of the Emperor Constantine and in that capacity played a leading role in the disputes connected with the Arian heresy.

As an apologist Eusebius composed a monumental two-part work, *The Preparation of the Gospel* (written about 314)[58] and *The Proof of the Gospel* (about 320).[59] The 15 books of the former survive intact; out of the 20 books of the latter only the first 10 and a fragment of the 15th still exist. Shortly before his death, perhaps about 333, Eusebius wrote a briefer resumé of the main arguments in the two works just mentioned. This summary, the *Theophany* (or *Divine Manifestation*),[60] survives in a slavishly literal Syrian translation, though not in the original Greek. Eusebius also wrote 25 books, which have perished, in reply to Porphyry's *Against the Christians*.

It is customary to deplore his lack of originality. Whenever possible he establishes his points by quoting from other authors. But notwithstanding the multitude and length of these excerpts, Eusebius's apologia does have a genuine unity of design and argument. In the *Preparation* he answers the principal objections of pagans such as Porphyry who accuse the Christians of infidelity to the Greek religious heritage; in the *Proof* he absolves the Christians from the Jewish accusation that they have been unfaithful to the religion of the Hebrew Scriptures. In the *Preparation* Eusebius proceeds first negatively, by showing the absurdities of Greek polytheism, and then positively, by showing the vast superiority of the Hebrew faith. In the *Proof* he defends the Christians from the Jewish charges that they have misinterpreted the Scriptures and have illegitimately claimed the benefits of God's covenant promises without accepting the burden of conformity to the Mosaic Law.

Eusebius would be valuable, if for no other reason, because he has gathered up almost everything of real importance in the apologetics of the Greek Fathers, especially Clement and Origen. In the *Preparation* he also quotes extensively from Greek historical and philosophical works. He shows the highest esteem for Plato and for Porphyry, both of whom he quotes more often to agree with than to differ from, even though Porphyry is thought to have been the adversary whom Eusebius chiefly had in mind.

In the first few books of the *Preparation* Eusebius restates more thoroughly than earlier Greek apologists the Christian case against Greek polytheism. The demons, he contends, have seduced men into the idolization of pleasure, and the cult of pleasure has led to moral degeneracy. The wisest philosophers of Greece, Eusebius contends, ridiculed the gods of the Greek pantheon.

In Book 5 of the *Preparation* Eusebius goes on to develop a fairly original polemic against the deceptiveness of the Greek oracular religion, which leads him into Book 6, a long and by no means superficial discussion of fate and free will. Beginning with Book 7 he examines the religion of Moses and the Hebrew Prophets. Like his predecessors Eusebius exaggerates the antiquity and perfect unanimity of the Biblical writers. His own philosophic interests betray him into depicting the early Hebrews as deeply concerned with reflection on the causes of the universe and with the cultivation of the inner man. In his comparisons between Greek philosophy and Hebrew theology, which take up the last five books of the *Preparation*, Eusebius Platonizes the Bible almost as much as he baptizes Greek speculation. He finds strong confirmations of the Christian doctrine of the

Trinity in the Old Testament doctrine of word and spirit and in the Plotinian doctrine of the three primary hypostases.

The *Proof of the Gospel*, less tied to Greek philosophy than the *Preparation*, is perhaps of greater contemporary interest. Books 1 and 2 are a prolegomenon for the remainder. To enhance the antiquity of Christianity, Eusebius holds it to be a republication, in more explicit form, of the religion of the Patriarchs. He dismisses the Mosaic Law as an unfortunate departure that God permitted after the Israelites had been weakened by demonic assaults in Egypt. The Mosaic Law, unlike the patriarchal religion, was incapable of founding a truly universal religion; it therefore had to be superseded in order that the prophetic promises of the OT might be fulfilled.

Book 3, which shows Eusebius at his best, focuses on Jesus Christ. For the sake of the Gentiles, who are not likely to be moved by deductions from the Hebrew Scriptures, Eusebius here argues directly from the NT. He calls attention to the surpassing moral stature of Christ and the sublimity of evangelical doctrine, which agrees with, and at the same time outstrips, the best in Greek philosophy. Then he turns to the miracles of Jesus as demonstrations of divine power. In order to validate the miracle stories, Eusebius appeals to the credibility of the Apostles. If one supposes them to have been deceivers, he asks, whence come their agreement, their willingness to abandon home and riches for the apostolate, their readiness to die for their message? Ironically he suggests that perhaps one should suppose that they entered into an insidious pact to this effect: Let us manufacture untruths that will profit neither ourselves nor those being deceived, nor indeed Christ Himself. What could be finer, ask the Apostles, than to renounce all things just to deceive and be deceived?

The remaining books of the *Proof of the Gospel* deal mostly with the OT prophecies of Christ. Here Eusebius takes up with his accustomed thoroughness the various texts that had by his time become traditional. More the advocate than the judge, he is determined to establish that each of these texts is really Christological. If Eusebius surpasses his predecessors in the handling of these prooftexts, his superiority lies not in his better judgment but in his more careful attention to textual and hermeneutical problems that others tended to neglect.

Strongly in favor of the Constantinian union of Church and State, Eusebius tends to view the Christianization of the Empire as the universal goal of history. With his historian's eye he cannot forget that the time of the Incarnation coincided with the unification of the world under a single Empire. At this time, he says in the *Theophany*, warlike hatred between nations came to a complete end. When the Gospels were written, who could have foreseen that their message would one day be extended to the entire world? Yet the power of truth has proved invincible. No longer do the demons hold men's minds in the grip of idolatry. No longer do the ambiguous replies of oracles confuse and torment anxious seekers after truth. 'Every word about fate has been rendered unavailing: every war-making necessity too has been removed far away: the Divine peace-making Word is hymned throughout the whole earth: the race of man is reconciled to God its Father; and peace and love have been restored to all nations.'[61]

Few if any of the early apologists have so stressed the signs of the times as arguments for the Christian faith. Eusebius, the court theologian, did not need to be taught the worldly relevance of revelation. But the very skill with which he adapted his apologetic to his own times has made his work less serviceable for posterity. Twentieth-century man, with a long and mournful chronicle of wars among supposedly Christian nations behind him, finds it difficult to respond to the triumphant enthusiasm and grandiloquent rhetoric of Eusebius. If he was correct in believing that the gospel had power to reconcile men to one another and to bring them into an all-embracing society, he underestimated the difficulty of fully converting men to the gospel.

Athanasius of Alexandria (*c.* 295–373), who composed his youthful works of apologetics about the same time that Eusebius was authoring his learned treatises, registers a similar mood of triumphant joy. Educated at the famous catechetical school, Athanasius grew up during the last and greatest persecution, which ended in Egypt in 311. His two little books, the *Treatise Against the Pagans* and *The Incarnation of the Word of God*, were composed about 318, for the instruction of a friend and recent convert. They reflect the glorious springtime when the Church had begun to benefit from the Edict of Milan and had not yet suffered the setback of the Arian heresy.

The *Treatise Against the Pagans*[62] has little originality. Following the main lines of Judeo-Christian polemics since the Book of Wisdom, it reiterates the standard arguments against idolatry and polytheism. Athanasius appears to be especially indebted to Athenagoras and Clement.

The Incarnation of the Word of God[63] is still one of the most widely read pieces of patristic theology. In its vibrant enthusiasm it recalls the *Protrepticus* of Clement. The main emphasis is not negative and polemical but positive and doctrinal. As a theologian Athanasius is far superior to Minucius Felix, Arnobius, and even Lactantius. His warm and eager commitment to Christ is more winning than the vitriolic eloquence of a Tertullian. Unlike Origen and Eusebius, who are much more thorough, Athanasius writes in swiftly moving prose and does not become bogged down in points of erudition.

The first portion of this little book is a brief dogmatic discussion of the problem, *Cur Deus homo?.* Athanasius concludes, somewhat as Anselm was to do, that there was no other way in which God could satisfy both His justice and His mercy. He then goes on to establish against the Jews that Jesus really fulfilled the messianic promises. He cites the standard prooftexts without recognition of their ambiguities and asserts confidently that the 70 weeks of Daniel[64] had run their course at the moment of the Incarnation. In the last portion Athanasius refutes Hellenistic objections to the doctrine of the Incarnation.

Justly famous in this treatise are the passages in which Athanasius argues to the reality of the Resurrection on the ground that Christ is presently active in the world. All His disciples, says Athanasius, despise death as an enemy already overcome. Drawn by Christ, men of all nations are streaming into the Church. Since the time of Christ, the pagan oracles have fallen silent, the shrines of the idols are being abandoned, the heroes and gods of the pagans are being exposed as mere mortals, and magic is being trampled under foot. 'Anyone who likes may see the proof of glory in the virgins of Christ, and in the young men who practise chastity as part of their religion, and in the assurance of immortality in so great and glad a company of martyrs.'[65]

Like Eusebius, then, Athanasius writes with high enthusiasm at the moment of the Church's greatest triumph. Not suspecting the difficulties to the faith that might arise (and that he himself would later experience) at the hands of an absolutist emperor seeking to regulate the affairs of the Church, Athanasius pointed with evident satisfaction to the signs of the times. 'Demons, so far from continuing to impose on people by their deceits and oracle-givings and sorceries, are routed by the sign of the cross if they so much as try. On the other hand, while idolatry and everything else that opposes the faith of Christ is daily dwindling and weakening and falling, see, the Saviour's teaching is increasing everywhere.'[66] An effective manifesto to his own generation, the *Incarnation of the Word of God* will continue to reveal its power whenever men vividly recall that moment of glory and whenever like revivals of faith and fervor occur.

As in the West, so also in the East, the last three quarters of the 4th century were a period of decline in apologetics. There was no major stimulus for new apologetical efforts until the reign of Julian the Apostate (361–363), who looked on himself as mystically called to restore the pagan heritage of Greco-Roman civilization, using Neoplatonism as an intellectual base. Julian wrote three books *Against the Galileans* (363), the contents of which are only vaguely recoverable from Christian refutations. He sought to show, among other things, that Christianity was a debased form of Judaism with pagan accretions. A number of pagan intellectuals and some Jews rallied to Julian's support, though only a few accepted his plan to establish a kind of pagan church on the Christian model.

Julian's attempt to overthrow Christianity provoked a flurry of hasty responses. In his own lifetime he was answered by the great Antiochene scholar, Diodore of Tarsus, who rose to defend the divinity of Christ. Shortly after the emperor's death, Gregory of Nazianzus composed two impassioned orations against him. John Chrysostom, in an early panegyric of St. Babylas of Antioch (about 382),[67] gloated over Julian's recent failure to restore the worship of Apollo at the site of the martyr bishop's grave.

Chrysostom's main apologetical treatise is his relatively brief and apparently incomplete *Demonstration to Jews and Greeks that Christ is God* (about 381–87).[68] Against the Greeks he here argues that Jesus has done what no mere man could do, namely, to win over men of all nations from corruption to a new way of life. This he has done through the preaching of a small band of ignorant Galileans. Fired with enthusiasm for the new faith, martyrs still lay down their lives, as may be observed today among the Persians. In a second part of the treatise, directed against the Jews, Chrysostom contends that the messianic promises have been fulfilled and that the Christian faith, according to the predictions of Christ Himself, is spreading irresistibly.

Chrysostom's notorious eight *Homilies against the Jews*,[69] preached at Antioch about 387, are more an embarrassment than an asset to Christian apologetics. With surprising lack of empathy, Chrysostom accuses the Jews of stubborn blindness, demands that they renounce their errors, and warns the faithful against their diabolical malice. He paints a vindictive picture of Christ Himself: 'Yet, O Jew, herein lies the wonder, that He whom you crucified did afterwards pull down your city, scatter your people, and disperse your nation throughout the whole world.'[70] It is scarcely surprising that the Jews were not won over by such argumentation. In partial extenuation of Chrysostom one may allude to historical factors such as the support that some Jews had given to Julian, the aggressive tactics of the Jewish community at Antioch, and the exaggerations characteristic of sermon and satirical literature. But it still remains true that Chrysostom's work set an unfortunate precedent for medieval polemics against the Jews. In this respect Chrysostom compares unfavorably with Justin, who showed himself at least capable of dialogue.

Toward the end of the 4th century Apollinaris of Laodicea (*c.* 310–*c.* 390) made a major contribution to apologetics with his 30 books against Porphyry and his treatise *On Truth* directed against the Emperor Julian. Unfortunately, however, these works have perished and are known now only from passing references in Jerome, Sozomen, and others.

Of Cyril of Alexandria's lengthy treatise *For the Holy Religion of the Christians against the Impious Julian* (*c.* 435–440)[71] only 10 of the original 20 (or perhaps 30) books survive. Without personal synthesis, Cyril follows his adversary step by step, somewhat as Origen had done with Celsus. However, he is far less successful. Antipathetic to classical culture and science, he adopts the position that no books beyond the Bible are necessary for a perfect formation in piety and letters. In his zeal to convict Julian of every type of absurdity he does not hesitate to distort the latter's obvious meaning.[72]

For all practical purposes the patristic age in the apologetics of the Eastern Church comes to a close with the great Antiochene theologian, Theodoret of Cyrrhus (*c.* 393–485). Probably in his youth, as a monk at Nicerte near Antioch, he composed a magnificent *summa* against paganism entitled *The Cure of Pagan Maladies; or, The Truth of the Gospels Proved from Greek Philosophy.*[73]

In his preface Theodoret explains the necessity of refuting three main objections raised against Christianity by cultured Hellenists: that the Christians, despising reason, rely upon blind faith; that the Biblical writers were ignorant and unpolished; and that the cult of martyrs is a senseless superstition. The answers to these objections that emerge in the course of the treatise are much what one might expect. To the first he replies in Book 1 that even the philosophers demand human faith from their disciples and that in the mystery religions only a few hierophants understand the meaning of the sacred rites. If such credit can be extended to human authorities, how much more should it be accorded to the divine Teacher! In this connection Theodoret engages in an interesting discussion of the mutual priorities of faith and reason. He explains how every student first believes in order that he may be able to understand but that belief itself always presupposes a modicum of understanding.

As to the second objection, Theodoret turns it aside by pointing out (also in Book 1) that elegance of style, which is admittedly found more among Greeks than among barbarians, can be deceptive. Socrates, as one reads in the *Apology*, was not ashamed to use simple and uncouth language. The wisest Greeks were humble enough to learn from the barbarians, whose wisdom is far more ancient and venerable.

When he turns to the third objection, in the latter part of his treatise (Book 8), Theodoret points out that God Himself has glorified the martyrs by working extraordinary wonders through their relics. The ex-votos bearing witness to these cures are evident everywhere. It is quite natural, then, that idols are being abandoned and that crowds should flock to the shrines of martyrs.

As the treatise evolves, it turns into something vaster than a reply to these random objections. In effect Theodoret outlines a whole system of dogma and Christian morality, as may be seen from the subject matter of the 12 books. In Book 1, he discusses the nature of faith and the interrelationship between faith and reason. Then in Book 2 he deals with God, the first principle. Thereafter he treats of the angels, demons, and false gods (Book 3), the material world (Book 4), the nature of man (Book 5), and divine providence (Book 6). The next three books deal with practical questions: sacrifices (Book 7), the cult of martyrs (Book 8), and laws (Book 9). Then, after a discussion of true and false oracles (Book 10), Theodoret concludes with treatises on death and judgment (Book 11) and the nature of true virtues (Book 12).

In dealing with these various problems his method is almost constant. He shows, first, that the philosophers disagree but that some of the best philosophers, including Plato, hold views that at least approach the Christian doctrine. The Greek sages, however, do not do justice to their own best intuitions, nor are their lives up to the level of their doctrine. The Bible, on the other hand, speaks unanimously. It heralds decisively what the philosophers are tentatively groping toward, and gives men power to live accordingly. Those who accept Christianity, even though they be unlearned, possess wisdom and virtue accessible to very few pupils of the philosophers.

The net result of Theodoret's disquisition is an impressive synthesis between the testimony of the Bible and the highest insights of Platonic and Neoplatonic speculation. Theodoret made an important contribution to Christian humanism and was to be highly esteemed by Ficino and other Renaissance Platonists. As apologetic his argument is persuasive up to a point but leaves many unanswered questions. Theodoret is open to the charge of selecting what he likes from Greek philosophy and rejecting what does not please him. Why are the philosophers to be approved whenever they agree with the Bible and reprobated when they disagree, unless one is willing to assume the very point at issue, namely, the revealed character of the Biblical message? If Theodoret had been proficient in philosophy he might have been able to show that the points he accepts from the philosophers are capable of being solidly demonstrated, while those he repudiates are based on faulty reasoning. But Theodoret was no philosopher. His work therefore cannot be exonerated from the charge of superficiality.

In emphasizing the accord between Platonism and Christianity, Theodoret unwittingly transforms the latter. He gives the impression that Christianity is a revealed philosophy or at best a school of virtue. His approach to the faith is doctrinaire and moralistic rather than historical and kerygmatic. The strong Christological devotion that gives life and warmth to the apologies of Clement and Athanasius is absent in Theodoret. He brings in the Incarnation as a kind of appendix to the treatise on providence.

Like Clement and Eusebius, Theodoret is fond of quoting pagan as well as sacred authors. Indeed he quotes almost the same passages, presumably gathered from Christian florilegia, but he weaves them more successfully into his own work than Eusebius had done. His arguments, likewise, are borrowed from earlier apologists. To read *The Cure of Pagan Maladies* after studying the other Greek apologies can therefore be a disappointing experience. But for one who has to make a choice of some one treatise, Theodoret's commends itself as much as any. There is perhaps no apologetical work that better illustrates the strengths and weaknesses of Greek apologetics in the patristic age.

AUGUSTINE AND HIS DISCIPLES

Thanks to his rare combination of speculative power, erudition, and literary eloquence, Aurelius Augustine (354–430) occupies a place of unique eminence in the story of patristic apologetics. As a thinker he is the equal of Origen; as a scholar he ranks not far below Origen and Eusebius; and as a writer he outclasses even Clement and Lactantius. He is the first Western apologist to achieve true eminence as a theologian. Whereas others were content to achieve tactical victories or to negotiate profitable alliances, Augustine was able to situate the approach to Christian faith within the framework of a highly developed metaphysic of religious knowledge. He gave new precision to the distinctions between authority and reason, faith and understanding, which have remained classic since his time. Besides recapitulating all that was best in the patristic tradition before him, Augustine formulated an original response to the philosophical onslaught of pagan Neoplatonism and to the political critique of Christianity on the part of Roman patriots. For all these reasons he deserves to be treated at some length.[74]

For an understanding of Augustine the apologist it is indispensable that one have some familiarity with the early philosophical dialogues that he composed in his retreat at the villa of Cassiciacum, near Rome, in the winter 386–387, while preparing to be baptized. His dialogues *On the Happy Life, An Answer to Skeptics (Contra academicos), Providence and the Problem of Evil (De ordine)*, and his *Soliloquies* stem from this period.[75] The following year (388) he wrote his twin treatises *On the Catholic and Manichaean Ways of Life (De moribus ecclesiae catholicae* and *De moribus manichaeorum)*,[76] which are likewise strongly apologetic. Other anti-Manichaean works such as the treatises *Of True Religion* and *On the Usefulness of Belief* (probably to be dated respectively in 390 and 391)[77] present his views on the role of authority in religious knowledge, and outline his demonstration of the truth of the Catholic faith. From Augustine's middle period, the dialogue *On Free Will* (about 395–396),[78] the *Reply to the Letter of Manichaeus Called Fundamental* (about 397), and the *Confessions* (about 397–400) are of importance for the apologetic theme. Of his later works the most pertinent is his monumental *City of God* (413–426).[79]

The point of departure for Augustine's apologetic is subjective and psychological rather than objective and systematic. He notes within man an inescapable drive toward happiness and, once the possibility of immortality becomes known, a drive toward eternal life. As he observes at the conclusion of his dialogue *On the Happy Life*: 'This, then, is the full satisfaction of souls, this the happy life: to recognize piously and completely the One through whom you are led into the truth, the nature of the truth you enjoy, and the bond that connects you with the supreme measure.'[80]

Augustine holds that human reason is capable of establishing by indubitable arguments the existence of God. His favorite argument is taken from the 'eternal truths.' Truth, Augustine holds, is absolute; it is above men's minds, which are above their bodies and the whole material world about them. 'If there is anything more excellent than wisdom, doubtless it, rather, is God. But if there is nothing more excellent, then truth itself is God. Whether there is or is not such a higher thing, you cannot deny that God exists. . . .'[81]

In depicting the effort of the mind to reach upward beyond all material and changeable things to the eternal, invisible Godhead, Augustine relies heavily on his Neoplatonic philosophic heritage. But he finds numerous Scripture texts in his favor. He is fond of quoting from Paul: 'Look not on the things which are seen, but on the things which are not seen. For the things which are seen are temporal, but the things which are not seen are eternal' (2 Cor 4.18). He also quotes from 1 Jn 2.15: 'Love not the world or the things which are in the world. For everything that is in the world is the lust of the flesh, the lust of the eyes and the ambition of this world.'[82] To approach God with the mind demands suitable moral dispositions—detachment from the senses, restraint of the passions, and earnest longing for enlightenment.[83]

Because Plato so acutely perceived the necessity of rising above matter and the senses he was, according to Augustine, very close to Christ. If Plato were to return to life, Augustine assures us, he would be delighted to find the churches full of men seeking spiritual and intelligible goods, animated by hope of eternal blessedness.[84] Augustine is confident that Socrates and Plato, if they lived today, would become Christians 'as so many Platonists of recent times have done.'[85]

While reason is in principle capable of knowing something of God, Augustine is no rationalist in natural theology. He asserts that for the mind to see God it must be illuminated by God Himself.[86] At best, one's knowledge of God in this life is negative rather than positive. God is 'better known by knowing what he is not.'[87] Many men have failed entirely to achieve the knowledge of God through reason. The philosophers disagree among themselves about whether one should worship many gods, one God, or no god.[88] Since wisdom is so scarce and difficult to attain, the path of skepticism is a very tempting one. Augustine was himself inclined toward the view of the skeptics until he became aware that God draws the soul not only by reason but by authority.[89]

In matters of great importance, pertaining to divinity, Augustine maintains, one must first believe before he seeks to know.[90] One ought to believe that God exists because 'that is taught in the books of great men who have left their testimony in writing that they lived with the Son of God, and because they have written that they saw things which could not have happened if there were no God.'[91] In other words, Augustine proposes an approach to the existence of God that is integral with and inseparable from his belief in miracles and in the Christian testimony. The normal order is first to believe such matters, and then later to arrive at some rational understanding of them. This agrees with the text from Isaiah so frequently quoted by Augustine, 'Unless you believe you shall not understand' (Is 7.9, LXX).

Augustine, however, is quite aware that the priorities between reason and belief are mutual. Nobody, he says, 'believes anything unless he is first convinced that it ought to be believed.'[92] Before he can lend credence to anyone, one must have reasons for accepting him as an authority.[93] But this brings one face to face with a grave difficulty. How can one know who is wise unless he himself is wise? Wisdom, unlike material things, is of such a nature that it cannot be known except by those who possess it; and if one is seeking it, he does not possess it. Hence he is in no position to judge what teacher is or is not wise.[94]

In some of his writings Augustine gives a pragmatic answer to this difficulty, based on the alternative possibilities with which he, as a religious inquirer, found himself confronted. His argument may be traced in the latter part of his anti-Manichaean treatise *On the Usefulness of Belief*. The Manichaeans, he says, raised certain specious objections to the Catholic doctrine of the causes of evil as they understood it, and then proposed their own explanation as one that could be justified by demonstrative reasons. But Augustine found that when he pressed them, they gave not reasons but rhetoric. While purporting to dispense with authority, they actually invoked it. They invited men to learn from them rather than the Catholic Church and frankly sought to bring men to belief in Christ. Thus they implicitly contradicted themselves.

Now if one is to believe in Christ, Augustine replied, this cannot be done on the basis of personal acquaintance with Him. The choice is between believing in Him on the unanimous authority of the great and ancient Church, which traces its history back to the original companions of Christ, and doing so out of respect for the Manichaeans, who are of recent origin, few in numbers, and discordant among themselves. If one believes in Christ through others than the Manichaeans, why should he come to them for instruction about Christ? Let them advise one rather to consult the leaders of the great mass of believers.[95]

Influenced, no doubt, by Tertullian, Augustine looked upon the Bible as the book of the Catholic Church. He himself came to the gospel through the influence of Catholics, and he argued that anything tending to weaken the authority of the Church would inevitably undermine his confidence in the gospel. If the Manichaeans, then, wished to lay weight upon their alleged arguments from the gospel, they ought to support the claims of the Catholic Church! In this context Augustine wrote his famous sentence: 'I should not believe the gospel except as moved by the authority of the Catholic Church.'[96]

Augustine, then, had strong pragmatic grounds for beginning his own religious investigations with Catholicism. The Catholic Church recommended itself to his consideration, first, by reason of its size, antiquity, and the relative unanimity of its teachers; and second, by reason of the fact that it was the one in which he had been brought up. In the religious crisis of his early 30s he resolved to remain a catechumen in that Church until he was persuaded either that it taught the truth he was in search of or that nothing was to be gained from seeking.[97]

The story how Augustine proceeded from his practical decision to investigate Catholicism to his conviction that it was a divine revelation is well known to all readers of his *Confessions*. In Book 8 he tells how he was struck by learning of the heroic virtue of the monks and virgins who dedicated their lives to God, in poverty and chastity, according to the example of Anthony. In their example he found hope and confidence that he himself could be delivered from the enslavement of lust and ambition by embracing the Christian faith with his whole heart.

In his apologetical works, Augustine, mirroring the route he had followed in his own religious pilgrimage, frequently argues to the truth of Christianity on the basis of the concrete reality of the Catholic Church. The history of the Church in the past few centuries seemed to contain an evident lesson:

After all the Christian blood shed, after all the burnings and crucifixions of the martyrs, fertilized by these things churches have sprung up as far afield as among the barbarian nations. That thousands of young men and maidens contemn marriage and live in chastity causes no one surprise. Plato might have suggested that, but he so dreaded the perverse opinion of his times that he is said to have given in to nature and declared [in]continence to be no sin. Views are accepted which it was once monstrous to maintain, even as it is monstrous now to dispute them. All over the inhabited world the Christian rites are entrusted to men who are willing to make profession and to undertake the obligations required. Every day the precepts of Christianity are read in the churches and expounded by the priests. Those who try to fulfil them beat their breasts in contrition. Multitudes enter upon this way of life from every race, forsaking the riches and honours of the present world, desirous of dedicating their whole life to the one most high God. Islands once deserted and many lands formerly left in solitude are filled with monks. In cities and towns, castles and villages, country places and private estates, there is openly preached and practiced such a renunciation of earthly things and conversion to the one true God that daily throughout the entire world with almost one voice the human race makes response: Lift up your hearts to the Lord.[98]

Augustine's principal argument for the truth of Catholicism takes the form of what today might be called a demonstration that the Church is a moral miracle. His clearest development of this theme is found in his tract *The Way of Life of the Catholic Church*, in which he extols the beneficent influences of the Church as the 'true mother of Christians.'[99] In this apologia he shows that the argument is not invalidated by the faults of 'those who, while professing the name of Christian, neither understand nor manifest the nature of the faith they profess.'[100]

In discussions such as this Augustine often alludes to the marvel that in spite of all opposition from worldly powers, the Church succeeded in converting what he hyperbolically calls the human race.[101] While he does not unequivocally characterize this expansion of the Church as a miracle, he suggests as much. In the *City of God* he speaks of three incredibilities: 'It is incredible that Christ should have risen in His flesh and, with His flesh, have ascended into heaven; it is incredible that the world should have believed a thing so incredible; it is incredible that men so rude and lowly, so few and unaccomplished, should have convinced the world, including men of learning, of something so incredible and have convinced men so conclusively.'[102]

According to the received accounts, the Apostles converted the nations with the help of miracles. The skeptic may deny this, but if so, he makes it more difficult for himself to explain the conversion of the civilized world. 'We are still left with the one stupendous miracle, which is all we need, the miracle of the whole world believing, without benefit of miracles, the miracle of the Resurrection.'[103]

In his discussion of the Church as a marvel, Augustine does not overlook the constancy of the martyrs, which had so impressed Tertullian and others. Contrasting the behavior of Christians with that of Romans who allegedly believe in the divinity of Romulus, Augustine asks: 'Has anyone ever chosen death rather than deny, when commanded to deny, that Romulus and Hercules and the rest were gods?'[104] The Christians, on the contrary, went joyfully to their deaths for the sake of Christ and defiantly continued to preach Him openly to every people in the world, notwithstanding every prohibition and penalty. As a result, says Augustine, the blood of martyrs watered the seeds of hope implanted in the world by Christ's rising from the dead. 'The result was that the truth that the world once rejected with all the fury of hate, it now sought with the fervor of faith.'[105]

In various tracts and sermons Augustine presents materials for an exceptionally rich and thorough treatise on physical miracles. He is fully cognizant of the problem of the historicity of the miracle stories told in Scriptures and elsewhere, and he honestly faces up to the task of distinguishing between true miracles and the wonders of magic and necromancy. Aware of these difficulties, he does not demand too much from an apologetic of miracles.

Most of all, perhaps, he stresses the pedagogical value of miracles. They serve to call man's attention to things he might not otherwise notice and to remind him of the power and goodness of God, which he might otherwise forget. The miracles of Christ, he says, speak eloquently of God's goodness and mercy, and attract men's hearts. Miraculous signs were particularly needed in the early years of the Church, when the witnesses of the faith were few and unlearned, but they became less essential once the Church had been diffused throughout the world. God did not allow miracles to continue in great numbers 'lest the mind should always seek visible things, and the human race should grow cold by becoming accustomed to things which when they were novelties kindled its faith.'[106] Yet miracles have not utterly ceased. In the *City of God*, Book 22, ch. 8, Augustine gives circumstantial descriptions of some familiar to him at first or second hand.

On the basis of Scripture and the claims of the non-Christian religions, Augustine admits that there are many prodigies that cannot be attributed to the God of Christians. He therefore recognizes two classes of prodigy, those that are demonic and those that are angelic or divine. Christianity has in its favor certain extraordinary miracles —such as the Virgin Birth, the Resurrection and the Ascension of Christ—that are not paralleled in pagan religions.[107] If the historicity of these miracles is contested, Augustine calls on the confirmatory arguments from fulfilled prophecy and from the marvelous expansion of the Catholic Church. These three types of argument converge and interlock, forming an unbreakable chain of evidence.

Second, Augustine maintains that true and false miracles can be

distinguished on the basis of their religious effects. In his refutation of
the Neoplatonist Porphyry, in the 10th book of the *City of God*,
Augustine argues that any miracles that tend to divert men from the
worship of the one true God 'in union with whom, as even the
Platonists abundantly testify, all blessedness is found,' are demonic,
whereas those that augment one's faith in God and one's love for
Him are genuine and heavenly.[108] The marvels of magic are meant to
persuade men to worship many gods or to adore the created spirits
who perpetrate them, but true miracles, such as those recounted in
Scripture, draw one to adore the God above all gods.[109]

In the apologetic writings of his early period Augustine gives
little weight to the argument from prophecy, which presumably
played no important part in his conversion. But in some of his later
works, composed after his elevation to the episcopate, e.g., in Book 18
of the *City of God* and in *De consensu evangelistarum*, *De fide rerum
quae non videntur*, *Contra Faustum*, and *Adversus judaeos*, he does
attempt to prove the truth of Christianity from the fulfillment of
what was promised in the OT. He progresses beyond earlier apologists
in that he does not limit himself to texts that imply miraculous precog-
nition on the part of the Prophets or hagiographers. Rather he looks
upon the total experience of the people of God under the old law as a
providential foreshadowing of what was to be accomplished in Christ
and the Church. This permits him to engage in a mystical or allegorical
interpretation of virtually any text from the OT. While this form of
exegesis may be helpful for Christian spirituality, it creates some
difficulty in apologetics, inasmuch as it depends on interpretations
that are not evident except, perhaps, to those who are previously convinced that Christ is the fulfillment of the Law and the Prophets.
Modern critics object, with some justice, that Augustine relies too
much on forced interpretations and adaptations totally foreign to the
minds of the sacred writers.[110]

One of the pieces in which Augustine most presses the argument
from prophecy is his sermon *In Answer to the Jews*, probably preached
sometime after 425. Like Chrysostom's *Homilies Against the Jews*,
this seems to have been intended primarily to warn the Christians
against falling prey to Jewish objections and influences. But Augustine
is free from the harshness of Chrysostom. After giving Christian
interpretations of a number of texts from the Jewish Scriptures, he
exhorts his hearers:

Dearly beloved, whether the Jews receive these divine testimonies
with joy or with indignation, nevertheless, when we can, let us

proclaim them with great love for the Jews. Let us not proudly glory against the broken branches; let us rather reflect by whose grace it is, and by how much mercy, and on what root, we have been ingrafted. Then, not savoring of pride, but with a deep sense of humility, not insulting with presumption, but rejoicing with trembling, let us say: 'Come yet and let us walk in the light of the Lord,' because His 'name is great among the Gentiles.' If they hear Him and obey Him, they will be among those to whom Scripture says: 'Come yet to him and be enlightened: and your faces shall not be confounded. . . .'[111]

While Augustine accepted the traditional argument from prophecy and utilized it in his debates with Jews and Manichaeans, it does not seem to have been of crucial importance for his own faith. Even miracles were for him important only insofar as they provided a clue as to how the Catholic faith had spread in the age of persecution. For his personal faith he relied very much on the divine wisdom that he found in Catholic teaching, and second on the authority of the Church, 'inaugurated by miracles, nourished by hope, enlarged by love, established by age.'[112] To these motives he adds, in the same passage, the continuous succession of popes and bishops, and the very name of Catholic, which no heresy has ever been able to wrest from the true Church.

Thus far we have referred only occasionally to Augustine's *City of God*, which occupies a unique place among his works by reason of its length and majestic architecture. It was occasioned by the pagan charges that the sack of Rome under Alaric (410) was a punishment for Rome's infidelity to the ancient gods. As Augustine explains in his *Retractations*,[113] the first 10 books of the *City of God* are primarily apologetical and polemical; they are designed to refute the view that pagan religion is necessary for man's welfare. In Books 1 through 5 he proves this with regard to man's temporal life and in Books 6 through 10 with regard to the life beyond death. Then in Books 11 to 22 he develops his own theology of history, tracing the concurrent and interacting vicissitudes of the cities of God and of man.

The polemic against paganism in the first 10 books is eminently successful and doubtless did much to undermine whatever prestige paganism still enjoyed at the time. In Book 1 Augustine shows that the atrocities of the sack of Rome were those customary in war but that the moderation practiced by the victors, and especially their respect for the churches as places of sanctuary, were due to the power of Christ's name. If many Christians suffered as the pagans did, this is partly because if God were to spare them such calamities, men would be drawn to the faith for unworthy motives. Yet the Christian doctrine of the Cross and Resurrection enables Christians to suffer with a patience and hope not available to others. The afflictions visited on Rome were a just punishment for its moral degradation.

In Book 2 Augustine dilates further on the vices of pagan society, which the Greco-Roman religion, far from arresting, actually fostered. Book 3 demonstrates the powerlessness of the gods worshipped by the Romans to prevent previous calamities such as the Punic Wars, the revolt of the Gracchi, and the civil wars under Marius and Sulla. In Book 4 Augustine points out the impossibility of ascribing the expansion of the Roman Empire to divinities such as Jupiter or the various others (Victory, Felicity, Fortune, and the like) who are sometimes invoked. On the other hand, the history of the Jews shows that their kingdom was preserved as long as they were faithful to the Mosaic religion. In Book 5 Augustine goes on to show that the rise and fall of empires is not ruled by chance, by fate, or by the stars but only by the true God, who wills to confer earthly glory upon those who live up to the moral standards of the earthly city. Beyond these temporal rewards, Christian emperors look forward in hope to the fullness of happiness in the life to come.

Books 6 to 10, probing more deeply into speculative questions, aim to exhibit the futility of looking to the pagan gods for salvation in the future life. In Book 6 Augustine argues that if the gods cannot give temporal prosperity, they are even less capable of bestowing eternal blessings. This incapacity, according to Book 7, affects even those whom Varro classified as the 'higher' gods of 'physical theology.' These gods, indeed, are in many cases nothing more than personified natural forces. Having previously disposed of the old paganism, Augustine turns in Books 8 and 9 to the religion of Plato and the Neoplatonists. In Book 8, after showing that these schools excel all other philosophical sects, he cautiously accepts the common view that Plato was probably indebted to Moses for some of his crucial insights.[114] Then he goes on to reprobate the polytheism and demon worship of the later Platonists, especially Plotinus and Apuleius. In this connection he argues (in Book 9) that the angels, though they are instruments of Providence, should not be worshipped with divine honors. Finally in Book 10 he shows that Christ's sacrifice was supremely pleasing to God and contends, against Porphyry, that the divine nature was in no way stained by taking on human flesh.

This first half of the *City of God*, here summarized all too briefly, is the most brilliant of all the Christian refutations of pagan religion thus far examined. No less brilliant is the second half, which seeks to lay the groundwork of a total theology of history, from the moment of creation to the final restoration of all things in Christ. In this survey it seems permissible to omit these last 12 books, since they pertain more directly to dogmatic than to apologetical theology. The points of greatest apologetical interest in these pages, such as the observations on miracles and prophecies, have been discussed above.

In connection with Augustine's *City of God* some mention should be made of two of his younger contemporaries, the Portuguese presbyter Orosius and the Gallic presbyter Salvian.

Paulus Orosius, having come to Carthage about 414 to put himself under Augustine's tutelage, wrote at the latter's request *Seven Books of History Against the Pagans*.[115] This is a history of the world from the great Flood to A.D. 417. The aim, as Orosius explains in his preface, was to supplement the early books of Augustine's *City of God* by adducing examples not only from Roman history but from secular history of other nations. The work comes to a climax with the birth of Christ, who is represented as the spiritual counterpart of Caesar Augustus. Just as Augustus shunned vainglory and established temporal peace throughout the world, so Christ, who was born at the time of Augustus' census, ushered in an era of spiritual peace. The 10 Roman persecutions are paralleled to the 10 refusals of the Pharaoh to allow the Hebrew people the freedom God wanted for them. These persecutions were punished by natural disasters comparable to the 10 plagues. In addition to these temporal calamities, the persecutors will 'receive the lot of perpetual damnation to burn with everlasting torments,' thus vindicating the justice of God. The entire work is intended to show that the wretchedness of humanity was even greater under paganism than it has been in Christian times. 'As a result of this, I would, in any way whatever, permit Christian times to be blamed freely, if, from the founding of the world to the present, any equally fortunate period can be pointed out.'[116]

During the years 439–451 Salvian, as a monk at Lerins, wrote his work *On the Present Judgment*, more commonly known under the title *The Governance of God*.[117] Focusing on the disasters that had befallen the various Roman provinces in his own generation, Salvian contends that, far from being an objection against God's justice, they are evidence in its favor. For the Roman people, even when they became Christian in name, continued to practice gluttony, drunkenness, impurity, and other vices, which Salvian castigates with exuberant oratory. A central thesis of the book is indicated by the following quotation:

I know the Romans can say and give complete proof that God does not watch over human affairs, because, in the old days, the Romans as pagans conquered and ruled, but now as Christians they are conquered and enslaved. What I said a little while back about almost all pagan nations could suffice for the refutation of this charge. My argument is that they who know God's Law and neglect it sin more than they who, in their ignorance, do not act according to the Law.[118]

Salvian contends that the Romans of old were blessed because of their natural justice and that they are now being punished because of their moral corruption. Unlike Augustine, Salvian seems convinced that the Roman Empire has seen its day and that the future lies in the hands of the barbaric tribes, whose virtues he idealizes.

Orosius and Salvian were by no means lacking in talent, but they do not as theologians in any way rival Augustine. Orosius writes as a tendentious historian, Salvian as a moralizing preacher. Neither of them has any real interest in the speculative problems of apologetics.

CONCLUSION

In the period from the 3d to the 6th centuries, just surveyed, apologetics continues to be, as in the 2d century, a lively branch of theology. The truth of Christianity is a very personal problem to the apologists themselves. Many of them—Clement, Cyprian, Arnobius, and Lactantius, among others—are converts. Others such as Augustine are former Christians who return to the Church. Some of the most vigorous opponents of the faith in this period, as in more recent times, are former Christians, e.g., Porphyry and Julian.

Superficially, many of the structures of 2d-century apologetics are retained. The Christian apologists continue to insist, as did their Jewish predecessors, that the Mosaic books give the most ancient and reliable account of cosmic origins and that the pagan religions lead to all manner of moral degradation. Against the Jews they still urge, most of all, the testimony of the messianic prophecies. These prophecies they continue to interpret in a tendentious and unconvincing way. Compared with modern apologists, the Fathers make little capital out of the miracles of Jesus, His Resurrection, and His personal sanctity. They prefer to argue from the effects of the gospel on the minds and hearts of believers.

On a deeper level, however, apologetics is transformed from the 3d century onward. With Clement and Origen, and even more with Eusebius, Theodoret, and Augustine, the overriding problem concerns the relationship between Christianity and Platonism in its various forms. The leading apologists are almost unanimous in opting for a synthesis of Biblical faith with classical culture. They take over many of the characteristic theses of Ammonius Saccas, Plotinus, and Porphyry. In the perspectives of a later age these concessions will appear to be a limitation, if not a defect. Did not the Christians and Neoplatonists, it will be asked, fall into identical errors in their excessive reverence for personal religion, for eternal truths, and for sacred tradition? The personal religion of both Platonists and Christians of this period is in danger of becoming too individualistic and otherworldly to satisfy the demands of the Bible. Their search for 'true doctrine' somewhat obscures the concreteness of the gospel message. Their veneration for tradition incurs the risk of making Christianity, like Neoplatonism, too antiquarian. These three developments all had a debilitating effect on the world-transforming dynamism of the gospel.

Another great event that affects the apologetics of the 3d through the 5th centuries is the amazing success of Christianity. From Tertullian to Augustine the apologists are able to point with pride to the rapid advances of the new faith, the constancy of its martyrs, the heroism of its saints. With the conversion of Constantine this pride verges, for a moment, on complacency: it is as though the golden age were at hand.

Eusebius, more than any other single thinker, introduced what one may call the apologetic of world history. Under more sobering circumstances Augustine and his disciples carried this apologetic to greater heights. Partly to cope with the pressing problem of evil, and partly to give scope to his metaphysical dualism, Augustine cushioned this apologetic with a pronounced distinction between the City of God and the earthly city.

The historical apologetic of the later Fathers was destined to be eclipsed for a time by the mystical and metaphysical preoccupations of the Middle Ages. But it would be revived by Bossuet and would see a vigorous future in the 20th century, when human thought would find itself, more than ever before, under the sign of history. Christian apologists must remain eternally indebted to the Fathers of the Church for their boldness in seeking to relate the Biblical revelation to the whole of human culture, human philosophy, and human history.

CHAPTER THREE

The Middle Ages

The foregoing survey of the patristic period has traced the encounter of the Biblical faith with peoples whose connatural modes of thought were shaped by the classical heritage. In order to commend itself to such a civilization, Christianity absorbed into itself many of the riches of pagan philosophy and letters. So successfully was this done that the pagans themselves found the new Christian-Hellenistic synthesis more appealing than the ersatz religions of Julian and the Neoplatonists.

In the Middle Ages the unity of Greco-Roman culture with the Christian faith was taken for granted. To the barbarians who invaded the Empire, the Church appeared as the mother of the arts and letters, philosophy and law. To reject the Church was to make oneself a social and cultural as well as a religious outcast.

The apostolic struggle of Christianity in this period was not with the old pagans or the young barbarians but with other races that had a rich cultural heritage of their own. In the West there were pockets of unconverted Judaism, living by the Mosaic Law and the Talmud. To the East there was the constantly growing power of Islam, which represented a cultural and military as well as a religious challenge to Christendom. Against Jews and Arabs the medieval theologians would direct their strongest apologetic endeavors. A third strand of medieval apologetic was reflective. The effort of the scholastic theologians to discern the rational grounds for their own commitment to Christ and to the Church would furnish materials for later apologetic encounters with skeptics and freethinkers.

DISPUTES WITH SARACENS AND JEWS: 600–1100

The last representatives of the patristic age are the true founders of the Middle Ages. In the East John Damascene (d. *c.* 754) is often designated as the last of the Fathers; in the West, Isidore of Seville (d. 636). These two great synthesizers provided models for medieval apologetics in the East and the West respectively.

John Damascene was born at Damascus late in the 7th century. As a youth he was probably an associate of his father, who was a Christian employed by the Saracen caliph to collect taxes from the Christian community. John first attracted attention about 727, when he wrote a striking apology defending the veneration of images against the Iconoclastic emperor, Leo the Isaurian. About 745 he entered the monastery of St. Sabas, near Jerusalem, where he composed his masterpiece, *The Source of Knowledge*. The third part of this work, entitled *The Exact Exposition of the Orthodox Faith*, was to become very influential in the West in a 12th century Latin translation.

At the opening of his *Orthodox Faith* John Damascene gives some comments on the relationship of natural knowledge to divine faith.[1] After affirming that all men 'naturally' know God, he specifies as channels of this knowledge the existence, conservation, and government of created things, the Law and the Prophets, and finally the only begotten Son of God, Jesus Christ, as known to men through the Evangelists and Apostles. Accepting the Biblical revelation as the highest disclosure of God, John Damascene then proceeds in his treatise dogmatically rather than apologetically. Only in Book 4, chapter 23, does he pause momentarily to refute Jewish objections to the effect that Christians disregard the law of the Sabbath.[2]

Among the minor works of John Damascene are several apologetical dialogues. In his best known, *Dialogue between a Saracen and a Christian*,[3] he touches briefly on the source of evil in the world and on the ways in which Christ, the Son of God, took on certain human and creaturely defects.

Probably the most accomplished apologist of the early Middle Ages was John Damascene's disciple, Theodore Abu Qurrah, the Melchite Bishop of Kara (or Harran) in Mesopotamia. A native of Edessa, he lived *c.* 740 to *c.* 820. Although he wrote extensively against the Christian heretics and the Jews, he is best known for his treatises in Arabic against the Moslems. His *God and the True Religion*, as J. H. Crehan remarks, 'shows that Eastern Christians were at this time far ahead of the West in the depth and range of their apologetics.'[4] In this treatise Abu Qurrah confronts squarely the problem of choosing among the various religions that claim to be revealed: Zoroastrianism, the Samaritan religion, Judaism, Christianity, Manicheism, and the sects of Marcion, Bardesanes, and

Mohammed. After examining the points of similarity and difference, Abu Qurrah proposes an allegory. A certain king, he narrates, had a son who had never seen him. In a foreign land the son fell ill and sent to his father for medical advice. Several messages came, one from the father, the others from the latter's enemies. The son, assisted by the advice of a doctor, scrutinized each message from the point of view of what it indicated about the author, the understanding of the disease, and the reasonableness of the proposed remedy, and accepted the prescription that best satisfied all three criteria. Applying the allegory to the choice of a religion, Abu Qurrah tries to show that Christianity presents the most plausible idea of God, exhibits the fullest understanding of man's actual religious needs, and prescribes what appear to be the most appropriate remedies. As auxiliary evidences, Abu Qurrah invokes the traditional arguments from miracles and from the expansion of Christianity.

Abu Qurrah was by no means the only important Christian apologist of the Middle Ages to write in Arabic. From about the 10th century there is a noteworthy apology ostensibly written by a certain Abd Al-Masih Al-Kindi. Its complete title is a lengthy one: *The Epistle of Abdallah ibn-Ismaîl al-Hâshimi to Abd-al-Masîh ibn-Ishâc al-Kindi, inviting him to embrace Islam; and the Reply of Abd-al-Masîh, refuting the same, and inviting the Hâshimite to embrace the Christian Faith.*[5] As reasons for preferring Christianity to Islam Al-Kindi focuses on the prophecies and miracles that testify in favor of Christ but not in favor of Mohammed. Further he remarks on the wonderful spread of Christianity through the miracles, example, and preaching of the Apostles as contrasted with the extension of Islam by the sword. The favorable treatment given to Nestorian beliefs in Al-Kindi's letter has convinced many scholars that it may have been the work of a Nestorian.

Isidore of Seville, like his Eastern counterpart John Damascene, is chiefly distinguished as a transmitter of the patristic heritage to the Middle Ages. His encyclopedia, the 20 books of *Etymologies*, is a disorderly compilation of miscellaneous information and misinformation. At the request of his sister Florentine, Isidore composed a work *Against the Jews: On the Catholic Faith from the Old and New Testament.*[6] Like Cyprian's *Testimonies* it lines up a multitude of prooftexts, but unlike Cyprian Isidore arranges the texts in a somewhat logical order and points out briefly how each of them bears on the point at issue. The treatise was evidently written more to support Christians in their encounters with Jews than with the direct aim of converting the latter.

During the Dark Ages the energies of the Western Church were chiefly consumed with civilizing and evangelizing the barbarians—a task scarcely calling for learned apologetical treatises. The period did witness the publication of some vehement diatribes against the Jews, such as those of Agobard, Archbishop of Lyons, who composed tracts *On the Insolence of the Jews* and *On the Judaic Superstitions*.[7] Both of these were written about 826–827. No less fierce is the *Book Against the Jews* by Agobard's successor, Amulo, who was archbishop from 841 to 852.[8]

During the 11th century, as the level of culture was rising, Christians began to support their attacks on the Jews with more rational exposition of the supposedly messianic texts of the OT. Fulbert of Chartres (d. 1028) in his brief *Tract Against the Jews*[9] dwells particularly on the implications of the text, 'The scepter shall not depart from Judah, nor the ruler's staff from between his feet, until he comes to whom it belongs, and to him shall be the obedience of the peoples' (Gen 49.10).

Cardinal Peter Damian (1007–72), notwithstanding his deep involvement in the practical reformation of the Church, found time to study Origen and the other Church Fathers.[10] Since he was no friend of purely rational explanation his work is not the place to look for detached philosophical arguments in favor of Christianity.[11] He did, however, compose two polemical opuscules against the Jews. In the first of these, *A Reply to the Jews*,[12] he begins by admonishing his fellow monks that it is more important to make war upon the vices of the flesh, which are always with us, than upon the Jews, who are all but extinct; but still: 'It is unfitting for a churchman to be silent out of ignorance in the face of calumniators, and to flee, conquered and confused, from the insults of the enemy. In many cases such lack of skill and such inordinate simplicity not only stimulate rashness in infidels but also beget error and doubt in the hearts of the faithful.' Shunning all vain disputes, such as Scripture censures, one should therefore set forth before the Jews the most evident prophetic testimonies to the Christian faith. With this introduction Peter goes on to comment on a series of OT texts that, to his mind, clearly refer to the Trinity, the Incarnation, and the sufferings of Christ.

In a sequel to this tract, entitled *A Dialogue between a Jew Asking Questions and a Christian Responding*,[13] Peter Damian replies to 10 difficulties raised by the Jew against Christianity. Most of these difficulties have to do with nonobservance of laws such as those prescribing circumcision and observance of the Sabbath, the dietary prescriptions, and the laws concerning animal sacrifices. At the conclusion of this dialogue Peter impatiently scolds the Jews for their incredulity.

As the 11th century drew to a close Christian apologetics against the Jews and Moslems increased remarkably in volume and in quality. This development was partly due to the rebirth of interest in philosophy that resulted, in part, from the internal stability of the West.[14] In part, also, it was due to the growing contacts between the East and West at the time of the first crusade (1095–99) and to the outbursts of missionary zeal attendant upon this effort. Now that Christians were being asked to bear arms against the Moslems in the East, they reflected more on their missionary responsibility toward the Jews in their home territory.[15]

There exist several records of public disputations held between Christians and Jews in various countries about this time. A good example is afforded in the *Dispute against a Jew Named Leo Concerning the Advent of Christ the Son of God*, contained in the works of Odo of Cambrai (d. 1135).[16] The dispute here recorded occurred at Senlis in 1106. More important for the purposes here is the theological disputation with a Jew in London (possibly Simon of Trèves) that occurred by 1092 at the latest and that forms the basis of the *Dialogue between a Jew and a Christian Concerning the Christian Faith* by Anselm's friend and disciple Gilbert Crispin, Abbot of Westminster.[17] Content in this work to employ the standard arguments from Scripture, Crispin allows it to appear that these texts do not fully dispose of the objections of the Jew. In an effort to supplement his earlier dialogue, Crispin later composed a *Disputation of a Christian and a Heathen Touching the Faith of Christ*,[18] in which he ponders more philosophically on certain difficulties raised by the Jew in the earlier dialogue against the Incarnation. He attempts to show that this does not involve mutability in God and that the taking on of human flesh is not unworthy of God. Crispin's second dialogue appears incomplete, possibly because the author felt that his purposes had been better accomplished by Anselm, who would have just completed his *Cur Deus homo*.

ANSELM

Anselm (1033–1109), the great Benedictine abbot who became Archbishop of Canterbury in 1093, is important to the history of apologetics not so much because of his formally apologetical writing as because of his reflections on the relationship between faith and reason, which were to have an important influence on the apologetics of the high Middle Ages. His teaching on this point may be studied in his *Monologion* (1076), his *Proslogion* (1077–78), and his *Cur Deus homo* (begun about 1094, completed 1098).[19] The first two of these treatises deal with the existence and attributes of God (including the Trinity), the third with the reasons for the Incarnation and hence with the theology of Redemption.

The *Cur Deus homo* has special apologetical significance, being cast in the form of a dialogue between the author and the monk Boso, who objects on the part of the infidel. As many scholars have pointed out,[20] the *Cur Deus homo* stands in the tradition of the Jewish-Christian polemical dialogues of the Middle Ages, from Isidore to Gilbert Crispin. There are grounds for supposing that it was under Gilbert's influence that Anselm was induced to complete his *Cur Deus homo.*[21]

All three of Anselm's works, however, are basically similar in method. He regularly begins in faith, accepting as true whatever is taught by the Scriptures and the creeds. He then seeks through the use of reason to achieve understanding of what he already believes. The necessity of beginning in faith is particularly stressed in the beginning of the *Proslogion*: 'I do not seek to understand that I may believe, but I believe in order to understand. For this also I believe—that unless I believed I should not understand.'[22] Similarly in the *Cur Deus homo* Anselm declares: 'Right order requires us to believe the deep things of Christian faith before we undertake to discuss them by reason.'[23] Although the theologian does seek reasons, his faith in no way depends upon the success of this effort. 'Since I thus consider myself to hold the faith of our redemption, by the prevenient grace of God, so that, even were I unable in any way to understand what I believe, still nothing would shake my constancy.'[24] Anselm is therefore far removed from rationalism as it has developed since the Enlightenment.

But if understanding presupposes faith, still it remains true according to Anselm that faith can issue in understanding. The movement from faith to understanding is for him the essence of theology. To his *Proslogion* he therefore gives the title 'Faith Seeking Understanding' and to his *Monologion* the title 'An Example of Meditating on the Logic of Faith.'[25] For Anselm, to understand is nothing other than to grasp the objective reasons, the *rationes,* that underlie and illumine the data of faith.

That faith is objectively rational is a cardinal principle of Anselm's whole theological enterprise. God, he holds, is supreme truth and hence eminently intelligible; and all that God does is conformed to

D

reason. He cannot act arbitrarily or irrationally. Man, insofar as he is by nature an image of God, participates through his faculties of memory, intellect, and will in this self-luminous divine nature. If there are truths too sublime for human reason to fathom—and Anselm repeatedly insists that there are—this is not because they are above reason itself but because man, especially in his present fallen condition, is not fully rational. Thus Anselm prays:

> Lord, I acknowledge and I thank thee that thou hast created me in this thine image, in order that I may be mindful of thee, conceive of thee, and love thee; but that image has been so consumed and wasted away by vices, and obscured by the smoke of wrong doing, that it cannot achieve that for which it was made, except thou renew it, and create it anew.[26]

Hence theology must be conducted at every moment under the leading of divine grace, and the theologian must continually maintain the attitude of prayer.

While he values the guidance of Scripture and Church teaching and the help of prayer and grace, Anselm does not underestimate the importance of seeking the inner intelligibility of the truths of faith. Authorities can correct the theologian when he goes astray, but they do not take the place of cogent reasons. Theology, as Anselm conceives it, must necessarily be conducted *sola ratione.*[27] In the *Monologion* he agrees to write in such wise 'that nothing from Scripture should be urged on the authority of Scripture itself, but that whatever the conclusion of independent investigation should declare to be true, should, in an unadorned style, with common proofs and with a simple argument, be briefly enforced by the cogency of reason, and plainly expounded in the light of truth.'[28]

In the *Cur Deus homo,* where Anselm is dealing not with anything resembling natural theology but with soteriology, he adopts the rule of proceeding by 'leaving Christ out of view (as if nothing had ever been heard of him).'[29] In this treatise Anselm does, it is true, assume the validity of other doctrines not under dispute, such as the existence and attributes of God, man's fallen condition, and man's destination to eternal beatitude. On the basis of these other doctrines he seeks to establish, by rational argument, the necessity of a redemptive Incarnation. The reasons that Anselm seeks are the objective reasons that prompted God to decree the Incarnation. To penetrate such reasons is to grasp more fully the data of faith.

Anselm sets forth various motives for his rational inquiry. He does not write to cure his own doubts or those of the monks who are his interlocutors or of the readers he envisages. All of these, he assumes, are convinced Christians, whose faith is solidly established on the word of God. Precisely because they do believe, however, they are in search of understanding. Faith is a restless form of knowledge, always in search of the intrinsic reasons that account for its own data and make them assimilable to man's faculty of understanding. Understanding as a form of contemplation affords delight.[30] This delight, as Anselm explains in the dedicatory epistle of *Cur Deus homo* to Pope Urban II, is a kind of opaque anticipation of the beatific vision. 'Since I conceive of the understanding to which we can attain in this life as a middle term between faith and the [beatific] vision, I judge that, the more anyone attains to it, the closer he comes to the vision to which we all aspire.'[31] Not to cultivate such understanding would be, in Anselm's estimation, a kind of negligence.[32]

Another benefit that Anselm has in mind for his readers is the properly apologetic one, that 'as far as possible they may always be ready to convince anyone who demands of them a reason of that hope which is in us [cf. 1 Pt 3.15].' Infidels, he mentions, often ridicule Christian simplicity as absurd. Why should God have sent His own Son into the world to die when it seems that He could have restored life to the world by some other being, angelic or human, or merely by His will?[33] In chapter 3 he explains in further detail that infidels, ridiculing the simplicity of Christians, 'charge upon us that we do injustice and dishonor to God when we affirm that he was born of a woman, that he grew on the nourishment of milk and the food of men; and, passing over many things which seem incompatible with the deity, that he endured fatigue, hunger, thirst, stripes and crucifixion among thieves.'[34]

The aim of theological reasoning, therefore, is partly to equip believers to deal with unbelievers. In meeting these difficulties Anselm is concerned to speak in terms meaningful to the unbeliever. The common ground between them and believers is not faith but reason. 'For although they appeal to reason because they do not believe [and thus have no alternative], and we, on the other hand, because we do believe; nevertheless, the thing sought is one and the same.'[35]

Quite evidently, Anselm did not have in mind a distinct science of apologetics, which would operate by principles and methods distinct from dogmatic theology. To attribute any such aim to Anselm would be as anachronistic as to imagine that he thought in terms of two distinct spheres of truth, some attainable by reason and some only by revelation. While such distinctions may be a legitimate prolongation of his thought, they do not seem to have occurred to Anselm himself. For him theological knowledge was a single science; it operated by reason under the guidance of faith; but the arguments, insofar as they were based on cogent reasons, could be meaningful to those who lacked faith.

All three of the works here examined are apologetical insofar as they aim to set forth reasons capable of convincing unbelievers. At the end of the *Proslogion* Anselm exclaims that he now understands God's existence so clearly that even if he no longer wanted to believe he would be unable to question or deny it.[36] In the Appendix to the *Monologion* he declares himself satisfied that he has given a proof of God that compels the assent of the 'fool' who denies God's reality.[37] And at the end of the *Cur Deus homo* he claims to have given a demonstration of the validity of the entire Biblical revelation. In the words of Boso:

> All things which you have said seem to me reasonable and incontrovertible. And by the solution of the single question proposed do I see the truth of all that is contained in the Old and New Testament. For, in proving that God became man by necessity, leaving out what was taken from the Bible, viz., the remarks on the persons of the Trinity, and on Adam, you convince both Jews and Pagans by the mere force of reason. And the God-man himself originates the New Testament and approves the Old. And, as we must acknowledge him to be true, so no one can dissent from anything contained in these books.[38]

Anselm is the ancestor of a whole line of apologists, from Richard of St. Victor and Raymond Lull to Hermes and Hegel, who seek to find demonstrative reasons for the Trinity, the Incarnation, and other central doctrines. The difficulty in all such approaches, as in Anselm himself, is that they seem to convert faith into reason and thus to render faith itself—in the sense of assent on authority—only provisionally necessary.

In Anselm's own writing one finds no clear solution to the apparent inconsistency in his views that faith is necessary and reason sufficient. Various groups of disciples, claiming to be faithful to Anselm, have attempted to resolve the ambiguity in their own way. Some, such as Barth and Bréhier, make Anselm out to be a fideist, holding that reason cannot operate correctly except within the framework of faith. Others make him a rationalist, on the ground that the deepest mysteries of faith are in his system accessible to unaided reason. Anselm's Catholic disciples in the Middle Ages will follow neither of these two extreme solutions. Some, such as Bonaventure, will hold that there are objectively necessary arguments for the mysteries of the Trinity and the Incarnation but that the human mind in this life cannot grasp the reasons with such clarity as to render faith superfluous.[39] Others, such as Thomas Aquinas, will prefer to transform Anselm's necessary arguments into mere arguments from suitability (*ex decentia, ex convenientia*).[40] In raising so clearly the question of the intrinsic demonstrability of Christian faith Anselm made a portentous contribution to the history of apologetics.

THE TWELFTH CENTURY

In the more strictly apologetical literature of the 12th century, as represented by the tracts against Jews and Moslems, intrinsic arguments for the truths of faith played only a minor role. Several of the most interesting works were composed by convert Jews. The Spaniard Peter Alphonsi (1062–1110), who became a Christian at the age of 44, dedicated to his godfather, Alphonso I of Aragon, a *Dialogue with the Jew Moses*, in which he combined a vigorous attack on Islam with ridicule for the Talmud.[41] Another convert, Hermann of Cologne (1108–98), having entered the Church at about the age of 20, subsequently as a Premonstratensian monk wrote an edifying account of his own conversion.[42] He tells how he was drawn by the ideal of Christian charity as set forth in the Gospels and as exemplified in the lives of some Christian churchmen whom he met.

In one of the more interesting controversial pieces of this century, entitled *Dialogue between a Christian and a Jew*, the traditional theologian Rupert of Deutz (*c.* 1075–1129) focuses on the miracles of Scripture as a primary evidence. Having depicted the Jew as grounding his faith in Moses in the signs and prodigies of the Old Testament, Rupert replies in the person of the Christian by pointing to the marvelous signs that accompanied the preaching of the Apostles.[43]

The most eminent 12th-century apologist was Peter the Venerable (1094–1156), the last great abbot of Cluny. The longest of his works is a hortatory apology, *Against the Inveterate Obstinacy of the Jews*.[44] Unlike many medieval works of similar titles it is primarily intended not for the instruction of Christians but for the conversion of Jews, for whose salvation the author is deeply concerned. Familiar with the work of Peter Alphonsi, he puts it to good use in his earnest efforts to meet objections based on the Hebrew text of the Bible and on the Talmud. The main thesis of this apology is that the coming of the divine Messiah, His humiliations, and His establishment of a spiritual kingdom were accurately foretold by the Israelite Prophets. In an interesting excursus Peter discusses the credibility of Jesus' miracles and those connected with the true cross and the holy sepulcher.[45] As a criterion for the authenticity of miracles Peter insists upon utility. No arbitrary marvels, genuine miracles are intended to prepare the whole man, body and soul, for the glorious risen life. Like other theologians of his time, Peter does not adequately explain the connection between the reality of miracles and the truth of the doctrine they allegedly confirm.[46]

More important than Peter the Venerable's answer to Judaism was his apologetic against Islam.[47] The military action of the Crusades, he believed, would come to nothing unless supplemented by a work of evangelization. The errors of Islam, however, could not be refuted until there were scholars proficient in Arabic and familiar with the Koran. About 1143 at Peter's behest the English astronomer Robert of Ketton translated into Latin the life of Mohammed and the Koran. Using these materials Peter then composed a brief summary of Islamic doctrine[48] and later, failing to interest Bernard of Clairvaux in the project of refuting Islam, himself wrote *A Book Against the Sect or Heresy of the Saracens.*[49] In this work Peter reassures the Moslems that he approaches them, not 'as our people often do, by arms, but by words; not by force, but by reason; not in hatred, but in love.' He then appeals to the objectivity of philosophical study as a model for the impartiality that should characterize religious debate. His actual refutation of Islam reflects the influence of the work of Al-Kindi, which Peter had had translated into Latin. He argues that the Moslems are obliged by the Koran to look upon the Christian Bible as divinely authoritative but that the Bible attests not to Mohammed but only to Jesus Christ as the true teacher. Thus in following the Bible one is compelled to reject Mohammed.

Toward the end of the 12th century the standard arguments from the OT prophecies and the Sibylline Oracles were set forth with rhetorical skill by the humanist Peter of Blois (d. 1202) in his *Against the Perfidy of the Jews.*[50] In this work he repeatedly warns his Christian readers against the devious and diabolical tactics by which the Jews seek to evade the force of the evidences. In another work, designed for the instruction of the Sultan of Iconium, who was said to be considering conversion to the Christian faith, Peter insisted primarily on arguments from the suitability of the Incarnation, the virginal conception, the Passion, and the Resurrection of Christ.

Among the scholastic theologians of the 13th century the problem of the relationship between faith and reason, so acutely raised by Anselm, continued to excite considerable interest. Peter Abelard

(1079–1142), without being a rationalist in the 18th-century sense, gave considerable scope to reason in the area of religious conviction. Reversing the traditional Augustinian order, he maintained that human reason, making use of objectively accessible evidences, could achieve some kind of inchoative faith, paving the way for the supernatural act of faith elicited under the influence of grace and charity.[51] In opposition to Bernard, Abelard argued that the 'blind faith' of Abraham (see Rom 4.18) is an exceptional grace and is hence not normative for ordinary Christians. He cautioned against precipitate faith, quoting from the Ecclesiast: 'One who trusts others too quickly is lightminded' (Sir 19.4).[52]

In his remarkably modern and unpolemical work, *A Dialogue between a Philosopher, a Jew, and a Christian*,[53] Abelard discusses at some length the rational grounds for faith. Near the beginning the philosopher complains that religion lags behind the other sciences and fails to progress because believers do not sufficiently question the traditions in which they have been reared. To this the Jew responds that while the authority of one's family and compatriots exerts a legitimate influence on the faith of the young, the faith of adults should be based on rational choice. Later in the dialogue the philosopher praises Christians because instead of childishly relying on miracles and other visible signs—as do the Jews—they make use of rational arguments. The best evidence in favor of Christianity, according to the philosopher, consists in its demonstrated capacity to convert educated men, such as the Greeks of old. The philosopher then deplores the fideism of some Christian preachers (did Abelard have Bernard in mind at this point?), an attitude that compares unfavorably with Augustine's respect for the role of rational inquiry. If reason were silenced, complains the philosopher, believers would have no way of answering an idolater who held up a piece of wood and demanded that it be adored as God! At the very least, says the philosopher, reason is needed to select what authority one is going to follow.[54]

The apologetic proposed by the Christian in the *Dialogue* highlights the moral superiority of Christianity, with its ethic of charity, over all other religions, including Judaism. The Christian shows to the satisfaction of the philosopher that man's highest good must consist in a happiness to be granted in the other world as a reward for virtue. The great contribution of Christ is to have held forth a sure promise of this goal.

In his *Christian Theology*, and less fully in several other works, Abelard takes up the theme so dear to Justin, Clement, and Augustine that the divine Logos had shed its light not only on the Jewish Prophets but also on the Greek philosophers, preparing them for the clear revelation of the Trinity in the New Testament.[55] Like Augustine Abelard exploits the Trinitarian implications of the Neoplatonic doctrine of the divine emanations in the form of Mind (*Nous*) and Worldsoul. To this Abelard adds the brief but significant remark that even the Brahmans of India acknowledged the divinity of the Word and of the Spirit.[56]

Taking up the objection that Christians are opposed to all others in their acceptance of the Trinity, Abelard simply denies the alleged fact. Both Jews and Gentiles, he says, admit that God has 'made all things in wisdom' (cf. Ps 103.24 Vulg) and that He radiates goodness. 'From this I believe that we can find an easy opportunity of converting all others to our own faith, if by such reasoning we can convince them that they already have a community of faith with us, so that even while they do not confess with their mouths as we do, since they misunderstand the meaning of our words, they still hold to it in their hearts, as it is written, "By the heart a man believes unto justice" (Rom 10.10).'[57]

In his zeal to build bridges from Christian orthodoxy to alien religions and philosophies and to close the rift between faith and reason, Abelard may have tended to rationalize the faith too much and to minimize what was distinctively Christian. Quite predictably he excited the opposition of zealous monks whose views were more rigid than his own. His most powerful adversary, Bernard of Clairvaux, rivalled Peter Damian in distrust of dialectics. The contest between Abelard and Bernard has remained vivid in the memory of Western man, for it symbolizes the tension between two Christian attitudes that recur in every generation—an apologetically inclined mentality, which seeks to find as broad a common ground as possible with the non-Christian, and a strictly dogmatic stance, which would safeguard the integrity of the faith even at the price of placing severe limits on the free exercise of reason.

Soon after the time of Abelard, perhaps about 1155, Richard of St. Victor composed his splendid treatise *On the Trinity*, in which he combines the traditional insistence on external signs of revelation with a serious quest for necessary reasons. Wishing to proceed from faith to understanding, Richard searches for intrinsic arguments for the Trinity that are not simply probable but truly necessitating. In order to justify his initial stand in faith, however, he appeals to the extrinsic evidence of miracles. In a well known passage he declares:

For us who are truly faithful, nothing is more certain and unshakable than what we apprehend by faith. So many, so great, and so wonderful are the divine prodigies attesting the heavenly revelation made to the Fathers, that to have the slightest doubt about them would seem to be a form of madness. For such manifold and extraordinary miracles could not be done except by God. In proclaiming and confirming our faith we employ signs in place of arguments, prodigies in place of experience. Would that the Jews would pay attention and the pagans take notice! With what great security of conscience on this score can we appear before the divine tribunal! Could we not say to God with perfect assurance: Lord, if this be error, you yourself have deceived us: for these things have been accredited to us by great and remarkable signs and prodigies such as you alone could have wrought.[58]

Toward the end of the 12th century some very interesting reflections on Christian evidences were set forth by Alan of Lille (d. 1202). Convinced that the Moslems could not be moved by Christian arguments from Scripture—since they could always question the authenticity and the interpretation of the texts—Alan felt it necessary to rely on intrinsic arguments for the truth of the various Christian doctrines. Inspired by Boethius and some pseudo-Hermetical writings, Alan sought in his *On the Catholic Faith against the Heretics of His Time*[59] to demonstrate the Christian faith from a few simple maxims. The work is divided into four parts, addressed respectively to the Albigensians, the Waldensians, the Jews, and the Pagans.

Another work of Alan—the authenticity of which is disputed—*The Art of the Catholic Faith*,[60] is more specifically directed against Moslem tenets. Alan here advocates a universally valid rational technique of quasi-geometrical demonstration. His proposal anticipates in many ways the 'great art' of Raymond Lull.

THOMAS AQUINAS

With the advent of the 13th century the intellectual environment shifted radically. The cathedral schools were in decline; the universities (Paris, Bologna, Padua, Oxford, and others) were on the rise. The monastic orders were losing their hegemony; the mendicant orders were assuming religious leadership. The spiritual theology of Augustinianism was declining in popularity before the new spirit of scientific learning. The main philosophical works of Aristotle were being recovered, edited, and translated. For the first time since the patristic age Christians were offered a scientific vision of the universe that did not depend on the religious imagery of the Bible. University theology found in these developments a new possibility of deeper Christian understanding, but conservative theology reacted against the 'profane novelties' of the schools and warned against the corruption of the faith.[61]

The situation of Christendom vis-à-vis the Moslem world was radically altered first by the failure of the Crusades to bring Islam to its knees and second by the penetration of Arabic culture and science into the Western world. Arabic philosophy came to be known principally through the work of the Spanish Arab Averroes (1126–98), who looked upon Aristotle as the highest possible exponent of philosophical truth and who composed an immensely influential series of paraphrases, compendia, and commentaries on the works of the master. The commentaries of Averroes were diffused in the West about 1230, nearly the same time that Aristotle's principal works became available.

Although Averroes himself professed fidelity to Islam, he was regarded as unorthodox by his coreligionists and died in disgrace as a heretic. He seems to have looked upon the Koran as a crude, imaginative presentation of truths known to philosophy with greater clarity and precision. According to his philosophy the world is eternal and absolutely necessary. The only immortal element in man, moreover, is the agent intellect, which each individual shares in common with the entire human species. Averroistic Aristotelianism ran afoul of many Christian doctrines, such as the freedom of creation, the origin of the world 'in time,' the predicted end of the world, divine providence, and personal immortality. It precluded the whole concept of an economy of Redemption—Incarnation, Church, and Sacraments.

The penetration of Averroes into the European universities precipitated a major spiritual crisis. The leading theologians of the 13th century were compelled to spend much of their time and energy in efforts to resist the Averroist tide. At Paris the Averroist movement began in the early 1250s. In 1256, at the behest of Pope Alexander IV, Albert the Great composed a work *On the Unity of the Intellect Against Averroes*. Under teachers such as Siger of Brabant and Boetius of Dacia, however, the forbidden philosophy continued to gain ground. A new turn in Christian apologetics was demanded by this situation, and this need was met to the fullest extent by Albert's more eminent disciple, Thomas Aquinas.

Thomas Aquinas (1225–74), after his theological studies at Paris and Cologne, taught at Paris from 1256 to 1259 and again from 1268 to 1272. Like his master, St. Albert, he felt that the errors of

Aristotelianism could best be met by erecting a Christian Aristotelianism that incorporated the best insights of the Stagirite.[62] To this end St. Thomas wrote a series of philosophical commentaries on Aristotle, seeking to interpret the master in a way more favorable to Christianity than his Arabic commentators had done. On certain points, he conceded, Christian revelation had corrected and completed what Aristotle had seen in a deficient manner.

The apologetics of Aquinas is most fully set forth in his great doctrinal synthesis, the *Summa contra gentiles*, which bears in some manuscripts the more descriptive title, *On the Truth of the Catholic Faith against the Errors of the Unbelievers*. This work he composed either between 1258 and 1264 or, according to a more recent view, between 1270 and 1272, at the request, apparently, of the former master-general of the Dominicans, Raymond of Pennafort, who was much concerned with the apostolate toward the Saracens. According to the early chronicler, Peter Marsilio:

> Furthermore, strongly desiring the conversion of unbelievers, Raymond asked an outstanding Doctor of Sacred Scripture, a Master in Theology, Brother Thomas of Aquino of the same Order, who among all the clerics of the world was considered to be, next to Brother Albert, the greatest, to compose a work against the errors of unbelievers, by which both the cloud of darkness might be dispelled and the teaching of the true Sun might be made manifest to those who refuse to believe. The renowned Master accomplished what the humility of so great a Father asked, and composed a work called the *Summa Against the Gentiles*, held to be without equal in its field.[63]

While there is no reason to question the substantial accuracy of this account, it would seem that if Thomas wrote for the benefit of Christian missionaries in Spain, he also had in mind the needs of scholars at Paris and in the universities generally where Averroism was becoming a major threat. Perhaps one may say with Chenu, 'It is rather a whole lot of *errantes* [erring], pagans, Moslems, Jews, heretics, who are examined and censured.'[64] The *Summa* is an all-embracing apologetical theology drawn up with an eye to the new challenge of the scientific Greco-Arabic world view.

In Book 1, chapters 1–9, Thomas sets forth his apologetical method. First he shows that the wise man is the one who considers all things in the light of the supreme truth, that is, the truth that pertains to the first principle from which all reality derives. The refutation of error, moreover, belongs to the same science as the discovery and exposition of truth. Thus the theologian, who contemplates reality in the light of the divine wisdom, has the task of refuting errors in religious teaching (1.1).

Thomas then explains that his aim in this work is to make known the truth that the Catholic faith professes and to confute the errors opposed to it. But to proceed against particular errors is difficult for two reasons. First, Thomas himself has not been made familiar by actual experience with the views of the adversaries and therefore feels unqualified to rebut their contentions by arguments that they would recognize as valid. In this respect, he explains, he is in a worse position than the early apologists, who had themselves been pagans or had at least lived in daily contact with paganism. Second, some of the adversaries, such as the Moslems and pagans—unlike the Jews and the heretical Christians—deny the sacred character of the Christian Scriptures and therefore cannot be refuted by arguments from authority. For these two reasons, Thomas decides to proceed positively rather than negatively and to argue from reason rather than authority. As he establishes each point in his argument, he will point out the contrary errors that his demonstration implicitly excludes (1.2.).

In chapter 3 Thomas sets forth a basic principle of his apologetic, derived, perhaps, from the Spanish-Jewish theologian Maimonides (1135–1204). The human mind in its effort to discover the divine ground of all things has limited competence. It can establish the existence of the one personal God and many other important religious truths, but there is a higher sphere of truths that remain impenetrable to man unless God is pleased to make them known by revelation (1.3).

It would be an error, however, to confine the content of revelation to truths of the latter class. On the contrary, there are good reasons why God should wish to reveal even naturally knowable religious truths. If He did not do so, such truths would be known only by a few men and by them only after long years of study, with many uncertainties and not without admixture of error. Revelation, on the other hand, puts such truths in their purity within easy access of even the young and the untutored (1.4).

At this point Thomas goes on to prove that it is suitable for God to reveal truths of the second class—those beyond the range of rational inquiry. For such knowledge is in many ways profitable to man. It inflames his love for God and enables him to direct his life to God. A very imperfect knowledge of these high and recondite truths, Thomas holds, is more satisfying than a thorough knowledge of truths that lie easily within man's grasp (1.5).

As the remainder of the *Summa contra gentiles* exhibits, apologetics takes on different forms when brought to bear on each of these types of revealed truth. Truths of the first class can be established by philosophical argument. In Books 1 through 3 Thomas proposes both demonstrative and probable arguments on behalf of these revealed doctrines. Book 1 deals with the existence and attributes of the one God. Book 2, which treats of the nature of creation and the variety of created being, includes a lengthy section refuting the Averroistic thesis that the world is necessarily coeternal with God.

Book 3 takes up the end of man. Like Abelard, Thomas thinks it possible to prove from reason that the highest human felicity can consist only in the uninterrupted contemplation of God. Thomas adds that since man cannot attain to a clear vision of God by his own powers and since his natural desire for such a vision cannot be in vain, God must provide after man's death a special light enabling the human soul to behold Him as He really is. Likewise in Book 3 Thomas discusses the operations of Providence—which extends, contrary to the Averroistic opinion, to all particulars immediately— and deals at some length with miracles, as works that God alone can perform. Later in Book 3 Thomas treats of divine law, rewards and punishments, and grace. He gives arguments from reason for the view that God must come to man's help by His grace in order that man may appropriately tend to the supernatural end that Thomas has assigned to man in Book 2.

In Book 4 Thomas turns to truths that by his own admission are beyond the investigative powers of human reason. These center about the Trinity, the Incarnation, the Sacraments, the resurrection of the body, the last judgment, and the consummation of the world. In dealing with such topics Thomas reverses the apologetic method of the preceding books. He leads not with reason but with authority; for, on the supposition that these truths are not knowable without revelation, it would be futile to seek to prove them philosophically. Apologetics must show, first of all, that the teaching of the Church is securely founded, and this Thomas does by citations from Scripture. Then he goes on to refute the opposed heresies. He is able to show in the first place that the Catholic position is not absurd: it does not contradict anything held by faith or evident from experience. Further, he can generally show that the heretical positions (e.g., those of Arius, Nestorius, Eutyches) do involve contradictions either with naturally known truths or with fundamental Christian doctrines.

In some cases Thomas takes his argument one stage further. He goes on to prove that the Catholic position, while not rigorously demonstrable by necessary reasons, is supported by probable arguments. As an illustration, one may point out what is said in Book 4, chapter 54, on the suitability of the Incarnation. Responding to a number of objections against this doctrine, Thomas maintains: 'If one earnestly and devoutly weighs the mysteries of the Incarnation, he will find so great a depth of wisdom that it exceeds human knowledge. In the Apostle's words: "The foolishness of God is wiser than men" (1 Cor 1.25). Hence it happens that to him who devoutly considers it, more and more wondrous aspects of this mystery are made manifest.' Thomas then proceeds to explain how magnificently the Incarnation shows forth the wisdom, justice, and mercy of God, employing many of the same arguments already seen in Athanasius and Anselm. Then he concludes: 'These points, then, and similar ones make us able to conceive that it was not out of harmony with the divine goodness for God to become man, but extremely helpful for human salvation.'[65] Again, in chapter 56 Thomas gives a series of arguments to prove that it was suitable that Christ, having redeemed man by His incarnate life, should have instituted Sacraments to apply the effects of His Redemption to men in the Church.

It might be thought that, in view of the powerful arguments for the Catholic doctrines in Book 4, St. Thomas might claim that unbelievers should be converted by a study of the arguments. But Thomas himself cautions against this view. In the introduction to the whole *Summa* he writes:

> For that which is above reason we believe only because God has revealed it. Nevertheless, there are certain likely arguments that should be brought forth in order to make the divine truth known. This should be done for the training and consolation of the faithful, and not with the idea of refuting those who are adversaries. For the very inadequacy of the arguments would rather strengthen them in their error, since they would imagine that our acceptance of the truth of faith was based on such weak arguments.[66]

But the question still remains: why should one accept doctrines that are neither demonstrable nor refutable? Would it not be more reasonable to adopt toward them an attitude of modest agnosticism? At this point Thomas might perhaps have appealed to the grace of faith, but he preferred to carry the scope of apologetics one step further. He invoked extrinsic signs. God, in revealing things beyond the scope of human reason to His chosen messengers, equips the latter with a grace of speech to enable them to herald His word accurately and effectively.[67] He also accredits His messengers with miracles, which are, so to speak, the seal by which He identifies His doctrine.[68] Besides this, He sometimes enables His emissaries to predict future contingent events that would not be certainly known by anyone except God.[69] These extrinsic signs of credibility, while they do not directly prove the truth of any individual articles of belief, guarantee the contents of the faith in general.[70] The average Christian, in adhering to the Church as organ of revelation, implicitly accepts all that the Church believes and teaches even though he does not know the contents of the faith in detail.[71]

In proposing signs of credibility to the unbeliever, Thomas, as contrasted with the patristic apologists and with the anti-Jewish controversialists of the Middle Ages, puts very little stress on the argument from prophecy. But he frequently returns to the argument from miracle, which seems to play an essential role in his account of credibility.[72] He defines miracles in the strict sense as works that only God could perform,[73] for, he adds, if such works could be performed by the natural powers of created causes they would not be beyond the natural order of things, considered in its totality.

For a brief presentation of Thomas' argument from miracles one may consult *C. gent.* 1.6, where he declares that the divine Wisdom, 'in order to confirm those truths that exceed natural knowledge . . . gives visible manifestation to works that surpass the ability of all nature. Thus there are wonderful cures of illnesses, there is the raising of the dead, and the wonderful immutation in the heavenly bodies; and, what is more wonderful, there is the inspiration given to human minds, so that simple and untutored persons, filled with the gift of the Holy Spirit, come to possess instantaneously the highest wisdom and the readiest eloquence.'[74] Unlike Augustine, Thomas gives no indication that he sees any difficulty in establishing the historicity of such happenings or in showing that, if they did happen as described in Scripture, they were worked by God. Nevertheless Thomas goes on to add the argument so effectively used by Augustine—the miracle of the conversion of the ancient world to the faith in spite of the fact that Christianity curbed the pleasures of the senses, spurned the goods of the world, and invited men to poverty and persecution.

This wonderful conversion of the world to the Christian faith is the clearest witness of the signs given in the past; so that they should be further repeated, since they appear most clearly in their effect. For it would be truly more wonderful than all signs if the world had been led by simple and humble men to believe such lofty truths, to accomplish such difficult actions, and to have such high hopes. Yet it is also a fact that, even in our own time, God does not cease to work miracles through His saints for the confirmation of the faith.[75]

At this point, in one of the few really polemical passages of the *Summa contra gentiles*, Thomas confirms this argument by contrasting the spread of Christianity with that of Islam. Mohammed, he says, seduced the people by promises of carnal pleasure. His precepts gave free reign to men's lower appetites. He taught no new and sublime truths but only what men of moderate intelligence are capable of discovering for themselves. And even this truth, in the Koran, is mixed with fables and errors. Mohammed, moreover, performed no miracles and fulfilled no prophecies. Those voluntarily converted to his religion were brutal inhabitants of the desert, ignorant of letters and philosophy. The further expansion of Islam took place by force of arms. Thus it is clear, Thomas concludes, that those who trust Mohammed's words believe lightly (1.6).

By any standards the *Summa contra gentiles* is a masterpiece. It stands to other medieval apologias somewhat as Augustine's *City of God* does to the output of the patristic age. But Augustine and Thomas are very different in mind and spirit. Where Augustine used Neoplatonism, Thomas has recourse to Aristotle. Where Augustine argued through the interpretation of history, Thomas depends primarily on metaphysics. Where Augustine uses the persuasion of rhetoric, Thomas uses careful and dispassionate reasoning. The *Summa contra gentiles* towers above all previous apologetic treatises by its absolute clarity, its perfect coherence, balance, economy, and precision.

Yet the very clarity of this work is perhaps the source of its greatest weakness. It is almost too systematic to be convincing. Neither Thomas's predecessors nor his successors in our own day are easily satisfied with a sharp line of demarcation between truths attainable to reason and those beyond its grasp. What kind of reason is it that can establish by its own powers all the attributes of God as conceived by medieval scholasticism—e.g., eternity, omnipotence, omniscience? Who today would dare to say that unaided reason can prove that man is ordered to an eternal contemplation of the divine essence as his ultimate goal and that God must attune the soul to this by bestowing grace in the present life? Yet Thomas treats these as matters not beyond the investigative powers of the human mind.

On the other hand, Thomas excludes from natural knowledge

certain doctrines that Athanasius, Augustine, Anselm, and Abelard had evidently regarded as demonstrable through reason, most notably the Trinity and the Incarnation. On reflection it does not seem evident that the Incarnation is any less demonstrable by reason than sanctifying grace, which in the present dispensation derives from it. Perhaps there lies at the basis of the whole dichotomy a certain obscurity about what reason really means. Is Thomas here speaking about what man could know in a hypothetical state of pure nature, or about his capacities in the present state of fallen and redeemed nature?

Because of this cleavage Thomas seems to be too rationalistic in his proofs of the naturally knowable doctrines of faith (the *praeambula fidei*)* and too extrinsicist in his arguments for those that allegedly evade the scope of reason. His argument from miracles is scarcely capable of sustaining the load that it ought to bear if one takes the introductory chapters at face value. As Van Hove and others have shown, Thomas does not really drive home his theory about the verifiability and discernibility of miraculous occurrences in a manner that would meet the critical exigencies of the modern mind.[76] Indeed, Thomas hints that a special grace may be needed to discern whether an apparent miracle is really divine in origin or is a magical or diabolical counterfeit.[77] If Thomas falls back on such an appeal to charisms in order to verify miracles, what becomes of the allegedly rational structure of his apologetic?

As for that miracle that Thomas calls the most evident of all, the 'conversion of the whole world' through the instrumentality of 'simple and untutored persons,' one may put a good many questions that Thomas does not answer. To show that this was not explicable through natural causes would require an unimaginably complicated historical and psychological investigation. In an Augustine, whose tactics are manifestly rhetorical, this argument seems quite appropriate; but in Thomas, with his penchant for metaphysical correctness, it is hardly satisfying.

---

* In 19th- and 20th-century manuals the term *praeambula fidei* came to convey the notion of a body of truths that an individual must know with natural certitude before he could make an act of faith. Among such truths were commonly reckoned the existence and veracity of God and the fact of revelation. For St. Thomas, however, the *praeambula fidei* are simply those truths of faith that are also within the grasp of natural knowledge; they are not necessary preconditions of the judgment of credibility. The fact of revelation, moreover, is not one of the *praeambula* for St. Thomas, for he never looks upon concrete contingent facts as demonstrable. On this whole question see the important article of Guy de Broglie, 'La Vraie notion thomiste des "praeambula fidei," ' Greg 34 (1953): 341–389; 36 (1955): 291–292.

But if one does not insist too much on the program set forth in the first few chapters of Book 1, it is possible to reach a more favorable judgment on the *Summa contra gentiles*. In point of fact, the extrinsicism of the 4th book is alleviated by an abundance of rational argument. As already stated, he develops some very long and persuasive proofs based on the total harmony of revealed truth, the accord between revelation and naturally known truths, and the correspondence between the Christian dogmas and the needs of man. Although he does not consider that he has rigorously demonstrated the strictly revealed truths from self-evident principles, Thomas does give very serious reasons in their favor. Thus the argumentation in Book 4 comes far closer to that in the first three books than Thomas's own introductory remarks would lead one to expect. His method comes closer to that of Anselm and Abelard than to the extrinsicist apologetics of a Rupert of Deutz or a Peter the Venerable.

In perusing the *Summa contra gentiles* one is struck by the completeness, sublimity, and inspirational power of the total synthesis. Just as Clement and Origen, Eusebius and Augustine had shown the wonderful harmony between Christian revelation and the highest insights of the Platonic tradition, so Thomas was able to show, in a manner not less impressive, the capacity of the Biblical revelation to absorb, correct, and complete the most brilliant achievements of Aristotle and his Arabian commentators.

MISSIONARY APOLOGISTS: 1250–1320

In connection with the *Summa contra gentiles* there already has been occasion to mention Raymond of Pennafort (1176–1275), the great Catalan Dominican who became the leading missionary strategist of the 13th century. Having served in Rome as grand penitentiary and as master-general of the Dominican order and later as chaplain to Pope Gregory IX, this eminent canonist returned to Barcelona, where he interested himself in the problems of winning over Jews and Moslems to the faith. Convinced that the Christians were greatly hampered in this apostolate by their ignorance of Oriental languages, he succeeded in setting up schools for Dominican friars to be trained in Arabic and Hebrew. One of the original group to be sent in 1250 to the *studium arabicum* in Tunis was another Catalan Dominican, Raymond Martini (*c.* 1220–*c.* 1285).[78]

Martini's earliest known work, *Explanatio symboli apostolorum*, (1257), attempts to set forth the basic articles of Christian belief in a manner convincing to Jews and Saracens. Taking an Augustinian viewpoint not far removed from ontologism, he holds that discursive proofs for the existence of God are superfluous. In 1267 Martini composed a polemical work, *A Muzzle for the Jews (Capistrum judaeorum)*, which somewhat impatiently exhorts the Jews to embrace Christianity. Deploring their evasive tactics in debate, as Peter of Blois had previously done, Martini holds that in refusing to give direct answers to the Christian arguments the Jews show themselves to be a stubborn and perverse people, rebellious to the Law of God as proclaimed by the Incarnate Son.

Martini's principal work, *The Dagger of the Faith (Pugio fidei)*, was completed in 1278. Shortly afterward he was assigned to teach Hebrew at the Dominican *studium hebraicum* in Barcelona, where he spent his declining years and died.

The *Pugio* is an extraordinarily learned and ambitious treatise, enriched with innumerable quotations from the Hebrew Bible, the Talmuds (of both Jerusalem and Babylon), the Midrashim, and numerous sages of the Moslem world. In his Preface the author explains his aim and method. Since, as the ancients held, no plague is more injurious than the enemies of one's own household, Martini is principally concerned with winning over the Jews, who live in the Christians' very midst. He trusts that his 'dagger' will serve to divide with them the bread of the divine word or, in the alternative, to destroy their impudent madness. The same weapon may be turned against the Saracens and other enemies of the faith.

The treatise is divided into three main parts. Part 1, introductory in nature, contains a series of theological dissertations on disputed questions: the existence of God, the end of man, the immortality of the soul, the creation of the world, God's knowledge of creatures, and the resurrection of the body. In handling these speculative questions Martini shows no philosophical originality; he depends on Thomas Aquinas, and more particularly on the *Summa contra gentiles*. Martini's five proofs for the existence of God repeat those of Thomas almost to the letter. The lengthy discussions of the eternity of the world and of God's knowledge of creatures in their individual traits are reminiscent of the debates with the Averroists at Paris.

In the second part of his book Martini proves in 10 chapters that the Messiah has already come. He bases his argument on four principal texts from the Hebrew Bible: the '70 weeks' of Daniel (9.24–27), the promise of Gen 49.10–12, the dream of Nebuchadnezzar (Daniel, ch. 2), and the oracle of Malachy (1.11). To these texts added testimonies from the Talmud are then subjoined. The final five chapters of Part 2 take up various rabbinic objections, namely, that Jesus did not save the Jews as predicted; that His crucifixion proves His incapacity to save others; that He failed to establish Himself as king and judge of all the nations; that He did not appear on the clouds of heaven; and that He did not gather the Jews from among the Gentiles. To each of these objections Martini replies by making distinctions and justifying them by reference to approved Jewish traditions.

Part 3, the longest portion of the treatise, is comprised of three sections. The first of these attempts to prove the doctrine of the Trinity, not by a priori philosophical reasoning (as do, e.g., Anselm, Richard of St. Victor) but by Biblical texts and Talmudic commentaries. Section 2 deals with the creation of man, the Fall, and the Redemption. Section 3, still following the Hebrew Bible and tradition, gives arguments for the divinity of the Messiah. The final chapters of section 3 set forth some additional thoughts concerning the Sacraments (Baptism, Penance, and the Eucharist), the Passion, death, Resurrection, and Ascension of Christ, the sending of the Holy Spirit, and the reprobation of the Jews. In his final chapter Martini asserts that the Jews as a people will remain ignorant of the truth until the end of time, only a small minority of them being converted and saved.

The *Pugio fidei* merits respect as one of the most serious and erudite literary efforts to convert Saracens and Jews. Martini has mastered the Hebrew and Arabic languages and literature; he quotes Hebrew texts in the original and approaches the Bible with exceptional respect for the original Hebrew readings. But it does not seem that the *Pugio* made any great impression on Jewish or Arab readers. For the few Talmudic and Midrashic texts that Martini was able to twist to his purposes there were multitudes that spoke unfavorably of the Christian positions. The *Pugio fidei* holds an honored place among the apologetical efforts of the age of the crusades; it served as an armory of texts and arguments for subsequent Christian apologists.

The same missionary ardor that animated Raymond Martini is found in even greater intensity in his fellow Catalan Raymond Lull (*c.* 1235–1316). This singularly attractive and romantic figure, having been born and raised in Majorca, married early and lived a somewhat profligate existence until converted by a mystical experience in his 30th year. He then gave most of his goods to the poor, abandoned his wife and children, and devoted himself to the study of Latin, Arabic, and theology. A mystic and a man of prayer, a poet and a romancer, a logician and an apologist, a restless voyager in the service of Christ, he correctly described himself as 'the procurator of the unbelievers' and as 'a most fantastic man.' In spite of his lack of a theological degree, he was several times invited to lecture on his doctrine at the University of Paris. He made missionary expeditions to Asia, Africa, and Armenia, assisted at the Council of Vienne (1311–12), and wrote upwards of 200 books and brochures. As an octogenarian he made his last missionary voyage to Tunis and Bugia, where he courted and obtained a martyr's death.

Lull is chiefly famed, or ridiculed, for the 'great art' that he some-times called *ars compendiosa inveniendi veritatem*, a brief technique for finding truth. Essentially this was a means of using the memory in such a way as to exhibit combinations of truths that might otherwise be hidden. 'For Lull himself, the great aim of the Art was a missionary aim. He believed that if he could persuade Jews and Moslems to do the Art with him, they would become converted to Christianity. For the Art was based on religious conceptions common to all the three great religions, and on the elemental structure of the world of nature accepted in the science of the time. Starting from premises common to all, the Art would demonstrate the necessity of the Trinity.'[79]

To facilitate this use of memory, Lull devised an elaborate set of diagrams with concentric circles and revolving figures. Lull himself was convinced that by the mastery of this method it would be possible to answer the most difficult questions of theology, morality, physics, and other areas to the satisfaction of Saracens, Averroists, and Jews as well as orthodox Christians. Modern students, however, confess their inability to put the method to any good use.[80]

In the realm of apologetics Lull's best contribution is perhaps to be found in some of his narratives embodying theological debates. In this class are his *Book of the Gentile and the Three Wise Men*, an allegorical disputation probably composed about 1273, involving a pagan philosopher, a Jew, a Christian, and a Saracen; also his *Book of the Tartar and the Christian* (about 1286), and the *Book of the Five Wise Men* (1293), which describes the efforts of a Latin, a Greek, a Nestorian, and a Jacobite to convert a Saracen. Lull's *Disputation of Ramon the Christian and Hamar the Saracen* (1308) records in substance an actual debate he had with a learned Moor while in prison for the faith in Bugia. In several allegorical dialogues, such as his *Dispute between Faith and Understanding* (about 1303) and his *Book on the Harmony between the Objects of Faith and Understanding* (1309) Lull propounds his views on faith and reason.

Nothing if not ambitious, Lull was eager to debate with any adversary about the most recondite problems of theology. On several occasions he tells the allegedly true story of a Catholic friar who successfully convinced a Moslem king of the falsehood of Islam and then stopped short of proving the truth of Christianity on the ground that it was above reason. 'You have done me a poor service,' says the king, 'for while previously I was at least a Mohamme- dan, now I am neither a Mohammedan nor a Christian.'[81]

While some have argued that Raymond was heretical in his failure to give due primacy to faith over reason, this charge is too severe. In various writings he depicts the relationships differently, appealing to different metaphors. In general he insists that faith comes first in the order of time. But like Anselm and Richard of St. Victor, he was convinced that all the mysteries of faith could be supported by neces- sary reasons. If Lull was occasionally too confident in pressing his attacks against the infidel, this was, as Peers puts it, 'an excess of the enthusiast' and is not to be put down to a voluntary departure from the rule of faith.[82]

To conclude these remarks on the missionary friars at the end of the 13th century, brief mention should be made of the Florentine Dominican, Fra Ricoldus de Monte Croce (d. 1320), who after years of apostolic labor in the Near East produced several controver- sial works, the best known of which goes by the title *Confutation of the Koran*.[83] This work, which has been called 'the finest piece of anti-Moslem polemic in the Middle Ages,'[84] aims to demonstrate that the Law of Moses, not being confirmed by miracle and prophecy, is not the law of God. The author admits, however, that the Moslems have many religious virtues that the Christians would do well to imitate. Along with Raymond Martini's *Dagger of the Faith,* Ricol- dus's refutation became a popular source book for later apologists. Martin Luther, who owned a copy, translated it into German.

SCHOLASTICISM AFTER ST. THOMAS

Through the end of the 14th century scholastic theologians continued to debate the vexing questions that had arisen with Abelard and Bernard regarding the relationship between faith and reason and the motives for the judgment of credibility. Aquinas, distinguishing be- tween naturally knowable and strictly supernatural truths, had pro- posed a compromise solution. For doctrines of the former class he admitted the possibility of stringent proofs from intrinsic reasons; for the latter, while admitting *rationes convenientiae* of a probable character, he made the reasonableness of faith turn chiefly on extrinsic evidences.

Many theologians of the Augustinian tradition, however, continued to hold that the central truths of faith should be defended by fully demonstrative internal arguments. St. Bonaventure (1221–74), the first great theologian of the Franciscan order, is closer to Anselm than to Aquinas. While holding that faith itself is the result of a divine illumination, he makes room for rational investigation that discovers supporting reasons. Such an investigation, he maintains, is profitable to refute the objections of adversaries, to sustain those weak in faith, and to afford delight to the strong.[85] In addition to extrinsic signs of credibility—such as the testimony of Scripture, miracles, and the consent of the Church—Bonaventure strongly endorses Richard of St. Victor's search for necessary reasons for the truths of faith. Such reasons, despite their demonstrative character, do not render faith superfluous, for, says Bonaventure, 'although they give a manner of certitude and evidence concerning divine matters, that certitude and evidence is not altogether clear so long as we are in this life.'[86]

Several 13th-century Franciscans, loyal to Bonaventure, accused St. Thomas of excessive timidity in shying away from intrinsic arguments. The English friar William of la Mare, who received his master's degree in theology about 1274, strongly pressed this charge. He composed a *correctorium* (correction) of St. Thomas that the Franciscan Order officially adopted at its general chapter of 1282.[87]

Several years later the Italian Franciscan Bartholomew of Bologna maintained that faith is reasonable not primarily because it is guaranteed by extrinsic signs and testimonies but rather because the truths of revelation are objects of the divine intellect. Thus he too, somewhat in the manner of Anselm, concerns himself with the *rationes internae* that give inner intelligibility to the mysteries of faith.[88]

Within the Franciscan school, with its emphasis on affectivity, one finds some very interesting suggestions regarding the role of religious experience in the assent of faith. Peter Olieu (Petrus Joannes Olivi, d. 1298), who stands close to the Franciscan Spirituals, regarded all signs of credibility—including miracles and testimonies—as mere media through which God, so to speak, comes personally and makes His presence felt by a kind of spiritual touch. Olieu therefore felt entitled to speak of a *certitudo experimentalis* available to believers.[89]

The English Franciscan John Duns Scotus (1266–1308) gave greater weight to the extrinsic evidences in supporting the judgment of faith. While stoutly maintaining that God alone was the true motive of faith, he insisted that this act could be objectively justified before the bar of reason in such wise as to refute adversaries and to prepare the way for inquirers to believe. In a passage of considerable apologetical import[90] he lists the following 10 reasons for the credibility of Holy Scripture:

1. *Praenuntiatio prophetica*, i.e., fulfilled prophecies
2. *Scripturarum concordia*, i.e., the concordant teaching of the Scriptures, as contrasted with the disagreements of the philosophers
3. *Auctoritas scribentium*, i.e., the claim of the writers to speak in the name of God
4. *Diligentia recipientium*, i.e., the careful discrimination of the Church in drawing up the canon
5. *Rationabilitas contentorum*, i.e., the harmony of the teaching of Scripture with the demands of reason and natural morality
6. *Irrationabilitas errorum*, i.e., the evident unreasonableness and immorality of those who reject the Scriptures
7. *Ecclesiae stabilitas*, i.e., the long duration of the Church according to the prediction of Christ to Peter (Lk 22.32) and in conformity with the criterion of Gamaliel (Acts 5.38–39)
8. *Miraculorum limpiditas*, i.e., the miracles by which the world was converted to Christianity—including, most importantly, the great miracle of the conversion of the world (with reference to the often-cited text from Augustine's *City of God* 22.5)
9. *Testimonia non fidelium*, for example, the testimonies to Christ purportedly given by Flavius Josephus and by the Sibyl (Scotus here follows Augustine's *City of God* 18.23)
10. *Promissorum efficacia*, i.e., the fidelity with which God, as He has promised, gives light and consolation to those who sincerely inquire and adhere to the Christian faith

Another Franciscan of the early 14th century, Nicholas of Lyra (1270–1349), the great Biblical commentator who taught at the University of Paris for some years after 1309, makes interesting use of the extrinsic signs of credibility in his two apologetical works against the Jews, entitled respectively *A Proof of the Time of the Incarnation of Christ* and *An Answer to a Certain Jew who Denounced the Gospel According to Matthew.*[91] As one would expect from Nicholas's special competence, he bases his Christian demonstration principally on the messianic texts of the OT. Like Raymond Martini, with whose *Pugio fidei* he seems to have been familiar, he finds Trinitarian passages in the Old Testament.

In connection with the scholastic controversies current at the time, it is noteworthy that Nicholas lays down some theoretical principles on the reasonableness of faith. The truth of a doctrine that cannot be verified by experience or intrinsic arguments may, he asserts, be established by divine testimony, provided God authenticates this testimony by miracles exceeding the power of any created agent. Christ, who clearly claimed to be the Messiah promised in the Old Testament, established His claims by working many such miracles—for example, the cure of the man born blind and the raising of Lazarus from the dead. The historical truth of these miracle stories, moreover, is sufficiently attested by the general trustworthiness of the Bible and by the non-Biblical traditions of Jesus' wonderful powers, admitted even by His enemies.

At the outset of his *Proof of the Time of the Incarnation* Nicholas concedes that the apologetical proofs from Scripture are not completely cogent. Even arguments from the New Testament, which generally speaks with greater clarity than the Old, are sufficiently obscure so that heretics may, and in fact do, contest them. Thus the proofs from OT prophecy can at best have a contestable certitude—one that in modern parlance would be called moral.

In the latter half of the 14th century the theory of credibility was further perfected by Henry Totting of Oyta (d. 1397). He distinguishes with great clarity between intrinsic and extrinsic evidence.[92] Although the human mind naturally seeks to grasp things through intrinsic reasons, there are many elevated truths that cannot be known except by divine revelation and hence are not susceptible of such inner demonstration. All the alleged proofs of the Trinity and Incarnation attributed to Plato and the Hermetic books actually fail to establish the desired conclusion with sufficient rigor and exactitude.

In the absence of necessary internal reasons, the act of faith requires for its rational justification external reasons giving at least a well founded probability. (The concept of moral certitude not being in use as yet, Henry speaks in this connection of *rationes probabiles*.) In one of his questions on the *Sentences* Henry sets forth 12 general principles by which the extrinsic grounds of faith may be established. These principles constitute in effect a brief apologetical summary, as may be gathered from the following: 'Any man of reasonable and uncorrupted judgment, considering the Law of the Christian Church and the upright wisdom of that Law, the fittingness of the worship and morals of the Christian people, the miraculous origins of the Church, the stability and power of the Christian name, must rightly conclude that all the books which it by its Law asserts to be divine or written by divine revelation should unhesitatingly be held to be such' (Principle 10).[93]

Henry of Oyta's contemporary Henry of Hainbuch (of Langenstein; d. 1397) provides even clearer outlines for an apologetical proof of the divine origin of the Christian religion. In an address that he delivered as rector of the University of Vienna on the Feast of St. Catherine of Alexandria, 1396, he set forth the following 10 principles:[94]

1. First, one should propose to him [the unbeliever] the first principle of the Catholic faith, namely that there is but one God, who is the last end and rewarder of all.
2. Then it should be proposed to the unbeliever . . . that God is all good and unimaginably perfect.
3. In the third place it should be proposed to the unbeliever that God is free with the freedom of contradiction, most powerful, most perfect, most wise, most truthful, incapable of being deceived or of deceiving, and immense without qualification.
4. Fourth, let it be proposed to him that if anything has been revealed by God, it is true.
5. . . . Let a man of holy and approved life, or several such, propose to the unbeliever that once there was a certain people who faithfully worshiped the one God of heaven and earth.
6. Sixth, let it be proposed that this people for a long period had eminent and very famous Prophets, signalized by various miracles, who predicted to this people what would happen to them and to other nations.
7. Seventh, let it be proposed that God in the Scriptures promised to send to the Jews and to all people one Savior.
8. Eighth, let it be proposed that this Savior has already come and long ago appeared in the world.
9. Ninth, let it be proposed to the unbeliever that this promised Savior was Jesus of Nazareth, whose birth was accompanied by many miracles and who Himself worked many and great miracles. . . .
10. Tenth and last, let His doctrine be proposed.

This outline reveals a high degree of systematization in the apologetical thought of scholastic theologians at the end of the 14th century. What is most striking is the virtual abandonment of any effort to ground the act of Christian faith upon any serious examination of the credibility of the doctrine itself. All the weight is shifted to the extrinsic signs, prophecies and miracles. Christianity is presented as a doctrine that must be accepted because of the signs that point to it from outside rather than because it answers any particular problems or needs on the part of man. The historian of apologetics sees that he has come a long way from Augustine and Aquinas but that the path has not been uniformly upward.

FIFTEENTH-CENTURY APOLOGETICS

Frequently mentioned in connection with the history of apologetics is the *Book of Creatures* (later called the *Natural Theology*) of the Catalan Raimundus Sabundus (also spelled Sibiuda, or, in French, Sebond). The author, a doctor of medicine who taught theology at the University of Toulouse, completed his work some weeks before his death in 1436. While the book is rarely read today, it is well known thanks to the fact that Michel de Montaigne later translated it into French and made it the theme of his 'Apology for Raimond Sebond.'

Sabundus's primary aim is contemplative rather than apologetic. He aims to give inner recollection and to stimulate devotion by allowing the mind to rise through the various stages of the ladder of being to God, the summit of all perfection. He is strongly influenced by Bonaventure's *The Mind's Road to God,* as well as by Anselm and by various works of his fellow Catalan Raymond Lull.

The main characteristic of the work is an exceptional confidence in the power of reason to prove almost the whole of the Christian faith without reliance on the authority of the Bible or the Church. A fundamental principle of the author's reasoning is that man ought to affirm 'whatever is more for his profit, good, and improvement, for his perfection and dignity and exaltation, insofar as he is a man, whatever promotes joy, happiness, consolation, hope, confidence, and security, and whatever expels sadness, despair. . . .'[95] On this basis Sabundus finds it easy to establish the existence of God as a belief that impels man to higher perfection and joy.[96] He then goes on to show that it is better to believe than not to believe that God is one, that God engenders a Son equal to Himself, that God perfects human nature by assuming it through Incarnation, and the other articles of the creed. Later in his work, when discussing the honor of God, Sabundus maintains that God could not have permitted Jesus Christ to usurp divine honors, misleading the human race, and that therefore Jesus must be in truth the Son of God.[97] From this he concludes that the Church, being founded by Christ, shares His authority and is likewise to be believed. The Bible too is to be believed insofar as Christ Himself approved of the OT and originated the NT.[98]

Sabundus then goes on to discuss the relations between the 'book of creatures' and the book of the Bible. Both, he holds, are fully authoritative and infallible, and therefore mutually concordant. The book of creatures, however, has priority insofar as no one would accept the Bible unless he were first convinced that God existed and were fully trustworthy. 'Thus the book of creatures is a gate, way, entrance, preface, and luminary for the book of Holy Scripture, which contains the words of God, and therefore the latter presupposes the former.'[99]

This doctrine of the 'two books given by God' is strongly set forth in the author's Prologue. The Bible, he declares, is the second book, given when man in his blindness became incapable of reading the first. The first book, however, retains the advantage of being accessible to all, even the unlettered, and of being beyond the power of heretics to mutilate or misinterpret. But in order to read the book of nature one needs to be divinely enlightened and cleansed of original sin. The pagan philosophers of old, lacking this aid, failed to read the book of creatures correctly.

Apparently because Sabundus seemed to exalt natural knowledge excessively and to minimize the supernatural content of special revelation his book was placed on the Index in 1559. In 1564 the prohibition was restricted to the Prologue, which was either altered or omitted in subsequent Catholic editions. But Sabundus had no heretical intentions. While he doubtless exaggerated the capacities of unaided reason, there can be no question of his pious acceptance of all the doctrines of the Church. His approach betrayed a generous heart and a loyal devotion. A certain lack of rigor in his argument impaired its apologetical value, but it undoubtedly assisted many convinced believers to contemplate the world in the light of Christian revelation.

The leading scholastic apologist of the 15th century was the ecstatic doctor, Denis the Carthusian. Born at Ryckel in Belgium in 1402, he wrote prolifically on Scripture and scholastic theology until his death in 1471. Eclectic in orientation, he combined a mastery and admiration of Thomas Aquinas, with leanings toward the Neoplatonizing mysticism of his namesake, Pseudo-Dionysius the Areopagite.

Denis's principal apologetical work is his *Dialogue Concerning the Catholic Faith* (*Dialogion de fide catholica*),[100] composed about 1436. Somewhat in the fashion of Anselm's *Cur Deus homo*, it is cast in the form of a discussion between a docile philosopher not yet a Christian, who asks questions and raises objections, and a wise theologian, who teaches and answers.

Book 1 is of decisive importance, since it brings the philosopher to the point of accepting the general stance of Christian faith. It begins with a discussion of the relations between faith and reason. The theologian explains that since faith is not a worldly form of wisdom it cannot proceed from self-evident principles but only from authority. The principles of Christian faith are the 12 articles of the creed. In matters of revelation one moves not from understanding to acceptance but from acceptance to understanding—an echo of the Augustinian *nisi credideritis non intelligetis*, 'unless you believe you shall not understand.'

The acceptance of Christian faith is, however, a reasonable and prudent act, because God authenticated the preaching of the Apostles by means of miracles. One can accept the veracity of the miracle stories about them because there is no other explanation of how ignorant and simple men, such as the Apostles are universally admitted to have been, could have converted the pagan world with its sophisticated philosophers. The theologian at this point pauses to expose the falsity of Avicenna's naturalistic explanation of miracles through the influence of the stars, as well as of the magical and demonic interpretations. Then follows a refutation of polytheism and an insistence on the necessity of Christian faith (either explicit or implicit) for salvation. Book 1 closes with a brief mention of two additional proofs for the truth of Christianity, namely, the fulfillment of OT prophecy and the heroic virtue of so many faithful Christians. After this the philosopher courteously thanks the theologian for his convincing presentation of the preambles (*praeinducta, praelibata*) of faith.

In Books 2 through 6 the theologian and the philosopher discuss the individual doctrines of the faith—the one God, the Trinity, creation (including the standard issue of the eternity of the world), Christology, the Eucharist, the angels, and the Antichrist. Book 7 develops at length the proof from OT predictions and refutes the 'errors of the Jews.' Book 8, an ample apologetic from miracles, makes liberal use of medieval legends.

Denis is grossly incompetent in historical criticism. He mistakenly identifies his patron Dionysius with the Areopagite converted by Paul, even through Abelard had shown the impossibility of this identification centuries before. He delights in classifying the angels according to the nine orders set forth in the *Celestial Hierarchies* of Pseudo-Dionysius—classifications that Dionysius, he thinks, proved beyond doubt to be divinely revealed. In Book 8 he narrates with relish how the Areopagite, after being beheaded for the faith, walked two miles carrying his head in his hands.

Quite evidently the *Dialogion* has small worth as an apologetic.

The author's real concern was no doubt to instruct students of dogmatic theology concerning the relations between faith and reason. Denis shows considerable dexterity in proposing and answering in scholastic form the most difficult metaphysical objections to doctrines such as the Trinity and the hypostatic union.

More properly apologetic in scope is Denis the Carthusian's polemic in four books, *Against the Perfidy of Mohammed (Contra perfidiam Mahumeti),*[101] composed shortly after the battle of Varna (1444) at the request of Nicholas of Cusa. This work is very negative in tone. Concentrating on the 'errors of Mohammed,' it refutes the Koran chapter by chapter. This refutation is prefaced in Book 1 with a general demonstration of the truth of the Christian faith. Five main arguments are given: the miracles of Christ, the fulfillment of the OT prophecies, the holiness of Christian life and doctrine, the definitive destruction of Jerusalem, and the expansion of Christianity in the face of persecutions.

The military successes of the Turks in the 15th century prompted many theologians to write treatises aimed at their conversion. In the East, Georgios of Trapezon composed about 1453 a respected book, *On the Truth of the Christian Faith to Amera the Mohammedan.* In the West Cardinal John Torquemada, a Dominican, published about 1460 his *Against the Principal Errors of the Miscreant Mohammed and of the Turks or Saracens.*

Among the creative theologians of this era who concerned themselves with the Islamic problem, the first place should probably be given to Cardinal Nicholas of Cusa (1401–64). It was at his urging, as already mentioned, that his friend Denis the Carthusian wrote his *Contra perfidiam Mahumeti.* In the winter of 1453–54, just after the fall of Constantinople, Nicholas, seeking to rouse himself from depression, composed his interesting dialogue, *On Peace or Concord in the Faith (De pace seu concordantia fidei).*[102] This work is a reverie, not an apologetic. It outlines what the author would consider the essentials of a world religion that could conceivably be adopted by all major groups—including pagans, Moslems, Jews, Tartars, and Hindus as well as Christians—if each would make all the concessions compatible with his conscientious commitments. The religious pact ultimately arrived at is a somewhat diluted version of Catholic Christianity. Nicholas's work reflects a weariness with religious strife and a longing for universal harmony that relates him less to predecessors such as Abelard and Raymond Lull than to successors such as Jean Bodin and Leibniz.

In 1460–61 Nicholas wrote his *Sifting the Koran (Cribratio*

Alchoran).[103] As the title indicates, it is an attempt to separate the good grain from the chaff rather than, as was then usual, simply to refute. Nicholas finds many points of agreement and attributes Mohammed's rejection of Christianity largely to the fact that he knew it only in a decadent Nestorian form. After showing in Book 1 that the Koran may be profitably used as an introduction to the truth of the gospel, Nicholas goes on in Books 2 and 3 to argue that the Moslems, on the basis of certain principles admitted by the Koran itself, should be prepared to accept the Trinity, the Incarnation, and the reality of Christ's death and Resurrection. Among the Islamic doctrines most deplored by Nicholas is the bestial sensuality he finds in the Koran's description of the joys of heaven.

In relation to most of his contemporaries, Nicholas of Cusa stands out as an exceptionally original and irenic thinker. Perhaps if apologetics had followed the lines indicated by Nicholas it would have spared itself much odium in later centuries.

Typical of the Italian Renaissance at its best is the apologetical work of Marsilio Ficino (1433–99), the first head of the Platonic Academy at Florence. Convinced that he was called to do for Platonic philosophy what his recent predecessors of the Renaissance had done for poetry and painting, he translated into Latin the works of Plato, Plotinus, Porphyry, and Proclus as well as the *Corpus hermeticum* and the works of Pseudo–Dionysius. His principal philosophical achievement was his *Platonic Theology*, a work on the immortality of the soul in 18 Books (written 1469–74). Having become a priest in 1473, he then wrote an apologetical work, *On the Christian Religion* (1474). In both these works he aims to bring *ratio platonica* to the support of Christian faith.[104] For him the 'religious philosophers' of the ancient world were precursors of Christianity in much the same way as were the Prophets of Israel. Plato, he believed, stood at the end of an inspired tradition handed down from Zoroaster, Hermes Trismegistus, Orpheus, Aglaophemus, Pythagoras, and Philolaus.

As Kristeller points out,[105] the question of God and of religion practically coincided for Ficino with that of the immortality of the soul. He believed that the tendency that is most distinctive to man, as opposed to the beasts, is the natural desire for the contemplation of God. If this religious striving were void, man would be made imperfect by the very thing that raised him above the brute animals, which would be contradictory and absurd. But in the present life, this natural desire finds no complete fulfillment. Hence one may legitimately argue from this desire to the immortality of the soul, as Ficino does especially in Book 13 of the *Platonic Theology*. God and the soul that eternally adores Him are for Ficino the objective and subjective aspects of one and the same act; hence both are proved by the same argument.

The question of the immortality of the soul was of crucial apologetical importance in 15th-century Italy, since immortality was rejected by the two leading branches of Aristotelianism at Padua (the Alexandrist and the Averroist schools). Shortly after Ficino's death, the Fifth Lateran Council was to define in 1513 the immortality of the soul against Pietro Pompanazzi and others.[106]

Since the Aristotelian philosophers of the time were almost unanimous in denying the immortality of the soul and the utility of religion, Ficino was convinced that the revival of Platonic philosophy was necessary for the defense of the Christian faith. In the preface to his *On the Christian Religion*[107] he laments the divorce between philosophy and religion, which he says leads to impiety in philosophy and to ignorance in religion. Originally, the philosopher and the priest were one and the same person, and if this happy condition cannot be restored philosophers should at least seek to penetrate divine mysteries with the help of religion, and priests, conversely, should esteem and cultivate philosophy.

All religion, in Ficino's view, is preferable to irreligion. The variety of religions is permitted by God and adds a certain luster to the beauty of the universe. But Christianity is the most perfect among religions and renders to God the most perfect worship.[108]

Grace, according to Ficino, is necessary for true blessedness, for the lower cannot by its own power raise itself to the form of the higher; it must be drawn from above. The Incarnation of the Word, in Ficino's system, is eminently suitable not only because it is the divinely perfect means of raising human nature to the divine and of compensating for the offense of original sin but also because by it all creation can in some way be brought into union with its divine source. Man, according to Ficino, is a microcosm: he is like God in unity, like the angels in intellect, like the animals in sense, like the plants in nutrition, and like inanimate things through essence.[109] Thus the infinite goodness, in desiring to communicate itself to all things, had to do so through union with human nature. When man is divinized through the grace of Christ, the whole universe is in some sort raised up and sanctified.[110]

Apart from these elements, which are distinctive to the apologetics of Ficino, there are many traditional themes. He argues at length with the Jews on the basis of the prophetic texts of the OT.[111] He insists likewise on the miracles of Christ, which he says are not denied by the Jews, the pagans, or the Moslems. He takes pains to show against contemporary superstitions that these miracles could not be due to the influence of the stars, a point already made by Eusebius.[112] To prove that miracles are not extinct, Ficino cites several recent incidents at Ancona and Florence.[113] He refutes Islam by tracing its errors back to Arianism and Manichean docetism, which he then proceeds to refute by the traditional proofs from the divinity of Christ and the reality of His death upon the cross. Throughout his apology he speaks with great respect of pagan Platonists. He quotes the patristic commonplace that Plato was only 'Moses speaking the Attic language'[114] and affirms that the Platonists 'made use of the divine light of Christianity to interpret their divine Plato.'[115]

During the lifetime of Ficino, the great Dominican preacher Girolamo Savonarola wrote at Florence, in 1497, an exceptionally attractive and balanced apologetical treatise. Entitled *The Triumph of the Cross*, the book begins with a vivid description of an imaginary triumphal procession in which the wounded and risen Christ is drawn through the city streets on a chariot, carrying the instruments of the Passion and the books of the Old and New Testaments. In depicting this procession Savonarola shows an artistic talent that relates him to the great muralists of Renaissance Florence. But then he becomes the faithful son of Thomas Aquinas and in the first books establishes those truths about God and man's ultimate destiny that can be proved from reason. In Book 2 he sets forth a series of apologetical grounds for accepting Christianity as a divinely revealed religion. Unlike many of the apologists so far examined he puts little emphasis on the proofs from prophecy and physical miracles. Far more central to his argument are the wisdom and goodness of Christ and the manifest effects that follow from a wholehearted acceptance of the gospel.

> One of the principal effects of the Christian life is peace, joy of spirit, and liberty of heart. For, besides the examples of our fathers, which we read or hear recounted, we have in our days, under our eyes, true Christians, whom the tempests and revolutions of this world do not move; who, on the contrary, glory in tribulation, and remain firm and stable in the confession of the faith of Christ. It is necessary, then, for us to seek out the source of these effects, to explain how it happens that the more one is attached to Jesus Christ by holiness, the more the soul progresses in liberty and serenity.[116]

In Book 3 Savonarola briefly enumerates the principal articles of Christian faith and moral teaching and seeks to show that none of

E

them is contrary to reason. Finally, in Book 4 he demonstrates the truth of Christianity negatively by showing the falsity of the alternative religions—paganism, Judaism, Christian heresy, and 'the sect of the Mohammedans,' which is described as a confusion of Judaism and heresy. In the section on paganism Savonarola includes a refutation of astrology and here makes reference to the work published several years before by his friend and protégé, Giovanni Pico della Mirandola, 'one of the marvels of the age for knowledge.'[117]

This orderly and well-written book contains nothing that would lead one to expect that its author would be burned at the stake a year later, with charges of heresy against him. His doctrine on nearly every point is that of Thomas Aquinas, of whom he said in a sermon, 'When I was in the world I held him in the greatest reverence. I have always kept to his teaching; and whenever I wish to feel small, I read him, and it happens always that he appears to me as a giant, and I to myself a dwarf.'[118] Yet Savonarola, as a Renaissance preacher, speaks with a warmth not found in the *summas* of St. Thomas. He strikes a modern note in the central position he gives to the person of the crucified Christ and to the experience of the Christian life.

CONCLUSION

At no time did the Middle Ages have ideal conditions for the development of apologetical theology. From the 6th to the 11th century the general level of culture was so low, and the social conditions were so unsettled, that theology had no real opportunity to establish itself as a science. From the 11th century on Catholicism was so much in possession and so tied up with the political and cultural life of the West that there was little occasion for successful communication with those of other faiths. Some efforts were made, especially in formal religious disputations, to discover the real points of controversy between Christians and Jews. A few scholars devoted countless hours poring over rabbinic texts. But these contacts were too rare, too narrow, too artificial for them to lead to anything like the free and fruitful exchange that had occurred among Stoics, Platonists, and Christians in the patristic age.

Apologetics against the Saracens suffered from an even greater cultural distance. While one must admire the assiduity of a Raymond Martini and the quixotic enthusiasm of a Raymond Lull, it seems clear that their apologetics failed to hit the mark. Western theologians were viewing the Moslem faith through Western eyes and failing to meet it as a living religion.

In two areas medieval apologetics made signal progress. First, from Anselm on, the scholastic theologians explored with great subtlety the relations between faith and reason. If they did not reach any agreed solution, they did develop a multitude of carefully chiselled theories, some more successful than others. The mediating positions of St. Thomas and St. Bonaventure continue to provide living options for the apologetical theologian today.

Second, some of the more reflective theologians of the Middle Ages, including Abu Qurrah and Abelard, opened up truly original perspectives on comparative religion. Looking upon Christianity as one among many great religions, they were able to grasp the underlying unity of the several faiths and to raise the question of God's approach to man through various religions. In the 15th century Nicholas of Cusa and Marsilio Ficino carried this approach still further.

Medieval apologetics rose to its highest level in the 13th century, with the *Summa contra gentiles* of Thomas Aquinas. Fourteenth- and fifteenth-century scholasticism failed to maintain the same level of speculative vigor. The later scholastics made some pertinent observations about the extrinsic signs of revelation, but they failed to follow up their theories with solid apologetical treatises. Doubtless the undeveloped state of textual criticism and of historical science at the time would have made it impossible to construct a fullblown apologetic for Christianity through miracles, prophecies, and other historical signs of revelation. This approach, which became prevalent in the 19th century, fits well with the theory of credibility worked out by the scholastics of the 14th and 15th centuries.

While patristic apologetics capitalized chiefly on the successes of the Church, medieval apologetics profited rather from the reverses of Christendom. In the 13th century the failure of the Crusading movement, together with the incursion of Arabic philosophy into the West, aroused thinkers such as Aquinas to build their giant syntheses. Then in the 15th century the fall of Constantinople and the sudden infatuation of the humanists with pagan antiquity afforded the needed impetus for Christian apologetics to break out of its scholastic mold. Nicholas of Cusa and Ficino, addressing themselves to the new world of their day, managed to put aside the excessive dogmatic preoccupations of their medieval predecessors and to deal with religion as a human phenomenon. Their keen appreciation of human and religious values and of the place of Christianity within man's total religious striving made them effective spokesmen for the faith in their own day and gave their ideas meaning and power for generations yet to come.

CHAPTER FOUR

From the Sixteenth through the Eighteenth Centuries

In the Middle Ages apologetics had been handicapped by the fact that the Catholic faith was taken too much for granted by most of the European populations. It was simply a part of the air they breathed. To find genuine objections to Christian faith the apologists were forced to seek out Jews and Saracens. This happy situation of religious unity was not destined to perdure. From the 16th century onward Europe was divided into hostile religious camps, and controversy became the dominant form of religious literature.

In the 16th century religious controversy was primarily an inter-christian affair. Most of it centered upon particular doctrines debated between Protestants and Catholics; for example, the Mass, indulgences, the invocation of saints, purgatory, the sufficiency of the Scriptures, and the authority of the pope. These domestic disputes among Christians were generally conducted on the presupposition that all parties to the discussion were convinced Christians. Hence the primary apologetical problem—the credibility of the Christian religion—scarcely arose in this literature. For this reason the interchristian polemics of the 16th century will be dealt with here only very briefly and, as it were, in passing.

In the 17th century one finds increasing evidences of skepticism and religious indifferentism, engendered in part by the hostility (including even religious warfare) among rival Christian groups. Under this external opposition Protestants and Catholics were to some extent brought together in a common effort to show the importance of religious convictions and the preeminent value of the Christian religion.

In the 18th century the forces of the Enlightenment staged a more blatant attack on the claims of Christianity, appealing to the positive sciences, especially history, to prove their case. Christian apologetics, seeking to answer in kind, concentrated increasingly on scientific historical evidences and relied rather less upon lofty metaphysical considerations.

THE PROTESTANT REFORMERS

The great new fact that conditions the development of apologetics from the 16th century onward is, of course, the Protestant Reformation. As the name indicates, this movement was directed toward an inner purification of the Church rather than toward an outward expansion of Christianity. None of the great reformers was deeply involved in the immediate problems of winning over non-Christians to the faith; hence they had little to say about apologetics in the strict sense of the term. Nevertheless, some of the great reformers, such as Luther, Melanchthon, and Calvin, through their discussions of the relations between faith and reason made notable contributions to the future of apologetics.

Martin Luther (1483–1546), while he occasionally polemicized against the Jews, constructed no formal system of apologetics. Not only would this have been foreign to his main purpose—the inner reform of the Church—but it ran counter to his idea of the relations between faith and reason.[1] Partly because of his background in the Ockhamist tradition, he distinguished sharply between two spheres: the natural, temporal, earthly sphere, and the sphere of the spiritual, the eternal, the heavenly. In the first sphere, he held, reason was the proper guide; properly used, it could sharpen man's natural prudence and could even lead to a certain civil righteousness. In the second sphere, however, reason was simply incompetent. When it strove to occupy itself with the heavenly and the divine it became insufferably arrogant—in Luther's vigorous language, the 'devil's whore.' Reason prior to faith, he held, could only raise objections and engender doubts. But if, on the other hand, reason was willing to submit to revelation, it could become a useful handmaid of faith. It could help one to interpret the Scriptures and to attain theological wisdom.

In Luther's eyes, the problem of faith and reason was not so much a matter of epistemology as of soteriology. To try to draw up a set of preambles of faith that would demonstrate the antecedent possibility or probability of revelation was for Luther an act of works-righteousness, smacking of Semi-Pelagianism. Thus apologetics, conceived as a natural preparation for faith, stood condemned by his doctrine of the sole efficacy of grace (*sola fide, sola gratia*).

While he rejected any naturalistic apologetics, conducted from a position outside of faith, his system did perhaps make room for a type of apologetics constructed from within faith. The development of such an apologetics—which would show the inner power of faith from the standpoint of the believer—would have to wait for authors such as Kierkegaard and Barth, both of whom were strongly influenced by Luther's dynamic and existential concept of reason.

Luther's close associate and systematizer, Philipp Melanchthon (1497–1560), in his early years as a theologian was totally won over by Luther's views on the relationship between faith and reason. In the first edition of his *Loci communes* (1521) he adopted a negative stance toward autonomous reason and philosophy. But several years later he regained his youthful devotion to classical philosophy and to Aristotle in particular. By the 1536 edition of the *Loci communes* Melanchthon was ready to declare that philosophy was not only useful within faith, as the servant of theology, but was also a propaedeutic device for leading men to the gospel. He came to hold that reason could establish without the aid of revelation that God exists; that He is eternal, wise, truthful, just, pure, and beneficent; that He created the world, conserved all things in existence, and punished the wicked.[2] More and more Melanchthon relied upon the natural evidences in favor of Christianity.

> Accordingly the later editions of the *Loci* contain a formal apologetic for Christianity as a divinely revealed philosophy. The antiquity of the Christian revelation, which includes the Old Testament, the excellence of its doctrine, the continued existence of the Church, in spite of the hostility of the world, the flesh, and the devil, the attestation by miracles—all these are cited in support of the gospel in good traditional fashion.[3]

Although many of Melanchthon's theological positions were repudiated by the normative Lutheranism that established itself in Germany in the latter part of the 16th century, his Aristotelian scholasticism won acceptance. As a result Lutherans of the 'age of orthodoxy,' such as Johann Gerhard (1583–1637) and particularly Abraham Calov (1612–88), took over many of the medieval Thomistic theses to justify the assent of faith before the bar of natural reason. David Hollaz (1647–1713) drew up an elaborate natural theology in which he established not only the existence and attributes of God, as Melanchthon did in the passage cited above, but offered philosophical proofs for the resurrection of the body. He also tried to demonstrate that the mystery of the Holy Trinity did not contradict anything in sound philosophy. 'In an effort to demonstrate the plausibility of the Christian faith, many Orthodox theologians made extravagant claims for reason and philosophy, so that to many an observer it must have seemed that there was very little actually remaining for divine revelation to supply after philosophy had done its best to discover the true nature of reality.'[4]

The Lutheran dogmaticians of the 17th century strove energetically to construct a rational proof for the doctrine that Scripture is an inspired and infallible source of faith. Summarizing the views of these theologians, one modern historian[5] enumerates eight external criteria and eight internal criteria that are supposed to be capable of engendering at least a human conviction regarding the divine authority of Scripture. These criteria are basically similar to the ones already noticed in Duns Scotus and those that had by this time been set forth by Calvin and his disciples.

John Calvin (1509–64), the most systematic of the 16th-century reformers, sets forth an integral fundamental theology in the first book of his *Institutes of the Christian Religion* (definitive edition, 1559).[6] He admits in theory that man can by the contemplation of creation arrive at a knowledge of God's existence, life, wisdom, power, goodness, mercy, and other attributes (1.1–5). But he goes on to say that man's inherited depravity is such that he inevitably falls into idolatry unless God assists him by positive revelation. In order to correct man's faulty vision, God must, so to speak, equip man with a pair of spectacles. The special revelation of God is contained, for all practical purposes, in Scripture alone (1.6). Thus for Calvin the reasons for accepting Scripture as divine coincide with the reasons for accepting the Christian faith.

As the primary and sufficient reason for admitting the divine origin of Scripture, Calvin alleged the inward testimony of the Holy Spirit (1.7), but then he adds auxiliary proofs from reason that serve to confirm what one already knows by inspiration. In Calvin's view these rational arguments suffice, so far as human reason goes, to render the Scriptures (and hence Christian revelation) fully credible. The *indicia* that he lists at this point are not very different from the traditional apologetical arguments for Christianity.

For the OT Calvin lists the following signs of credibility: the sublimity of the matter (its heavenly doctrine, savoring of nothing earthly); the majesty of style (at once humble and eloquent); the antiquity of the books (which in his estimation 'far outstrip all other writings in antiquity'); the honesty of the writers (e.g., in reporting the disgraces of the Patriarchs); the miracles, publicly attested; predictive prophecies, later fulfilled; and finally the wonderful preservation of the original text throughout all the vagaries of history (1.8.1–10). Turning to the NT, Calvin gives still other arguments more specially adapted to this part of the Bible, such as its authorship by untutored men, the universal consent of the Church as to its authority, and the blood of so many martyrs who died as witnesses to its veracity (1.8.11–13).

Arguments such as these, Calvin maintains, are available in case anyone should wish to establish the validity of the Scriptures on rational grounds; but Calvin admits that the arguments do not give full conviction unless confirmed by the inner testimony of the Spirit. On the other hand, he who has the Spirit's own witness does not need to rely on any rational arguments.

Calvin's apologetical arguments do not today appear very impressive. Like other apologists since Justin, he vastly overestimates the antiquity of the OT as compared with the writings of other civilizations, e.g., Egypt. His appeal to the miracles and much of his argument from prophecy move in a vicious circle; for the reliability of the Biblical reports of miracles and fulfilled prophecies is the very thing in question. Some of Calvin's arguments, no doubt, give valid grounds for a high esteem of the Christian Scriptures, but they do not lead necessarily to the conclusion that they are divinely inspired and completely free from error. Still less do they provide, as many Calvinists wished them to, a practical norm for determining the limits of the canon.

THE COUNTER REFORMATION AND BAROQUE SCHOLASTICISM

The Catholic polemicists who responded to Luther in his own lifetime—most of whom wrote in Germany and the Low Countries— were concerned with particular points controverted among Christians and not with a general Christian apologetic. For this reason it will suffice to mention only the names of theologians such as Johann Eck (d. 1543), Johannes Cochlaeus (d. 1552), the Franciscan Nicholas Herborn (d. 1534), and the Louvain controversialists, John Driedo (d. 1535), Albert Pigge (d. 1542), and Jacobus Latomus (d. 1544), all of whom stoutly defended papal primacy and the Catholic teaching concerning the Sacraments and justification. Under the distinguished leadership of Cardinal William Allen (d. 1594) and Thomas Stapleton

(d. 1598) Douay and Louvain became in the latter part of the 16th century important centers for the training of missionary priests for England. Several of these (such as the Jesuits Campion, Southwell, and Persons) were capable pamphleteers for the Catholic cause.

Catholic apologetics in a more traditional style continued to be written in Italy and Spain throughout the 16th century and well into the 17th. In the first quarter of the 16th century churchmen in Italy continued to oppose the new paganism, especially in the form of Averroistic Aristotelianism. Cardinal Adriano of Corneto (d. 1521), in his *On True Philosophy from the Four Doctors of the Church*,[7] argued on the authority of the great Latin Doctors of the Church that faith should take precedence over reason. The Florentine Platonist Gian Francesco Pico della Mirandola (d. 1533), following in the footsteps of his distinguished uncle, Giovanni Pico, inveighed against the philosophical errors of the Epicureans and the Aristotelians.[8] The Augustinian Bishop Agostino Steucho of Gubbio (d. 1548) in his *Perennial Philosophy*[9] defended the Christian view of God, man, and the universe from the testimonies of the pagan philosophers, especially the Neoplatonists.

About the same time several brilliant Italian Dominicans were laying the foundations for the revival of Thomism in the 16th century. Sylvester of Ferrara (d. 1525) and Tommaso de Vio (Cajetan; d. 1534) were drawn to some extent into polemics against the Averroists and the Lutherans, but their main importance lies in their contribution to the Thomistic renewal.

The greatest systematizer of Catholic polemics against the Protestants was the Italian Jesuit St. Robert Bellarmine (1542–1621), who began his teaching career at Louvain (1569) and was subsequently called to the Roman College, where he lectured to missionary students from 1576–86. He was created a cardinal in 1599. The three volumes of his *Disputations concerning the Controversies of the Christian Faith against the Heretics of this Age*[10] put order and coherence into the chaotic exchange of arguments in the theological literature of the previous 60 years. The popularity of this work is attested by the fact that it went through 100 editions in the next century and a half.

Bellarmine's friend, the Oratorian Cardinal Caesar Baronius (1538–1607), made a contribution to Catholic apologetics by his *Ecclesiastical Annals*,[11] a 12-volume work intended to offset the propagandistic effect of the Lutheran account of Church history published by the Centuriators of Magdeburg in 1560–74.

Apologetics in Spain was relatively untouched by the Protestant

Reformation. The Spanish humanist and educator Juan Luis Vives (1492–1540) composed a serene and systematic apologetical *summa*, *On the Truth of the Christian Faith* (Basel, 1543).[12] Book 1 is a survey of naturally knowable religious doctrines, not unlike the first book of Savonarola's *Triumph of the Cross*; it centers about God and the human soul. Book 2 gives a summary treatment of the principal revealed mysteries, beginning with the Trinity but focusing chiefly on the Incarnation, life, death, and Resurrection of Jesus. Book 3, cast in the form of a dialogue between a Christian and a Jew, deals principally with the messianic prophecies of the OT. Book 4 is a dialogue with a Moslem concerning Mohammed and the Koran. The final book then points out the superiority of Christianity over all other religions.

Vives's work is well structured and profits from much of the literature already examined. He shows himself thoroughly familiar with Augustine, on whose *City of God* he had written a commentary, Thomas Aquinas, and Ficino. In his fourth book he draws heavily—though without explicit acknowledgement—on Ricoldus de Monte Croce.[13] While Vives lacks the originality of Nicholas of Cusa, the vividness of Savonarola, and the philosophical depth of Ficino, the amplitude, balance, and fine Latin style of his work were to assure it considerable influence in the coming century. Melchior Cano, Philip du Plessis Mornay, and Hugo Grotius put Vives to good use.

Aside from the great work of Vives, the most interesting Spanish apologetical work of the mid-16th century is perhaps the *Against All Heresies* (Paris, 1534) of the Salamanca professor Alfonso de Castro (1495–1558).[14] Composed in the form of an apologetical dictionary, this work sets forth the various deviations, old and new, from Catholic orthodoxy.

An important work for the development of fundamental theology was the posthumously published *De locis theologicis (On Theological Sources)* of Melchior Cano, o.p. (1509–60).[15] Profiting from an earlier manual written by Johannes Eck in response to Luther and Melanchthon, Cano discussed in this work 10 fonts of theological proof. Although not primarily apologetical in intent, this work might almost as well have been called *On Apologetical Sources*. In a final, 14th, book, never actually written, Cano was to have explained the use of the *loci* for purposes of controversy against non-Catholics.

Beginning about the middle of the 16th century, Spain witnessed an extraordinary revival of scholasticism, which included great commentators on St. Thomas, such as the Dominicans Báñez and John of St. Thomas, and some more original or eclectic thinkers, such as the Jesuits Suárez and Lugo. The scholastics of this period did not develop any special treatise on apologetics such as Thomas Aquinas had set forth in his *Summa contra gentiles,* but they did give considerable attention to the motives of credibility in their treatises on the virtue of faith, especially when commenting on the 2a2ae of the *Summa theologiae.* With a few examples it may be possible to indicate the kind of materials that lie hidden in these little-read tomes.[16]

Gregory of Valencia, s.j. (d. 1603), is notable for his insistence that the arguments of credibility are not strict demonstrations but are sufficient to render the decision of faith reasonable and prudent. In his notion of the goal of apologetics he includes the idea of motivating the will of the prospective convert so that he positively desires to believe.[17]

Francisco Suárez, s.j. (d. 1617), in his discussion of the motives of credibility, puts primary emphasis on the inner qualities of Christian doctrine—its purity and holiness—and on its efficacy in leading men to a higher moral life.[18] These factors weigh more heavily for Suárez than miracles, though he also takes pains to establish the relationship between miracles and the divine truth that they guarantee.[19]

The Jesuit Caspar Hurtado (d. 1646), accepting the view that the arguments of credibility are not demonstrative but only indicative, anticipates to some extent Butler and Newman by pointing out that the convergence of so many signs in favor of the Christian revelation is such as to found a legitimately firm conviction.[20]

Juan de Lugo, s.j. (d. 1660), while giving considerable weight to the intrinsic qualities of Christian doctrine, as pointed out by Suárez and others, puts more weight on miracles, which he terms the 'clearest and strongest source' (*illustrissimum et potissimum caput*).[21]

Among the Dominicans Domingo Báñez (d. 1604) holds with Gregory of Valencia that apologetical arguments are not strictly demonstrative but that the faith is reasonably credible through a multiplicity of probable arguments. There is no stringent proof, he observes, that the conquest of Jerusalem or the overcoming of idolatry in the first Christian centuries were providentially decreed.[22]

John of St. Thomas (d. 1644) makes much of the Augustinian and Thomistic argument for Christianity from the rapid conversion of so many nations, especially through such humble instruments as the Apostles and their companions. At times he somewhat overextends the argument from universal consent, writing almost as if everyone accepted the Christian faith.[23]

The French Thomist, Jean Baptiste Gonet, o.p. (1616–81), while generally following in the footsteps of the Spanish Dominicans, gives greater emphasis than they do to the proof from prophecy, declaring, 'this argument is the weightiest of all.'[24] He likewise adduces a number of additional arguments of dubious value, such as the predictions of the Sibyls, the pagans, Jews, and Moslems, and the admirable agreement of ecclesiastical writers with one another.

Two Spanish Jesuit apologists, writing in the latter part of the 17th century, introduce a certain rigorism foreign to the scholastics just discussed. Miguel de Elizalde (1616–78) and his disciple Thyrsus Gonzalez de Santalla (1624–1705) seem to have been influenced by the mathematicism of Descartes. Elizalde in his *Method of Seeking and Finding the True Religion*[25] is one of the first to insist that the truth of Christianity can be rigorously demonstrated from the rational evidences prior to the gift of faith. Against Suárez and Lugo he vigorously maintains that the 'fact of revelation' is not something believed in faith but rather something proved.

Thyrsus Gonzalez, who is principally known as an opponent of probabilism in moral theology, wrote an apologetical treatise on the manner of converting Mohammedans[26] in which he displays the same kind of supernaturalistic rationalism already noted in the work of Elizalde.

FRANCE BEFORE 1650

In France from the mid-17th century the chief apologetical questions concerned the dangers and values of doubt, tolerance, and religious indifferentism. A subtle form of religious indifferentism was inculcated by the political theorist Jean Bodin (1530–96), who in his interreligious dialogue *Heptaplomeres*[27] allows seven participants to set forth their views on religion. The participant who contends that no religion is demonstrable and that all are of equal value evidently speaks for the author.

Michel de Montaigne (1533–92) managed to combine an almost cynical diffidence regarding the powers of the human intellect with an apparently sincere adherence to the Catholic faith. In his *Apology for Raymond Sebond* (written 1575–76) he takes the position that Sabundus should not be severely censured for his paralogisms, because the human mind is powerless to deal cogently with philosophical and religious questions. The only safe course is to adhere humbly to the teaching of the Church.[28]

Skeptical currents such as these, in addition to the turmoil of the Wars of Religion, set the background for the voluminous apologetical productivity of the period on the part of both Protestants and Catholics. The leading Protestant apologist of the 16th century in France is undoubtedly the Huguenot layman Philip du Plessis-Mornay (1549–1623), a close adviser of Henry of Navarre before the latter became a Catholic and ascended the throne of France. In 1578 Mornay published a polemical but not very original *Treatise on the Church* directed against Roman Catholicism.[29] Three years later, during a period of repose in Holland, he composed his most important work, *On the Truth of the Christian Religion*,[30] which entirely avoids controversies among Christians themselves.

In his preface Mornay explains his purposes in writing, namely, to combat both the antipathy to religion and religious indifference on the part of many nominal Christians as well as to strengthen their convictions to the point where they will be motivated to live up to the demands of the gospel. Turning then to apologetical method, Mornay calls attention to the necessity of arguing from principles that are accepted by the adversary as well. In the case of pagans one may appeal to self-evident principles and to demonstrable philosophical truths; in the case of Jews, to the OT. Regarding the relations between faith and reason Mornay does not materially differ from many Catholic writers of the scholastic tradition.

Like most apologetical treatises since the *Summa contra gentiles*, Mornay's begins with philosophical demonstrations. The first 19 chapters deal with the existence and nature of God, the creation of the world, providence and evil, the immortality of the soul, original sin, and the last end of man. In his doctrine of God Mornay includes two chapters on the Trinity. He seeks to demonstrate this first from created effects and analogies, using the Neoplatonists and other pagan philosophers as witnesses. Then, following Raymond Martini, he invokes rabbinic authorities to support a Trinitarian exegesis of certain texts from the OT.

Chapter 20, a crucial turning point in the treatise, demonstrates the necessity of religion if man is to attain his last end, union with God. Here Mornay makes use of Ficino. Then he lays down three notes by which the true religion is to be recognized: it must promote worship of the one true God; it must rely on God's revelation as to the way in which He wills to be worshiped and served; and it must offer effective means of reconciliation with God. In the remaining chapters Mornay shows that these characteristics are verified in the Jewish religion of the OT and even more perfectly in Christianity, which is the fulfillment of the messianic hope of Israel.

Mornay's *Truth of the Christian Religion* has the strengths and weaknesses of similar treatises issued in early modern times. Its main importance is perhaps that it introduces into Protestant circles the same kind of apologetical writing that had been customary for centuries in the Catholic world.

A generation after Mornay, another Huguenot author, Moïse Amyraut, published *A Treatise Concerning Religions, in Refutation of the Opinion which Accounts All Indifferent* (1631).[31] As the title indicates, this work is specifically directed to the problem of religious indifference. It deals successively with three types of error: that of the Epicureans, who deny divine Providence; that of the 'philosophers,' who admit Providence but deny any supernatural revelation; and that of the indifferentists, who admit that God has made a revelation but do not wish to hold men to profess any particular religion. Amyraut has no difficulty in showing that this last attitude is contrary to the tenets of all the great religions that purport to rest on revelation—Judaism, Islam, and Christianity. As signs of the true religion Amyraut specifies that it should comprehend the human situation, that it should effectively help to reconcile man with God, that it should maintain itself against its enemies, and that it should be accredited by great and signal miracles.

Catholic apologetics after Montaigne continues to make use of a combination of skepticism and fideism and to pave the way for faith by exposing the feebleness of reason. A very interesting, though somewhat perverse, representative of this tendency is Montaigne's friend and disciple, the Abbé Pierre Charron (1541–1603). His best known work, *The Three Truths*,[32] is primarily a reply to du Plessis-Mornay's *Treatise on the Church*. As his first truth Charron declares that there is one God—and then proceeds to support this thesis on the ground that atheism presumptuously pretends to grasp the nature of the God whose existence it denies. Second, Charron seeks to show that the non-Christian religions proudly claim an unattainable knowledge of God. In the third and longest part of his book he maintains that the Protestants, claiming to have access to the Christian revelation without the guidance of the Church, rely too much on the capacities of their own minds.

Other Catholic apologists of the period, such as Bishop Jean-Pierre Camus, St. François de Sales, Cardinal du Perron, and the Jesuits Juan Maldonat and François Veron seek to undermine Calvinism by proposing a series of skeptical difficulties.[33] In particular they deny that the meaning of Scripture can be known by private interpretation. Their arguments have a certain efficacy if one grants that the Catholic faith is 'in possession' and that anyone who wishes to depart from it must be able to give adequate reasons for doing so.

The Franciscan apologist Jean Boucher, while he reprimands the Pyrrhonism of Montaigne and Charron, shows an acute consciousness of the limits of human reason. In his *Triumphs of the Christian Religion*[34] he returns frequently to the Augustinian thesis that even in worldly matters man can understand almost nothing unless he first makes the venture of believing. J. F. Senault in his *L'Homme criminel* (1644) bases his apologetic not on abstract rational considerations but rather on a concrete descriptive anthropology. His portrait of man's paradoxical situation, to be caught in the toils of his own self-love, prepares the way for Pascal's existential 'logic of the heart.' 'Pascal, therefore, can claim no distinctive contribution to Christian apologetics in his use of the psychological approach and in his emphasis upon the moral aspect of Christianity, which constitute his two main points of departure from the traditional apologetic method.'[35]

FRANCE IN THE SECOND HALF OF THE SEVENTEENTH CENTURY

Blaise Pascal (1623–62), after making extraordinary discoveries as a youth in the fields of mathematics and physics, underwent a thoroughgoing religious conversion in 1655 and thenceforth applied the full force of his genius to the service of religion. At the convent of Port-Royal, where his sister was a nun, he imbibed a strict Augustinism and became convinced that the certainties of faith are unattainable except to the heart that loves. About 1656, while seeking to win over two of his friends—charming but worldly 'freethinkers'—he conceived the idea of writing an apologetic for the Christian religion.

Pascal's projected apologetics remained incomplete. It comes down to the present day in the form of scattered sentences and paragraphs, known as the *Pensées*. Although many have tried to reconstruct how these fragments would have fitted together in a single work, the evidence is too sparse to permit more than frail conjectures. Many modern critics accept in substance the plan set forth by Filleau de la Chaise that purports to rest upon the latter's recollection of a lecture given by Pascal in 1658 concerning his proposed apology. If this plan is applied to the materials in the *Pensées*, one would get an apologetic in three main sections, somewhat as follows.

In Part 1 the author discusses the enigmatic situation of man. Addressing himself to a typical 'libertine' of the day (i.e., one who considered himself emancipated from religious belief and religious norms of conduct), Pascal describes this person as self-satisfied, engrossed in present pleasures, indifferent to all questions concerning God and the afterlife. From this indifference Pascal seeks to rouse him. 'Seeing the blindness and misery of man, looking upon the whole mute universe, and man without light, abandoned to himself, without knowing who put him there, nor what he has come to do, nor what will become of him when he dies, incapable of all knowledge, I am overcome by dread like a man who has been brought in his sleep to a savage desert island, who wakes up not knowing where he is and without any way of escaping. . . .'[36]

With extraordinary psychological insight Pascal dissects the nature of man showing both his nobility and his wretchedness. He shows the paradoxes of the human situation, man's foolish pride and vain imaginings, his weakness before the wild powers of nature, and his superiority over those powers insofar as he knows his misery, repents of his failures, yearns for all truth and goodness. 'Man is but a reed, the feeblest in all nature, but he is a thinking reed. . . . All our dignity, then, consists in thought' (n. 347).

Unlike previous apologists, Pascal makes no effort to give metaphysical arguments for the existence of God. He ridicules those who argue: there is no vacuum, hence God exists (n. 243). Even if such proofs were valid, to what would they lead except an empty deism? What good would it do to arrive at a God whose only importance is to have given the world an initial fillip, setting it spinning on its way. Deism, for Pascal, is almost as remote from Christianity as atheism. The only God he cares to know is the 'God of Abraham, Isaac and Jacob . . . the God of Jesus Christ' (n. 556; cf. Pascal's *Memorial*).

Instead of proving the existence of God in the abstract, Pascal draws attention to the strange fact that human nature can neither comprehend God nor do without Him. 'If man was not made for God, why is he never happy except in God? If man was made for God, why is he so contrary to God?' (n. 438).

Particularly impressive is the dialectic by which Pascal leads the libertine to admit that the question of immortality concerns himself. He contrives a speech that he puts on the mouth of the freethinker. After describing the weakness and ignorance in which he finds himself, the freethinker says: 'And from all this I conclude that I should then pass all the days of my life without thinking of investigating what will become of me. Perhaps I could find some enlightenment for my doubts, but I do not want to take the trouble, or move one step to search . . .' (n. 194). Such an attitude, concludes Pascal, is contrary to a man's own evident self-interest and can win him no esteem in the eyes of others. Only two kinds of people are reasonable: those who, knowing God, serve Him with their whole heart; and those who, not knowing Him, seek Him with their whole heart (n. 194).

In what might have made up the second major part of his apology, Pascal makes an inventory of the various philosophies and religions. Do they give a plausible account of the actual state of man and do they offer any remedy that could give man happiness? Most religions and philosophic systems either confirm man in his foolish pride or involve him more deeply in passion or condemn him to despair. Biblical religion, however, is an exception. By attesting that man was made in the image of God, it establishes his true greatness. By its doctrine of the Fall the Bible sufficiently accounts for his present inclination to frivolity and evil. Finally, the Bible speaks worthily of God. It makes Him lovable by the doctrine that God Himself comes to make atonement for man's sin and lead him to salvation.

At this point Pascal has brought the libertine to the point of wishing that he could believe, without having yet proved that Christianity is true. Here, perhaps, Pascal would have inserted his famous wager. If Christianity is true, you have everything to gain from embracing it; if false, you have lost nothing (n. 233). But suppose the libertine objects: I should gladly make this bet, but I cannot believe. Pascal replies: imitate the actions of those who have staked everything on the truth of Christianity. Take holy water, have Masses said, etc., and you will soon find yourself able to believe (n. 223). To the one who says, I would quickly give up my pleasures if I had the faith, Pascal replies, 'you would quickly have the faith if you surrendered your pleasures' (n. 240).

Pascal profoundly analyzes the relations between faith and reason. Like Augustine he finds a unity within difference, a concord within contrast. Nothing is more reasonable, he maintains, than for reason to submit to authority (n. 272). In its decision to submit, reason is not governed by probative evidences but rather by 'reasons of the heart' (n. 277). This term in Pascal does not mean emotion or blind sentiment but rather an intuitive type of logic. It issues not from the *esprit de géometrie* but from the *esprit de finesse* (n. 1). The man who seeks stringent evidence for the truth of Christianity will not find it. God has so arranged things that there is 'enough light for those who desire only to see, and enough obscurity for those who have the contrary disposition' (n. 430). Those who are able to believe without proofs do so because God inclines their hearts (n. 284).

The third and last section of the apology, according to the plan here being followed, would have been a historical demonstration of the truth of Christianity. Perhaps the following paragraph was intended as its outline:

> PROOF. 1. The Christian religion, by its establishment, having established itself so powerfully, so gently, while so contrary to nature.—2. The holiness, sublimity, and humility of a Christian soul.—3. The wonders of Holy Scripture.—4. Jesus Christ in particular.—5. The apostles in particular.—6. Moses and the prophets in particular.—7. The Jewish people.—8. The prophecies. —9. Perpetuity. No religion has perpetuity.—10. The doctrine, which gives an account of everything.—11. The holiness of this law.—12. By the conduct of the world. [n. 289]

Pascal's treatment of the Biblical evidence is strongly Christocentric. Jesus Christ, he says, is the center of both Testaments: of the Old as looking forward to Him, and of the New as its model (n. 740). In a lengthy paragraph, 'The Mystery of Jesus,' Pascal expresses his deep devotion to his Lord (n. 553). This devotion is integral to his apologetic. The great marvel of Jesus Christ is that outside of Him one can understand neither God nor himself: 'Outside of Jesus Christ we cannot know what is the meaning of our life or our death, nor what God is, nor what we ourselves are' (n. 548). With an implicit reference to the opening passage of Paul's letter to the Corinthians, Pascal says that although signs and wisdom may prepare a man to accept Christianity, the acceptance itself involves submission to the folly of the cross (n. 587).

The arguments from miracles and prophecies, Pascal stresses, are not absolutely convincing but are of such a nature that one cannot say it is unreasonable to believe (n. 564). Miracles, as an external and bodily sign, are necessary because man is not a pure spirit: the whole man, body and soul, must be convinced (n. 806). The process of discerning miracles involves a dialectical relationship between miracles and doctrine: miracles discern right doctrine, and right doctrine discerns miracles (n. 803).

The prophecies, Pascal maintains, are 'the greatest of the proofs of Jesus Christ . . . for the event which fulfilled them is a subsistent miracle from the birth of the Church to the end of time.' Following the then accepted view of Biblical scholars, Pascal imagines that the first five books of the OT were written by Moses himself; consequently, he exaggerates the element of predictive prophecy in the OT. He marvels, for instance, that Moses should have been able to foresee

so many details of the history of the people under the old covenant
(n. 711). In addition to prophecy, Pascal finds typological or figurative
meanings in many OT realities, as related to their NT counterparts.
For instance he holds that the Flood and the Red Sea are types of
the water of Baptism. This, too, is evidence of divine inspiration
(cf. nos. 643–692).

Unlike many apologists, Pascal does not seek to establish the
authenticity of the OT by external testimonies regarding its authorship. But he argues from the portrait of Jesus in the Gospels. 'Who
taught the Evangelists the qualities of a perfectly heroic soul, to paint
it so perfectly in Jesus? Why do they make him so feeble in his
agony? . . . But when they make him so troubled, it is when he
troubles himself, and when men trouble him, he is perfectly strong'
(n. 801). To prove the truthfulness of the apostolic testimony, Pascal
like Eusebius[37] shows the absurdity of imagining the Twelve plotting
to claim falsely that Jesus had risen from the dead and then dying as
witnesses to their own lies (n. 801).

Pascal gives only a few indications of how he would have argued
to the truth of Christianity from the Church as sign. The Church, he
maintains, has the three marks of true religion: perpetuity, virtuous
conduct, and miracles (n. 844). 'A thousand times,' he writes, 'the
Church has been on the verge of total destruction, but each time that
it was in this condition, God raised it up again by extraordinary
feats of power' (n. 613).

At the end of his apologetic Pascal is careful not to claim too
much. 'It is indubitable,' he writes, 'that after all this one should not
refuse, considering what life and religion are, to follow the inclination
to accept it, should this come into our hearts; and it is certain that
there are no grounds for mocking those who accept it' (n. 289).

The reconstruction made here of the approximate order of
Pascal's ideas is very tentative. But even when one does not know how
to assemble them, the fragments are more impressive than the finished
masterpieces of others. With Pascal thought and life, piety and reflection, were inseparable. His apologetic is shot through with a profound
grasp of the human heart and a deep Christian spirituality, only
slightly tarnished by the rigorism of Port-Royal. Like other apologists
of his day Pascal directed his arguments to the religiously indifferent
intellectuals. His style almost miraculously combines passion and
clarity. Few of his arguments, taken in themselves, are truly original.
He has evidently made considerable use of Augustine's *De vera
religione* for his views on the relations between faith and reason. For
his Scriptural arguments he refers occasionally to Raymond Martini

and Grotius. His analysis of the human predicament relies partly on Montaigne. But Pascal has known how to select what is most effective, to give it the stamp of his personal genius, and to express it in immortal prose. Few if any apologetical works have brought so many unbelievers on the way to faith.

The only apologetic work of the 17th century that from a literary point of view bears comparison with the *Pensées* of Pascal is the *Discourse on Universal History* (1681) by the celebrated court preacher and bishop Jacques-Bénigne Bossuet (1607–1724). Appointed by Louis XIV to serve as Tutor to the Dauphin, Bossuet fulfilled this charge very conscientiously from 1670 to 1681. Writing in a simple style for the benefit of his royal pupil (who seems not to have been overendowed with intellectual interests and capacities), Bossuet divides his work into three parts. Part 1 summarizes in about 100 pages the main stages of world history; Part 2, about 200 pages, deals with the continuity of religion; and Part 3, less than 100 pages, discusses the successive empires from the Scythians to the Romans.

Part 1, which concentrates on Biblical history, with a few glances at Greece and Rome and a concluding section on the history of Christian Europe, is a rather dry and shapeless chronicle, but it provides the background for Part 2, which is obviously of far greater interest to the author. Here Bossuet shows that the key to the meaning of world history is to be found in religion, which relates events to God, who has fashioned for Himself a chosen people under the old law and under the new:

> You can easily follow the history of these two peoples, and notice how Jesus Christ effects the union of the one with the other, since he, as expected or as given, has at all times been the consolation and the hope of the children of God.
> Hence you see that religion is always uniform, or rather always the same, since the beginning of the world. The same God has always been recognized as author, and the same Christ as Saviour, of the human race.[38]

In the following chapters Bossuet gives an admirably compact and persuasive narrative of the salvation history of the Old and New Testaments. He accounts for the delay of more than 4,000 years between the creation and the Incarnation on the ground that men had to learn from bitter experience their need of a Redeemer (2.1, p. 132). In the OT section he makes much of the prophetic testimonies to Christ, but his exegesis, it must be confessed, is weak even by the standards of his own age. The following paragraph illustrates the synthetic vision, rhetorical power, and untroubled confidence with which Bossuet proposes his arguments. After a number of quotations from the Davidic Psalms, he continues:

> The other prophets did not see less of the mystery of the Messiah. There is nothing great or glorious which they did not say of his reign. One sees *Bethlehem, the smallest* town of Judah, made illustrious by his birth, and at the same time, rising to a still greater height, he sees another birth by which he *issues from all eternity* from the bosom of his Father (Mi 5:2). Another sees the virginity of his mother, an *Emmanuel,* a *God with us* (Is 7:14), coming forth from this virginal womb, and an *admirable* child, whom he calls God (Is 9:6). This one sees him coming *into his temple* (Mal 3:1); this other one sees him *glorious in his tomb,* in which death was overcome (Is 11:10, 53:9). In publishing his glories, they are not silent concerning his disgraces. They saw him *sold;* they knew the number and the use of the *thirty pieces of silver with which he was purchased* (Za 11:12–13). At the same time as they saw him *great and* exalted (Is 52:13), they saw him *despised and hardly recognizable in the midst of men,* the *object of the world's wonder* as much by his humiliation as by his greatness; *the most abject of men, the man of sorrows, laden with all our sins: doing good, and unacknowledged; disfigured by his wounds and thereby healing ours; treated as a criminal; led to punishment with the wicked* and peacefully *delivering himself up to death* like an innocent *lamb.* They saw a *long posterity being born* from him (Is 53) by this means, and vengeance wreaked upon his unbelieving people. In order that nothing should be wanting to the prophecy, they counted the years until his coming (Dan 9); and unless a man blinds himself, there is no longer any possibility of failing to recognize him.[39]

Aware of the complexity of the total argument from the fulfillment of prophecy, Bossuet wisely chooses to concentrate on a few essentials. God, he declares, has chosen to make various palpable facts, 'attested by the whole world,' so evident that their significance is apparent to even the most untutored—namely, 'the desolation of the Jewish people and the conversion of the gentiles, both taking place at the same time, and both likewise coinciding with the moment when the gospel was first preached, and when Jesus Christ appeared.'[40]

In his chapter on 'Jesus Christ and His Teaching' Bossuet very appealingly presents what is most novel and inspiring in the personality and doctrine of Jesus. 'He announces lofty mysteries, but he confirms them with great miracles. He commands great virtues, but at the same time gives great lights, great examples, and great

graces.'[41] Bossuet's pages in this chapter on the new precept of charity
and on the 'law of the cross' merit a place among the great pages of
apologetical literature. Time has not dimmed their luster.

More questionable, however, is the apparent complacency with
which Bossuet dwells on the desolation of the Jews, which he interprets as their definitive rejection as the people of God. He does not
hesitate to accuse the Jewish people collectively of the crime of
deicide and to depict the legions of Titus as mere instruments in the
hands of an avenging God.[42] The termination of the Aaronic priest-
hood and the commingling of the families of Israel are for Bossuet
evident proofs that the Old Law has ceased and that the Messiah
must have come.

With his customary eloquence Bossuet describes the conversion of
the Gentiles. While he exaggerates the rapidity with which the Church
expanded and the simplicity of those who preached the gospel, he
effectively develops the Pauline thesis that the foolishness of the
Cross has triumphed over the wisdom of this world.[43]

In the concluding section of Part 2 Bossuet extols the strength and
stability of the Church triumphing over all idolatry and all heresies.
'This Church, always attacked, but never conquered, is a perpetual
miracle, and testifies brilliantly to the immutability of the divine
counsels.'[44] Bossuet makes much of the uninterrupted succession
that can be traced from Peter to Innocent XI. Against the Catholic
Church, strongly built on the rock of Peter, all heresies and persecutions beat in vain.

Although Part 3, from a literary point of view, is not inferior to
Part 2, it need not be considered here. Bossuet's consideration of the
succession of empires, while it contains many religious reflections, is
not directly apologetical in content.

While Charron and others had sharply distinguished between the
apologetic for Christianity and the apologetic for Catholicism, these
two phases of apologetics practically coincide in the thought of
Bossuet. He rejects Protestantism because he does not find in it the
qualities that draw him to Christianity itself. In his principal controversial work, *A History of the Variations of the Protestant Churches*
(1688), Bossuet impugns Protestant Christianity for its lack of
unity and stability. The Catholic Church, in contrast to the Protestant
sects, 'so unalterably attached to decrees once pronounced, that not
the least variation can be discovered in her, shows herself a Church
built upon the rock, always in full security from the promises she has
received, firm in her principles, and guided by a Spirit who never
contradicts Himself.'[45] This exaltation of the changeless uniformity of

Catholicism was well suited to an age that identified change with degradation and diversity with chaos.

Bossuet represents almost to perfection the self-understanding of the Church as it would have appeared to a leading churchman of the *grand siècle*. His work shows the classical order and balance that mark the painting of Poussin and the drama of Racine. He is perfectly confident of his positions and seems to experience no need to agonize in the search for truth. The critical problems with which Biblical scholars such as Richard Simon[46] were beginning to wrestle have no interest for Bossuet. 'The difficulties raised against the Holy Scriptures,' he writes in the *Discours*,[47] 'are easily overcome by men of good sense and good faith.' It is precisely this unawareness of the precariousness of his own positions that gravely weakens the apologetic of Bossuet. He has no realization how difficult to justify is his own decision to view world history in the light of the Bible and, even more narrowly, in reference to Christ as its center and summit. Pascal, who would not have rejected Bossuet's interpretation of history, has the advantage of greater sensitivity to the personal options involved. Pascal, with his personal anxiety before the mystery of the universe, speaks more powerfully to our troubled century than the self-assured Bishop of Meaux.

While Bossuet was serving as tutor to the Dauphin, Louis XIV in 1670 appointed as his assistant Pierre Daniel Huet (1639–1721), a prodigiously erudite man who later became Bishop of Avranches. In several philosophical works on faith and reason[48] Huet repudiated Descartes' identification of clarity with certitude, maintaining on the contrary that demonstrations based on moral experience are more solid than mathematical proofs. In religion, he contended, the motives of credibility cannot give more than probability, but grace inclines the intellect to assent with a certitude surpassing any rational proofs.

Huet's major apologetical work, *A Demonstration of the Gospel to his Highness, the Dauphin*,[49] is a bulky folio volume with 650 pages of text and 75 additional pages of indexes. In great part it is a response of Christian orthodoxy to the rationalistic critique of the Bible contained in Spinoza's *Tractatus theologico-politicus* (1670). Influenced no doubt by Spinoza, Huet constructs his apologetics on the analogy of geometry. In the preface he explains that the gospel can be proved by reasons as valid in their own order as geometrical demonstrations are in the mathematical order. He then lays down seven definitions, two postulates, and four axioms. The body of the treatise consists of 10 propositions.

Huet's argument in substance comes down to this: All the Biblical books were written at the times to which they are attributed and by their commonly supposed authors. But the OT prophesies many events to be accomplished in the life of the Messiah. These prophecies were fulfilled in the career of Jesus, who must therefore be acknowledged as the Messiah. The Christian religion is therefore true. As a corollary it follows that all other religions are false and impious.

The major part of Huet's effort is taken up with vain efforts to prove what few modern apologists would consider even faintly probable—for example, that Moses wrote the entire Pentateuch and that all the religions in the world trace their ancestry to Moses. In his proofs of the Messiahship and divinity of Jesus Huet heaps up such a mass of arguments that the reader is virtually crushed. For all the titles of Jesus (e.g., light, fire, sun, star, flower, font, rock) Huet quotes parallel texts in the Old and New Testaments.

If the learned Huet contributed something to the systematization of Catholic apologetics, his clumsiness offset whatever gains he achieved. The unconvincing character of most of his arguments made it quite evident that the geometrical form of his treatise was ill-adapted to the subject matter.

The most popular apologetical work of 17th-century France, and one of the best, was the three-volume work of the Huguenot pastor Jacques Abbadie (1654/1657–1727). In Volumes 1 and 2, together entitled *Treatise on the Truth of the Christian Religion*,[50] this work demonstrates successively the existence of God, the necessity of religion, the truth of the Jewish religion, and the truth of the Christian religion. Then in a separate work entitled *Treatise on the Divinity of Our Lord Jesus Christ*,[51] later published as the third volume of the treatise just mentioned, Abbadie undertakes to prove that Jesus Christ was true God, 'of one same substance with his Father.'

Abbadie's apologetic reflects both the merits and defects of his century. Highly systematic, he orders his questions with the utmost clarity. Familiar with the OT criticism of Spinoza and with the paleontological speculations of La Peyrère, he makes a genuine effort to come to grips with new and urgent questions. At the same time he is a man of piety, who like Pascal can employ the 'logic of the heart.' In one of the best sections of his book he shows how the intrinsic attributes of the Christian religion correspond with the religious needs of man.

Like most of his contemporaries, however, Abbadie is given to a rigid, syllogistic type of logic that cannot deal easily with literary and historical questions. Complacent in his orthodoxy, he is not seriously open to any evidence that tends to undermine established positions. He is totally committed to the proposition that Moses wrote the Pentateuch and to the fact that the world could not possibly be older than one would gather from computing the years from Adam to the present day, on the basis of the Biblical accounts. In his volume *The Divinity of Jesus Christ* Abbadie assumes an almost defiant tone toward all adversaries. If Jesus was not of one substance with the Father, he argues, then Mohammedanism would be better than Christianity, Jesus would have been justly condemned to death by the Sanhedrin, and, indeed, religion itself would be indistinguishable from superstition and magic. This minatory type of argumentation is better calculated to foster apostasy than to convince doubters. For a type of apologetic better adapted to a scientific and empirical era, one will have to turn to Holland and England.

SEVENTEENTH-CENTURY HOLLAND

The leading Protestant apologists of Holland in the 17th century were Arminian Calvinists, theologically close to du Plessis-Mornay. The most popular Protestant apology of the century was probably that of Hugo Grotius (Huig de Groot, 1583–1645). Originally published in verse form in Dutch (1621) for the use of sailors traveling to non-Christian parts of the globe, *The Truth of the Christian Religion*[52] was expanded and transformed by the author himself into a Latin treatise in 1627. It soon appeared in many European languages as well as in Persian, Arabic, Malayan, and Chinese.

In his preface Grotius respectfully acknowledges the work of his many predecessors, mentioning by name Sabundus, Vives, and Mornay. His own work is not remarkably different in structure, but several significant changes are introduced.

Book 1, dealing with the general truths of natural religion, is brief and easy to follow. The existence and attributes of God, the immortality of the soul, future rewards and punishments, and the necessity of religion are all established by popular arguments chosen more for their persuasive force than for their demonstrative rigor.

Book 2, which seeks to vindicate the preeminence of the Christian religion, begins more positivistically than the works here previously examined. First Grotius argues to the historical existence of Jesus, alleging the testimony of pagan authors and the admissions of anti-Christian polemicists. Then he goes on to establish the credibility of the apostolic testimony to the miracles and Resurrection of Jesus. After these extrinsic proofs he examines the intrinsic arguments for the supremacy of Christianity: the excellence of the rewards it promises, the purity of its precepts, and the moral qualities of Jesus. Then Grotius argues from the marvelous expansion of Christianity, adding the usual comment that if this had occurred without miracles the occurrence itself would be miraculous.

Book 3 differs from the works seen thus far by introducing a somewhat serious effort at source criticism. It attempts to establish, first, that the NT is by the authors to whom it has traditionally been ascribed, and second, that these authors were well informed and honest and hence are worthy of credence. In answer to the objection that the Bible contains contradictions, Grotius maintains that the apparent inconsistencies are minor, are not insoluble, and establish the lack of collusion between the Biblical witnesses.

The last three books (4–6) are directed respectively against paganism, Judaism, and Islam. They are not remarkable for originality; but the section on Judaism has the merits of being reasonably brief and of seeking to meet the real objections of the Jews.

From a speculative and dogmatic point of view, Grotius is disappointing. He has little interest in metaphysical argument. He gives no clear indication as to whether he accepts the orthodox dogmas regarding the Trinity and the Incarnation. He consequently omits the usual *rationes convenientiae* in favor of the Incarnation. The main merits of Grotius are, first, that he began to apply documentary criticism to the Bible, especially the NT, and, second, that he wrote in a clear and readable style. Although he makes use of very numerous references to pagan philosophers, historians, and rabbinic commentaries, he relegates much of his supporting evidence to footnotes, thus adapting his work better to the ordinary reader without sacrificing scholarly thoroughness.

In the course of the 17th century Holland became a refuge for theologians of unorthodox opinions, both Jewish and Christian. It was here that the Jew Baruch Spinoza (1632–77) set forth his pantheistic philosophy and launched his attack on the inspiration of the Bible. He was answered by the contentious Calvinist Pierre Jurieu (1637–1713), also known for his ardent polemics against Bossuet and other Catholics. Jurieu took into his protection the apostate Catholic Pierre Bayle (1647–1706) and gave him a teaching post at Amsterdam. When Bayle, however, wrote in favor of the toleration of atheists, Jurieu denounced him as a secret atheist and terminated his academic career. Taking advantage of the ensuing leisure Bayle then composed his gigantic *Historical and Critical Dictionary* (1697), which was to be used by the 18th-century *philosophes* as the 'arsenal of the Enlightenment.'

In the closing decades of the 17th century two other Dutch Arminians, close in mind and spirit to Grotius, made significant apologetical contributions. Philip van Limborch (1633–1712), Scripture professor at the Remonstrant College in Amsterdam, published a very successful dialogue *On the Truth of the Christian Religion: A Friendly Conversation with a Learned Jew.*[53] By moderate arguments Limborch defends the superiority of the Christian over the Mosaic revelation.

Limborch's colleague at Amsterdam, the Swiss-born Jean Leclerc (1657–1736), while primarily famed for his work in Biblical criticism, deserves mention as an apologist. In *Treatise on Incredulity*[54] he examined the sources of unbelief and came to the conclusion that it was largely the result of the worldliness, indifference, immorality, and intolerance of Christians. In two appended letters, Leclerc gave positive grounds for the acceptance of the Christian religion. In this area of his thought he shows considerable dependence on Grotius, whom he greatly admired.

ENGLAND IN THE SEVENTEENTH AND EIGHTEENTH CENTURIES

In the latter part of the 17th century the intellectual leadership of Europe passed for a time from France to England, and to England one must look for the most creative advances in apologetics. The dominant mood of the 17th century is one of exuberant confidence in the divinely established harmony between reason and nature. The approach to God through reason and nature, rather than through positive historical revelation, gave rise to deism.

In its early phase deism is best represented by Edward, Lord Herbert of Cherbury (1583–1648), who came into contact with skeptical ideas during his service as ambassador to France (1618–24) and attempted to construct an antidote to skepticism. Having published his treatise *On Truth*[55] in 1624, he later expanded it under the title *On the Religion of the Gentiles* (*De religione gentilium,* posthumously published, 1663). Taking the universal consent of mankind as the infallible index of truth, Herbert maintains that God has impressed upon all men certain common religious notions. He specifies the following five (without however denying that there are others):

1. There is a supreme Power (whom one may call God).
2. This sovereign power must be worshiped.
3. Virtue combined with piety constitutes the principal or best part of divine worship, as has always been believed.

4. All vices and crimes are hateful and should be expiated by repentance.

5. There are rewards and punishments after this life.

All who subscribe to the truths of natural religion are in Herbert's opinion members of a Church that truly deserves to be called Catholic and outside of which there is no salvation. He does not entirely reject the idea of revelation, but he denies that it communicates additional truths. Rather, he says, it makes us more than ordinarily certain of things known by reason and gives us an experience of God's gracious approach to man. Later Deists, going beyond Herbert of Cherbury, tended to reject entirely the idea of a supernatural order, including the notions of grace, revelation, incarnation, and miracle.

Among the early opponents of deism was Robert Boyle (1627-91). While firmly convinced that the progress of science helped to manifest the creative hand of God, Boyle argued in numerous short tracts for the existence of revealed truths beyond the range of human reason.[56] In a late work, *The Christian Virtuoso* (1690), Boyle defended the truth of the Christian revelation on the basis of three main proofs: the sublimity of Christian doctrines, the testimony of miracles, and the beneficial effects of the Christian religion on the history of the human race.

In his will Boyle set up a foundation for an annual series of eight lectures to be delivered in a parish church of London 'for proving the Christian religion against notorious infidels, viz., atheists, theists, pagans, Jews, and Mahometans, not descending lower to any controversies that are among Christians themselves.'

The first Boyle lecturer was the classical scholar, Richard Bentley (1622-1742), who chose for his topic in 1692 *The Folly of Atheism and What is Now Called Deism, even with Respect to the Present Life.* These lectures were essentially an argument against Thomas Hobbes, whose *Leviathan* had been published 40 years earlier. The first lecture dwells on the evil consequences of atheism both for the individual—whom it deprives of life's best hope—and for society, which is securely founded on religious faith. In his second lecture Bentley seeks to prove the existence of God from the faculties of the human soul. Lectures 3 to 5 proceed to establish God's reality from the design of the human body; and lectures 6 to 8, taking advantage of Newton's *Principia* (1686), aim to prove God's existence from the wonderful order of the heavens.

In 1694 Bentley delivered a second series of Boyle lectures, *A Defense of Christianity*, but they were never printed, and the manuscript copies have been lost. The very fact that he gave this course is, however, a reminder that Bentley was not content to let the matter rest with natural theology. Already in his first series of lectures he asserted that there 'is a wide difference between what is contrary to reason and what is superior to it and out of its reach.'[57] Thus he subscribed to the classical conception of revelation as the manifestation of things above the grasp of reason.

Isaac Newton (1642–1727) enthusiastically endorsed the apologetical use that Bentley in his first volume had made of the *Principia*. In a letter to the author he declared: 'When I wrote my treatise about our system, I had an eye upon such principles as might work with considering men for the belief of a Deity; and nothing can rejoice me more than to find it useful for that purpose. But if I have done the public any service this way, it is due to nothing but industry and patient thought.'[58] Newton's own theology was Latitudinarian, probably even Unitarian, but he did not yield to the most orthodox divines in his esteem for the Scriptures. Among his posthumously published papers are his curious speculations entitled *Observations upon the Prophecies of Daniel and the Apocalypse of St. John*, in which he asserts (1831 ed., p. 25) that to reject the prophecies of Daniel is to reject the Christian religion.[59]

In the full glow of the Newtonian illumination theologians appealed with increasing confidence to the reflections of the divine attributes in the order of nature. John Ray (1627–1705), who may be regarded as the founder of modern botany and zoology, produced an influential volume on *The Wisdom of God in Creation* (1691), in which he dwells enthusiastically on the teleological structure of living organisms and the marvels of animal instinct. Somewhat less penetrating but equally characteristic of the time are the Boyle lectures of William Derham (1657–1735), later published (1713) as *Physico-Theology, or a Demonstration of the Being and Attributes of God from His Works of Creation*. Derham finds in the design of the world innumerable proofs of God's power, wisdom, and goodness. As for the apparent deficiencies in nature, one cannot, he says, censure God for them, for the full purposes of God's will escape men's limited minds.

Among the most influential of the Boyle lectures were the two series delivered by the Anglican Samuel Clarke (1675–1729) in 1704–05. Although Clarke has been accused of Arianism in theology, the peculiarity of his doctrinal position has no great effect on his apologetic. His first volume, entitled *A Demonstration of the Being and Attributes of God*, was specifically intended as an 'answer to

Mr. Hobbes, Spinoza, and their followers' and seeks by a set of highly metaphysical deductions to establish successively that there must be a necessary being, eternal, infinite, omnipresent, unique, intelligent, free, omnipotent, omniscient, and infinitely good.[60] What Clarke does is essentially to reconstruct the natural theology of medieval scholasticism on the basis of Newtonian rather than Aristotelian physics. Like Newton, Clarke accepted the quaint idea that absolute space is the *sensorium* of God—a notion possibly derived from the Cambridge Platonists of the 17th century.

The second volume of Clarke's Boyle lectures, directed against the Deists, deals with *The Unchangeable Obligations of Natural Religion and the Truth and Certainty of the Christian Revelation.* The gist of the argument is that any Deist who sincerely confronts the claims of Christianity will inevitably embrace it and that any Deist who refuses to do so is on a path that leads logically to atheism. The doctrines of Christianity, Clarke maintains, are agreeable to unprejudiced reason; they have a natural tendency to improve human conduct and, taken in unison, constitute the most consistent and rational system of belief ever known. To this pragmatic approach Clarke then appends the customary extrinsic arguments from the miracles of Jesus, the fulfillment of OT prophecies, and the testimony of the Apostles. Appealing to the authority of Eusebius, Clarke contends that 'all the books of the New Testament were either written by the Apostles; or, which is the very same thing, approved and authorized by them.'[61] The written testimony of the Apostles, he concludes, 'was the most credible, certain and convincing evidence that ever was given to any matter of fact in the world.'[62]

In the preface to his second volume of Boyle lectures Clarke felt obliged to take notice of the 'indecent and unreasonable reviling' of his older contemporary, John Locke (1632–1704), who had objected to the facility with which Clarke concluded to the essential properties of matter and of God. Locke in his *Essay Concerning Human Understanding* (1689) found fault with the theory of innate ideas and sought to base religious knowledge upon man's experience of the world about him.

In particular, Locke assails the innatism of Herbert of Cherbury, whose five principles of natural theology, he maintains, are neither evident nor universal.[63] Locke nevertheless regards the idea of God as 'naturally deducible from all parts of our knowledge' with a certitude equal to that of the most evident geometrical theorems.[64] In Book 4, chapter 10, he sets forth a rather crude demonstration of God's existence based on the principle of causality.

By means of this proof he concludes to the reality of an eternal and powerful being that stands at the origin of the world.

Locke, as a convinced Christian, unhesitatingly accepts the idea of revelation. In a famous passage he writes:

> Reason is natural revelation, whereby the eternal Father of light, and fountain of all knowledge, communicates to mankind that portion of truth which he has laid within the reach of their natural faculties: revelation is natural reason enlarged by a new set of discoveries communicated by God immediately, which reason vouches the truth of, by the testimony and proofs it gives that they come from God. So that he that takes away reason, to make way for revelation, puts out the light of both, and does much-what the same as if he would persuade a man to put out his eyes, the better to receive the remote light of an invisible star by a telescope.[65]

Locke explicitly discusses the criteria of revelation in his *Discourse on Miracles* (1703). Taking for granted as a presupposition the existence of God as creator and governor of the world, he maintains that a divine mission cannot be credited except under three conditions: (1) it must deliver nothing derogating from the honor of the one, only, true, invisible God or inconsistent with natural religion and the rules of morality; (2) it must not inform man of things indifferent, or of small moment, or easily knowable by the application of their natural powers; and (3) it must be confirmed by supernatural signs. Miracles may be reasonably taken to be divine until such time as disproved, by a contrary mission attested by yet greater wonders. 'His [God's] power being known to have no equal, always will, and always may be, safely depended on, to show its superiority in vindicating his authority, and maintaining every truth that he hath revealed.'[66]

Locke simply takes for granted the historicity of the Biblical miracles. In his *The Reasonableness of Christianity as Delivered in the Scriptures* (1695),[67] a work designed to show that the one essential of Christian belief is the acceptance of Jesus as Messiah, Locke holds that Jesus established His messiahship both by His many miracles and by His fulfillment of OT prophecy (par. 58–59). Locke dwells particularly on Isaiah ch. 9, Mic 5.2, Dan 7.13–14, and Dan 9.25.

Although Locke's version of the Christian creed was, by traditional standards, a very attenuated one, he remained a committed Christian who accepted the idea of supernatural revelation attested by supernatural signs. Some of Locke's disciples, however, were to use their master's epistemological principles in support of an antisupernaturalistic deism.[67a] In 1696 John Toland, an admirer of Locke, published the treatise *Christianity not Mysterious*, which rejects the Lockean idea that there could be a revelation superior but not contrary to reason. The only possible function of revelation, in Toland's deistic position, would be the clarification of naturally knowable religious truths.

Typical of the radical deism of the 18th century is *Christianity as Old as Creation*, a work published by Matthew Tindal in 1730. Radicalizing Locke's positions, Tindal argues that the Bible is nothing but a republication of the religion of nature.

The early part of the 18th century witnessed a great proliferation of apologetical works in defense of supernatural revelation against the Deists.[68] Noteworthy among these was the immensely popular monograph of Thomas Sherlock, *The Trial of the Witnesses of the Resurrection of Jesus* (1729), a work that concludes with the verdict that the Apostles are not guilty of having given false witness. A thorough vindication of the historical basis of the Christian faith was given by Nathanael Lardner (d. 1768) in his *The Credibility of the Gospel History* (published in 13 sections from 1727 to 1755). The Puritan minister of Dublin, John Leland (1691–1766), who has been called 'the indefatigable opponent of a whole generation of Deists,' wrote, partly against Toland, a well known treatise on *The Advantages and Necessity of the Christian Religion* (1733). The Irish bishop and philosopher George Berkeley (1685–1753) composed in 1732 a dialogue, *Alciphron, or the Minute Philosopher*, in which Christianity is defended against the skeptics on the ground of its tendency to good, its superiority to the other religions, its natural harmony with man's needs, as well as the usual arguments from miracles and prophecy. William Warburton (1698–1779), who had been a lawyer before becoming an Anglican priest, published in 1737–41 six books on *The Divine Legation of Moses*, more conspicuous for the vehemence of their asseverations than for the lucidity of their reasoning.

The most successful of these responses to deism was undoubtedly that of Joseph Butler (1692–1752), an Anglican clergyman who became Bishop of Bristol in 1738 and Bishop of Durham in 1750.[69] In his work, significantly entitled *The Analogy of Religion, Natural and Revealed, to the Constitution and Course of Nature* (1736), Butler writes as a religious empiricist who has reflected deeply on the phenomena of nature and has assimilated the lessons of Locke's treatise on probability.

Butler takes for granted in this work what would have been conceded by his adversaries, and indeed by practically all his contemporaries—namely, that there is an all-powerful author and governor of nature. He asks himself what is to be inferred from this with regard to natural and revealed religion. In Part 1 he shows that the observed course of nature gives strong reasons to suppose that this present life may be a probation leading to a future state in which man will be rewarded or punished for what he has done on earth. It is therefore altogether likely that moral improvement may be the chief purpose of his life on earth. Although the argument from natural analogy is not, Butler concedes, such as to exclude all doubt, it gives sufficient credibility 'to engage men to live in the general practice of all virtue and piety.'[70]

In Part 2 Butler directly confronts the question raised by the Deists, whether natural religion gives sufficient guidance so that any additional, supernatural revelation must be judged useless and hence incredible. To this he replies, first, that the principles of natural religion are not widely recognized except among peoples to whom the Biblical revelation has been authoritatively proclaimed. Then he adds that although the greater part of Christianity may indeed be a republication of the religion of nature, it cannot be reduced to this alone. If it be true that Christ is man's divine savior and that the Holy Spirit is his sanctifier, these facts are far from unimportant. Thus all men are under an obligation to 'search the Scriptures' in order to determine whether these claims are credible.[71]

In chapters 2 and 3 Butler goes on to show that there can be no a priori presumption against miracles and revelation on the ground of their singularity, for nature itself is full of irregularities and singularities. He then contends (ch. 4) that if an ostensibly revealed religion is more self-consistent and conducive to virtue than systems of admittedly human devising, there is a presumption in favor of the truth of its claims. Even if man, with his limited human grasp, cannot eliminate all the apparent anomalies and obscurities in Biblical faith, this is no more an argument against its divine origin than the unaccountable phenomena of nature are proofs against the divine authorship of the world (which the Deists do not question). So too, Butler continues (ch. 5), the manner in which creatures come into being through the instrumentality of others and depend on others for their sustenance and growth makes it antecedently likely that God might communicate the goods of Redemption through a mediator. The want of universality in the Christian religion, he argues (ch. 6), proves nothing against its truth, for it is evident from the course of nature that Providence, while extending its care to all, does not confer upon all the same kind and degree of benefits.

F

Only in chapter 7 of Part 2 does Butler turn to the positive evidence tending to prove that Christianity, besides being antecedently likely, is factually revealed. His principal arguments are from miracles and prophecies, but unlike most previous apologists he does not attempt to prove individual supernatural events taken separately. Rather he weaves a single general argument from the whole course of Biblical history and from the fortunes of Judaism and Christianity since NT times. Only within this global framework does he think it profitable to weigh the evidence in favor of any particular miracle or prophecy. The very multitude of these signs, he points out, is a factor in their favor. 'Upon the whole: as there is large historical evidence, both direct and circumstantial, of miracles wrought in attestation of Christianity, collected by those who have writ upon the subject; it lies upon unbelievers to show, why this evidence is not to be credited.'[72] So too with prophecy: 'A long series of prophecy being applicable to such and such events, is itself a proof that it was intended of them.'[73] Although some or all such utterances taken separately might be explained naturally as referring to other events, it remains to be explained why the whole series of them is applicable to Christ and the Church. In summary, Butler's argument is cumulative and convergent. 'For probable proofs, by being added, not only increase the evidence, but multiply it.'[74]

In his final chapter (2.8) Butler raises against himself the difficulty that his arguments from presumptions and probabilities are not powerful enough to induce men to make great sacrifices and to stake their whole lives upon the result. To this he replies that in almost all the practical decisions of life, including those of gravest consequence, man acts 'upon evidence of a like kind and degree to the evidence of religion.'[75]

In this connection he refers back to a point made earlier (2.6) in connection with the common objection that if God wanted to make a revelation He would surely signalize it in a way that all could recognize as indubitable. To this Butler replies that the objection would hold if God unconditionally wanted all men to accept the revelation, but it might well be that God intends His message only for those who are serious and upright in their motivation.[76] If so, it should not be surprising if those who are frivolous, careless, or desirous of evading moral obligations should fail to be convinced. Here again the analogy from natural knowledge helps. Quite clearly, levity, passion, and prejudice impede one's perception in areas other than religion. Why then should this not be true in the moral and religious sphere?

Once the nonbeliever recognizes that his own faults may lie at the root of his doubts, he will be shaken out of his complacency and will awaken to his serious duty to investigate. If this does not bring him to firm conviction, it should at least make him aware how rash it would be to vilify and scorn Christian belief.

In this classic work Butler breaks away completely from the standard format of apologetical treatises since the Middle Ages. He avoids the complacent apriorism of the Enlightenment and the authoritarian extrinsicism of late scholasticism. Shunning the lofty flights of metaphysical reasoning, he keeps close to empirically known facts. With the pragmatic instincts of the typical Anglo-Saxon, he makes deft use of presumptions and probabilities. If this be in itself an inferior type of evidence, it is appropriate, he thinks, for beings of limited intelligence who depend so heavily upon the senses. For man, he maintains, probability is the very guide of life.

Like Pascal, Butler is able to accept obscurities in the evidence and to account for them. He sees that geometrical clarity has little place in the moral and religious sphere. But Butler, the cool and reflective churchman, is far removed from the personal mysticism of Pascal. While the convert of Port-Royal is on fire with devotion to the God of Jesus Christ, Butler looks upon religion objectively as the potential source of a series of truths by which to regulate one's moral conduct. His originality consists in his use of empiricism to provide an epistemological footing for evidence of a moral and historical character. His mastery of the complexities of convergent evidence is unique among apologists up to his time and links him with his great 19th-century disciple, John Henry Newman.

British apologetics in the 2nd half of the 18th century was largely taken up with answering David Hume (1711–76), who did much to weaken the complacent optimism of the Deists and the dogmatism of the orthodox. In his *Dialogues on Natural Religion* (composed 1751, published posthumously), Hume criticized the traditional arguments from design and raised the difficulty that from contemplating the universe one might well conclude that there is no governor except 'blind nature, impregnated by a great vivifying principle, and pouring forth from her lap, without discernment or parental care, her maimed and abortive children.'[77] In his *Natural History of Religion* (1757) Hume seems favorable to the theistic position but is highly critical of the superstitions that often accompany the desire to propitiate a supernatural being. Earlier, in his *Essay on Miracles*, defining miracle as a violation of the laws of nature established by firm and unalterable experience, he took the view that human testimony could never be sufficient to establish such an event, since it is always more probable that the witness is mistaken or untruthful than that such an extraordinary event has occurred.

Among the most important defenses of miracles in reply to Hume, the following three are noteworthy: William Adams (1707–89), *Essay on Mr. Hume's Essay on Miracles* (1752); George Campbell (1719–91), *Dissertation on Miracles* (1763); and John Douglas (1721–1807), *Criterion, or Miracles Examined* (1756). The best arguments in these works were to be recapitulated by Paley, the leading representative of the evidential school.

William Paley (1743–1805)[78] did for 18th-century England what Abbadie had done for 17th-century France: he summed up in clear and systematic form what was best in the arguments of his predecessors. Paley is still remembered for his *Principles of Moral and Political Philosophy* (1785), which proposes a Christian utilitarianism. In *Horae paulinae* (1790), his most original work, he amasses arguments for the reliability of the historical indications contained in the 13 Pauline Epistles, making use of parallels found in Acts and elsewhere. His two best known works are even more directly and deliberately apologetical. In 1794 he published *A View of the Evidences of Christianity*, so successful that it remained compulsory reading for all seeking entrance to Cambridge University until the 20th century. In 1802 he issued his *Natural Theology*, one of the classical presentations of the argument from design. Something deserves to be said about both of these major works.

Underlying Paley's apologetic is a moralistic and utilitarian theory of revelation. The purpose of revelation, he holds, is to influence human conduct by informing men of the rewards and punishments that await them in the future life.[79] In the opening pages of the *Evidences* he argues skillfully for the antecedent likelihood of revelation, granted the existence of a wise, beneficent creator and the need that man experiences for additional light and assurance. He then replies to Hume's argument against the discernibility of miracles. The argument does not hold, he maintains, for there can be no presumption that miracle stories must be false. If God is capable of intervening in the world, if revelation is likely, and if miracles are the appropriate way of sealing revelations, then miracles are likely in the context of what appears to be a revelation.

In the first major division of Part 1 Paley aims to show that there is satisfactory evidence that the original witnesses of Christianity were converted to a radically new manner of life and passed their lives in labors, dangers, and sufferings in order to bear witness to their beliefs. Those beliefs, moreover, were substantially the same as contained in the NT and therefore centered on the miraculous history of Jesus. In this connection Paley demonstrates at length the credibility of the NT accounts, drawing on the voluminous work of Lardner, mentioned above. Then Paley concludes that the testimony of the NT must be true for it is evident that the Apostles would not have gone about lying in order to teach virtue.

In the second major division of Part 1 Paley seeks to establish, by comparison with other religious movements, that there is no satisfactory evidence 'that persons pretending to be original witnesses of any other similar miracles have acted in the same manner, in attestation of the accounts which they delivered, and solely in consequence of their belief of the truth of those accounts.'[80] He takes up in particular the alleged miracles of persons such as Vespasian and Apollonius of Tyana and shows how unimpressive and poorly attested are these miracles compared with those of Christ. In these pages Paley leans heavily on the arguments drawn up by Adams and Douglas in their answers to Hume.

In Part 2 Paley furnishes nine other arguments, which he considers auxiliary, for the truth of Christianity. They are the arguments from prophecy, from the originality of the NT code of morality, from the character and doctrine of Christ, from the candor of the NT writers, from the agreements of the NT writers in their portrayal of Christ, from the originality of Christ's character, from the agreements between the NT and profane history, from the undesigned coincidences among the NT writers, from the impossibility of accounting for the Easter faith without supposing the real Resurrection of Christ, and, finally, from the rapid and extensive propagation of the Christian religion. All of these arguments are traditional. Paley expounds them persuasively but without much originality.

In Part 3 Paley takes up seven popular objections that might seem to militate against his own arguments for Christianity. He explains, for instance, why many Jews and pagans did not accept the Christian message and why miracles were not greatly stressed by the early Christian apologists. To the objection that 'if God had given a revelation, he would have written it in the skies,' Paley replies with arguments borrowed from Bishop Butler to the effect that if revelation has the same author as nature one might expect it to contain a like obscurity and that there might be good reasons why God would not wish to compel man's assent with overpowering evidence.

While the fame and popularity of Paley's *Evidences* are sufficient testimony to its merits, the book has little more than historical interest today. Paley was a skillful advocate, but he remained on the surface of things. He did not probe deeply into metaphysics or criteriology and therefore failed to justify his extrinsicist view of revelation and his extraordinary insistence on the evidential value of miracles. His argument from the Biblical miracles, although it may have seemed solid in the 18th century, has lost much of its force because it presumes that the Gospels and Acts are, on the whole, eyewitness reports. Paley knew nothing of oral tradition, of the complex processes by which legends are formed, or of the subtle shades of difference between various forms of popular history. For him, as for Abbadie and others, there were but two alternatives: factual history and imposture.

The *Evidences* presupposed the existence and the essential attributes of God. Only later, in his *Natural Theology*, did Paley give his rational justification for this presupposition. This work begins with the famous (though even in Paley's time far from original) comparison between the world and a watch. As it would be irrational to assert that a watch required no maker, so, he reasons, it is necessary to postulate a designer for the world. Following the basic lines of argument already developed by writers such as John Ray and William Derham, Paley proceeds to give a lengthy analysis of the manifold instances of design in the world. Like Ray, he prefers to concentrate less on astronomy than on biology. Drawing on medical and anatomical literature, he expatiates on the structure and functions of plants, insects, mammals, and especially on the organs of the human body. The examination of the human eye, he holds, would itself be a sufficient cure for atheism.[81]

Here, as in the *Evidences*, Paley presents his case with remarkable force and clarity but with a dissatisfying lack of profundity. While he piles up illustrations, he fails to examine the logical steps and presuppositions in a manner that meets the obvious objections. He does not go into the difficulties of Hume, whom he had read, or of Kant, whose *Critique of Pure Reason* (1781) was probably unfamiliar to him. He accepts the mechanistic assumption, that 'the problem of creation was, "attraction and matter being given, to make a world out of them." '[82] If this is one's view of nature, one can easily surmise that the world owes its purposiveness to an external designer. But has Paley given enough value to the intrinsic purposiveness of living organisms? Largely as a result of the work of Darwin, whom Paley greatly influenced, the argument from design as previously proposed is no longer convincing.

GERMANY IN THE SEVENTEENTH AND EIGHTEENTH CENTURIES

In no other European country was there so creative an apologetical encounter between theology and unbelief as in England. One may therefore summarize more briefly what occurred in continental Europe.

In Germany the tone for the discussion in the 18th century was to a great extent set by Gottfried Wilhelm Leibniz (1646–1716). This remarkable mathematician, physicist, historian, and jurist wrote several major philosophical works touching on religious questions. In his youthful *De arte combinatoria* (1666) he proposed the development of a universal logic along the lines suggested by Raymond Lull. In 1669 he outlined the plan of a definitive apology entitled *Demonstrationes catholicae* that was intended to reestablish the religious unity of Europe and to prepare for the successful evangelization of the world. According to Leibniz's outline this work was to consist of a series of Prolegomena dealing with logic, metaphysics, physics, and practical philosophy, to be followed by four parts: (1) A demonstration of the existence of God; (2) a demonstration of the immortality of the soul; (3) proofs of the Christian mysteries; and (4) proofs of the authority of the Church and of holy Scripture.[83]

Leibniz was intent upon forging a philosophical system that would reconcile the new developments since Descartes and Spinoza with Aristotle and the ancients. In a letter to his former professor Jakob Thomasius, dated April 30, 1669, he expressed the apologetical importance he attributed to this task: 'I venture to assert that atheists, Socinians, naturalists and skeptics can never be opposed successfully unless this philosophy is established. I believe this philosophy is a gift of God to this old world, to serve as the only plank, as it were, which pious and prudent men may use to escape the shipwreck of atheism which now threatens us.'[84]

Leibniz strongly rejected the contention of Pierre Bayle that faith is contrary to reason and that the act of faith must therefore be blind and irrational. In his 'Discourse on the Conformity of Faith with Reason,' prefixed to his *Theodicy* (1710), Leibniz replies that faith, while in a certain sense above reason, is never contrary to it. But unlike Locke he is not content with a juxtaposition of faith and reason on the basis of mutual noninterference. He holds that truths of faith necessarily agree with the a priori principles of reason, such as the principle of contradiction and the principle of sufficient reason. Revelation and miracles, while they go beyond the physical powers of created agents, are within the scope of reason insofar as God must have a sufficient reason for decreeing such exceptions. Whether such interventions have in fact occurred is for Leibniz a question of fact, to be established by historical evidence. He has no personal doubts but what the revelation attested in the Bible is sufficiently founded on reliable testimony and is therefore to be accepted.

In the case of Leibniz, as in that of many other apologists, the effort to defend the faith was inseparable from a critical rethinking of Christian doctrine. He labored to show, for instance, that the Catholic doctrine of transubstantiation and the Lutheran doctrine of consubstantiation could both be properly understood in a sense that did not go against self-evident rational principles. Approximating in some ways the tradition of the Calvinist churches, he regarded the presence of Christ in the Eucharist as a substantial but spiritual presence. So too he sought to defend the eternity of hell by the somewhat novel suggestion that the souls of the damned continually perform new acts of sin. In his *Theodicy*, replying to Bayle, he attempted to account for evil in the world without prejudice to the power and goodness of God and in this connection propounded his famous thesis that this is the best of all possible worlds. In other works Leibniz sought to give a rational demonstration of the immortality of the soul. He considered that those who based their acceptance of this doctrine on faith alone unduly weakened the rational foundation of Christian faith.

In various controversial writings Leibniz engaged in debates with Locke, Hobbes, and Spinoza. In lengthy correspondence with Samuel Clarke he combated Newton's view that it was necessary for God to interfere in the world in order to keep the universe in operation. Against the Socinians he wrote an essay, *Defense of the Trinity by Means of New Logical Inventions* (1671).

Leibniz's disciple Christian Wolff (1679–1754) early in his career composed an outline of apologetics under the title, *The Method of Demonstrating the Truth of the Christian Religion* (1707).[85] He insists on a geometrical, a priori method that starts with the existence and perfections of God and goes on to demonstrate, in view of man's actual state, the necessity of immediate divine revelation and of its expression in prophetic and apostolic writings. In his most mature religio-philosophical work, *Natural Theology*,[86] Wolff sets forth stringent demonstrations both a priori and a posteriori of the existence and attributes of God. He adds refutations of errors such as atheism, deism, and naturalism.

In 18th-century Germany the deistically inclined 'physico-theology' that had already become popular in England won wide acclaim. Johann Albert Fabricius (d. 1736) translated two major works of Derham, and he himself wrote works entitled *Hydrotheology* (water) and *Pyrotheology* (fire). Other enthusiasts of the movement published works with such odd titles as *Phytotheology* (plants), *Petinotheology* (birds), *Brontotheology* (thunder), *Lithotheology* (stones), and *Insectotheology*.

Somewhat similar in orientation was the apologetical work of the Dutch mathematician Bernard Nieuwentijdt, *The Right Use of the Contemplation of the World for the Knowledge of the Power, Wisdom, and Goodness of God and also for the Persuasion of Atheists and Unbelievers* (1715). This vast and ambitious treatise exploits numerous areas of scientific information for signs of the attributes of God and only in a concluding section deals with properly revealed mysteries. Bodily resurrection is defended on the basis of analogies in plant and insect life.

Later in the century the Swiss botanist Charles Bonnet erected a bold and original religio-cosmological system on the basis of Leibnizian principles. In his *Contemplation of Nature* (1764–65) he speculates on the worlds above man. In 1769 he published a two-volume work, *Philosophical Palingenesis*, which propounds a scientific basis for the doctrine of immortality by linking the soul to a tiny imperishable organism composed of subtle matter. In the final portion of this work, later published separately under the title *Philosophical Reflections on the Proofs for Christianity* (1770), he deals with revealed truth. He proposes a naturalistic explanation of miracles on the basis of a theory of preestablished harmony. In the closing section, dealing with the credibility of the Bible, he stresses the wonderful doctrines and effects of Christianity as the primary signs of its credibility.

As in England so in Germany there were deistic rationalists hostile to all revealed religion. The best known representative of this tendency is Hermann Samuel Reimarus (1694–1768), the orientalist from Hamburg, who composed a bulky *Apology for or Defense of the Rational Worshipers of God*, five sections of which were published after his death by Lessing under the title, *Wolfenbüttel Fragments* (1774–77). Reimarus, like Toland and Tindal, holds that the world itself is a sufficient revelation of God and that a purely rational religion is sufficient. He vigorously attacks the whole conception of historical revelation and rejects miracles as unworthy of God. He finds the OT crude and childish in its teachings and repulsive in the immorality of its heroes. Turning to the NT he finds the Resurrection accounts too conflicting to serve as a basis of faith. In a final fragment published by Lessing in 1778, *On the Purpose of Jesus and His*

Disciples, Reimarus argues that Jesus was a deluded fanatic, that His disciples perpetrated a deliberate deception, and that the Christian religion is therefore a colossal fraud.

The dramatist Gotthold Ephraim Lessing (1729–81), who had begun his career as a divinity student, retained a lifelong interest in religious questions, even if he did not staunchly adhere to the Lutheranism of his fathers.[87] In some of his writings he seems to stand close to the Deists, but to their philosophy he added at least the idea of progress. In his *The Education of the Human Race* (1777), building on a favorite theme of Irenaeus and Origen he takes the view that the Biblical religion, and Christianity as its culmination, have led humanity to insights concerning God that would never have been achieved by unaided reason. In particular Lessing valued the religions for promoting the ideals of sincerity, tolerance, and brotherly love—though he also criticized religion when it interfered with these values. His exaltation of tolerance and his critical attitude toward positive religion best appear in his play *Nathan the Wise* (1779).

While not an apologist in the ordinary sense, Lessing made some provocative observations on the question of Christian evidences. He published Reimarus not because he fully agreed with the latter's dogmatic anti-supernaturalism but because he thought that Reimarus had successfully destroyed the possibility of defending Christianity on the basis of the Biblical proofs from prophecy and miracle.

Lessing's own views on apologetics may be gathered at least in part from his brochure *On the Proof of the Spirit and of Power*, written in reply to a pamphlet by Johann David Schumann (1777), which had 'reaffirmed the traditional historical arguments for Christianity in answer to Reimarus. Lessing took exception to the idea set forth by Bonnet and others that although historical truth cannot be demonstrated yet one must believe the Biblical prophecies and miracles as firmly as truths that have been demonstrated. 'Accidental truths of history,' he maintained, 'can never become the proof of necessary truths of reason.' The passage from historical truth to the truths of faith, he reasoned, was an illegitimate leap from one genus of discourse to another, over 'the broad, ugly ditch which I cannot get across.'[88]

Lessing did not himself reject all proofs for Christianity. At the conclusion of his pamphlet against Schumann he asserts that one can accept Christianity on the basis of its inner truth, insofar as this speaks with certainty to one's heart. One no longer has to rely upon miracles and prophecies, though these signs may have been necessary to procure the acceptance of Christianity by the multitude at the time when the religion was strange and new. Now that the building is complete, the scaffolding may be torn down. Faith is sustained by the 'ever continuing miracle of Christianity itself.'[89]

In addition to the bold and creative thinkers thus far discussed, 18th-century Germany and Switzerland had their share of tradition-ally orthodox controversialists. For example, the Swiss mathema-tician and physicist Leonard Euler (1707–83) in his *Defense of Divine Revelation Against the Objections of Freethinkers*,[90] after replying to the deistic objections against revelation, concludes that one can rely firmly on all the gospel promises because they are accredited to man by the supreme miracle of Christ's Resurrection. The Swiss scientist and poet, Albrecht von Haller (1708–77), in a collection of letters, replied to the Deists and Encyclopedists of England and France, respectively.[91] Theodor Chr. Lilienthal (1717–82), professor at Königsberg, composed in 1760–82 16 volumes of lengthy but un-original arguments against the objections of Deists and unbelievers.[92] The Göttingen professor Gottfried Less (1736–97), after publishing a work on the Gospel accounts of the Resurrection against Reimarus, wrote several volumes of general Christian evidences much read in their day. His succinct treatise, *The Authenticity, Uncorrupted Preservation, and Credibility of the New Testament*,[93] in which he presents some of the early testimonies to the NT writings previously assembled by Lardner, was translated into English. To show the credibility of the Gospels he gives a somewhat oversimplified picture of how 'thirteen poor, inconsiderable, unlearned, and almost unknown men' spread the Christian message to the 'whole world.'

CATHOLIC APOLOGETICS IN FRANCE AND ITALY

In Roman Catholic countries the apologetics of the 18th century took the form of a series of defensive reactions against the new philosophies of the Enlightenment.[94] The Benedictine François Lamy (or Lami; 1636–1711), a disciple of Nicolas Malebranche, published a philosophical polemic, *The New Atheism Overthrown, or, Refutation of the System of Spinoza*.[95] He sought to refute Spinoza's monism by proving that man is, as Descartes had contended, a composite of two substances, body and soul. Against Spinoza's determinism Lamy alleged the immediate experience of free will. He argued further that Spinoza's pantheistic system, if accepted in practice, would lead to disastrous moral consequences.

In other works Lamy set forth the positive grounds for accepting

Christianity. His *Evident Truth of the Christian Religion*[96] is a rather jejune demonstration of the 'fact of Christian revelation' from miracles, prophecies, and the testimonies of the witnesses to Jesus Christ. In a later and more elaborate apologetic, *The Unbeliever Led to Religion by Reason,*[97] he sets forth the Christian evidences in nine rather tedious dialogues between Arsile and Timandre. He gives both a priori arguments from the antecedent necessity of a mediator and a posteriori arguments from the NT witnesses.

As the 18th century progressed, French apologists, like their colleagues in England, showed an increasing tendency to shift their ground from philosophical reasoning to historical evidence. This development is already discernible in the work of the Oratorian Alexandre Claude François Houtteville (or Houteville; 1686–1742), who issued in 1722 *The Christian Religion Proved by Facts.*[98] Book 1, the most original part of this work, demonstrates that the miraculous events narrated in the Gospels are worthy of acceptance according to the general laws of historical evidence. In the first place, he observes, since miracles are not selfcontradictory, they are worthy of serious investigation (ch. 6). Further, the Gospel miracles are vouched for by contemporary eyewitnesses (ch. 7) who were sincere and truthful (ch. 8). The Gospel facts, moreover, were public and of general interest (ch. 9). They stand at the basis of certain later facts, such as the willingness of the early Christians to die for their faith (ch. 10). The miracles of Jesus were admitted by the Jews and pagans of the first Christian centuries, although it would have been to the interest of these adversaries to deny them (ch. 11). Finally, the miracle stories have been handed down without corruption (ch. 12). In Book 2 Houtteville sets forth the conventional arguments from OT prophecies of Christ, and in Book 3 he replies to 14 major objections raised by the Deists to the veracity of the Gospels. At the end he appends a dissertation on the systems that the unbelievers propose as alternatives to Christianity.

Houtteville's work is clear and well-ordered. His efforts to apply exact historical method to the Gospels represented a real advance, but the undeveloped state of historical science in his day has, of course, made his work quite obsolete by modern standards.

From about the middle of the 18th century, Catholic apologetics was compelled to reply to brilliant antagonists such as Jean-Jacques Rousseau (1712–78), who advocated a kind of sentimental deism; Voltaire (1691–1778), who mordantly satirized the ideas of providence and election in a cascade of pamphlets, novels, and historical works; and the Baron Paul d'Holbach (1723–89), who propounded, especially in his *Système de la nature*, a thoroughgoing atheistic determinism.

The most prolific Catholic adversary of the *philosophes* was the Abbé Nicolas Sylvestre Bergier (1718–90), whose collected works in Migne's edition comprise eight bulky volumes. Against Rousseau he wrote *Deism Refuted by Itself*,[99] a successful popular work in the form of 12 letters. The first three deal respectively with the possibility, necessity, and factual existence of supernatural revelation; the fourth takes up the authority of the Church as a divine teacher, and the remainder answer various objections that Rousseau, or his mouthpiece in *Émile*, the 'vicar of Savoy,' had raised against Catholic Christianity. Bergier's primary tactic is to expose the internal inconsistencies in Rousseau's position—a task not too difficult in the case of this particular adversary. Bergier's own proofs for Christianity are primarily drawn from the NT miracles that, as in the case of Houtteville, are viewed as incontestable supernatural facts. Less subtle than Pascal, Bergier holds that while doctrine is proved from miracles, the converse is never the case.[100]

In 1767 Bergier published, in reply to the now forgotten Fréret, a work entitled *The Certainty of the Proofs of Christianity*,[101] which undertakes to defend traditional Christian apologetics from Eusebius to Houtteville against the historical objections that have been raised. Without insisting on the strict authenticity of the NT books, Bergier regards their trustworthiness as demonstrable and the efforts to degrade them to the level of the NT apocrypha unavailing. He upholds the argument from miracles and denies that it is weakened by the alleged parallel of the false miracles worked at the tomb of the Jansenist, Abbé Pâris. The gospel miracles, says Berthier, won converts, but the Jansenist miracles succeeded only in convincing those who were previously confirmed Jansenists (Migne ed. 8:108).

In response to the Baron d'Holbach's *System of Nature* (1770), Bergier brought out his *Examination of Materialism*,[102] in which he takes up d'Holbach's points one by one. In Part 1, examining the cosmos and man, he seeks to show that materialism is incapable of accounting for movement in the world and, a fortiori, for what is characteristic of human life. He defends the freedom of the will, the spirituality of the soul, and personal immortality. In Part 2 Bergier refutes d'Holbach's atheism not so much by proposing arguments for the existence of God as by proving that d'Holbach's objections against Clarke and others do not hold.

Bergier was a very industrious, well informed, and lucid apologist. His great forte was his ability to pick out inconsistencies in the positions of his opponents, and his principal foible was his failure to rise above the common assumptions of the intellectuals of his day. Thus in writing against Rousseau he seems to accept the latter's extrinsicist view of revelation. In reply to Fréret he falls into a positivism of 'miraculous facts,' and in refuting d'Holbach he seems to accept the deistic notion of God that d'Holbach is rejecting. Unlike the great apologists, Bergier failed to develop a positive theory of Christian credibility that could commend itself to later generations.

Voltaire, the leading publicist for deism in 18th-century France, stirred up a host of Catholic adversaries. The Jesuit Claude François Nonnotte (1711–93) published several works in answer to the sage of Ferney, most importantly his two-volume *The Errors of Voltaire*,[103] which politely and moderately points out where Voltaire misrepresents the facts of history. The wittiest and most effective answer to Voltaire was the *Letters of Certain Jews to Monsieur Voltaire*,[104] by Antoine Guénée. Voltaire is chided for his ignorance of the ancient languages and his shortcomings as a Biblical scholar, as exhibited in many of his generalizations about the religion of the Jews.

Italian Catholics in the 18th century looked on with horrified anxiety as the waves of deism and atheism swept over England and France. Already schooled by their predecessors of the 17th century to detest the heresies of Luther and Calvin, the Italian apologists regarded the new errors as the natural and inevitable outcome of the Protestant principle of private judgment. Faith, in their view, depended in very large measure on the living authority of the Church, especially that of the pope. This general trend to center apologetics on the question of the Church and to refute all the other sects and religions from the standpoint of Catholic Christianity characterizes, for instance, the works of the Jesuit pulpit orator Paolo Segneri[105] and those of the Dominican apologists Moniglia, Concina, and Gotti. Cardinal Vincenzo Gotti's *The True Church of Jesus Christ*[106] is a milestone in the development of the apologetics of the Church.

One of the most popular and typical apologies of the period was the *Truth of the Faith*,[107] by the Italian Redemptorist St. Alphonsus de' Liguori (1696–1787), a work in which the author recapitulates the main points of two of his earlier tracts against modern unbelief and heresy. The book consists of three main parts. Part 1, against the atheists and materialists, establishes the existence of God and the spirituality of the human soul. Part 2, prefaced by a brief chapter on the necessity of revelation, sets forth the standard arguments from prophecy and miracle to prove, chiefly against the Deists, the fact of Christian revelation. This part closes with a series of chapters on divine providence, the immortality of the soul, and future rewards and punishments. Part 3, directed primarily against the Protestants, undertakes to show that the Roman Catholic Church alone is legitimate, as may be seen from its historical continuity with the apostolic Church and from the continuing miracles within it (including the liquefaction of St. Januarius's blood). The Protestant Churches are dismissed as false because their founders had no divine mission and because they have no stable rule of faith. In the closing chapter Alphonsus takes a strong position in favor of the infallibility of the pope, which was to be defined as a dogma a century later.

Less typical of Italian apologetics at the time was the Barnabite Cardinal Hyacinthe-Sigismond Gerdil (1718–1802). Born in Savoy, he taught some years at Turin before being called to Rome as a cardinal. Although French was his native language, he composed the majority of his more important works in Italian. In a number of shorter treatises Gerdil attacked the empiricism of Locke, the liberalism of Montesquieu, and the naturalistic educational theories of Rousseau. In his early work he defends the ontologism and occasionalism of Malebranche, but by the time he wrote his lengthy *Introduzione allo studio della religione*[108] he had evolved toward an eclectic Platonism. Appealing to figures such as Plato, Descartes, Newton, Leibniz, and Wolff, he argues against Bayle and others that the wisest men of the most enlightened centuries have esteemed religion and have known how to distinguish it from popular superstition. Religion, he maintains, is necessary, for without it men would not have the motivation to adhere to the demands of justice. The Catholic religion, offering certitude, excels all others. Protestantism, by its doctrine of free examination, contains the seeds of its own destruction.

While Gerdil differs from most of the Italian apologists of his century by reason of his positive attitude toward modern philosophical developments, he resembles them in his infallibilist tendencies and in his antipathy to Protestantism. In no country did 18th-century Catholic apologists take an active share in the creative development of new forms of thought, as the Anglicans were doing in England or the Lutherans in Germany.

CONCLUSION

The period from the Protestant Reformation to the end of the Enlightenment was marked by so many diverse trends of thought that it is no easy task to summarize its contribution to the progress of apologetics. Three main points may perhaps be made.

First, these years did not produce any grand apologetical syntheses comparable in magnitude and depth to those of Augustine and Aquinas. The authors who did compose summas on a vast scale, such as Vives, Mornay, Abbadie, and Paley, were not notable thinkers in their own right. Bossuet, whose *Discourse on Universal History* has a certain grandeur, lacked the learning and critical spirit that his project called for. For the most part, the apologists of these centuries were too disinterested in metaphysics to attain a lofty, comprehensive vision of reality comparable to that of their patristic and medieval forebears.

Second, partly as a result of the weaknesses already noted, the initiative in this period no longer lies with the protagonists of the Christian cause but rather with the adversaries. The apologists, rushing to answer one objection after another, are vexed and harassed, anxious and defensive. They seem unable to turn the tables on the adversaries by mastering and correcting the new currents of thought —as Origen had done for middle Platonism, Augustine for Neoplatonism, and Aquinas for Averroistic Aristotelianism.

Third, significant progress is made in sorting out and analyzing the various kinds of apologetical evidence—subjective and objective, deductive and inductive, historical and contemporary.

The efforts of some to construct fully demonstrative and quasi-mathematical proofs for the truth of Christianity (Huet, Elizalde, Gonzales, Wolff) are generally recognized to be unsuccessful. Others, veering to the opposite extreme, seek to establish the need for blind faith in the teaching of the Church to compensate for the feebleness of human reason (Montaigne, Charron). In appealing to skepticism they are playing with a dangerous instrument that could easily be turned against faith itself.

Pascal, building on the work of the skeptical fideists, sets forth with singular power the contrast between 'reasons of the heart,' serviceable in apologetics, and 'reasons of the mind,' valid in the scientific sphere. His insight into the role of subjectivity in the decision of faith was not developed further until the 19th century.

The British and German apologists in their dialogue with deism grappled seriously with the relationship between the natural sciences and Christian evidences. This problem, which seemed to have been solved in a way favorable to Biblical faith by the time of Paley, was to break out with new violence in the 19th century, especially in connection with the evolutionary controversy.

British apologists such as Butler and Paley, building on the empiricism of Locke and Hume, made effective use of probabilities and presumptions in apologetics. While their common-sense approach injected a healthy note of realism, they sometimes fell into an unfortunate legalism that their greater disciple, Newman, was to detect and correct.

Partly through the assaults of adversaries such as Spinoza and Reimarus, modern Biblical criticism began to develop in the late 17th and early 18th centuries. Moderate Christian thinkers, such as Simon, Grotius, Leclerc, and Lardner, made use of this incipient science to enrich their apologetics. In a similar way, controversialists such as Houtteville, seeking to exhibit the force of the evidences, advanced the methodology of historiography.

The almost exclusive insistence on Biblical and historical evidences in the 18th century involved certain dangers for apologetics. The 'fact of revelation' came to be considered too positivistically as an arbitrary intervention from on high, and the reasonableness of faith was made to depend too much on bookish erudition. Better than his more orthodox opponents, Lessing perceived this danger and pointed to the need for grounding one's conviction in the contemporary performance of the Church. Many apologists of the 19th century, from their own point of view, were to look for present 'proofs of the Spirit and of power.'

In summary, then, the centuries considered in this chapter are transitional. Apologetics is beginning to reorient itself, almost reluctantly, to the problems and thought forms of the modern mind and is thus preparing the paths of the future.

CHAPTER FIVE

The Nineteenth Century

The 18th century, as has been seen, opened up a rich variety of options for the apologist. He might construct a rational, metaphysical justification for faith, as did Huet, Leibniz, and Wolff; or a more concrete apologetic based on the analogies of nature with the supernatural, as did Ray and Butler; or a Biblical-historical apologetic, as did Grotius, Lardner, and Houtteville; or, finally, an inward apologetic of the heart, based on the aspirations of the human spirit, as did Pascal.

It was the last of these options that most attracted the first generation of 19th-century apologists, both Protestant and Catholic. At this point in history man seems to have become more conscious than ever before of his own individuality and subjectivity. He sought contact with the higher world not through abstract reason but rather through feeling and the movements of the heart. This approach is evident in many leading apologists in the first part of the century, such as Schleiermacher in Germany, Kierkegaard in Denmark, Coleridge in England, and Chateaubriand in France.

The path for this new apologetics was cleared by Immanuel Kant (1724–1804). In his *Critique of Pure Reason* (1791) Kant portrayed the speculative reason as hardly more than a calculating machine, capable of organizing the data of sense experience but not of rising above empirical data and of dealing realistically with the transcendent or the divine. In his *Critique of Practical Reason* (1788) Kant supplemented this outlook by pointing out that the sense of moral obligation and the demands of conscience require man, for practical purposes, to postulate the reality of God, of freedom, and of immortality. Thus Kant made room for faith in a new sense of the term—

158

belief resting not simply on external authority but rather on personal motives that are subjectively compelling though objectively insufficient. In his *Opus postumum* Kant apparently identified the voice of conscience very closely with the divine presence within man, thus laying the foundations of what was to develop into the subjective idealism of Fichte.

Kant, while he sharply criticized the notion of historical revelation, gave a secure philosophical status to some of the fundamental Christian doctrines, notably in his *Religion within the Bounds of Reason Alone* (1793). His dualism of speculative and practical reason set the philosophical framework for much of the apologetics of the early 19th century, especially in the Protestant world. Many followed his suggestion that faith should be grounded in the voice of conscience and in the sense of moral obligation. Within the context of the Romantic revival, however, Kant's moralism was alleviated by a deeper regard for the feelings, his individualism by a keener sense of community, and his formalism by a deeper interest in historical concreteness.

PROTESTANTISM: 1800–50

Germany

As much as any single individual, Schleiermacher may be credited with having first fashioned an apologetic suited to Protestants of the new age. Raised among the Moravian brethren, Friedrich D. E. Schleiermacher (1768–1834) retained a strong Pietistic bent. But at the same time he moved easily among the dechristianized professors and writers of Berlin. His mission, as he conceived it, was to mediate between the Pietistic Christianity of his fathers and the enlightened romanticism of his intellectual companions. In this sense he was a mediating theologian.

Schleiermacher's first book, *On Religion: Speeches to Its Cultured Despisers*,[1] was programmatic for his entire life work; it was also the manifesto of a sophisticated religious revival. He takes the offensive by beginning with an indictment of the spiritual poverty of the Enlightenment. 'Suavity and sociability, art and science have so fully taken possession of your minds, that no room remains for the eternal and holy Being that lies beyond the world.'[2] 'With pain I see daily how the rage for calculating and explaining suppresses the sense [of religion].'[3] But this sense is innate and cannot be permanently crushed out. If any man looks into his own heart he will find a

sense and taste for the infinite, which longs for satisfaction. Schleiermacher was profoundly convinced that the times were propitious for
bringing religion to the cultured men of the day.[4] His dominant
concern is well summarized in a sentence from his open letter to
Lücke: 'shall the knot of history be thus loosed: Christianity with
barbarism and learning with unbelief?'[5]

In his effort to mediate Schleiermacher takes pains to show that
religion should in no way be identified with the *bric-à-brac* of
traditional dogmas and practices. He tells his cultured readers how he
himself learned to cleanse his thought and feeling from the rubbish of
antiquity,[6] and he advises them to forget everything that usually goes
by the name of religion.[7] He proclaims that it is possible to be both
religious and fully abreast of new developments in science and
philosophy. As he reconstructs religion from the inside outward on
the basis of inward emotions and dispositions, he turns the apologetic
sword against traditional orthodoxy. In his second speech[8] he
radically redefines practically all the key concepts of religion, including miracle, revelation, inspiration, prophecy, God, and immortality.
Schleiermacher is not seeking, as some apologists have done, to sell
conventional Christianity by sugar-coating it: he is revising Christianity to make it something that he as a man of his times can accept.
The deliberateness with which Schleiermacher goes about this task is
something new.

As one who subscribes to the Kantian critique of speculative
reason, Schleiermacher has no intention of trying to demonstrate
either the existence of God or the fact of revelation. In his great
dogmatic synthesis, *The Christian Faith*, he attacks the arguments from
miracle and prophecy. These signs, he maintains, are not sufficiently
probative to bring conviction, although they may suffice to
corroborate the faith of those who already accept Christ as
Redeemer.[9]

In his own way, however, Schleiermacher does construct an
apologetic for Christianity. Negatively, as has been seen, he seeks to
show that the dogmas can be so reinterpreted that Christianity does
not prevent one from being a fully modern man. Positively, he
maintains that the religious sense achieves its highest fulfillment in
Christianity. In both *On Religion* and the *Christian Faith* he begins
this demonstration by showing that religion cannot flourish except
within a 'Church,' 'a communion or association relating to religion or
piety.'[10] 'If there is religion at all, it must be social, for that is the
nature of man, and it is quite peculiarly the nature of religion.'[11]
Then he goes on to show that a religion must be definite and that any

'Church' must be rooted in the characteristic religious experience of some great founder. Man is, in practice, faced by a choice between historically existing religions.

In the introductory section of his *Christian Faith* Schleiermacher gives his most elaborate vindication of Christianity as the highest religion. He begins by defining piety as man's immediate consciousness of absolute dependence. On the basis of this definition he has no difficulty in establishing the superiority of monotheism over polytheism, for man is not absolutely dependent on any of the gods of polytheism. There are three great monotheistic faiths: Judaism, Islam, and Christianity. Judaism, he argues, is not really an option because it is a particularistic religion, restricting the love of Yahweh to the race of Abraham, and because it is 'almost in process of extinction.'[12] Islam and Christianity, the two great monotheistic world religions, are of very unequal worth. Islam—sensuous, passive, and fatalistic— subordinates the moral order to the order of nature. Christianity, which by contrast subordinates the natural to the moral order, is spiritual, teleological, and conducive to human freedom. Christianity, therefore, is the highest form of monotheism; monotheism is the highest kind of religion; and religion is necessary for a truly human life.

Yet the fact remains, according to Schleiermacher, that the central affirmation of Christianity—the fact of man's Redemption by Jesus of Nazareth—cannot be verified outside of faith. To believe it one must experience Christ's redeeming power, imparted through the Holy Spirit. Under this influence one acquires a God-consciousness that finds its unsurpassable exemplar in the filial consciousness of Jesus. Only those who have undergone this experience, by opening themselves to it in love, are able to perceive that it raises man's God-consciousness to the highest pitch and thus validates itself.[13]

Schleiermacher was perhaps the first to construct a thoroughgoing 'inner apologetic' that proceeds through the progressive unfolding of man's innate longing for communion with God. He stands at the opposite extreme from the positivism of the evidential school and from the rationalism of the Wolffian supernaturalists. He is the prototype of all later apologists who look upon speculative reasoning as a mere accompaniment of the vital movement of the human spirit in its aspiration to dynamic self-fulfillment.

In his *Brief Outline on the Study of Theology* Schleiermacher set forth his program for apologetics. He proposed that the entire enterprise of Biblical, historical, and practical theology should be prefaced by a new discipline, called 'philosophical theology,' which 'has thus far never been exhibited or recognized as a unit.'[14] This new discipline, using the framework developed in philosophy of religion, seeks to present the essence of Christianity in such wise that it can be recognized as a distinctive mode of faith.

Philosophical theology, as Schleiermacher conceives it, is divided into two main branches, apologetics and polemics. Apologetics seeks to view Christianity in relation to religious communities in general; polemics, to detect and correct deviations within the Christian community. The task of apologetics, as Schleiermacher here describes it, is not to bring others into the community—a task pertaining rather to 'practical theology'—but rather to communicate to the faithful a 'conviction of the truth of the mode of faith' propagated in the Church community in such manner that it becomes intellectually acceptable.[15] Apologetics, then, must set forth a formula of the distinctive nature of Christianity, establish the claim of Christianity to a distinct historical existence, and show how the developments of the community have been in line with its initial orientation.

One of Schleiermacher's disciples, Karl Heinrich Sack (1789–1875), in volumes on apologetics and polemics tried to carry out his master's program for philosophical theology, and in so doing made a great contribution to the establishment of the discipline that would later be called fundamental theology. Sack's *Christian Apologetics*,[16] however, deviates somewhat from Schleiermacher's own intention, reverting to the conventional concept of apologetics as a rational grounding of the Christian faith in demonstrable divine facts. After first expounding the value of religion in general, Sack points out the deficiencies of the non-Christian religions. Then he turns to the idea of revelation as God's self-communication through personal witnesses and shows how this idea is surpassingly verified in the appearance of Jesus as the Christ. Next he points out how salvation, or Redemption, as the true and proper effect of revelation, is offered by Christ, who in this respect fulfils the prophecies and types of the OT. He then demonstrates that Christianity has singular power to foster religious and moral life, thus contributing to human freedom and progress. Finally, in his concluding section he grounds the lifegiving power of Christianity in the Word of God and in the Holy Spirit.

The philosophy of religion continued to develop in close relationship to idealistic philosophy, thanks to thinkers such as J. F. Fries (1773–1843) and M. W. L. De Wette (1780–1849). The latter constructed a phenomenology of revelation, viewed as the inbreaking of something radically new that nevertheless fulfilled man's previous aspirations. The Christian revelation, he argued, was unique in that it had given a wholly new direction to the religious spirit in the world.

The philosophy of religion was carried to new heights by Georg W. F. Hegel (1770–1831). Somewhat in the spirit of the Anselmian faith seeking understanding, he sought to make his philosophy a rational appropriation of the Christian patrimony. In his youthful romantic period he wrote eloquently of the religion of Jesus as a gospel of love, life, and freedom. In his mature work he sought to show how the principal Christian dogmas (Trinity, Incarnation, Redemption) were but a symbolic or imaginative projection of the rational truths set forth in his own system of dialectically evolving pantheism.

Some of Hegel's disciples, such as his editor, Philipp Conrad Marheineke (1780–1846), attempted to combine the philosophical idealism of their master with orthodox adherence to Church teaching. In his *System of Christian Dogmatics*[17] Marheineke interpreted the Church as the locus in which the Absolute attains full self-consciousness, concretely actualizing the presence of the Spirit in history. In a certain sense this fusion of philosophy and dogma may be viewed as an apologetic, for it tended to exhibit the rational basis for traditional Christian doctrine.

A more radical member of the Hegelian school, David Friedrich Strauss (1808–74), drastically reinterpreted the Christian message, deliberately subordinating traditional orthodoxy to the interests of a new evolutionistic philosophy. Strauss's famous *Life of Jesus*[18] maintained that the union of finite and infinite has its realization not in a single individual, Jesus Christ, but in the whole of humanity, as the latter becomes divinized. The Christ of the New Testament was for Strauss a myth bearing the true and revelatory idea of God-manhood. Since the major part of Strauss's *Life of Jesus* was devoted to exposing the historical unreliability of the Gospel stories, his work was enthusiastically hailed by unbelievers and passionately condemned by committed Christians.

Many of the most significant answers to Strauss came from apologists of the Schleiermacher school. One of them, Carl Ullmann (1796–1865), exemplifies a devotional type of apologetics not uncharacteristic of the times. His best known work, *The Sinlessness of Jesus: An Evidence for Christianity*, argues apologetically from the NT portrait of Jesus and from Jesus' testimony concerning Himself to the conclusion that Jesus was in fact sinless, as befits the Redeemer of mankind. To the objection that the Gospel portrait might be a fiction Ullmann replies, with Rousseau, 'The inventor of such an image would be more astonishing than his subject.'[19] Then he adds that the effects of the manifestation of Jesus in the religious regeneration of the world would not have a proportionate cause except in a real person. 'He especially who has felt in his own heart the peculiar power experienced by the Gospel delineation of the Lord Jesus, will entertain no kind of doubt as to its reality and origin.'[20]

In reply to Strauss Ullmann wrote two articles that he later combined into a pamphlet, *Historical or Mythical?*[21] When Strauss later maintained that the only religion left to modern man is the worship of genius, Ullmann replied with a brochure, *The Worship of Genius.*[22] Here and in a brief reply to Feuerbach, *The Distinctive Character or Essence of Christianity*,[23] Ullmann contends that the singular unity of the human and the divine in Jesus surpasses all achievements of human genius and is reliably attested both by the Gospels and by the abiding influence of Christ in the Church.

Likewise influenced by Schleiermacher is the Pietistic brand of apologetics found in August Tholuck (1799–1877). In reply to De Wette's *Theodore; or, The Skeptic's Conversion*,[24] a book that countenanced the ordination of agnostics to the ministry, the youthful Tholuck wrote his early, and partly autobiographical, *Guido and Julius; or, Sin and the Propitiator Exhibited in the True Consecration of the Skeptic.*[25] Using the device of a highly emotional exchange of letters between two university students, the one in theology, the other in classical philology, Tholuck extols the joyful experience of regeneration through Christ and maintains that the new life impressed upon men's hearts by the Holy Spirit is its own guarantee.

In a later work, *The Credibility of the Evangelical History*,[26] Tholuck takes Strauss to task for his aprioristic rejection of miracles and for his exaggerated efforts to find inconsistencies in the Gospels. But Tholuck himself is aprioristic in his assumption that miracles are possible and that the Gospels can always be harmonized. His reply to Strauss, like that of other mediating theologians in the Schleiermacher school (e.g., August Wilhelm Neander and Johann Peter Lange) suffers, as Albert Schweitzer remarked, from the false supposition that the Fourth Gospel provides an authentic historical framework into which the Synoptic pericopes can somehow be inserted. The Strauss controversy had a good result insofar as it finally drove NT scholars to forge better techniques for appraising the historicity of the Gospel accounts. This achievement, however, belongs not to the Schleiermacher school but to the Liberals of the second half of the century.

Denmark

Few theologians have been more violent in their attacks on apologetics than the Danish journalist-philosopher, Søren Kierkegaard (1813–55). And yet Emil Brunner has said of him with good ground: 'We may indeed claim that no other thinker has ever worked out the contrast between the Christian Faith and all the "immanental" possibilities of thought with such clarity and intensity as he has done. Kierkegaard is incomparably the greatest Apologist or "eristic" thinker of the Christian faith within the sphere of Protestantism.'[27]

Kierkegaard exposed the weaknesses of estheticism, of self-complacent bourgeois morality, and the mass spirit. But above all he directed his invective against the efforts of the Hegelians to commend Christianity by adapting it to the exigencies of their rationalistic view of history. The seminary professor H. L. Martensen (1808–84), one of Denmark's foremost Hegelian theologians, suffered the fiercest blows from Kierkegaard's rhetoric.

In many passages Kierkegaard seemed to reject the entire apologetical effort as illegitimate. 'If one were to describe the whole orthodox apologetical effort in one single sentence,' he wrote, 'but also with categorical precision, one might say that it has the intent to make *Christianity plausible*. To this one might add that, if this were to succeed, then would this effort have the ironical fate that precisely on the day of its triumph it would have lost everything and entirely quashed Christianity.'[28] Rational proofs, he maintained, were out of place in theology. 'For whose sake is it that the proof is sought? Faith does not need it; aye; it must even regard proof as its enemy. But when faith begins to feel embarrassed and ashamed . . . , when faith thus begins to lose its passion, when faith begins to cease to be faith, then a proof becomes necessary so as to command respect from the side of unbelief.'[29] But such proofs are unavailing, for 'to defend anything is always to discredit it.'[30]

The proofs, moreover, were logically invalid. In the early pages of *Philosophical Fragments*[31] Kierkegaard, following Kant, tries to show the paralogisms in the usual demonstrations of God's existence. In his *Postscript* he argues characteristically that 'to prove the existence of one who is present is the most shameless affront, since it is an attempt to make him ridiculous.'[32]

In many of his works he rejects all avenues of demonstration of the divinity of Christ, which he considers to be the central, if not the unique, fact of the Christian faith. The proofs from the antiquity of the true religion he mocks as a rhetorical 'showerbath.' 'Eighteen centuries have no greater demonstrative force than a single day, in relation to an eternal truth which is to decide my eternal happiness.'[33] To prove the truth of Christianity from the reliability of the Gospel history is equally fruitless. At best this procedure would result in putting one in the position of the original witnesses, who saw only 'a humble human being who said of himself that he was God.'[34] As for the miracles, it is idle to mention them, for 'whoever does not believe does not see the miracle.'[35]

More fundamentally Kierkegaard was concerned with the impassable ditch that Lessing had discerned between the accidental truths of history and the desperately essential truth of salvation. Historical truth, he argued, was simply incommensurable with an 'eternal decision.' The passage from the one to the other was a 'leap' into a new category.[36]

Repeatedly in his writings Kierkegaard insisted that there can be no access to faith through objective logical thinking. For him the doctrine of the Incarnation was the central Christian affirmation, and it meant that the Creator had become a creature, the infinite finite, the eternal temporal, the necessary contingent. Such a union of incompatible attributes was strictly contradictory and inconceivable, and any attempt to make it plausible could amount only to adulteration.

In a curious way—Kierkegaard suggests, without developing the thought—a kind of apologetic can be developed out of the very absurdity of the Christian affirmation. Faith itself is a miracle, he declares.[37] The very fact that some people have believed that God appeared on earth in the humble figure of a man is so astounding that it provides an occasion for others to share the faith.[38] Christianity is the only historical movement that has ever proposed to base man's eternal happiness on his relationship to an event occurring within history. Since no philosophy or mythology has ever had this idea, Kierkegaard finds it possible to conclude that 'it did not arise in the heart of any man.'[39]

Kierkegaard was familiar with the ironical conclusion of Hume's *Essay on Miracles*, that while historical evidence is not capable of establishing miracles in the past, still 'whoever is moved by *Faith* to assent to it [Christianity], is conscious of a continued miracle in his own person, which subverts all the principles of his understanding, and gives him a determination to believe what is most contrary to custom and experience.' As Lowrie points out, Kierkegaard was deeply struck by Georg Hamann's comment on this passage: 'Hume may have said this with a scornful and critical air, yet all the same, this is orthodoxy and a testimony to the truth from the mouth of an enemy and persecutor—all his doubts are proofs of his proposition.'[40]

In spite of certain extreme affirmations Kierkegaard clearly did not think that the value of Christianity consisted in its absurdity alone. Rather it answered a real human need. According to his anthropology man does not come into the world a fully constituted self. In many of his works Kierkegaard describes the inner tensions in man between the finite and the infinite, the temporal and the eternal, the contingent and the necessary.[41] Man's task is to achieve some kind of creative synthesis of these opposite tensions. Anticipating the phenomenology of Blondel and others, Kierkegaard describes the 'stages on life's way' by which man rises from the demonic detachment of the aesthete to the sweet reasonableness of the 'ethical man,' and finally to the courageous commitment of religious faith. The passage from philosophic reason to faith is achieved not through objective reasoning but through passionate subjectivity and cannot be made without 'fear and trembling.' But the step taken in the personal responsibility of the Christian decision is warranted because without it man cannot attain the fullest degree of inwardness and authenticity.[42]

In *Sickness Unto Death* Kierkegaard clarifies this existential logic by showing how all man's efforts to evade the religious decision, proposed in the most challenging form by the Christian paradox, lead ultimately to despair. Sin is despair before God; it is the surrender of hope of becoming an authentic self. The central Christian paradox, for Kierkegaard, offers the only valid answer to the sickness of despair.[43] Despair is the failure to have faith, but paradoxically also, despair is the first fact of faith, for it arises from man's ineluctable drive toward the acceptance of a life transcendentally grounded in God. The experience of despair rouses his spirit from dullness to the passionate interest needed for truth and faith considered as subjectivity.

For Kierkegaard, then, faith was ultimately irrational, but it was the consummation of an existential dialectic and thus, in a paradoxical way, a fulfillment of reason. Through passionate subjectivity man found a way beyond the sterile dichotomies of philosophical reason. 'The highest pitch of every passion is always to will its own downfall; and so it is the supreme passion of the Reason to seek a collision, though this collision must in one way or another prove its own undoing.'[44] Because man is essentially paradox, his thinking is a participation in something transcending himself. Thus the destruction of reason in faith is at the same time the supreme achievement of what reason aspires to do.

There would be much to add by way of criticism of Kierkegaard's form of apologetic. In order to throw the reader back on inwardness and subjectivity, Kierkegaard hardens to an extreme the trans-rational elements that Christian theology has traditionally recognized under the rubric of mystery. He takes over from rationalist theology the idea that God must be 'absolutistically' conceived as the necessary, the immutable, the infinite, and he rejects without discussion all the distinctions by which classical theology had sought to remove the apparent contradiction from the Incarnation. Undoubtedly Kierke-gaard stands in need of some correction on points such as these; but he performed a salutary and much needed service by calling attention to the scandal and offense of the gospel, and to the fact that philosophic reason itself stands under divine judgment. In his profound phenomenological analysis of the role of subjectivity and the 'leap of faith' he thematized with true genius the inner logic of the existential decision. Many important insights that had begun to surface in Pascal and Schleiermacher received in Kierkegaard their classic form of expression.

Great Britain

Something of the same intense subjectivity that guided Schleiermacher in Germany and Kierkegaard in Denmark was introduced into England by the poet, essayist, and polymath Samuel Taylor Coleridge (1772–1834). Without being a specialist in theology, Coleridge never ceased to concern himself with religious questions.[45] In his early Bristol lectures, 1795, corresponding to his Unitarian period, he presented a rather rationalistic apologetics based on Butler and Paley. After being converted a decade later to Trinitarian theology, he propounded an original and highly personalistic epistemology of faith, influenced on the one hand by modern German philosophy (Lessing, Kant, Schelling) and on the other hand by Neoplatonism, which he knew from personal study and from the writings of the Cambridge Platonists.

At this stage in his career Coleridge became convinced that apologists such as Paley, by uncritically accepting the empiricism of Locke, had destroyed their own capacity to answer effectively the objections of Hume. In his *Aids to Reflection* Coleridge repeatedly castigated the evidential school for forgetting that Christianity is not just a theory but rather spirit and life. In a famous passage he wrote:

Hence I more than fear the prevailing taste for books of Natural Theology, Physico-Theology, Demonstrations of God from Nature, Evidences of Christianity, and the like. EVIDENCES OF CHRISTIANITY: I am weary of the word. Make a man feel his WANT of it, and you can safely trust to its own Evidence—remembering only the express declaration of Christ Himself: No man cometh to Me unless the Father leadeth him.[46]

In his theory of knowledge Coleridge makes a sharp distinction, somewhat similar to Kant's, between understanding—the faculty that deals with sense data—and reason, which can rise to the spiritual order. Faith, for Coleridge, is an exercise of the 'higher reason,' a term that in his use of it closely resembles Kant's practical reason but that, unlike the latter, includes imaginative and emotional elements derived from religious experience. In view of his doctrine of higher reason, Coleridge can say that—strong as are the historical evidences in favor of Christianity—'the truth revealed in Christ . . . has its evidence in itself, and the proof of its divine authority in its fitness to our nature and needs;—the clearness and cogency of this proof being proportionate to the degree of self-knowledge in each individual hearer.'[47]

Proceeding on these premises Coleridge holds with Augustine that faith must precede understanding. Without the prevenient grace of God, which elevates and attunes the higher reason, one would be incapable, he judges, of responding to the divine signs that come to him through history and experience. Hence Coleridge can write, much in the fashion of Schleiermacher: 'Miracles are parts of our Religion and Objects of our Belief, not Grounds of it.'[48] And again:

My whole & sincere opinion is this: that Miracles are a condition & necessary accompaniment of the Christian Religion; but not it's specific & characteristic Proof. They were not so even to the first eye-witnesses; they cannot be so to us. I believe the Miracles, because many other evidences have made me believe in Christ; & thus, no doubt, the faith in miracles does then react on it's cause, & fills up & confirms my faith in Christ.[49]

Coleridge's friend and disciple, Frederick Denison Maurice (1805–72), followed up on this rejection of the authoritarian, extrinsicist view of revelation and on the system of evidences that had been built up around that view. In his *What Is Revelation?* polemicizing against H. L. Mansell's Bampton Lectures of 1858, Maurice bewailed 'the unfortunate rage for apologetic literature in the

Christian Church'[50] and lamented the baneful effects of Paley's *Evidences* on the faith of clergy and laity alike. At a time when England was being rocked by the controversy growing out of Strauss's *Life of Jesus,* Maurice maintained that the current debates about documents could never lead to any religiously satisfying results. In faith, he argued, one knows God as He personally imparts Himself to man in experience, and this personal communion is for the believer its own evidence.

Maurice's actualistic, personalist view of revelation obviously called for a different type of apologetic than was current at the time, but he himself did not supply this need. He gave no convincing reasons for holding that Christians really possessed the type of communion with God that he so glowingly described. As Vidler remarks, 'If we are looking for Christian apologetics—meaning by that the argumentative defence of Christianity—we shall turn to Maurice in vain.'[51]

Coleridge and Maurice, of course, spoke for only a minority of the Anglicans of their day. The evidential tradition represented by Mansell had a brilliant advocate in Richard Whately (1787–1863), the eccentric Oxford logician who in 1831 was appointed Anglican archbishop of Dublin. In 1837 Whately composed a remarkably clear and persuasive volume, *Introductory Lessons on Christian Evidences,* addressed to younger readers. As primary evidences Whately stressed the OT prophecies, the NT miracles, and the unstudied candor of the Evangelists. Whately also composed a pamphlet, *Historic Doubts Relative to Napoleon Buonaparte* (1819), in which he tellingly satirized the historical skepticism of Hume.

The evidential school in Scotland was capably represented by the Scottish evangelical preacher Thomas Chalmers (1780–1847), chiefly renowned for the part he played in the disruption with the Established Church. His popular manual, *The Evidence and Authority of the Christian Revelation,* was gradually expanded in successive editions until it became the two-volume *Miraculous and Internal Evidences of the Christian Revelation.* Like Paley and Whately, Chalmers makes his demonstration turn chiefly on miracles, prophecies, and the historical reliability of the NT testimony to Jesus. Then he analyzes the excellence of the 'moral system contained in the Bible' and its wonderful agreement with the light of conscience. The self-evidencing power of the Bible, he holds, 'makes its doctrines portable to every understanding, and its lessons portable to every heart.'[52] While one cannot help but respect the author's staunch devotion, the chief value of his treatise is to show how congenial

Christianity as he understood it is to Biblically and morally oriented persons like himself.

The watchmaker type of apologetics likewise reappears in Chalmers, especially in his *Discourses on the Christian Revelation Viewed in Connexion with Modern Astronomy* (1817) and the *Natural Theology* that comprises the first two volumes of his *Works*.

A more experiential type of apologetics may be found in the work of Chalmers's countryman, the layman Thomas Erskine (1788–1870). Sometimes called the Scottish Schleiermacher, Erskine was on cordial terms with F. D. Maurice. Like both these theologians he looked to the inner life of the believer for the rational basis of faith. In his best known work, *Remarks on the Internal Evidence for the Truth of Revealed Religion* (1820), he stresses the moral influence of the gospel and bypasses the usual arguments from miracles, prophecy, and eyewitness testimony. The Biblical teachings, he declares, 'not only present an expressive exhibition of all the moral qualities which can be conceived to reside in the Divine mind, but also contain those objects which have a natural tendency to excite and suggest in the human mind that combination of moral feelings which has been called moral perfection.'

Among the various difficulties that could be raised against this approach, perhaps the most obvious is that Erskine's own ideas of God and morality, like those of Chalmers, were in fact drawn principally from the Bible. His strong appeal to natural religion was criticized for its lack of a philosophical and empirical basis, and in a prenote to the later editions he remarked, rather lamely: 'I am aware also that there is considerable vagueness in the term "natural religion," but there is no other word for it, and a metaphysical accuracy is not of much moment here.'[53] Perhaps Erskine would have done better to admit that there was some circularity in his apologetics. As a testimony to the inner life of a deeply convinced Christian, Erskine's *Internal Evidence* is not unimpressive.

CATHOLICISM: 1800–50

France

The Romantic movement in France assumed a form less vehement but on the whole more sentimental than in Germany. Its effects may be discerned in Catholic apologetics under the Revolution, the first Empire, and the Restoration. Toward the end of the 18th century French apologists abruptly turned away from positivistic, documentary types of argument and from rationalistic philosophy of the Cartesian sort. This could be abundantly illustrated from authors who flourished during the Revolution and the first Empire.

Cardinal César de La Luzerne (1738–1821) in his *Pastoral Instruction on the Excellence of Religion* laid down the principle that since the enemies of religion are seeking to make it odious, the apologist must concentrate on manifesting its beauties. 'Our goal is less to make you see how true religion is than to make you feel how beautiful it is.'[54] Archbishop Adrien Lamourette (1742–94) in his *Thoughts on the Philosophy of Unbelief* bases an argument on the sweet tears of the devout congregation at Mass ('quelles larmes délicieuses!').[55] Abbé de Crillon, in his *Philosophical Memoirs*[56]—the fictional autobiography of a German baron—recommends religion as the sole remedy for the new sickness from which youth has been suffering since Goethe wrote his *Werther*. The young baron of the story is converted at the graveside of his deceased beloved.

The dramatist and literary critic Jean François de Laharpe (1739–1803) in his posthumously published *Fragments of an Apology for Religion* elegantly summarized the whole content of the Bible as a 'history of divine love.'[57] About the same time the illuminist philosopher Louis-Claude de Saint-Martin (1743–1803) proposed an apologetics of the heart in a highly mystical and theosophical style.[58]

The apologist who most gloriously rode the crest of the revolt against the Enlightenment was surely François René de Chateaubriand (1768–1848). After wrestling with many doubts in his youth, he regained his faith, partly through the effect upon him of the deaths of his mother and of one of his sisters. In terms reminiscent of Crillon he summarizes his own conversion in the sentence, 'I wept, and I believed.' His *The Genius of Christianity; or, Beauties of the Christian Religion*,[59] one of the most influential apologetic works of all time, remains high on the list of French literary classics. In the Introduction to Part 1 Chateaubriand explains his reasons for holding that a new apologetic is needed. The standard works, he contends, proceed deductively to prove particular doctrines on the basis of the mission of Jesus Christ. But today the basis itself is contested; hence one must take the opposite route, from effects to causes—'not to prove that Christianity is excellent because it is from God, but that it comes from God because it is excellent.'[60]

In Part 1 Chateaubriand treats of 'Dogmas and Doctrines.' 'There is nothing beautiful, sweet, and great in life except what is mysterious,' he begins. In this spirit he discusses the Trinity, the

Incarnation, the Sacraments, the decalogue, and the Mosaic books of Scripture. Then he proves the existence of God from the wonders of nature and the immortality of the soul 'from morality and sentiment.'

In Part 2, 'The Poetic of Christianity,' Chateaubriand seeks to demonstrate that Christianity stimulates the most splendid achievements of drama and poetry. By opening up the perspectives of heaven and hell, with their populations of angels, saints, and demons, Christian revelation gives a new range of sublimity and inner depth to human attitudes and emotions, thus enriching the possibilities of epic and drama, as may be seen from the work of Dante and Tasso, Milton and Racine. The Bible, he adds, vastly surpasses Homer in simplicity and poignancy of style.

Part 3 deals with the fine arts and literature. The benefits of Christianity to music are illustrated by Gregorian chant, its contributions to the visual arts by Raphael and Michelangelo, its architectural expression by the Gothic cathedrals. In philosophy, Chateaubriand asserts, 'Clarke in his *Treatise on the Existence of God*, Leibniz in his *Theodicy*, and Malebranche in his *Recherche de la vérité*, rose so high in metaphysics that they left nothing after them to be done.'[61] The Christian achievement in the realms of history and oratory is illustrated especially by Bossuet.

In Part 4, 'Cult,' Chateaubriand makes much of the beauties of the liturgy. After opening this part with an essay in praise of the melody of bells, he expatiates on the offices for the dead, on Christian tombs and cemeteries, and the like. He speaks briefly of Jesus Christ in order to introduce a section on the clergy and the religious life, followed by an eloquent survey of the Christian missions, which includes a highly idealized description of the Paraguay Reductions and a moving panegyric of the North American martyrs. The entire work closes with an enumeration of the many blessings that the Church has conferred upon mankind through its schools, its hospitals, and its other charitable works.

Chateaubriand's apologetic, while it may have proved next to nothing, succeeded in presenting Christianity in colors that appealed enormously to French readers of the day. It enlarged the scope of apologetics by viewing Christianity in the context of civilization and especially of the arts. Without being in any sense a theologian or even a profound thinker, Chateaubriand provided a much needed alternative to the scholarly hairsplitting in which apologetics had become involved. By calling attention to the many blessings brought into the world by Christianity he helped to restore the morale of a Church that had been too long on the defensive, and thus he evoked an

G

enthusiastic response among a people eager for a restoration of the glories of ancient France.

The typical seminary apologetics of the early 19th century, however, continued to follow essentially the pattern set by Grotius. The founder of the Sulpician school, Denis Luc de Frayssinous (1765–1841), before being raised to the episcopate in 1822, gave an immensely popular series of lectures at Saint-Sulpice in Paris from 1803 to 1809 and from 1814 to 1820. These were then printed under the title *A Defence of Christianity*.[62] Although he has been called 'the outstanding Catholic apologist during the Restoration period,'[63] Frayssinous shows neither philosophical depth in speculation nor methodical exactitude in the handling of historical evidences. He was still seeking to use the weapons of the 17th-century arsenal against adversaries of the Enlightenment.

Under the Restoration the most vital movement in French apologetics became the traditionalism of Maistre and Bonald. As Walter Horton has said,[64] traditionalism was essentially an émigré philosophy. Unlike Chateaubriand, Maistre and Bonald did not set out to woo the soul; rather they threatened and demanded that reason submit to the authority of God.

Joseph de Maistre (1754 [3?]–1821), while he wrote no systematic treatise on apologetics, was the true founder of the movement. This Savoyard nobleman, as a young man, had been a Freemason and had felt the influence of Saint-Martin's mystical illuminism. Disgusted by the excesses of the Reign of Terror, he soon became an avowed apostle of reaction. From his post as ambassador of the King of Sardinia to the Tsar of Russia (1802–17) he watched and encouraged the European powers in their struggle against Napoleon. His conversations with other intellectuals and émigrés at the Russian court were the basis of his *St. Petersburg Dialogues*.[65]

In these *Dialogues* Maistre sketched a theology of history partly inspired by Bossuet. He gave eloquent and passionate expression to his thoughts on divine providence and the problem of evil. Suffering is necessary, he argued, in order to expiate the evil of sin. All the horrors of the French Revolution were but a divine chastisement for the satanic insurrection against God and His Church set off by the proud speculations of the Enlightenment. To return to the way of salvation, both national and personal, men would have to recognize that their primary need is to be curbed under the double yoke of political and spiritual sovereignty.

The same mystique of authority permeates Maistre's anti-Gallican work *On the Pope*,[66] in which he contends that man is born into servitude but that he can be made free if he submits to the absolute authority that God has established in the world. The pope alone, thanks to his divine prerogatives, can make true freedom possible. This he can do 'in his character of sole head of that religion which was alone capable of moderating wills and which could deploy its full strength only through him.'[67]

Traditionalism was first developed into a thoroughgoing system—political, philosophical, and religious—by the Vicomte Louis de Bonald (1754–1840), a French nobleman who emigrated during the Revolution and who lived to publish his most important works under the Bourbon kings. The essential truths needed to live a human life, he argues, lie beyond the reach of rational inquiry, but they have been revealed by God since the dawn of history. Tradition, the bearer of these truths, has divine and infallible authority. The Catholic Church according to Bonald is indispensable because it alone transmits tradition in its plenitude. By his insistence on centralized authority in Church and in State Bonald deliberately set himself in opposition to the democratic tendency of the age. By appealing to political and intellectual reactionaries Maistre and Bonald, in the long run, performed an unwitting disservice to the Church.[68]

The theologian and evangelist of the 'new apologetic,' as it came to be called, was Abbé Félicité de Lamennais (1782–1860). Born like Chateaubriand at St. Malo in Brittany, he too fell under the spell of the *philosophes*. He read his way back into the Church, however, and after some private study was ordained in 1816. Almost immediately he began to devote himself with passionate ardor to the restoration of Catholic intellectual life and to the renewal of ecclesiastical studies.[69]

Less royalist and restorationist than Maistre and Bonald—he eventually became an extreme liberal—he shared their philosophical traditionalism and their religious Ultramontanism. Perceiving that an apologetics based on Cartesian and rationalist assumptions could never meet the difficulties of the modern mind, he sought to ground the justification of faith on a more realistic estimate of the powers of reason. This meant for him an antirational authoritarianism. As he wrote to Maistre in 1821:

> They ought to realize at Rome that their traditional method, according to which everything is proved by facts and authorities, is no doubt admissible in itself, and one neither can nor need abandon it; but it is insufficient, because it is no longer understood. Since reason has proclaimed itself sovereign, one must go straight to it, seize it on its throne, and compel it, under pain of death, to prostrate itself before the reason of God.[70]

Lamennais's apologetic is developed in the four volumes of his *Essay on Indifference in Matters of Religion*.[71] Volume 1 begins with a spirited but fundamentally conventional attack on indifferentism in three characteristic forms: the atheistic indifference of those who cynically use religion as a means of controlling the populace; the deistic indifference of those who reject revelation in favor of natural religion; and the fundamentalist indifference of those who deny the importance of all but a few central Christian doctrines. After refuting these three positions by exposing the contradictions into which their advocates have fallen, Lamennais turns to the constructive part of his apologetic. Religion commends itself, he declares, by conferring immense benefits on individuals and societies, for it is the source of law, virtue, and sacrificial love. But religion cannot be stringently demonstrated; its acceptance is always a free and voluntary adherence to testimony.

Volume 2 contains the true heart of the Mennaisian apologetic. Cartesian doubt, he argues, can never lead to certitude about anything, for every proof depends on presuppositions that can themselves be doubted. True certitude, he holds with Bonald, must be sought from the *raison générale* or *sens commun*, which is infallible because it derives from the divine revelation that God implicitly obliged Himself to confer when He created man and that He in fact conferred upon the first parents.

Once one admits the universally attested truths of primitive revelation as a divinely guaranteed and certain source of knowledge, he will have to accept the existence of God and the importance of adhering to the true religion—for all mankind acknowledges these two points. The diversity of religions might seem to show that God has given no clear testimony of Himself; but in fact it proves only that it is possible for man to fail to use the means God has provided for recognizing the true religion. From all that precedes, it should be evident, Lamennais contends, that these means are authority and tradition. In chapter 20 he draws the crucial—but illogical—corollary that the true religion is that which rests on the greatest visible authority. From this point on, he has an easy time establishing that Christianity, in its Roman Catholic form, is the true religion. The authority of an infallible pope makes Catholicism the supremely authoritative, and hence the true, form of Christianity.

In Volumes 3 and 4, more in line with the conventional apologetics of the schools, Lamennais maintains that the true religion is discernible by the four marks of unity, catholicity, perpetuity, and holiness; since these marks, when conjoined in one body, carry the greatest possible measure of authority. At the conclusion he adds a brief and rather unoriginal presentation of the traditional arguments from prophecy, miracles, and the beneficent effects of Christianity.

It is to the credit of Bonald and Lammenais that they called attention to the social nature of man and religion, which had been all but forgotten in the individualism of the Enlightenment. They were justified, moreover, in pointing out that Christian apologists had too uncritically taken over the assumptions of Cartesian philosophy. They rightly pointed to the weakness of the deductive and historical proofs that awkwardly inserted a positivistically conceived Christianity into an almost deistic framework. But the philosophy of 'general consent' was hardly a satisfactory alternative to the defective apologetics of the past. From the premise that authority is needed somewhere, it scarcely follows that the most authoritative religion is the only true one. General consent could be used at least as easily in favor of a popular and democratic religion as in favor of papal sovereignty. Not surprisingly, many youthful enthusiasts for traditionalism, such as Alphonse de Lamartine, Victor Hugo, and Lamennais himself, were soon won over to radical republicanism and defected from the Church, if not from Christianity.

The apologist who best succeeded in combining the political liberalism of Lamennais with firm allegiance to the Holy See was perhaps the pulpit orator Henri-Dominique Lacordaire (1802–61), who became a Dominican in 1839. Associated with Lamennais in the editing of the newspaper *L'Avenir* in 1829–31, he submitted to Gregory XVI's condemnation of traditionalism (1832, 1834) and in 1834 wrote a refutation of the philosophy of 'common sense.' In his celebrated *Conférences de Notre Dame*, preached at Paris from 1835–36, 1843–46, and 1848–51, and in his course of sermons at Toulouse in 1854, he attempted to develop a new apologetic. As he wrote to a friend (Oct. 24, 1844): 'It is a wholly different point of view in the demonstration of Christianity than anything previous. Pascal, Bergier, La Luzerne, Frayssinous—all, in fact—demonstrate the truth of Christianity from the outside; my demonstration, on the contrary, is taken from within. It is a contemplation of the inside of faith and a view of its harmony with all the general laws of the world.'[72]

Instead of arriving at the Church as the conclusion of a protracted demonstration he begins by a consideration of the Church and shows how admirably it corresponds with the needs of human nature and the aspirations of modern society. Only then does he turn to a study of Christian origins and of the person of Jesus Christ.

Chateaubriand, de Maistre, Lamennais, and Lacordaire were all more eminent for their eloquence than for the depth and rigor of their thought. For a more philosophical approach to apologetics somewhat akin to traditionalism one may turn to the Abbé Louis-Eugène Bautain (1796–1867). Like Chateaubriand, de Maistre, and Lamennais, he fell away as a young student from the piety of his Catholic childhood. He became an outstanding disciple of the eclectic philosopher Victor Cousin and then plunged into an intense study of German idealism, which left him disillusioned as to the powers of speculative reason in the realm of metaphysics. With the help of a devout friend, Mlle Humann, he was rescued from skepticism and by meditation on the Gospels became a fervent convert to the faith. Dispensed from the ordinary course of seminary training (as Lamennais had also been), he was ordained in 1828. The remainder of his life he consecrated to the goal of converting the intellectuals of the day to Christianity. 'In our days,' he wrote, 'to return to Christianity one must begin by being a philosopher.'[73]

This thesis is illustrated in the *Philosophy of Christianity*,[74] two volumes of letters exchanged between Bautain and four of his disciples, three of whom were young Jews considering whether to enter the Catholic Church. These letters give a vibrant record of Bautain's apologetical method in action. His first step is to demonstrate negatively the incapacity of reason—and of Kantian critical philosophy—to give any coherent synthesis of reality. (Kant was for Bautain, as Montaigne was for Pascal, the Bible of the unbeliever.)[75] The bankruptcy of reason, according to Bautain, rules out the possibility of apologetics in its traditional form, for it demolishes all speculative proofs of the existence of God and of the fact of Christian revelation.

The only effective route to faith, for Bautain, requires the inquirer to pass through the stage of hypothetically accepting, on the basis of human faith in persons who already professed Christianity (perhaps here Bautain was thinking of his own relationship to Mlle Humann), the idea of Christian revelation. Once a man allows the contents of revelation, contained in the Bible and in Christian tradition, to be impressed upon himself, God begins to flood his soul with light. The power of the word acts upon him as physical light acts upon the eye. Revelation requires no discursive demonstration because it validates itself by its inherent luminosity.

Pressed by objectors who accused him of vaporous mysticism, Bautain gradually supplemented this intuitionist doctrine with reasoned arguments of credibility. Christianity, he maintained, established itself as the highest philosophy thanks to its power to enlighten man's existence and to supply answers to burning questions on which discursive philosophy is mute.

Bautain's rejection of traditional apologetics aroused fierce opposition in many parts of Europe. His local bishop, and later the Roman authorities, ordered him to sign various sets of propositions affirming the capacity of unaided reason to demonstrate the existence of God, the spirituality and immortality of the soul, and the fundamental principles of epistemology and metaphysics, as well as to recognize with certitude the fact of revelation as evidenced by miracles, by prophecies, and especially by the Resurrection of Christ.[76] Bautain made his submission sincerely, acknowledging that in his earlier writing, under the influence of Kantianism, he had unduly depressed the powers of human reason. But he continued to believe that, while in principle reason could achieve a demonstration of credibility on metaphysical and historical grounds, in practice conviction does not come this way. Because human nature has been corrupted by original sin, man cannot ordinarily arrive at faith unless he allows the word of God to heal and enlighten him. Thus the normal road to *divine* faith is through a provisional acceptance of the Christian message on the basis of *human* faith.

Bautain is commonly charged with having fallen into various philosophical and theological errors, but much of the difficulty came from the failure of his critics to understand the philosophical vocabulary he was using. In any case he had a far better grasp of the psychology of conversion than many of the professional apologists who opposed him. Like Lacordaire he is to be praised for improving on the rationalistic and extrinsicist apologetics that had established itself in the majority of seminaries.

Germany

Nearly all the German Catholic apologists of the early 19th century were, like Bautain, heavily influenced by Kant and the idealist philosophers. Georg Hermes (1775–1831), a priest and professor at Münster, was long troubled by religious doubts, but eventually hit upon a personal solution that, like Bautain's, made use of Kant's own weapons in the service of faith. In the preface to the first volume of his *Introduction to Catholic Christian Theology*[77] he tells of his anxious search for a criterion of certitude and his immense joy at finding an answer. The contents of Biblical history, including the very bestowal of Christian revelation, are in his view mere contingent facts and therefore not susceptible of demonstrative proof. While they elude speculative reason, they are nevertheless not beyond the grasp of practical reason, which makes it evident that one is obliged to believe whatever is required for man's observance of the moral law, whereby one is bidden to respect and promote the dignity of every man. In his second volume Hermes applies this principle and shows that to believe the contents of the NT—including the miracles wrought by Christ—is necessary if one is to live up to his obligations.

Hermes's Cartesian and Kantian methodology, while it aroused great enthusiasm in Germany, was offensive to Catholic ears in the Latin world. After his death his books were condemned by Rome. While his system was undoubtedly too rationalistic, he did make more allowance than is commonly recognized for the practical and existential considerations that normally prepare for the decision of faith.

The most outstanding German Catholic apologist of the period was Johann Sebastian von Drey (1777–1853), the founder of the Catholic Tübingen School. In his *Apologetics as a Scientific Demonstration of the Divinity of Christianity*[78] he did much to delineate the discipline of fundamental theology as it was to be understood by Catholics for the next century. Originally, Drey explains in the introduction, he had accepted Schleiermacher's view that apologetics should simply point out what is essential and distinctive to the Christian religion, but he came around to the view that apologetics must give a secure rational grounding for the fact of Christian revelation and thus provide a solid basis for the other theological disciplines. As a mixed discipline apologetics derives its formal principles from philosophy, especially the philosophy of religion, and its material content from the history of religions. Drey's view of apologetics, therefore, corresponds closely with that of Sack.

In Volume 1 Drey sets forth his general philosophy of revelation: its necessity for the proper development of religion, its purposes, its discernibility, and the conditions under which it can be preserved and disseminated in the world. Then in Volume 2 he examines the relationship of Christianity to Judaism and paganism. As the religion of revelation in its fullness, Drey maintains, Christianity is wholly centered on the Incarnation, the mystery by which God Himself enters history as Savior. The divinity of Christ is demonstrated by traditional arguments, primarily the arguments from miracle and prophecy.

Finally in Volume 3 Drey treats of tradition and especially of the Church as the organism whereby the Christian revelation is made present for successive generations. He demonstrates the credibility of the Catholic Church by direct arguments from Scripture and from the traditional four notes—one, holy, catholic, and apostolic.

Drey gives a remarkably complete and systematic presentation of Christian and Catholic apologetics, and handles both the theoretical and positive sections with the competence of a master. His work is valuable for its recognition of the historical character of the Christian religion, for its many-faceted analysis of the concept of revelation, and for its organic view of tradition and of the Church. For his concept of history and of society Drey drew heavily on Schelling and the Romantics.

Drey's disciple, Johann Adam Möhler (1796–1838), the glory of the Tübingen school, can scarcely be classified as an apologist, but his works on *The Unity of the Church*[79] and on *Symbolics*,[80] both of which synthesize Catholicism in terms of the Incarnational principle, are of apologetical interest insofar as they give an appealing and coherent presentation of the Catholic faith in its inmost essence. His *Symbolics* also marks an immense step forward in the development of a more irenic type of controversial theology than had been seen since the Reformation.[81] Although Möhler argues firmly for Catholic positions, he makes a genuine effort to present the guiding intuitions and inner coherence of the Protestant confessional writings.

Spain and Italy

In the Latin countries apologetics in the first half of the century was powerfully affected by the contest between anticlerical Liberals and Catholic restorationists in France. The leading Spanish apologist of the period, Jaime Balmes (1810–48), was a moderate conservative. A devout priest and professor, he left behind him no less than 32 volumes when he died at the age of 38. Although he touched on many areas of politics and philosophy, his consuming interest was apologetics. Even his philosophical works were motivated by an apologetical concern. In his *Criterion*[82] and his *Letters to a Skeptic on Religious Matters*[83] he concerned himself with the methodology of arriving at religious truth and sought to expose the confusions in current German and French philosophy. His four-volume *Fundamental Philosophy*[84] (1846), while by no means purely Thomistic in doctrine, is a precursor of the 19th-century revival of scholasticism.

Balmes is chiefly remembered for his eloquent *Protestantism and Catholicity Compared in Their Effects on the Civilization of Europe*,[85] a polemical work aimed to offset the influence in Spain of the French

Protestant historian, P. W. Guizot. Contradicting the latter, Balmes argues that Protestantism has done nothing to promote human liberty and progress, whereas Catholicism has always favored them. Further, he contends that Protestantism is faced by the dilemma of either admitting the principle of authority, thus throwing itself into the arms of the Roman Church, or denying that principle, and thus allowing all that it retains of true Christianity to be eroded. For purposes of the present survey, the most interesting feature of Balmes's book is its 'new demonstration of the divine origin of the Catholic Church.'[86] Anticipating Dechamps, Balmes argues that the Church exhibits its divine life in its ability to stand up under long and powerful opposition and in its capacity to draw together a multitude of great and independent minds into a wonderful unity of faith (ch. 3).

Less measured and more Ultramontane in tone and content is the work of the noble layman Juan Donoso Cortès (1809–53), who abjured Liberalism in favor of Catholicism relatively late in life. His *Essay on Catholicism, Authority and Order* is a highly rhetorical polemic against French Liberalism and socialism. 'Catholicism, in deifying authority, sanctified obedience, and in deifying the one and sanctifying the other, condemned pride in its most terrible manifestations, the spirit of domination and that of rebellion.'[87]

In Italy several of the leading men of letters lent a hand to the task of defending the Church. The poet and novelist Alessandro Manzoni (1784–1873) published in various editions *A Vindication of Catholic Morality*,[88] the primary aim of which was to refute the charges in Sismondo de' Sismondi's *History of the Italian Republics during the Middle Ages* (Paris, 16 vols., 1807–18).

Among the more theological apologists, Mauro Capellari (who later became Pope Gregory XVI) and the Oratorian Francesco Colangelo, may be mentioned. More original was the Theatine Gioacchino Ventura (1792–1861). Strongly influenced by French Romanticism and traditionalism, he composed in 1837 a brief work on the Epiphany that he later expanded under the title *The Beauties of the Faith in the Mysteries of Epiphany*. In the preface to this work of apologetics and devotion Ventura pays tribute to Chateaubriand for having revived apologetics and declares that 'the most effective apologies of the faith and of virtue are not so much those which make it believed as those which make it loved.'[89]

The dominant theologian at Rome during the mid-19th century was Giovanni Perrone, s.j. (1794–1876), who taught at the Roman College and closely advised several popes on theological matters. He sounded the alarm against the errors of Hermes and wrote several theological pamphlets against them.[90] He also helped Bautain to align his views with the accepted teaching on faith and reason, and was consulted by Newman on the development of doctrine. Perrone's *Lectures on Dogmatics*[91] were models of orderly systematization and did much to set the style and tone of Latin seminary manuals for the next hundred years. Perrone's general approach is positive and apologetical rather than dogmatic and speculative, as may be gathered from the fact that the first volume of his course is a rational introduction, *On the True Religion Against Unbelievers and Heretics*.[92] Part 1, directed against unbelievers, follows this outline:

1. The possibility of revelation
2. The necessity of revelation
3. The criteria of revelation
    a. Miracles
    b. Prophecies
4. The existence of revelation, proved from
    a. The miracles and prophecies of Christ, His Resurrection
    b. The excellence and sanctity of evangelical doctrine
    c. The admirable propagation of the Christian religion
    d. The conservation of the Christian religion
    e. The witness of the martyrs

Part 2, aimed against the 'heterodox,' establishes that the Catholic Church, since it alone possesses infallible teaching authority, unity, visibility, and perpetuity, is the true Church of Christ.

Perrone developed his anti-Protestant polemic at greater length in *Protestantism and the Rule of Faith*.[93] Against rationalistic critics of the Gospels (Paulus, Strauss, Renan) he later composed *On the Divinity of Our Lord Jesus Christ against the Unbelievers of this Century*.[94] Like many apologetical manuals of the ensuing century, this work begins with a defense of the authenticity and historical reliability of the canonical Gospels and only then goes on to prove by means of them the divinity of Christ.

Perrone's apologetic lacks nothing by way of clarity and logic, but it rests on narrow and uncriticized assumptions. His step-by-step movement from natural theology to Christian revelation, while highly suitable to classroom presentation, fails to correspond to the actual process by which the mind progresses toward religious truth. Like other apologists of the time Perrone falls into a type of supernatural rationalism that grew out of a combination of medieval Scholasticism and Cartesian mathematicism. Bautain and Newman, whose work he corrected, would have had much to teach him.

ENGLISH-SPEAKING CATHOLICS: 1800–1900

England

Until the middle of the 19th century most English Catholic apologists were content to leave to Protestants and Anglicans the general task of establishing Christian credibility and to confine their efforts to rebutting objections to Roman Catholicism. Even William Poynter (1762–1827) in his *Christianity; or the Evidences and Character of the Christian Revelation* (1827) is mainly concerned with vindicating the authority of the Roman Catholic Church as 'the depository and dispenser of the mysteries of Christianity.'

With Nicholas Wiseman (1802–65), the learned professor of Oriental Languages and Rector of the English College in Rome, who was to become Cardinal-Archbishop of Westminster in 1850, English Catholic apologetics emerges from the ghetto. In his *Twelve Lectures on the Connexion between Science and Revealed Religion*[95] he discusses the comparative study of languages, the natural history of the human race, the natural sciences, early history, archaeology, and Oriental literature. His aim, as he puts it, is 'to show the correspondence between the progress of science, and the development of the christian evidences.'[96] The very sciences which in their initial stages seemed to posit objections against religion, he argues, have as they developed gradually removed their own objections. Wiseman displays an impressive command of many fields of knowledge, but the apologetical value of his work has not endured; for it is based on the highly questionable assumption that Christian believers are bound to think of the OT as giving a scientifically accurate description of cosmic origins and of man's primeval history. His book served a good purpose insofar as it encouraged Christians to open their minds fearlessly to the latest discoveries in science.

In 1836 Wiseman delivered a course of *Lectures on the Principal Doctrines and Practices of the Church.*[97] These lectures deal only with those points of Catholic doctrine contested by Protestants (e.g., pope, purgatory, indulgences, transubstantiation) and are therefore beyond the scope of this investigation.

The leading Catholic apologist of the 19th century and one of the greatest of all time was John Henry Newman (1801–90). As a boy he accepted a Calvinistically tinged Anglicanism; as a student at Oxford he was influenced by the Broad Church views of his mentor, Whately; then he joined the High Church Oxford Movement, and in 1845 became a Roman Catholic. A cautious and reflective thinker, he was at every stage in his life deeply concerned with the criteria of religious knowledge. Already as an Anglican he wrote two *Essays on Miracles*.[98] His *University Sermons,* preached during the years 1826 to 1843, show the gradual development of his views on faith and reason, and foreshadow the main themes of his mature apologetic.[98a] In 1845 he published *An Essay on the Development of Christian Doctrine,*[99] in which he explained his reasons for thinking that the Roman Catholic Church is the authentic successor of the great Church of the early centuries. Three years later he intimated the motives for his conversion in a partly autobiographical novel, *Loss and Gain*.[100] In 1864 in response to the attacks of Charles Kingsley, he composed the history of his religious opinions, *Apologia pro vita sua*.[101]

Finally in 1870 Newman issued his last major work, *An Essay in Aid of a Grammar of Assent,*[102] wherein he sought to diagnose the manner in which men arrive at personal convictions, particularly in the area of religion. In Part 1 of this book, dealing with the Liberals' objection to dogmatic religion, he attempts to show that religious assent is real, not notional. While speculative theology may deal in logic and abstractions, the believer, when he recites his creed, adheres with his whole heart to the living God of revelation. Then in Part 2, addressing himself to the apparent discrepancy between the degree of conviction demanded by faith and the apparently slender grounds on which it rests, Newman evolves his doctrine of the illative sense as the faculty at work in informal inference.

Newman never believed that it was possible to amass a set of philosophical or historical arguments that would point ineluctably to the conclusion, 'I must become a Christian (or a Catholic).' For this reason he never saw eye to eye with Perrone, under whom he studied when in Rome. Of the Roman school he wrote:

They know nothing at all of heretics as realities—they live, at least in Rome, in a place whose boast is that it has never given birth to heresy, and they think proofs ought to be convincing which in fact are not. Hence they are accustomed to speak of the argument for Catholicism as a demonstration, and to see no force in objections to it, and to admit no perplexity of intellect which is not directly and immediately wilful. This at least is their tendency in *fact*, even if I overstate their theory.[103]

On many occasions Newman professes great admiration for Butler and a corresponding distaste for Paley and the evidential school. Butler recognized the necessity of relying on presumptions and of weighing sets of probabilities. Paley on the other hand asked only for a judicial neutrality, and sought to demonstrate Christianity to an impartial court. Newman felt that this purely objective and scientific approach would be incapable of bringing true religious conviction.[104] In his 'Letter to the Duke of Norfolk' he wrote: 'For myself, I would simply confess that no doctrine of the Church can be rigorously proved by historical evidence: but at the same time that no doctrine can simply be disproved by it.'[105] For this reason, he avoided making his argument turn on the miraculous occurrences narrated in Scripture, though he was far from denying that miracles had occurred.[106]

Recognizing the subjective element in all religious inquiry, Newman preferred to cast his apologetic in autobiographical form. 'In religious inquiry each of us can speak only for himself, and for himself he has a right to speak. His own experiences are enough for himself, but he cannot speak for others; he cannot lay down the law.'[107] His personal apologetic takes the form of what Walgrave has aptly called the 'existential dialectic of conscience.'[108] For Newman there are only two thoroughly consistent religious attitudes, atheism and Catholicism. Whatever inclines a man to reject the one tends, unless obstructed, to lead him to embrace the other. The logic here involved is not simply an affair of the mind, but a whole set of tastes and attitudes, a way of approaching questions that sets a man in motion in a certain direction rather than another.[109]

The atheistic alternative was unacceptable to Newman because of the testimony of conscience, which he regards as a specific and irreducibly distinct function of the human mind. Judgments of moral value, he maintains, have absolute imperative force as commandments from on high, and therefore imply the existence of a personal God—a supreme legislator, all-powerful ruler, and universal judge. Children and simple people, Newman contends, adhere naturally to conscience and therefore spontaneously accept the existence of God unless there are positive circumstances that interfere.[110]

A second fact, scarcely less evident than the existence of God, was for Newman God's absence. Looking about the world, he was filled with an oppressive sense of evil, which seemed to contradict the power and goodness of God. This could only be explained, he believed, by some primeval catastrophe whereby man had been alienated from his Creator. All nations in their religious rites bore witness to the sinfulness of man and the necessity of atonement. Yet the fact that men did engage in prayer and sacrificial ceremonies testified to an unquenchable hope of redemption. To Newman, with his profound conviction of the goodness of God and the indigence of man, it was scarcely thinkable that God would not have supplied what man so imperiously needs—a divinely given way of salvation, accompanied by a teaching authority sufficiently strong to withstand the arbitrary willfulness of man.[111]

Newman therefore approaches the Christian evidences with a whole set of presumptions and hopes that provide the clue to the complex materials of religious history. Natural religion, in his opinion, provides an anticipation that revelation will be given, an antecedent probability so strong that it could be for some minds 'almost a proof, without direct evidence, of the divinity of a religion claiming to be the true, supposing its history and doctrine are free from positive objection, and there be no rival religion with plausible claims of its own.'[112] For Newman, 'There is only one Religion in the world which tends to fulfil the aspirations, needs, and foreshadowings of natural faith and devotion,' for Christianity alone has 'a definite message addressed to all mankind.'[113]

With these presuppositions, Newman sets forth in the last section of his *Grammar of Assent* (ch. 10, part 2) an impressive historical argument for the truth of Christianity based on a convergence of probabilities. His point is not simply that of the 18th-century French apologist Amort, that Christianity is more probable than other religions, but rather that the accumulation of probabilities can give rise to legitimate certitude.[114] The argument includes two main parts, corresponding respectively to the history of the Jews and that of the Christian Church. First, he maintains, the history of the Jews shows an extraordinary tenacity of theistic faith in the face of the idolatry of the surrounding nations, together with a persistent and growing conviction concerning the coming Messiah. Jewish history, moreover, terminates in a final national disaster following upon the rejection of Jesus as this Messiah. Second, the history of Christianity exhibits the fulfillment (and partial correction) of the messianic expectation of Israel and agrees perfectly with Jesus' own prediction that His religion would spread to the ends of the earth and become a great empire 'not as other victorious powers had done, and as the Jews expected, by force of arms or by other means of this world, but by the novel expedient of sanctity and suffering.'[115] Christianity survives today not as a mere relic of the past but as a mighty moral force that successively masters all its persecutors.

In other works, notably the *Apologia*, Newman develops more fully the Catholic dimension of his apologetic. Divine revelation, he argues, if delivered over to the dominion of human reason, would inevitably deteriorate and dissolve into a chaos of confusion. Since no truth, however sacred, can stand up against the wild tendencies of unaided reason, it is not surprising that 'in these latter days, . . . outside the Catholic Church things are tending—with far greater rapidity than in that old time from the circumstance of the age—to atheism in one shape or other.'[116] Only an infallible living authority can effectively arrest this process of decline, and the only form of Christianity that even claims to exercise such authority is the Catholic Church. Its infallibility is 'a supereminent prodigious power sent upon earth to encounter and master a giant evil.'[117] In the *Essay on the Development of Christian Doctrine* Newman seeks to show more in detail that the Catholic Church has followed a line of organic development that is proof of its vital continuity with the revelation originally given in Biblical times.

With his remarkable combination of gifts—historical learning, religious piety, psychological discernment, and literary power—Newman unquestionably ranks with Augustine, Pascal, and a few others, among the finest apologists of all time. His apologetic, which reflects his own spiritual pilgrimage, offers endless matter for study and reflection. Not content with subjective desires and presumptions, he candidly faces the objective data in their full complexity, and constructs a vast and many-dimensioned synthesis. Avoiding the rationalism, naive biblicism, and philosophical modishness of many apologists of his day, he constructed a work of enduring value.

At the distance of a century, however, one cannot help but remark that Newman belonged to his own time. As a Victorian Englishman he loved culture and tradition; he was alarmed by the liberal and radical movements that were already threatening to shake the civilization of Europe. As a university don he cherished ideas and found satisfaction in a highly dogmatic faith. And with his sharp and sensitive conscience he loved to retire into meditative communion with God. Now that the Liberal revolution has so largely prevailed, few will share Newman's pessimism about the course of reason unrestrained by external authority. Men tend today to look forward with more faith in the future, or at least to be less convinced that the past can prove an adequate guide. And some, by temperament, will not be drawn to Newman. To the extrovert and activist he will appear too introspective and withdrawn.

No English Catholic of the 19th century is in a class with Newman as an apologist. For the sake of completeness, however, we should mention among his contemporaries Cardinal Henry Edward Manning, a convert to the Catholic Church in 1851, who touched upon apologetics in many of his works. In his four lectures on *The Grounds of Faith* he argued that to reject the divine authority of the Catholic Church is 'to make all authority for faith merely human' and consequently 'to convert all doctrine into the subjective imagination of each several man.'[118]

The anatomist St. George Mivart (1827–1900), who had been converted to Catholicism in 1844, made a contribution to apologetics by his efforts to reconcile evolutionism with the faith. He rejected Darwin's theory of natural selection and in his *The Genesis of Species*[119] maintained that God had established and concurred with natural laws in the production of the human body, while creating the soul *ex nihilo*. For his services to the Church in the realm of science, Mivart was awarded a doctorate by Pius IX in 1876. Shortly before his death he advanced a theory of the Church as an evolving organism which his bishop, Cardinal Vaughan, rejected and condemned.

The United States

Until the middle of the 19th century Catholic apologists in the United States, like their colleagues in England, were generally content to show that, supposing Christianity to be the true religion, Catholicism was its true form.[120] The missionary Prince Demetrius Gallitzin (1770–1849) and the Alsatian-born Jesuit Anthony Kohlmann (1771–1836) were largely taken up with defending Catholicism against unjust charges. In the following generation Archbishop Francis P. Kenrick of Baltimore (1796–1863) and his immediate successor, Archbishop Martin J. Spalding (1810–72), wrote systematic defenses of Catholic as opposed to Protestant Christianity. All these works were eclipsed by Cardinal James Gibbons' *The Faith of Our Fathers* (1876), the most widely read Catholic apologetical book ever published in the United States. Drawing upon his missionary experiences in North Carolina and Virginia, Gibbons succeeded in presenting the Catholic faith in a way eminently satisfying to 19th-century Americans. In successive chapters he gave a serene exposition of those points of Catholic doctrine chiefly disputed by Protestants, such as saints, images, purgatory, the Mass, indulgences, and clerical celibacy. In his chapter on civil and religious liberty he enthusiastically endorsed the separation of Church and State.

A more comprehensive form of apologetics, which attempted to justify Christianity itself in justifying Catholicism, was developed by two remarkable converts of the midcentury, Orestes A. Brownson (1803–76) and Isaac T. Hecker (1819–88). Brownson, after passing through Unitarianism and Transcendentalism, came to the Church in 1844 by way of French philosophy. He was much influenced—as Bautain had been—by the intuitionism of Victor Cousin and by the socialism of Saint-Simon. In Pierre Leroux he came upon the principles of hierarchy and communion expounded in secular form. Applying these principles to religion, Brownson concluded that the divinization of humanity cannot be achieved except through a supernaturally endowed mediator, Jesus Christ. In his autobiographical work, *The Convert*,[121] Brownson explained how this chain of thinking led him not only to supernatural faith but to Catholicism. The divine-human life that first became present in Jesus Christ could not be communicated, he believed, except through a Church in uninterrupted communion with the apostles.[122]

Immediately after his conversion Brownson turned his back on all kinds of Utopian dreams and practically lost interest, for a decade, in the social progress of mankind. But in the years 1854–64 he returned to his earlier interests and in several essays argued that Catholicism is necessary to sustain popular liberty. His study *The American Republic*[123] is an excellent presentation of his political philosophy within a religious perspective.

Isaac T. Hecker (1819–88), the founder of the Paulists, who had some associations with Brownson in connection with the Brook Farm experiment, likewise entered the Catholic Church in 1844. His first apologetical work, *Questions of the Soul*,[124] was partly autobiographical. It set a new pattern in Catholic evidences in that it offered no logical or historical defense of Catholicism but argued simply that man's innate yearning for authority and for union with something greater than himself was uniquely satisfied by the Catholic Church with its authoritative teaching and its sacramental system. In a second work, *Aspirations of Nature*,[125] Hecker is concerned to show that Catholicism is the religion which best harmonizes with the American tradition of respect for reason, freedom, human dignity, and universal brotherhood. To demonstrate that Protestantism does not meet these qualifications he quotes extensively from Luther's attacks on reason and free will. Regarding private judgment, Hecker distinguishes his position from that of Balmes. Catholicism in Hecker's view protects private, in the sense of personal, judgment in all that it is possible for man to know.

The posthumous life of Isaac Hecker by Walter Elliott, in a defective French translation with a glowing preface by Abbé Felix

Klein,[126] was one of the factors leading up to the condemnation of Americanism in Leo XIII's encyclical *Testem benevolentiae* (1899).[127] Among the errors singled out in this encyclical was a method of apologetics according to which Catholic teaching should be whittled down to suit modern civilization and to attract those not of the faith. Nobody was mentioned as holding this view, nor could Hecker be fairly accused of having taught this.

CATHOLICISM IN CONTINENTAL EUROPE: 1850–1900

France and Belgium; Vatican Council I

From 1850 to 1870 French apologetics continued along the same lines as in the first half of the century. Walking in the footsteps of his friend and master Bautain, Auguste J. A. Gratry (1805–72) championed an intuitive approach to the knowledge of God, notably in his *Guide to the Knowledge of God*.[128] Gratry is commonly accused of having assigned an excessive role to the heart and to emotion in the discovery of truth.

Following Lacordaire, a brilliant series of pulpit orators appeared from year to year to give the *Conférences de Notre Dame*. The Jesuit Gustave-Xavier de Ravignan (1795–1858) was perhaps the most outstanding of these pulpit apologists. In a more popular vein the lawyer from Bordeaux, Auguste Nicolas (1807–88), after publishing in 1842 two immensely successful volumes, *Philosophical Studies on Christianity*,[129] followed them up with volumes on *The Divinity of Jesus Christ*[130] and *The Art of Believing*.[131]

The Belgian Redemptorist Victor Dechamps (1810–83), who later became Bishop of Mechlin and in 1875 cardinal, received an early orientation toward apologetics when his father directed him in his boyhood reading of Lamennais. Among his major apologetic works the first place belongs to his *Conversations on the Demonstration of Christian Revelation*,[132] a dialogue some 500 pages in length that attempts to construct a more practical and realistic approach to Catholic belief than was available in the seminary textbooks. According to Dechamps' 'method of providence' it is sufficient to call attention to two facts—one interior and the other exterior—that lie within the experience of all men. By the 'interior fact' he meant the fact that man wants to live a good life but feels unable to do so without divine enlightenment concerning his ultimate destiny. By the 'exterior fact' he meant the Church itself, which claims to speak for God and to answer man's need for divine assistance. The correspondence between the psychological need and the external institution uniquely capable of satisfying it suggests the likelihood that the Church may be God's providential answer to man's need for divine help and guidance. To demonstrate the divine origin of the Church, according to Dechamps, it is not necessary to make a critical analysis of 1st-century source documents. It is enough to contemplate the Church as a present and obvious fact. Its unity, durability, universality, and holiness, Dechamps maintains, leave no doubt but that it is a 'subsistent miracle.'[133]

Vatican Council I (1869–70) took up the relations between faith and reason, which had become a storm center in the controversies with the rationalists. While the Council did not sponsor any particular apologetical system, it had much to say about the evidences of credibility. After pointing out that faith is not the mere result of rational argument but a gift of divine grace, the Council noted that in addition to the interior helps of the Holy Spirit, God has been pleased to supply external evidences in order that the decision of faith should be in full harmony with man's rational nature. In this connection the Council spoke of miracles and prophecies as being the primary signs, but the Council refrained from stating that the Biblical prophecies and miracles are a sufficient sign to be wholly convincing to the contemporary inquirer.[134]

In a later paragraph (Denz 3013) the Council spoke of the Church itself as a 'motive of credibility' and specified this further by calling attention to much the same properties as those that Dechamps— following Lamennais—had used in his description of the 'external fact.' Although some have thought that the Council's appeal to the Church as a moral miracle was attributable to the influence of Dechamps, who was himself present at the Council, recent study tends to show that the paragraph was primarily the work of Franzelin, who relied on Kleutgen and, indirectly, on the theologians of the Tübingen school.[135] It seems probable that Dechamps, through his friend Cardinal Dupanloup, influenced at least the language of the Council; and he was undoubtedly pleased at seeing his own line of apologetics endorsed by such high authority.

In the closing decades of the 19th century French Catholic apologetics entered the period of extraordinary ferment that was to last through the first quarter of the 20th century. A multitude of Davids came forth to meet the advancing Goliath of modern incredulity in its various forms, e.g., evolutionary idealism, monism, materialism, positivism, and agnosticism.[136]

In the 1880's primary attention was focused on the conflict

between science and religion. The greatest defender of the faith in this area was Msgr François Duilhé de Saint-Projet (1822–97), Rector of the Institut Catholique at Toulouse, who organized several Catholic scientific congresses. In 1855 he published his *Scientific Apology for the Christian Faith*, which went through many editions and was revised in 1899, after the author's death, by J. B. Senderens.[137] After an introductory section dealing with the relations between the different orders of knowledge—scientific, philosophical, and religious—Duilhé de Saint-Projet considered the various problems that had arisen in the domains of cosmology, biology, and anthropology. Writing somewhat in the spirit of Wiseman and Mivart, he recommended an attitude of positive openness to new scientific discoveries and even tried to find in them confirmations of the data of revelation. An unfortunate effect of this approach was that it led to a movement known as concordism. In a hasty and undignified manner apologists successively revised their interpretations of Genesis so as to make Moses agree with every new scientific theory about the origins of the universe, of life, and of man.

Perhaps the most productive French apologist of the late 19th century was the Abbé Paul de Broglie (1834–95), professor of apologetics at the Institut Catholique at Paris. His first apologetical work, *Positivism and Experimental Science*,[138] dealt with the theory of knowledge. During the remainder of his career he worked principally in the field of comparative religion. His 'method of transcendence' appears most clearly in his *Transcendence of Christianity*[139] and in his *Problems and Conclusions of Comparative Religion*.[140]

Although he recognized the legitimacy of the metaphysically based apologetics that had been traditional in the schools since the time of Thomas Aquinas, de Broglie considered that it could not be effective so far as the majority of men were concerned. As Thomas himself recognized, metaphysics is the most difficult of sciences, and one that presupposes a great deal of maturity and wisdom. In the present day, moreover, men are poorly disposed for metaphysics, since Kant has made a profound impression on modern thought. Seeking to meet the capacities and prejudices of the intellectuals of his day, the Abbé sought to draw up a purely inductive argument based on universally recognized historical facts. Applying the axioms of common sense to the facts of comparative religion, he concluded to the absolute transcendence of Christianity and hence, by virtue of the principle of causality, to its divine origin.

Like Eusebius of Caesarea, Paul de Broglie divides his argument into two main steps. First he compares the religion of the OT with that of the surrounding peoples; then he views primitive Christianity against the background of all other religions. The originality of Hebrew monotheism, he maintains, is such that it cannot be plausibly explained on natural grounds. Humanly speaking it would have been impossible for a few enlightened leaders to have imposed their faith upon a people dedicated to the worship of Baal, of Astarte, or of Moloch. Whether it arose early or late in the history of Israel, the persistent monotheism of this people is a wonderful fact, presupposing the power of a divine revelation behind it.

A second peculiarity of Israelite religion is the pervasive theme of messianic prophecy. From the promises made to Abraham to the predictions of Isaiah and Daniel, the people's religious hopes are concentrated on a future deliverer who will restore the glory of Israel and found a truly universal religion. In Christianity this promise was undoubtedly fulfilled. A scion of Israel extended to all nations in a new and higher form the worship of the God of Israel.

Second, Christianity is transcendent with regard to all that had preceded it. It is a harmonious living synthesis of all that is good in the various religions. It combines the monotheism of Israel, the Moslem insistence on the absolute sovereignty of the invisible God, the sacred rites and imagery characteristic of the mystery religions, and the asceticism of the Far Eastern religions. Yet it is not a merely artificial combination dependent on these elements. The Gospels make it clear that Christianity is an autochthonous reality.

The advances of comparative religion, therefore, may be judged to have made it more evident than ever that Chritianity owes its existence to an intervention from on high. This new form of demonstration, based on the history of religions, is particularly apt for the times. It does not replace but merely supplements the classical arguments from the sanctity of Jesus, His Resurrection, the conversion of the Greco-Roman world, and the homogeneous development of Catholic doctrine. Even when all the arguments are taken cumulatively, the apologist admits, they do not yield mathematical clarity. But for those who are drawn by divine love, the evidences are more than sufficient.[141]

The Abbé de Broglie unquestionably made a very impressive case for concluding that Christianity is the absolutely transcendent religion. He was well informed and relatively objective. But one may well ask whether it is possible for a scholar to become sufficiently familiar with the religions of other times and places to reconstruct their relationships with such assurance. Are not the data as elusive as the metaphysics that Paul de Broglie found beyond the reach of his contemporaries? And did he not assume too easily that, because religion had been a necessary support for human progress in the past, it must continue to be so in the future? Might not religion itself be a vestigial organ? These questions are perhaps more acute in the 20th century than they were in the 19th.

About the same time that Paul de Broglie was seeking to answer objections arising from the new science of comparative religion, others were heavily engaged in defending the historicity of the Bible. In this field the leading scholar was Fulcran Vigouroux (1837–1915), a Sulpician whose *The Bible and Modern Discoveries in Egypt and Assyria*[142] passed through six editions between 1877 and 1896. Vigouroux also edited the apologetically oriented *Dictionary of the Bible*[143] in five massive volumes (1895–1912). He was Secretary of the Biblical Commission from its establishment in 1903 until 1912. Chiefly concerned with apologetical questions, Vigouroux tended to be conservative in exegesis.

Germany

The main achievement of Catholic apologetics in the latter half of the 19th century in Germany was massive systematization. A number of distinguished textbooks, encyclopedic in size and scope, were issued by erudite professors. Three may be mentioned as representative.

Franz Hettinger (1813–90), professor of apologetics at the University of Würzburg, composed a learned and ably written *Christian Apology*[144] and followed this up with a more rigorously scientific *Manual of Dogmatic Theology*.[145] In both works the general pattern is the same. Beginning with religion in general, the author goes on to consider successively the possibility and necessity of revelation, the signs of revelation (miracles and prophecies), the credibility of the Gospels, the divinity of Christ (which is demonstrated from the claims of Jesus, in combination with His physical and moral miracles and especially His Resurrection), the fulfillment of OT prophecy in Christ, the wonderful expansion of Christianity, and the Church as a standing miracle. As a kind of 19th-century Paley, Hettinger incorporated into his apologetical *summae* nearly every argument known to earlier authors. He did so with balance and system but without originality.

Paul von Schanz (1841–1905), who taught apologetics at Tübingen, wrote a three-volume *A Christian Apology*[146] directed principally against positivistic adversaries. The first volume, on God and nature, deals at great length with scientific difficulties raised against the Biblical accounts of the Creation and the Flood. Volume 2, on God and revelation, begins with a very full discussion of the various races of men and their religions, and closes with a historical reconstruction of the life of Jesus. Volume 3, which deals with the Church, proves the validity of Catholicism from the usual four notes and, as might be expected, devotes many pages to the primacy and infallibility of the pope.

In response to Bismarck's *Kulturkampf,* a struggle against the Church in the name of modern civilization, it became especially necessary to show that Catholicism is not an obstacle to human progress. To meet this need Albert Maria Weiss (1844–1925), a Dominican and specialist in social questions, wrote an immense *Christian Apology from the Standpoint of Morals and Culture,*[147] in which he sought to establish the credibility of Catholic Christianity on the ground of its moral teaching and its beneficent social effects. Weiss wrote with fire and eloquence, but his work lacks order and conciseness; it is criticized by Protestants for being unjust to Luther and the Reformers.[148]

PROTESTANTISM: 1850–1900

Germany

In Germany, where Protestant authors published prolifically in the field of apologetics, theologians may be divided into two main groups, the one more conservative and Biblically oriented, the other more liberal and progressive. As examples of the first group one may take the Reformed theologian August Ebrard (1818–88) and the Lutheran Christoph Ernst Luthardt (1823–1902).

Ebrard, a professor at Erlangen, began his apologetical career with a resounding reply to Feuerbach and D. F. Strauss, *Scientific Criticism of the Gospel History.*[149] In later editions Ebrard expanded this polemic to take on F. C. Baur, Renan, and Schenkel for having impugned the historicity of the Gospels. His principal writing was a two-volume *Apologetics; or the Scientific Vindication of Religion.*[150] The major portion of this ponderous work is taken up with refuting on scientific grounds various modern theories concerning the origins of man and the early history of religion.

Luthardt, a mediating theologian in the tradition of Schleiermacher and Sack, was the most successful Lutheran apologist of the period. His fame rests chiefly on the first three volumes of his four-volume series of *Apologetical Lectures* delivered at Leipzig.[151]

Volume 1, *On the Fundamental Truths of Christianity*,[152] portrays, somewhat in the manner of Pascal, the enigmas of human life and points out that they demand a personal God who manifests himself as living love. Volume 2, *On the Saving Truths of Christianity*,[153] points out that the 'contradiction of all contradictions is sin' (p. 316) and that the only answer to this is the redemptive work of Christ. The essential truths concerning Jesus, according to Luthardt, are not mere casual historical facts but, by reason of their importance for our inner life, can be grasped with firm moral conviction. Volume 3, *On the Moral Truths of Christianity*,[154] warns against the illusions of seeking progress and culture without God, and advocates as the true path of happiness the harmonious union of culture with religion. Without being profoundly original, Luthardt gathered up some of the best thoughts of his predecessors in a basically conservative, devotional type of apologetics. He drew freely upon Catholic apologists such as Pascal, Nicolas, and Hettinger, as well as upon Protestants such as Ullman and Tholuck.

The liberal wing of German theology was dominated by the neo-Kantianism of Albrecht Ritschl (1822–89), who depicted the doctrine of the kingdom, conceived as a communion of love, as the heart of Jesus' message. This demanded a new type of apologetics that, instead of seeking to justify the dogmas of Christianity before the bar of speculative reason, would seek to show the reasonableness of faith as a practical judgment. Wilhelm Herrmann (1846–1922), one of the first theologians to ally himself with Ritschl, seems to have looked upon the Christian's experience of communion with God[155] as mediated through the figure of Jesus Christ, as self-validating, and hence beyond the need of apologetical justification. Critics of Herrmann, however, have difficulty in seeing how one could reach such intuitive certainty that the NT portrayal of Jesus is accurate.[156]

Of the Ritschlian dogmaticians Julius Kaftan (1848–1926) is notable for the attention he gives to apologetics. In his *The Truth of the Christian Religion*[157] he holds that faith, since it operates in the domain of feeling and of the practical judgment, can be neither proved nor disproved by scientific evidence. But apologetics, he says, must show on theoretical grounds why it is reasonable to make an act of faith in the Christian revelation. Kaftan's principal argument is that, without a revelation such as Christianity purports to be, there is no way of giving intelligibility to human history as a whole or of answering man's questions regarding the origin and final purpose of all things. Without Christianity, he says, 'our highest knowledge would remain incomplete, a Postulate or hypothesis.'[158]

Another Ritschlian, Hermann Schultz (1836–1903), in his *Outlines of Christian Apologetics*,[159] rests his defense of Christianity on ethical grounds. Christianity, he affirms, is uniquely conducive to a sound and unlimited development of human culture.[160] The gospel, being purely ethical and religious in scope, contains nothing that could conceivably be overthrown by scientific discovery.[161]

A similar defense of Christianity by means of drastic reduction of its content may be found in the celebrated lectures of Adolf von Harnack (1851–1930), *What is Christianity?*[162] Harnack appeals to scientific historical criticism of the NT to establish his thesis that the gospel, as originally preached by Jesus, centered about the 'higher righteousness' of love, a doctrine that commends itself by its simplicity and sublimity. Harnack, in his opening chapter, criticizes earlier apologists for seeking to defend nonessentials. In his version of the gospel, reformed according to the requirements of neo-Kantian philosophy, the miracle stories and the bodily Resurrection of Jesus can be left aside.

The English-Speaking Countries

During the latter part of the 19th century a great part of the Protestant and Anglican apologetical effort was expended on domestic controversy between radicals and conservatives within the Christian household. Most apologists in Britain and the United States were content to follow along the lines of the evidential school, although some paid greater heed to internal and moral evidences than to the traditional arguments from miracle and prophecy. Apologetical courses were often given in the form of founded lectureships.[163]

A great deal of the apologetics of this period centers about the historicity of the Gospels. George P. Fisher of Yale, in his *Essays on the Supernatural Origin of Christianity*,[164] took on Renan, Strauss, and the radicals of the Protestant Tübingen School. A little later in England, J. B. Lightfoot in his *Essays on the Work Entitled 'Supernatural Religion'*[165] used his massive learning in the field of Christian origins to devastate the brash statements of a British enthusiast for German radical criticism.

After the publication of Darwin's *On the Origin of Species by Means of Natural Selection* (1859), a multitude of conservative apologists took up the pen in defense of the Biblical creation narrative. Professor Charles Hodge, Princeton Theological Seminary's learned systematician, declared: 'A more absolutely incredible theory was never propounded for acceptance among men.'[166] Mark Hopkins rejected the Darwinian theory as essentially atheistic, and the British statesman William E. Gladstone was moved to write his *The Impregnable Rock of Holy Scripture*.[167] On the other hand, President James McCosh of Princeton University in his *Christianity and Positivism*[168] saw possibilities of reconciling Darwinism with Christian faith. Natural selection, for him, was but the reverse side of supernatural design. Many other Protestant theologians were likewise open to the new theory. The Scottish popular philosopher Henry Drummond (1851–97) in his *Natural Law in the Spiritual World*,[169] applying Butler's principles of analogy, attempted to construct an evolutionary interpretation of the kingdom of God.

The most distinguished apologetical manual in English in this period was that of the Scottish NT exegete, Alexander B. Bruce, *Apologetics; or, Christianity Defensively Stated* (1892). After explaining in his introduction the aims and methods of apologetics, he gives in Book 1 a brief sketch of the Christian view of the world and then weighs its merits against those of five alternative theories of the universe: pantheism, materialism, deism, Unitarianism, and Agnosticism. In his consideration of Spencerian agnosticism he concedes that the proofs of God are rarely convincing except to those who already believe on other grounds.[170] But if one takes the Christian idea of God as a hypothesis, he argues, he will find that everything else he knows tends to verify it. (Bautain might have said almost the same.)

In his consideration of Israelite religion (Book 2) Bruce admits at least for purposes of the argument the documentary hypotheses of Wellhausen and others concerning the development of the OT. In such systems of religious evolutionism, says Bruce, there is nothing detrimental to Christianity.[171] In the final chapter of this Part he acknowledges many defects in OT religion (querulousness, vindictiveness, legalism, exclusiveness) but holds that these present no stumbling block to intelligent Christian faith, since the OT revelation is not claimed as final and perfect.

In Book 3, on the Christian Origins, Bruce takes a relatively conservative position on the authorship and historical value of the four Gospels. The miracle stories, he admits, have little persuasive force for modern unbelievers; but they retain their didactic value for instructing believers with regard to the mission of Jesus. The physical resurrection of Jesus, on the other hand, cannot be explained away on natural grounds.[172] After further chapters on the Lordship of Jesus and on the various NT authors Bruce closes his work with a wise and moderate statement on the supreme religious authority that

Christ enjoys in the minds of the faithful. Christianity, he holds, is God's final word to men. 'On the simple principle of the survival of the fittest, it is destined to perpetuity and ultimate universality.'[173]

Unlike some of the German apologists Bruce does not delve deeply into problems of epistemology or natural science. His is a basically Biblical apologetic, prefaced with some considerations regarding natural theology. Within its limits it is a highly successful piece of work. With some updating on critical and exegetical questions it could still be serviceable today.

CONCLUSION

The 19th century is unquestionably one of the most fruitful in the entire history of Christian apologetics. The sheer complexity and volume of the material is overwhelming, but it is possible to pick out some clear directions and to register some solid gains. In this period apologetics establishes itself as a distinct theological discipline; it also relates itself in a new way to the philosophy of religion, to the political order, and to the positive sciences.

Schleiermacher first called for an apologetical prolegomenon to the whole of theology. This systematization was first put into effect for Protestants by Sack and for Catholics by Drey. It was worked out with an excessive—because deceptive—clarity by Perrone and the Roman school, who tended to isolate apologetics too much from dogmatic theology.

The relationship of apologetics to philosophy was promoted by remarkable advances in the philosophy of religion achieved by Kant and the idealists of the 1st half of the century. The net effect of this reflection was to set off religion more clearly as a distinct mode of knowledge, dissimilar to the purely speculative sciences. For some apologists this led to a certain fideism, an unwillingness to justify the assent of faith by any rational process—a tendency already noted in many Protestants, such as Kierkegaard, Maurice, and Herrmann, and in some Catholics, such as Bautain. For others the influence of critical philosophy resulted in an apologetics of the heart (Schleiermacher, Tholuck, and in an analogous way Chateaubriand and Ventura) or in intuitionism (Gratry) or in some form of religious pragmatism based on the postulates of practical reason (Hermes, Ritschl, Kaftan).

Normative Catholic theology, rejecting the Kantian critique, continued to insist on the demonstrability of the existence of God and of the credibility of revelation (Balmes, Perrone, Vatican Council I).

But in a thinker such as Newman the epistemology of religious knowledge is expressed with great caution and refinement. Many Catholic theologians of the period, impatient with long and tenuous historical evidences, base the reasonableness of faith upon the present reality of the Church as sign (Balmes, Dechamps, Vatican Council I).

Apologetics relates itself in an ambivalent way to political and social life. French traditionalism early in the century, shrinking back from the chaos of the revolution, views religion as a force that is capable of restoring order, unity, and discipline. Donoso Cortès and even Newman, with their horror of Liberalism, share something of the same orientation. But others, such as Lamennais, Brownson, and Hecker, look upon Catholicism as a force of progress. In a more defensive way the same is true of Luthardt and Weiss. While giving Christianity credit for fostering true freedom and human welfare, they warn against secular idolatry.

In the scientific area apologetics has to face challenges from the progress of natural and historical knowledge. A crisis is brought on by the Darwinian theory, but farsighted apologists such as Mivart and Drummond are able to take this in stride. Another crisis arises out of Biblical criticism. The radical NT exegesis of Strauss and the Protestant Tübingen school is at first answered heatedly and polemically. But scholars such as Lightfoot and Harnack are able to use scientific source criticism in support of the historical reliability of the Synoptic Gospels. Toward the end of the century Bruce takes a sane and balanced attitude toward scientific criticism of both the Old and the New Testaments. Catholics of the same period, such as Vigouroux, still adopt an unduly conservative attitude, which will not be abandoned until the middle of the 20th century.

A final challenge to traditional apologetics is offered by the new science of comparative religion. Paul de Broglie more than any other single theologian shows himself able to master the findings of this science and to utilize them as an additional source of Christian evidences. While his arguments are not rigorously probative—and are not intended to be—they are solidly persuasive and have not lost their value in the 2d half of the 20th century, although the state of the evidence and the questions being asked have somewhat changed in the past hundred years.

CHAPTER SIX

The Twentieth Century

Until the Enlightenment the Churches were on the whole quite secure in their own position. The apologist, speaking from the stable platform of official Christianity, had only to refute the adversary and to convince him of the error of his ways. With the rise of deism, and even more, under idealism and Liberalism, the lines between defense and attack became increasingly blurred. The type of Christianity that some apologists sought to defend appeared to many of their colleagues as a betrayal of the tradition. With thinkers such as Lessing, Hegel, Strauss, and even Harnack it is hard to know to what extent they are to be regarded as objectors and to what extent as upholders of the faith.

By the beginning of the 20th century is possible to speak of two basic types of apologetics: a defensive type that seeks to argue unbelievers into submission to the faith as traditionally understood and a revisionist type that seeks to forge a new synthesis between religious and secular knowledge. The thoughtful apologist increasingly finds himself in a no-man's land between conservative Christians and radical unbelievers. The new types of apologetical theology that develop in the 20th century—from Catholic Modernism and Protestant liberalism in the early decades to Christian existentialism in the 4th decade and Christian secularity in the 6th decade—are sources of scandal and conflict within the Churches themselves.

CATHOLIC APOLOGETICS

Blondel and the Modernists

The most vital center of apologetical thought at the turn of the century was undoubtedly France. The general atmosphere was, like a century

202

earlier, anti-intellectualist.[1] The exorbitant claims of positivistic science no less than those of the Enlightenment provoked a reaction against the objectivity of the calculating mind. The dominant philosophy in university circles was a neo-Kantianism that excluded belief from the sphere of competence of critical reason. Protestant fideism, which reached its highest apex in the theology of Auguste Sabatier and Eugène Ménengoz, maintained that faith rested upon no rational evidences.[2] From across the English channel came the ideas of the English statesman Arthur J. Balfour (1848–1930), who contended that all man's fundamental attitudes are determined by *authority*—a very wide term that in his usage included instinct, custom, and environmental conditioning.[3] To this was added the influence of the American pragmatist William James (1842–1910), who in various books translated into French called attention to the affective elements in faith and to the roots of religion in the psychology of the unconscious.[4]

In Catholic apologetics new movements attuned to the times were led by Léon Ollé-Laprune (1839–98) and Fernand Brunetière (1869–1906). The former, a professor at the École Normale in Paris, wrote a doctoral dissertation on moral certitude in which he stressed the free and voluntary character of faith; he advocated Catholicism on the basis of its harmony with the deepest aspirations of the human heart.[5] Brunetière, a renowned literary critic who became a convert to Catholicism, wrote the preface to the French translation of Balfour's work. Here and elsewhere he spoke of the 'bankruptcy of science' and its incapacity to furnish guidance for life. 'One does not demonstrate the divinity of Christ,' he wrote; 'one believes it or one does not.'[6]

It was in this antirationalist neo-Kantian atmosphere at Paris that Maurice Blondel (1861–1949) began his career as an apologist. His first publication, dedicated to his director of studies at the École Normale, Ollé-Laprune, was his dissertation, *L'Action*.[7] Strictly speaking it was a philosophical not an apologetical work. It addressed itself to the problem whether and how the question of the supernatural can legitimately present itself to an intellectual formed according to the demands of contemporary philosophy. Blondel attempted to show that human action, rigorously analyzed, inevitably raises questions regarding the destiny of man and the meaning of human life. The human will at its deepest level aspires to a fulfillment beyond anything this world can give. Man craves for a communion with God that he cannot obtain by his own effort. Every attempt to give oneself God without His giving Himself turns out, on examination, to be illusory and superstitious. Hence one must humbly wait and dispose oneself to become a participant in divine life, if God freely offers communion with Himself. Philosophy cannot establish the reality of the supernatural gift, but it can show that the idea of such a gift holds a necessary place in the total logic of life.

Toward the end of *L'Action* Blondel has some discussion of the manner in which a man might recognize and assimilate the thought and life of God, were the gift to be made. Without humility and abnegation one would not be disposed to receive. The presence of the supernatural, moreover, cannot be established by stringent proofs of a quasi-mathematical kind but only by a type of experimentation. If a man acts as though he had faith, he may discover through the expansion and intensification of his life that there are sufficient reasons for affirming the reality of revelation.[8]

In 1895 the editor of the *Annales de philosophie chrétienne* wrote an article, 'New Tendencies in Philosophical Apologetics,' in which he presented *L'Action* as a rejection of all metaphysical approaches to apologetics in favor of one that was purely psychological. This partial misrepresentation of his thought provided Blondel with an occasion to set forth his views on apologetics. He replied in a lengthy 'Letter on the Requirements of Contemporary Thought in the Field of Apologetics . . .'[9] The article consists of three main parts, the first two of which are pertinent to the present inquiry. Part 1 deals with current methods of apologetics. It begins with a general statement to the effect that apologetics should not opportunistically content itself with specious arguments that are practically persuasive but should limit itself to speculatively valid arguments that can stand the test of criticism. Then Blondel proceeds to criticize five forms of apologetics currently in use:

1. Scientific apologetics occupies itself with seeking to harmonize the conclusions of the positive sciences with the dogmas of the Church. This effort (Blondel may have had the work of Duilhé de Saint-Projet in mind) rests on the fallacious assumption that science is seeking to give a picture of reality whereas in fact science is using symbols functionally for pragmatic aims. This method, therefore, is a waste of time.

2. Others such as Paul de Broglie seek to establish Christianity as a historical fact, as though it could be known by ordinary historical testimony. This method erroneously presupposes that the supernatural can be scientifically verified. Furthermore this approach fails to explain why an individual is not at liberty to ignore the Christian fact, as he inevitably has to disregard many other alleged facts.

3. Still others such as Chateaubriand and Ollé-Laprune wish to prove Christianity on the ground that it is a source of cultural and moral benefits. This argument, says Blondel, has value for those who have some inner experience of Christianity, but it fails to establish that Christianity is more than a human doctrine. For nonbelievers such an inventory of spiritual treasures is meaningless and even irritating.

4. Georges Fonsegrive (1852–1917), in a conference on 'The Conditions of Modern Apologetics' (*Annales*, 1895) had called for recognition of 'the identity between Catholicism and life.' This identity, even if established, would point only to the natural truth of Catholicism. Fonsegrive, moreover, made some unfortunate statements about the 'parallelism' between dogma and the natural order that suggested that the two orders never interpenetrated.

5. The seminary textbooks rely chiefly on the order and completeness of the Thomistic system but fail to show that that system meets the questions and needs of contemporary man. Modern man, however, is justified in demanding that religious truth should be not only coherent in itself but also perfective of man.

In Part 2 Blondel expounds his own method. He begins by asserting that modern thought takes for granted the principle of immanence, namely, 'that nothing can enter into a man's mind which does not come out of him and correspond in some way to a need for development.'[10] To meet this exigency Blondel proposes what he calls the 'method of immanence.' In the rest of the section he summarizes in substance the dialectic already developed in *L'Action*. If a man seeks out the implicit affirmations that underlie all his actions he will see that philosophy cannot avoid the question of the supernatural. 'Only practical action, the effective action of our lives, will settle for each one of us, in secret, the question of the relations between the soul and God.'[11] If one acts in accordance with one's best lights, grace will enable him to experience that it is good and reasonable to believe.

Blondel was often accused of contradicting the doctrine of Vatican Council I on the motives of credibility. Partly to offset such charges he wrote under the name of his friend F. Mallet three articles comparing his system with that of Cardinal Dechamps.[12] He praised Dechamps for recognizing that the moral dispositions are not merely extrinsic and preparatory but permanent and constitutive for the approach to faith. He found in Dechamps his own conviction that 'apologetics must tend not only to make us know and believe but . . . also and primarily to make us be and act more and better.'[13]

H

Elsewhere Blondel praises Dechamps for his recognition that the Church provides an atmosphere in which the sacred fire of faith can be effectively transmitted.[14]

In many of his writings Blondel deplored the extrinsicism of the conventional argument from miracles. The miracle, he complained, is treated as a mere label 'simply detached from the facts and placarded at the entrance of the dogmatic fortress.'[15] For Blondel there was an unbreakable connection between the nature of the miraculous deed, its significance, and its evidential value. To recognize a miracle it is not sufficient that it be perceived as anomalous and enigmatic. Christian miracles move men to belief insofar as they are expressive symbols of God's extraordinary goodness in extending His offer of friendship to man.[16]

Influenced by the philosophy of indeterminism and by the scientific theory according to which all physical laws are merely statistical, Blondel vigorously rejected the definition of miracle, rather commonly accepted since the time of Hume, as an exception to the laws of nature. For him there could be no strictly scientific demonstration of miracles. Exceptional events, produced and intended by God as signs, miracles could not be recognized except by those who were attuned by suitable spiritual dispositions. For those properly prepared, miracles could be conducive to Christian faith. 'Miracles, then, are miraculous only in the eyes of those who are already prepared to recognize the divine action in the most ordinary events and acts.'[17]

Blondel's views on the recognition of miracles excited a long and heated controversy in France.[18] He was energetically attacked by conservative Catholic apologists such as Abbé Hippolyte Gayraud and especially by the Dominican Salvador Schwalm, who accused him of subjectivism and immanentism. He was defended, on the other hand, by his disciple Lucien Laberthonnière (1860–1932). This young and eloquent Oratorian priest was unfortunately suspected of Modernism and silenced by Church authorities, with the result that he never fulfilled his early promise.

Wounded as Blondel was by the attack from the right, he was even more gravely harmed by the acclaim he received from the theological left. Alfred Loisy (1857–1940), writing under the pen name Firmin, praised him for reviving the true Augustinian concept of miracle, which Loisy then proceeded to use in support of his own fideism. 'Miracle,' he wrote, 'is the train of the world, contemplated by faith, which alone penetrates its enigma.'[19] In much the same spirit the Bergsonian philosopher Édouard Le Roy (1870–1954) proclaimed that miracles, instead of generating faith, are engendered by it.[20] Blondel was much disturbed by Le Roy's exaggerations and answered them under the pen name of Bernard de Sailly in an article, 'La Notion et le rôle du miracle.'[21] He insisted again that the miracle is an objectively real occurrence that solicits faith and actually leads on to faith in the case of those who respond also to the interior prompting of grace.

The Modernists, with Loisy at their head, were strongly influenced by various evolutionary, pantheistic, vitalistic, and pragmatistic currents in contemporary thought. They looked upon faith primarily as a feeling or experience rather than as adherence to any definable truth. In their view apologetics ought to lead men to the experience of the Catholic religion rather than seek to persuade them by arguments that that religion is true. According to Loisy, 'The profound and universal reason for faith is nothing but the conformity of religion with the needs and aspirations of man.'[22] While admitting that arguments could be given, Loisy maintained that these arguments sufficed only to give probability and were not the true reason for assent.

George Tyrrell (1861–1909), who shared with Loisy the theological leadership of the Modernist movement, likewise espoused a vitalist apologetic, influenced by pragmatism. Purely objective and abstract arguments, he held, are ineffective. For apologetical evidences to win acceptance, they must be connected with man's religious life. An affective apologetics, which dwells on the beauties and advantages resulting from religion, to some extent fills this need, but its appeal is a mere seduction and temptation unless one can show that what is beautiful and satisfying is also true. Tyrrell's thesis is that every man is equipped with a religious sense 'whose developments, healthy or unhealthy, furnish an experimental criterion of belief, one whose verdict is often not less considerable than that of a strictly intellectual criterion.'[23] Applying the 'criterion of life, of spiritual fruitfulness'[24] he seeks in his *Lex orandi* to give an experimental proof of Christianity. The true reason one adheres to Christianity, he asserts, cannot be stated in apologetical arguments. 'The reasons we give to our mind are but after-justifications of an impulse that derives, not from reason, but from the sympathetic intuitions of the Spirit of Holiness.'[25] The touchstone, in the last analysis, is the collective verdict of the spiritual experience of the Church. *Lex orandi est lex credendi.*

Church authorities feared that Modernism at least in some of its most prominent representatives was leading toward naturalism, if not toward pantheistic monism, and was disfiguring the gospel. The reaction of Rome was strong; it uprooted some wheat with the chaff. The encyclical *Pascendi* in its discussion of apologetics appeared to condemn not so much Loisy as Blondel. Of the apologetics of Modernism it stated: 'The goal that it sets for itself is this: to lead a man who lacks faith in such a way that he undergoes that experience of the Catholic religion that, according to the Modernists, is the sole foundation of faith.'[26]

The encyclical goes on to deplore the views of those Catholics 'who, while rejecting the doctrines of immanence, nevertheless use it for apologetics and thus dangerously speak as though human nature possessed not only a capacity and suitability for the supernatural order—as Catholic apologists, with due reservations, have always shown—but a true exigency properly so called.'[27]

Another Vatican document, the Oath against Modernism (1910), reaffirmed with added emphasis what Vatican Council I had taught concerning the demonstrability of the existence of God and added with regard to the signs of revelation: 'I admit and recognize the external signs of revelation—that is, divine facts, and primarily miracles and prophecies—as most certain signs of the divine origin of the Christian religion, and I hold that these signs are excellently suited to the understanding of all ages and all men, even those of today.'[28]

Credibility and Apologetics: Scholastic Controversies in France

The controversy about miracles provoked by Blondel was only part of a far-reaching discussion of the motives of credibility and the nature of apologetics. The current textbooks and the seminary tradition at the time distinguished very clearly between two orders, natural and supernatural. The assent of faith, it was agreed, was gratuitously elevated and hence supernatural; but as a free moral action it had to measure up to the norms governing all such actions, including the norm of prudence. The prudence of the act was guaranteed by the reasonableness of the decision to believe. According to the standard authors this could be shown by an apologetical demonstration that did not rest upon any supernatural subjective aids.

By substituting a logic of action for a logic of objective inference and by utilizing God's interior call to communion with Himself as an ingredient in the apologetic process, Blondel struck at the foundations of the accepted approach. Many felt that he was undermining the rational character of the act of faith and the possibility of scientific apologetics. Some scholastic authors, however, sought to give the apologetic of immanence some status, at least secondary or supplementary, within a basically traditional approach. The most important effort along this line was that of the Dominican Ambroise Gardeil (1859–1931).

Gardeil's approach[29] is built upon a distinction between the normal and the exceptional approaches to faith. In the normal case, he holds, the prudence of faith is guaranteed by a speculatively certain judgment of credibility that relies on external evidences as judged by the natural light of reason. This judgment may be rigorously scientific or it may be a matter of ordinary knowledge, not rigorously methodical. The task of apologetics is to establish in a general way the credibility of Catholic dogma by arguments that are valid in themselves and capable of being appreciated by persons competent to follow historical and philosophical evidences. Apologetics, while it seeks to demonstrate the credibility of the Christian faith by stringent proofs, does not refuse to employ 'topical' arguments that have merely probable force.

Gardeil, however, admits that there are men who by reason of their lack of ability, their ignorance, or their prejudices are incapable of appreciating the objective arguments of credibility. For these too, he says, faith is possible thanks to various subjective helps that by motivating the will to believe compensate for the lack of objectively valid reasons. It is the merit of 'subjective apologetics,' he holds, to have underscored the appetibility of revelation. Gardeil distinguishes three types of subjective apologetics—basically those respectively of Blondel, of Ollé-Laprune, and of Brunetière. First, there is the 'apologetics of action,' which moves men toward faith by bringing out their incapacity to beatify themselves. Second, there is 'moral apologetics,' which calls attention to the harmonies between faith and man's moral aspirations; third there is 'fideist apologetics,' which prompts men to act on the hypothesis that faith is valid and thereby makes them more susceptible to the impulses of grace. Subjective apologetics, Gardeil believes, is too individual a matter to constitute a strict science; neither is it capable of furnishing objectively sufficient reasons for holding that Christianity is a divine revelation; but it should not be denied all place in apologetical literature. Gardeil suggests that there should be a special practical discipline adjoined to apologetics that would study the subjective conditions that can better dispose untutored persons or those confused by modern agnostic philosophies to receive the gift of faith.

A disciple of Gardeil, Ambroise de Poulpiquet, went beyond him in refusing to regard the affective and subjective elements in the approach to faith as mere 'suppléances,' whose function would be to compensate for a lack of intellectual capacity.[30] For anyone to arrive at faith, he argued, his will must be drawn by the desire to believe. A complete apologetics should therefore include both intellectual and affective elements. Whereas Gardeil had defined apologetics as the science of the credibility of Catholic dogma, Poulpiquet defined it as 'the demonstration of the credibility and of the appetibility of dogma.'[31]

The mediating positions of Gardeil and Poulpiquet were received with great interest on all sides. Traditionally oriented theologians such as the Jesuits J. V. Bainvel and H. Pinard de la Boullaye felt that in the case of the 'simple,' these authors had not sufficiently saved the reasonableness of faith. Pinard objected against both Gardeil and Poulpiquet that moral and spiritual impulses were not destitute of evidential value. Poulpiquet in addition failed to safeguard the unity of apologetics. This unity could be restored if credentity, rather than credibility, were taken to be the formal object of apologetics. 'We define apologetics as: the rational justification of the duty to believe.'[32]

For his part, Blondel was dissatisfied with the concessions made by Gardeil and Poulpiquet. In a brochure published under the name of B. de Sailly[33] he protested that Gardeil had driven a wedge between intellect and will, between credibility and appetibility, between objectivity and subjectivity. He separated men into two classes, some who believe (as St. Thomas's demons do) because coerced by the evidences and others who believe without an adequate rational basis, on the basis of 'subjective supplements.' Why should the 'faith of demons' be treated as the ideal or even the normal case? Poulpiquet had advanced beyond Gardeil in perceiving that the internal and volitional elements as well as the external and intellectual are normally necessary, but he went astray in constructing two kinds of apologetics, the one without motive power and the other without light.

In a number of important articles on the theology of faith published between 1910 and 1914, the young French Jesuit Pierre Rousselot (1878–1915) gave a more traditional expression to some of Blondel's theses regarding the evidences of credibility. Appealing to St. Thomas's views on the active dynamism of the intellect toward truth and on the role of connaturality in the knowledge of moral and spiritual matters, Rousselot found a basis in Scholasticism for the Blondelian doctrine that subjectivity plays an essential role in the discernment of signs. Rousselot went so far as to declare that without the subjective attunement of supernatural grace it is impossible for man to perceive the revelatory significance of the signs of credibility. He held that the judgment of credibility is temporally simultaneous with the act of faith itself. In his view, therefore, it is a serious error to limit apologetics as Gardeil and the modern Scholastics did to the establishment of a purely natural credibility. While giving Blondel credit for making great advances, Rousselot preferred not to rely on Blondel's arguments from man's restlessness toward the divine as 'an interior fact.' For Rousselot the function of grace was not to provide new evidences but to give man the 'eyes of faith,' thanks to which he could interpret the supernatural significance of the external evidences and grasp their probative value.[34]

While many theologians recognized that Rousselot had made an important contribution by pointing out that grace is normally at work in man as he approaches the decision of faith and that grace has an illuminating effect on the mind, Rousselot was vigorously attacked for his denial that there could be a purely natural judgment of credibility, and particularly for his efforts to attribute this doctrine to St. Thomas. While the principle of reciprocal causality was indeed a Thomistic one, Thomas does not seem to have held that faith and the judgment of credibility are mutually causative of each other. According to many competent scholars, St. Thomas taught that it was possible for men to reach, without the help of grace, a firm and objectively founded judgment that Christianity is a divine revelation.[35]

After Rousselot's death many of the best Catholic theologians made use of his theological insights for the renewal of apologetics. His influence was very great upon Jesuit apologetical theologians such as Huby, Bonsirven, Lebreton, and subsequently Guy de Broglie, Henri Bouillard, and Felix Malmberg. Outside the Society of Jesus, theologians such as Pierre Tiberghien and Eugène Masure applied Rousselot's principles to apologetics. Tiberghien in his *Does Science Lead to God?*[36] argued that the scientific and philosophical arguments for the divine origin of miracles are never conclusive unless the subject studying the evidences is enlightened by grace. Masure in *The Apologetical Highroad*[37] warmly approved of the apologetics of immanence. It was too little, he held, to call it—as some Blondelians had—a 'threshold apologetics' (*apologétique du seuil*); rather it was an 'apologetics of the crypt,' sustaining from below the entire structure of the evidences of credibility. He agreed with Tiberghien that miraculous signs do not have supernatural significance except for those who, thanks to the impulses of grace, are restless for personal communion with God.

A further problem much discussed by Catholic theologians in the early 20th century concerned the relationship between apologetics and theology. Gardeil, followed by X. M. Le Bachelet,[38] made a distinction between apologetics or 'apologetical science' on the one hand and apologetical theology on the other. Gardeil explains: 'Apologetical science moved from outside to inside, from reason to the credibility of the object of faith. Apologetical theology will move from inside to outside, from the object of faith and from its credibility, presupposed as beyond dispute, to the rational arguments that can defend these.'[39]

Gardeil's eminent pupil, Réginald Garrigou-Lagrange (1877–1964), in several articles published in 1919 and 1920 developed an alternative position, which he restates succinctly in the Prolegomena to his manual, *Revelation Declared through the Catholic Church*.[40] The apologist, he maintains, is not an inquirer but a defender of the faith. As a believer he makes use of the authoritative theological sources—Scripture and tradition in its various forms—to establish what revelation is and to what extent it can be rendered evident by external signs. Drawing upon his resources as a theologian the apologist is able to give his discipline the unity, order, integrity, and depth without which it would be defective as a science. While apologetics is a theological science, it differs from sacred theology properly so called insofar as the apologist does not presuppose faith in his readers and consequently does not argue from articles of faith. Under the direction of faith he constructs arguments that are valid before natural reason.[41] In establishing apologetics on a firm theological basis Garrigou-Lagrange made a clear step forward, but unfortunately his apologetical method remained imprisoned in the narrow rationalistic framework of the Roman textbook tradition. In the second volume of his manual he applied a step-by-step deductive approach to the question of Jesus as a divinely authoritative teacher.

The Refutation of Rationalism: 1910–50

In the early part of the century the reliance of apologetics on the teaching authority of Jesus Christ made it more urgent than ever to refute NT scholars such as Strauss, Renan, and Harnack, who questioned the divine claims and the miracles of Jesus. Many Catholic apologists therefore concentrated on the problem of Jesus.

The Swiss Capuchin Hilarin Felder (1867–1951) produced a prodigiously learned refutation of rationalist exegesis, *Christ and the Critics*.[42] After first vindicating the historical value of the NT sources this work establishes successively the messianic consciousness of Jesus, His divine consciousness, His intellectual and moral perfection, His miracles, and His Resurrection. Felder claims to conduct his investigation by the objective techniques of scientific history. Early in his work he proves to his satisfaction (if not to that of the reader) that the Gospels are 'in their full extent and in the strictest sense of the word, historical authorities and scientific evidence.'[43] Once this is granted he has a relatively easy time proving the absurdity of the difficulties raised by critical exegetes. After overthrowing the adversaries one by one, he arrives at the triumphant conclusion: 'And just as only that study of Christ which confesses the Messiahship and divinity of our Saviour can lay claim to the spirit of Christianity, so only can such a study claim to follow a scientific method. Every christological conception which regards Jesus as a mere man is, if historically considered, a fanciful monstrosity.'[44]

A more nuanced approach along similar lines was developed by the great French Jesuit Léonce de Grandmaison (1868–1927). Assigned by superiors in 1899 to teach a new treatise, 'De Christo legato,' he did so for more than ten years before composing his important article 'Jésus Christ' for the *Apologetical Dictionary of the Catholic Faith*.[45] In a preliminary section on method, he specifies that the problem of Jesus is to be solved apologetically not by faith itself but by an objective, critical approach that treats the Gospels as though they were merely human historical documents. In the first portion of his article he establishes that the Gospels are reliable historical sources. Then he goes on to demonstrate that Jesus presented Himself as a divine-human mediator, as Son of God. In a third section he shows that Jesus vindicated His claims by miracles and prophecies and, in the closing section, that the Father bore witness to Jesus by raising Him from the dead. Although the Resurrection, considered from the point of view of faith, transcends the dimensions of historical fact, it must be treated in apologetics, according to Grandmaison, in its human and historical dimensions.

In the last years of his life Grandmaison expanded this article into his great work, *Jesus Christ: His Person, His Message, His Credentials*.[46] A remarkable feature of this work is the series of valuable excurses on special problems in exegesis and the history of religions.

Grandmaison wrote with such a splendid combination of learning, style, and devotion that his work is simultaneously instructive, delightful, and inspiring. But in the light of a later generation it seems regrettable that he felt obliged to confine himself within the straitjacket of positivistic historiography. He shows some embarrassment in trying to handle, by the method he sets for himself, mysteries such as the Resurrection and the divinity of Jesus. Thanks to his personal faith and piety, his work is more impressive than the limitations of his method would seem to promise.

In the person of H. Pinard de la Boullaye (1874–1958), whose early work on apologetical method has already been mentioned here, the cathedral of Notre Dame found a distinguished successor to Lacordaire and Ravignan. In his Lenten conferences from 1928 to 1937, Pinard transported into the pulpit the fruits of his fundamental theology courses given at the scholasticate of Enghien in the previous 15 years. Of particular apologetical worth were his sermons of 1929 on the historicity of the Gospels and of Paul; those of 1930 on Jesus' messiahship and Resurrection; and those of 1931 on Jesus' miracles and prophecies. The published volumes containing these sermons are fully equipped with learned footnotes, but the style is unmistakably oratorical. The argumentation takes the positivist, historical form already examined in Felder and Grandmaison.

French Catholicism in the 1st half of the century produced some remarkable efforts of collaboration, the most outstanding being the *Apologetical Dictionary of the Catholic Faith* (DictApolFoiCath). It takes up the main subjects pertaining to fundamental theology (God, Christ, Church, Scripture, etc.), the other religions and the dissident Christian groups, and subsidiary questions in the fields of doctrine, history, science, etc. that have made for religious controversy. The editor, Adhémar d'Alès, gathered an exceptional team of scholars including not only Grandmaison and Le Bachelet, whose contributions have already been mentioned, but Lebreton (Trinity), Y. de la Brière (Church), Teilhard de Chardin (Man), Rousselot (Intellectualism), Bainvel (Faith), Mangenot (Canon), Duchesne (Gnosis), Harent (Modernism, Pope), Prat (Paul), Pinard de la Boullaye (Religious Experience), the Valensin brothers (Immanence, Doctrine and Method of),[47] and M. de la Taille (Insurrection).

On a somewhat less ambitious scale, but also very comprehensive, was the bulky tome *Apologetics* published in 1937 under the joint editorship of Maurice Brillant and Maurice Nédoncelle.[48] It contained articles by prominent scholars on the main questions taken up in the standard seminary apologetics course, e.g., the philosophy of religion, natural theology, the possibility of revelation, the historical value of the Old and New Testaments, the status of the dissident Churches and of the non-Christian religions, and the common objections to Catholic Christianity. The volume was reissued in 1948 with some revisions, especially as regards the relationship between science and religion. In the revised edition it was thought proper to reduce the article on the history of apologetics from eighty pages to ten!

On the occasion of the first edition of the publication just noted, one of the contributors, the Louvain Scripture scholar Joseph Coppens, in a frequently noticed essay, ventured to summarize the current state of Catholic evidences. [49] His summary comes down to an inductive apologetic reminiscent of Newman (whom he frequently quotes) and the Abbé de Broglie. 'The figure of Jesus,' he concludes at one point, 'is so transcendent and unique in religious beauty, both for Jews and for pagans, that souls in search of the truth will not hesitate, after having come to know him, to give themselves to him in an act of faith and trust as the best guide that history offers them on the road to religious truth and salvation.'[50]

The triumphs of atheistic Communism in Russia, in the judgment of some Catholics, called for a new *Summa contra gentiles*. In 1937 Yvan Kologrivov edited such a work. In 1950 it was thoroughly revised under the editorship of Jacques de Bivort de la Saudée and reissued in 1953 with several new chapters.[51] The work in its final form was intended not simply as a reply to Marxists but as a general refutation of scientific materialism on those points where this philosophy collided with Catholic orthodoxy. The work explored at some length questions such as the origins of man and the world, the spirituality of the soul, and the relations between the Church and capitalism. The contributions by Henri de Lubac on the origins of religion and by Y. M. J. Congar on the problem of evil—to mention only two—placed this work far above the normal level of apologetical symposia.

Meanwhile the flow of Latin seminary manuals on the Roman pattern continued unabated.[52] Commonly these works consist of two main parts: first a general Christian demonstration following the basic lines of Grandmaison's article, and then a Catholic demonstration that seeks to prove that the Church founded by Christ has the same essential characteristics as, and is historically continuous with, the Roman Catholic Church of today. Monotonously similar to one another, these manuals uniformly reject the 'method of immanence' and the theses of Rousselot regarding the discernment of supernatural signs. They hold that miracles and prophecies are certainly

knowable by unaided human reason and are the primary signs
vindicating the divine authority of Jesus Christ. They conclude that
the only reasonable position is to accept the credibility of Catholic
Christianity.

As already noted in the work of Perrone, the simplicity of the
argument in these scholastic manuals had obvious pedagogical
advantages over the bulky Teutonic treatises of the late 19th
century. But the apparent clarity of the demonstration is dissatisfying
to the critical reader. The manner in which the argument is structured
—in a series of theses, each of which presupposes its predecessors and
is independent of those that are to follow—makes it necessary to
claim certitude for every major affirmation and to overlook the
inductive logic of converging probabilities as developed by Butler,
Newman, and others.

The more perceptive Catholic theologians—especially those
influenced by Rousselot—were not unaware of these limitations of
seminary apologetics. In a notable article published as early as
1930[53] Henri de Lubac castigated 'the apologetics of yesterday'
as being too mean, too opportunistic, too superficial, and too
untheological. It remained too much in the area of extrinsic criteria
and failed to enter boldly into the sanctuary of revealed truth.
There is no valid apologetics, according to Lubac, which does not
begin and end in theology, understood as a quest for a deeper understanding of faith.

The most incisive Catholic critique of textbook apologetics was
perhaps that of Jean Levie, professor at the Jesuit scholasticate in
Louvain. In his *Under the Eyes of the Unbeliever*[54] he applies to
apologetics the ideas of Pierre Rousselot and of Joseph Maréchal
regarding the dynamism of the human intellect and will in their
restless search for communion with the infinite. Apologetics, he
maintains, must present Christ and the Church as living signs of
God's infinite charity toward men. Only when viewed in relation to
this center of intelligibility can the claims and miracles of Jesus, as
narrated in the NT, appear credible.

In the course of his argument Levie calls attention to five erroneous
postulates that underlie the scientific-historical apologetics of the
seminary manuals:

1. That the examination of the evidences of credibility can
   suitably be made without any consideration of the specific
   content of revelation
2. That the evidences of credibility are equally accessible to all
   men of good will, whether believers or unbelievers

3. That by rigorous application of profane historical method one can arrive at stringent conclusions regarding the religious significance of Christ
4. That the moral and religious dispositions of the subject play no positive role in the apologetical process
5. That each of the arguments of credibility is an independent whole, which can reach its conclusion without the concurrence of the others

By relentlessly criticizing each of these postulates, Levie intellectually demolished many of the specific positions of the Roman school and the popular apologetics deriving from that school.

A rather different approach, innocent of the theological sophistication of Lubac and Levie but keenly realistic in its handling of evidences, was developed by the French lay apologist Jean Guitton (1901–). His most popular work, *The Problem of Jesus*,[55] instead of beginning from Christianity as a position to be demonstrated seeks to trace the reflections of a sincere 'free thinker' attempting to find the most plausible explanation for the assertions of the NT. Anxious to avoid minimizing any objection, Guitton shows a keen awareness of the complexities of historical testimony and of the special difficulties inherent in the history of Jesus. What testimony, he asks, would be sufficient to establish the reality of such elusive facts as Jesus' divine sonship and His appearances from beyond the grave? In the final analysis, Guitton shows, the difficulties in accepting the Christian explanation of the documents are less than the difficulties in other interpretations. The total candor of Guitton's approach does much to offset the overbearing complacency of so many apologetical tracts. He leaves the reader with a new respect for the honest objections of nonbelievers and with a healthy realization that a sympathetic examination of the objections can purify and strengthen the faith of those who do believe.

The influence of Levie, Guitton, and others helped Catholic NT scholars from 1950 on to adopt a less defensive approach to the problem of Jesus and to face more courageously the real difficulties growing out of the texts. Xavier Léon-Dufour, for example, gives a scholarly and nuanced analysis of the problem of faith and history in the Gospel that takes advantage of the best results of Protestant Biblical scholarship.[56]

The official Roman directives since World War II have shown a gradual but hesitant relaxation of the anti-Modernist strictures in the area of fundamental theology. In his encyclical in Biblical studies (*Divino afflante Spiritu,* 1943) Pius XII accepted the literary principles of form criticism with regard to the Old Testament and New Testament—an acceptance later confirmed by Vatican II's Constitution on Divine Revelation (*Dei Verbum,* 1965). The encyclical *Humani generis* (1950), warning against an imprudent irenicism that would stray from the approved tradition of the Church, reiterated the possibility of a purely natural knowledge of God and of the moral law, and insisted that God had provided sufficient external signs of credibility so that the divine origin of the Christian faith could be certainly proved 'by the merely natural light of reason.' Vatican Council II, however, was remarkably silent on the cognitive powers of unaided reason in the area of religion. It made scarcely any mention of the traditional arguments from prophecy and miracle and from the wonderful properties of the Church. Whatever apologetics may be found in the documents of Vatican II takes the form of an appealing and irenic presentation of Catholic doctrine.

The Apologetics of Restoration

A very influential stream of Catholic apologetics in the 1st half of the century took the form of a critique of modern culture. It maintained that the modern West in rejecting the divine authority of the Church was ineluctably plunging toward the abyss of nihilism and despair. This approach is especially evident in works by converts seeking to win others to the Catholic faith.

Some of the Catholic apologists of this period were converts from high Anglicanism (e.g., R. H. Benson, R. A. Knox, S. P. Delaney) much concerned with technical points disputed between Anglicans and Roman Catholics, such as the problem of Anglican Orders. But the majority of the converts, both in England and the United States, came from broad and liberal types of Protestantism. They had become convinced that civilization would fall apart without a strong religious authority such as Catholicism alone could offer. Zealous laymen such as David Goldstein and Frank Sheed, as well as highly apostolic priests such as Fulton Sheen, Martin Scott, and John A. O'Brien, swelled the volume of Catholic apologetical writing.

The themes of the convert literature show little variety. Outside the Catholic Church religion was rapidly declining; dogma was evanescing, Church membership was shrinking (Knox). 'Protestantism was splintered into a myriad of groups' (Murray Ballantyne). The Protestant churches were in utter bewilderment on moral questions such as birth control, divorce, and spiritualism; only the

Catholic Church consistently dared to speak up against the spirit of the times and with accents of authority (Chesterton). Western civilization was still living off the accumulated capital of the ages of faith; but it was illusory to suppose that 'it is possible to conserve all of positive and constructive value in the Christian order while removing from it belief in God' (Rosalind Murray). Protestantism had an inner affinity with subjectivism and with the ultimate denial of reason; it had sired empiricism, pragmatism, and was leading to revolt against the very idea of God (Ross Hoffman). To become a Catholic was to assume a part in 'an Armageddon-fight between the old culture in which Europe was cradled, and the sharply defined materialistic forces of today' (Knox). 'The craving for unity, for consistency, for certainty . . . can be satisfied only where the principle of authority, established by Christ, stands like the rock of Gibraltar against the shifting winds of private fancy' (John A. O'Brien). 'The cold clear light of reason is all the guidance a man needs to find his way to the Church' (Lunn).

The spirit of the convert literature is reflected in some of the titles: *Rebuilding a Lost Faith* (John L. Stoddard), *Restoration* (Ross Hoffman), *The Good Pagan's Failure* (Rosalind Murray), *The Flight from Reason* and *Now I See* (Arnold Lunn), *I Had to Know* (Gladys Baker), *All or Nothing* (Murray Ballantyne)—and even by Thomas Merton's Dantesque title, *The Seven Storey Mountain*. The mood was at once rationalist and authoritarian, and on both counts restoration-ist. The world could save itself only by going back to *The Thirteenth, the Greatest of Centuries* (James J. Walsh).

Converts from English-speaking Protestantism were in general very negative toward the Church they had left. They often took the position that Protestantism as a faith was dead. Their arguments were directed toward men who loved civilization and reason rather than to firm Protestant believers. Rather different in this respect is the Catholic convert literature published on the European continent in the 1950s. Writers such as Cornelia de Vogel, Willem van de Pol, Heinrich Schlier, and Louis Bouyer continued to revere the Protestant principles upon which they had been reared; but they argued that these principles were supplemented and better protected within Catholicism. Not untypical is the chapter in Bouyer's *The Spirit and Forms of Protestantism*[57] entitled, 'The Catholic Church Necessary to the Full Flowering of the Principles of the Reformation.' The principles of the Reformation—e.g., grace alone, faith alone, Scripture alone—were still a live issue on the Continent in the 1950s as they had not been in the English-speaking world for a generation.

A similar restorationist spirit undergirded the revival of scholastic philosophy under the leadership of two brilliant French laymen, Étienne Gilson (1884–) and Jacques Maritain (1882–). Both of them were convinced that modern philosophy could not revive unless it returned to the metaphysics of *philosophia perennis* and that metaphysics itself could not survive outside of the Christian atmosphere in which it had achieved its highest development.

Gilson, who was primarily a historian of medieval philosophy, began to set forth his personal convictions in the 1930s and 1940s. In his Gifford Lectures of 1931–32 he formulated with masterly clarity his notion of Christian philosophy: 'I call Christian every philosophy which, although keeping the two orders formally distinct, nevertheless considers the Christian revelation as an indispensable auxiliary of reason.'[58] *The Spirit of Mediaeval Philosophy* by Gilson is an apologia for such a philosophy, and hence indirectly for Christianity itself. It traces the healthful impact of the Judeo-Christian revelation on medieval philosophy and shows how the scholastics were able to rise to a greater rationality thanks to their divinely given knowledge of the origin and goal of man and the world.

Several years later in *The Unity of Philosophical Experience*[59] Gilson contended that the various efforts to revive philosophy after the Middle Ages had inevitably come to nothing because they had neglected to return to the metaphysics of being, the keystone of medieval philosophy.

Speaking at the Harvard tercentenary in 1936, at a time when Hitler was rising to the peak of his power, Gilson pleaded for a restoration of medieval universalism. 'The aim and purpose of this communication,' he began, 'is to describe a certain aspect of medieval thought and medieval culture that can rightly be considered as typical of that period, and whose lasting value is so high that everything should be done to revive it under some form suitable to our own times.'[60] The principle was that truth is universal in its own right and that it belongs to mankind as a whole. The rampant nationalism of the day, according to Gilson, was the natural result of a process that began with the rejection of the authority of God. 'The sad fact is that after losing our common faith, our common philosophy, and our common art, we are in great danger of losing even our common science and exchanging it for state-controlled dogmas.'[61] The clear implication was that men should return to a common faith, authoritatively determined, in order to safeguard the values of science and philosophy.

Jacques Maritain, a convert to the faith in 1906, devoted his life to the dissemination of Thomism, which he viewed as a philosophy that had been born in and could not survive outside of a Christian atmosphere. 'I am convinced,' he wrote, 'that what the world and civilization have lacked in the intellectual order for three centuries has been a philosophy which would develop its autonomous exigencies in a Christian climate, a wisdom of reason not closed but open to the wisdom of grace.'[62]

Believing in the *de facto* dependence of nature on grace and of reason upon revelation, Maritain advocated as the basis for society a theistic and Christian humanism.[63] There were basically only two forms of humanism, he believed: an anthropocentric humanism that so deformed the image of man that it invited the demons of Communism and Fascism; and a theocentric humanism—or humanism of the Incarnation—that acknowledged both man's dignity in relation to God and man's sinfulness in relation to the Fall and the Crucifixion. 'The only way of regeneration for the human community is a rediscovery of the true image of man and a definite attempt toward a new Christian civilization, a new Christendom.'[64] This new Christendom would differ from that of the Middle Ages in that it would be secular rather than sacral, but it would be authentically Christian insofar as the leaven and inspiration of the Gospel would be permitted to penetrate all the structures of life and thus sanctify the temporal order. In many of his finest books Maritain explored the relationship between the democratic ideal and the Christian outlook on the world. Maritain even more than Gilson was concerned to recommend Thomism—and hence indirectly Catholic Christianity—on the basis of its relevance to contemporary secular life.

Teilhard de Chardin

The philosophy of Gilson and Maritain, while it cannot fairly be called reactionary, took for granted the stability and essential permanence of the world order and of the systems of thought corresponding to the real. The Jesuit paleontologist Pierre Teilhard de Chardin (1881–1955), on the other hand, espoused a radically evolutionary world view. Early in life he became convinced of his vocation to be an apologist to the world of science. As he wrote in 1926, referring to a recent lecture by a Harvard professor on the dawn of thought in the animal series:

> However farfetched the notion might appear at first, I realized in the end that, *hic et nunc*, Christ was not irrelevant to the problems that interest Professor Parker; it only needed a few intermediate steps to allow a transition from his positivist psychology to a

certain spiritual outlook. This realization cheered me up. Ah, there lie the Indies that draw me more strongly than those of St. Francis Xavier![65]

In other early letters one finds him saying: 'To tear away the mask of atheism from these new currents of thought and to express them as Christian—that is my great hope, and I need not tell you that it urges me on as a vocation.' 'To point out this strong, genuine and total coherence [between science and Christian revelation], this will be my whole "apologetic."'[66]

The great objection brought against Christianity in his time, Teilhard de Chardin believed, was the suspicion that it isolates its adherents from the rest of the human family and lessens their interest in man's common tasks. Even convinced Christians, feeling cut off from their nonbelieving colleagues, were sometimes prompted to ask themselves whether they had not lost touch with the mainstream of human development. 'One of the first apologetic duties of the Christian is to show, by the logic of his religious views and still more by the logic of his action, that the Incarnate God did not come to diminish the magnificent responsibility and splendid ambition that is ours: *of becoming our own self.*'[67] In his many books, which began to be published after his death, Teilhard tried to establish that Christianity represents the highest fulfillment of personal life and lies on the main axis of the progress of the universe.

The formal structure of Teilhard's apologetic is succinctly stated in a memorandum, *How I Believe*, in which he analyzes the sources of his own conviction that Christianity is valid. Proceeding on the premise that any articulate faith arises out of a more basic and primitive faith, which must keep developing in order to maintain itself, Teilhard probes the depths of his own fundamental faith and seeks to show how it finds in Christianity its most coherent development. At the bedrock level of his own faith he finds, first of all, a belief in the *world* as a coherent system, somehow capable of being grasped as a unity. Contemplating the world, he concludes that its unity is dynamic and evolutionary; he sees it in movement toward life and consciousness. As a second article of his creed, Teilhard therefore states that he believes in *spirit* (thought, freedom, reflective awareness) as the term toward which the world is moving. Third, he sees spirit itself in man striving forward by the implicit logic of action toward an indestructible result. (Here Teilhard refers to Blondel's searching analysis of action.) If there were not an unlimited horizon ahead, the sources of man's effort would dry up. Fourth, Teilhard affirms that immortality must be personal. If life is meaningful, the best that is in man must survive—but if his personality became extinct, the best would perish. 'My personality, that is, the particular center of perception and love that my life consists in developing—it is that which is my real wealth.'[68] As the universe tends toward its consummation, persons converge in unity. For the unity to be one that preserves and develops the individuality of each, it must be a union in love. For love, instead of absorbing and annihilating what it unites, preserves the distinctness of lover and beloved. 'Union differentiates.'

In a second portion of *How I Believe* Teilhard discussed the choice of a religion. Some religion is necessary, for religion is an essential dimension of the developing collective consciousness of mankind as it seeks to relate itself to the universe as such. For himself, Teilhard confessed, no extrinsic norms, such as miracles, could be decisive; he looked rather to harmony with the personal credo expressed in the preceding pages. There seemed to be three main types of religion to be considered: the ancient Oriental religions, the new secular humanism of the West, and the Biblical faiths, among which Christianity alone appeared to Teilhard as a living option. In the Eastern religions Teilhard admired the mystical sense of cosmic unity and the yearning for transcendence, but he found that these religions gave too little place to human personality and earthly progress. He was greatly attracted to the humanitarian pantheism of the modern West, which accentuated the very elements overlooked in Asiatic religion; but Western humanitarianism stopped with the second article of Teilhard's personal creed. Since it failed to open up the prospect of personal immortality, its ceiling was too low.

Christianity appealed to Teilhard because it was *par excellence* the religion of the imperishable and the personal, but in its existing forms it seemed to give insufficient weight to man's corporate progress on this earth. Teilhard felt that some Christians were asking him to cut his ties with the earth and to scale the clouds. This defect, however, appeared remediable if Christianity could absorb what was valid in the creeds of secular science. Teilhard's was the religion of the universal Christ upon whom, as he saw it, all the religions of the world were converging.

In his masterpiece, *The Phenomenon of Man*,[69] Teilhard sketches the forward movement of the universe from the dawn of life to the present day. This progress he attributes to the influence of a real goal, a 'prime mover ahead,' called Omega. Turning then to the current situation he describes, somewhat in the style of Pascal, the 'giddiness and disorientation' that seizes upon man as he wakes up to the terrifying realization that he now stands at the spearhead of the universe, holding in his own hands the future of evolution.[70] Man cannot rise to the next level, Teilhard concludes, except through the actual influence of Omega as an operative force in the universe.

The NT idea of the cosmic Christ, Teilhard believed, super-abundantly verifies the specifications of the scientific hypothesis of Omega. This idea assures us that Omega is not just an abstract idea but a present center of attraction, a personalized star capable of eliciting and focusing the highest energies of love. The love of Christ can overcome individual and corporate egotism and assist in the planetization of mankind in a way that no human philosophy such as Marxism is capable of doing:

> Failing such a center of universal coherence, not metaphorical or theoretical but *real*, there can be no true union among totalized Mankind, and therefore no true substance. A world culminating in the Impersonal can bring us neither the warmth of attraction nor the hope of irreversibility (immortality) without which individual egotism will always have the last word. A veritable *Ego* at the summit of the world is needed for the consummation, without confounding them, of all the elemental *egos* of Earth. . . .
>
> I have talked of the 'Christian view,' but this idea is gaining ground in other circles. Was it not Camus who wrote in *Sisyphe*, 'If Man found that the Universe could love he would be reconciled'? And did not Wells, through his exponent the humanitarian biologist Steele in *The Anatomy of Frustration*, express his need to find, above and beyond humanity, a 'universal lover'?[71]

Teilhard was one of the most daring and original apologists the Church has ever known. With prophetic singlemindedness he concentrated upon what was to become, a decade after his death, the most serious problem of apologetics: the Christian significance of the secular. Not content with a superficial concordism between the current theories of science and of theology, he sought to pioneer new interdisciplinary methods. If neither science nor theology has fully accepted his results, could this not be because each remains too isolated in its own sphere?

Considering his limitations as a philosopher and a theologian, it is not surprising that Teilhard left many problems unanswered. The most serious is the question he expressly put to himself: once we have 'panchristized' the universe, integrated Christianity into cosmogenesis, and generalized Christ the Redeemer into Christ the Evolutor, 'is this still really the Christ of the Gospel?'[72]

Teilhard, of course, was convinced of the affirmative, but many other capable thinkers judge otherwise. Gilson, for instance, wrote: 'The Teilhardian theology is one more Christian gnosis, and, like gnoses from Marcion to the present, it is a *theology-fiction.* . . . I am not sure whether an Omega point of science exists, but I feel perfectly sure that in the Gospel, Jesus of Nazareth is quite another thing than the "concrete germ" of the Christ Omega.'[73] Maritain agrees with this criticism and also with Cardinal Journet, who regards Teilhardianism as a misguided apologetics—able for a time to attract some devotees of science but tending in the long run to seduce men away from orthodox Christianity. The Peasant of the Garonne asks leave of his readers to speak bluntly: 'Is it the function of apologetics to lead minds to the truth by using the seductions and approaches of any error whatever . . . or do apologetics have to lead us to Truth *via* truth?'[74]

German Apologists

Many of the Catholic apologists in Germany, while keeping an eye on developments in France and Belgium, followed a somewhat independent course, influenced by the German philosophical tradition, both the idealism of the 19th century and the phenomenology of the 20th (Brentano, Husserl, Scheler, Heidegger . . .). From the beginning of the 20th century, German apologetics showed a healthy concern with the inner unity of the Christian message and with its adequacy as an answer to man's total quest for meaning and value.

The 'new apologetic' that aroused such commotion in France at the turn of the century made only a slight impression across the Rhine. The Tübingen apologist Paul von Schanz, then in the last years of his life, commented that the scholarly tradition had failed to take sufficient account of the psychological and moral aspects of the approach to faith, which were now being fortunately reemphasized by Blondel and his associates.[75]

The most prominent fundamental theologian in the first decade of the century, Herman Schell (1850–1906), professor of apologetics at Würzburg from 1884 to 1906, tried to renew apologetics with the help of a dynamic and actualistic philosophy partly influenced by the personalism of Franz Brentano.[76] Desiring to renew Catholicism and bring it into close contact with the modern world, he wrote a book on *Catholicism as a Principle of Progress,*[77] but this, like some of his other works, was placed on the Index through the influence of more conservative Catholics.

In his works on *God and Spirit*[78] and *Religion and Revelation*[79] Schell showed himself generally in agreement with Blondel's view of the weaknesses of the prevalent forms of apologetics, but he felt that Blondel was in danger of falling into a naturalistic immanentism. In his two-volume *Christian Apology*[80] Schell tried to strike a balance between intellectualism and voluntarism, between immanentism and extrinsicism. The most important signs of credibility, he argued, were the two internal marks of wisdom and holiness, which answer respectively to man's drives for meaning and for value and to his dual aspiration for union with God in mind and will. These internal criteria of the Christian religion are, however, supplemented by two external marks, miracle and prophecy, which exhibit the coherence of revelation with the whole of reality. Miracle shows revealed religion as a victorious inbreaking of God's kingdom into the world, turning back the forces of evil. Prophecy identifies the revelation as a unified and progressive realization of God's salvific plan in human history.

In the spiritual crisis in Germany following World War I, when all values seemed to be threatened by skepticism and nihilism, the value-oriented phenomenology of Husserl and Scheler had a revivifying effect on apologetics. Max Scheler (1874–1928), who had been converted to Catholicism in his days as a student, became active as a university professor in the intellectual apostolate, especially at Cologne, where he began to teach philosophy in 1919.[81] Several years later, at the time of his divorce and remarriage, he broke with the Church and fell into a religious depression from which he seems never to have recovered.

During his Catholic period, influenced by the religious phenomenology of Rudolf Otto, Scheler argued that the experience of the holy was an irreducibly distinct act. For apologetics this implied, negatively, the futility of seeking to prove the transcendent by inference from ordinary experience. On the positive side this meant that to intuit the transcendent man must open himself in humble attentiveness to the loving self-disclosure of God, to which he must be prepared to submit in loving adoration. 'Pascal was right when he said, "Do thou but kneel, and faith will come." And so we should thus advise our man: "Try to perform the moral acts and ritual which this religion lays down, then see whether or how far you have gained in religious understanding."'[82]

The Tübingen theologian Karl Adam (1876–1966), following up on the religious phenomenology of Otto and Scheler, evolved an original value-oriented theology of faith. In his first apologetical work, *The Spirit of Catholicism*,[83] he assailed the critical theology of the past century for being mistakenly committed to the kind of scientific method suited only to the profane sciences and for behaving 'as though the living Christian faith can be resolved into a series of ideas and notions which might be examined, considered, and classified according to their provenance.'[84] The Catholic, Adam asserts, does not know Christ by piecing together the fragmentary evidences of the NT considered as an academic historical document but through the living faith of the Church as the mystical body of Christ.

In *The Son of God* and other Christological works Adam applies this approach to the problem of Jesus. Faithful to the principles of phenomenological method, he insists that the subject-matter of any investigation necessarily conditions the attitude to be taken by the inquirer and the act by which it is to be apprehended. Religious knowledge, he maintains, is specifically distinct from every kind of secular knowledge; it involves not merely the intellect but the whole man, including the will and the emotions. Thus, one seeking to solve the question of Jesus by the techniques of secular history finds that 'the critical boring tool breaks off when the real question first emerges, that of the supernatural being and activity of Christ.'[85]

In accordance with his declared method Adam does not hesitate to present a deeply religious and even theological apologetic. On every page of his study he confronts the reader with profoundly existential questions of faith. He concentrates on the inner life and divine consciousness of Jesus rather than on the exact chronology of His words and deeds. When he comes to discuss the Resurrection he views it as a supernatural manifestation of Jesus as Lord and Savior. Like Karl Barth, Adam was able to face with equanimity and even with some satisfaction the collapse of the 19th-century 'quest of the historical Jesus,' whose funeral oration had been pronounced by Albert Schweitzer. The immense popularity of Adam's books among seminarians and laity alike were clear signs that he met a religious need not adequately filled by the scholastic textbooks of the day.

Since World War II the dominant influence in Catholic apologetics has perhaps been that of the systematic theologian Karl Rahner (1904–). Working on the basis of an original blend of the transcendental Thomism of Joseph Maréchal and the existential phenomenology of Martin Heidegger, Rahner has delved deeply into the philosophy of religion and the credibility of the Christian proclamation. His early work *Hearers of the Word*[86] takes up the Blondelian question of man's obligation to concern himself with the question of supernatural revelation. On the basis of a sound philosophical anthropology and natural theology, Rahner maintains, it is antecedently clear that God could freely reveal Himself and that if He were to do so His revelation would have to come to man in a social and historical way (that is, a way proportioned to man's nature as a socio-historical being). Man's highest task, therefore, is to interrogate the history of the human race for signs as to whether God has disclosed Himself. In certain polemical passages Rahner argues that the Protestant philosophy of religion falls either into a modernistic rationalism *à la* Schleiermacher or into a fideistic agnosticism *à la* Barth.[87] Everything leads up to the conclusion: 'Whoever reckons with the possibility that a specific portion of human history, to the exclusion of others, may be God's history, is bound to believe a revelation in the Catholic sense.'[88]

This early excursion into the philosophy of religion does not, even in the revised edition, do justice to Rahner's mature thought. His later writings on the approaches to faith are profoundly affected by his conviction that the reason of all men is supernaturally elevated by grace and therefore oriented toward explicitly Christian faith.[89] To awaken explicit faith, then, one must never present the contents of Christian revelation as an extraneous element foreign to the hearer's personal experience but rather as an interpretation of that which the individual in his depth experience has already encountered through the inner workings of grace. The primary task of the apologist, then, is to exhibit how the whole system of Christian teaching is the one complete answer to the primordial question that man is to himself. To the ineluctable question, how the transcendent ground of being is related to human existence, Christianity responds: as merciful intimacy in the radical self-communication of God in Jesus Christ.

To furnish a scientific historical demonstration of the Christian fact today, according to Rahner, is an immensely complex task, beyond the normal possibilities of the individual believer or even those of the individual theologian. But belief is nevertheless a reasonable attitude. To one who has opened himself to the Christian interpretation of man as divinized through Christ, every other view of human life seems less meaningful and less inspiring. The objections from the various sciences are too peripheral and trivial to outweigh the total vision of man's nature and destiny offered by the gospel as understood in the Catholic Church.[90]

In his recent writings Rahner has been more concerned with the implications of the gospel for man's life in the world. He accepts the Teilhardian vision of man as the shaper of his own innerworldly destiny, with all the terrible responsibility that this implies. Without renouncing his original transcendental Thomism, he accepts an evolutionary and future-oriented doctrine of man and religion. He sees the religions of the world as flowing together into a single stream in the present age of planetization. In integrating certain elements of secular theology with a basically Thomistic personalism, Rahner has received much support and occasional criticism from younger colleagues such as Edward Schillebeeckx (1914–) and J. B. Metz (1928–), two of the outstanding Catholic proponents of Christian secularity.

In any complete account of 20th-century German apologetics it would be necessary to discuss many other writers. In this cursory sketch of the main lines of development, significant authors such as Hans Urs von Balthasar—several of whose major works might be considered apologetical in character—as well as apologists of a more traditional sort such as Alois Riedmann, Albert Lang, and Heinrich Fries will be left aside. From the perspectives of a later generation, it will doubtless be easier to discern their contribution to the total development of Catholic apologetics.

PROTESTANT APOLOGETICS

English-Speaking Conservatives and Liberals

At the beginning of the 20th century conservative Protestant apologetics was ably represented in both England and the United States. One such able conservative was Benjamin B. Warfield (1851–1921) of Princeton Theological Seminary. In an encyclopedia article on apologetics published in 1908 he maintained that the business of apologetics is to establish the truth of Christianity as the absolute religion, directly and as a whole. Apologetics consequently takes its place 'at the head of the departments of theological science, and finds its task in the establishment of that knowledge of God which forms the subject-matter of these departments.'[91] He set himself in opposition to the Ritschlian bifurcation between theoretical and religious knowledge, which in his view would undermine apologetics by asserting that religion is not the object of rational proof.

In the face of mounting attacks on the inspiration and inerrancy of the Bible, followers of Warfield's type of rational apologetics found themselves ranged on the conservative side of the Fundamentalist-Modernist controversy that rocked American Protestantism in the 1st third of the century. Beginning with the publication, in 1909, of the first volume of *The Fundamentals*, fundamentalist apologists were heavily engaged in polemics against liberal Protestants regarding specific points such as Biblical criticism, the Virgin birth, Christ's atoning death, the evolution of man, and the social gospel.

Meanwhile, an apologetics of accommodation was being practiced by liberal theologians. A moderate representative of this school may be found in the English 'liberal Catholic' prelate Charles Gore (1853–1932). In the preface to a programmatic work that he edited under the title *Lux mundi* Gore expressed the aim of his lifetime apostolate. 'Our purpose,' he wrote, 'was to "succour a distressed faith" by endeavouring to bring the Christian Creed to its right relation to the modern growth of knowledge, scientific, historical, critical; and to the modern problems of politics and ethics.'[92] In *The Reconstruction of Belief*[93] Gore analyzed the major shocks to religious belief that had come from the Darwinian theory, Biblical criticism, comparative religion, and the revolt of the modern conscience against the Calvinistic ideas regarding hell and atonement. He sought to show how faith could be renewed on the basis of a critical reappraisal of the Biblical and traditional heritage, taking advantage of all the tools of modern scholarship. In a volume replying to his critics, *Can We Then Believe?*[94] Gore restated his conviction that it is possible to find a *via media* between blind conservatism and rootless modernism.

Both conservative and liberal apologetics were taken to task by Harvard's Willard L. Sperry in his *'Yes, But—' The Bankruptcy of Apologetics*. In either form, says Sperry, apologetics is but an unsatisfactory compromise between the old faith and new knowledge. 'The religious mind does not like to qualify its beliefs and the scientific mind does not care to qualify its truths.'[95] The apologist is drafted for the 'sorry service' of trying to defend religion against the honest efforts of the human mind to discover what is so. After first taking the position that new scientific theories are false, apologetics is forced in the end reluctantly to concede the validity of new theories.[96] Religion deserves no credit for conceding at a late date truths it should have gladly welcomed from the beginning. In place of apologetics the religious mind should content itself with seeking the truth and be prepared to follow wherever the evidence may lead. Yet toward the end of his book Sperry, the convinced Christian, falls into something like apologetics himself. He says that 'the closer one seems to come to the man [Jesus] himself the more impertinent and irrelevant conventional apologetics become. We should have the courage and generosity to go as far as is historically possible in letting him stand in his own right and speak his own words, whether we hear or whether we forbear. That is the only useful Christian apologetic.'[97]

In the aftermath of World War II there was a certain revival of conservative Evangelical apologetics in the United States. The Northern Baptist theologian Carl C. F. Henry composed a number of apologias, such as *Remaking the Modern Mind* (1946) and *Giving a Reason for Our Hope* (1949), in which he castigated the relativistic and naturalistic tendencies of modern philosophy and argued that Christian faith in revelation was the highest rationality.[98] As contrasted with classical Thomism, this school of apologetics denies the power of the unredeemed intellect to reason correctly about religious questions; but it asserts with Luther and especially Calvin that redeemed reason can see the validity of the Christian evidences. These authors generally make only minimal concessions to modern historical and scientific criticism, and keep close to the 'obvious sense' of the Bible.

Dialectical Theology

In the period between the two world wars the most potent opposition to liberal theology within Protestantism came not from evangelical conservatism but rather from the dialectical theology developed by Karl Barth (1886–1968) and his circle. In general Barth is antipathetic to apologetics. In the early chapters of his *Church Dogmatics*[99] he raises the question whether prolegomena should be admitted as a pretheological discipline. The usual answer, he says, is that of Emil Brunner, who holds that in this day, when the very existence of God and of revelation is widely called into question, it is necessary to show initially that there is in the human situation a point of contact for the divine message and that the Word of God is a gratuitous fulfillment of what reason by itself cannot achieve. Barth rejects this position on three grounds. First, he argues that these times are not singular, for there has always been opposition to the Christian faith. The contention that revelation is a fulfillment of religious aspirations rests on the false supposition that Christianity is merely a special case within the genus of revelation as a whole.

Second, Barth objects that no amount of anthropological study can establish man's capacity to discern divine revelation. Revelation creates within man the capacity to perceive it; hence there is no justification for an extratheological basis for theology. If it be true that the revelation, when it comes, must be presented with a view to the concrete situation of men, this is not a prolegomenon for dogmatics but rather a consequence flowing from the knowledge of revelation.

Third, according to Barth a really up-to-date dogmatic theology will establish its own relevance to modern man by appearing 'on the spot, as the witness of faith against unbelief. . . . There has never been any other effective apologetic and polemic of faith against unbelief than the unintended one . . . which took place when God Himself sided with the witness of faith.'[100] When apologetics as a special discipline assumes the task of going out to meet the unbeliever, it runs the risk of losing its own theological character, and by separating itself from theology it leaves theology out of contact with the modern world.[101]

In the chapter on Schleiermacher to which allusion has already been made,[102] Barth gives a portrayal of the dangers involved in the type of apologetics that seeks to commend the Christian message to the world of the day. The apologist, says Barth, must go out to the enemy 'carrying a white flag' and must seek to mediate between belief and unbelief from a superior position, from which he can be just to both parties.[103] This cannot but be damaging to Christianity.

In a later volume of his *Church Dogmatics*, however, Barth makes room for a 'supplementary, incidental and implicit apologetics' that proceeds from revelation and from the constraint that the word of God imposes on man, and seeks to differentiate between the true knowledge of God and the false knowledge of idolatry.[104] In his study of Anselm, Barth gives an illustration of how the believer can go out to meet the unbeliever without compromise or betrayal of the faith. Anselm, he suggests, in his desire to convince the unbeliever, crossed the gulf 'on this occasion not in search of a truce . . . but . . . as a conqueror whose weapon was the fact that he met the unbelievers as one of them and accepted them as his equal.'[105] This tactic could be successful, Barth intimates, because the grace of God went ahead of the defender of the faith. In the end, therefore, Barth seems to make room for an apologetic that proceeds from faith and that addresses itself at least in appearance to unbelievers.

Of Barth's companion in arms in the early days of dialectical theology, Emil Brunner (1889–1966), it has been correctly said that his 'entire theology has an apologetic character.'[106] By apologetical, or as he prefers to call it, eristic, theology Brunner means the intellectual discussion of the Christian faith in the light of the ideologies of the present day that are opposed to it.[107] The principal task of apologetics, according to Brunner, is not to set Christian faith on the platform of some previous rational understanding of reality, still less to prove it by reference to this, but rather to reflect on faith with a view to exposing the falsity of reason's understanding of itself. Apologetics thus aims to defend Christian faith against the misunderstandings that originate from man's sinful abuse of reason. Since these objections are identical with the believer's own temptations against the faith, apologetics is not, according to Brunner, self-righteous.

In Brunner as in many other contemporary Protestant theologians (even Barth might perhaps be included) apologetics is not a distinct discipline but rather a dimension of all theology. A few years before his death, Brunner wrote: 'As a matter of fact these two tasks, apologetics and dogmatics, cannot be separated from each other. Every dogmatic statement is at the same time an apologetic-polemic statement and vice versa.'[108]

Rudolf Bultmann (1884–   ) takes an attitude toward apologetics that might be described as intermediate between the predominantly negative view of Barth and the highly positive stance of Brunner. With regard to the celebrated dispute about whether there is in human nature a 'point of insertion' for the gospel, he sides rather with Brunner than with Barth. Man, he says, has a necessary and permanent relationship to God, in advance of God's revelation in Christ. 'Man's life is moved by the search for God because it is always moved, consciously or unconsciously, by the question about his own personal existence. The question of God and the question of myself are identical.'[109] But man's personal relationship to God, which is decisive for faith, can be made real only by God and cannot be discovered by man himself. 'God's revelation is not at the beck and call of human criteria: it is not a phenomenon within the world, but his act alone. And he alone must know whether and how he wishes to speak to us.'[110] Not even the so-called facts of revelation—the great and wonderful deeds of God—can constitute grounds of faith except 'as perceived by faith itself.'[111] The effort to secure faith by rational proofs, according to Bultmann, undermines faith by making it depend on something else—and this something else proves in the long run to be insecure. 'He who thinks that it is possible to speak of wonders [miracles] as of demonstrable events capable of proof offends against the thought of God as acting in hidden ways. He subjects God's action to the control of objective observation. He delivers up the faith in wonders to the criticism of science and in so doing validates such criticism.'[112]

As a New Testament critic Bultmann feels that he is in no way undermining faith when he casts doubt upon the historical accuracy of various reports concerning the miracles and Resurrection of Jesus. For with him it is a principle that God's action in Jesus Christ is 'not a fact of past history open to historical verification.'[113] 'We cannot buttress our own faith in the resurrection by that of the first disciples and so eliminate the element of risk which faith in the resurrection always involves.'[114]

In spite of Bultmann's apparent indifference to any positive program of apologetics, his famous demythologizing program is partly motivated by an apologetic intent. Holding that the stumbling block of faith cannot and should not be removed, he adds that one should remove the false stumbling block that is presented for contemporary man when he is asked to accept the Christian preaching in mythological form. 'To demythologize is to deny that the message of Scripture and of the Church is bound to an ancient world-view which is obsolete.'[115]

Barth is therefore on good ground when he suggests that although 'Bultmann and his disciples are annoyed if we call him an apologist,' Bultmann is concerned, as Schleiermacher was, 'to make Biblical exegesis, theology in general, and preaching in particular, relevant and interesting for its cultured despisers.' And, Barth adds, 'Surely theologians have always been apologists in some sense; they could hardly help it.'[116]

A fourth major representative of dialectical theology, Paul Tillich (1886–1965) developed an original and penetrating doctrine regarding the nature and value of apologetics. He adverted to the present disrepute into which apologetics had fallen and ascribed this to two main reasons.[117] In the first place—and here his statements resemble those of Sperry—apologists have often tried to take advantage of the gaps in scientific knowledge in order to find room for the divine. This has involved apologetics in a series of graceless and humiliating retreats. Each time science increased its capacity of explanation, theology had to find new lacunae as the loci of the divine mystery.

Second, as Barth and the kerygmatic theologians point out, theology endangers its proper autonomy when it seeks to ground itself in knowledge that does not depend on revelation. Once theology has to appeal to criteria that can be verified outside of faith, it is in danger of sacrificing its distinctive character and of falling away from the kerygma that should be the criterion of all theological statements.

Tillich, however, does not draw the Barthian conclusion that the Christian message must be thrown 'like a stone' at those who stand outside the believing community. He holds that theology, without loss of its proper principles, can show that the Christian message is relevant to man in the existential situation in which he finds himself. In Tillich's 'method of correlation' apologetics has the task of showing that the symbols used in the Christian message respond to man's existential questions—the profoundly personal questions that are 'we ourselves.'

For Tillich, therefore, apologetics is not a non-theological preamble to theology; it is not a sheerly philosophical or historical discipline having a merely extrinsic relationship to faith. For him as for Brunner apologetics is 'an omnipresent element and not a special section of systematic theology.'[118] 'The method of correlation explains the content of the Christian faith through existential questions and theological answers in mutual interdependence.'[119] It is not as though man operating independently of God asked the questions, and God subsequently by a supernatural intervention supplied the answers. Rather, according to Tillich, 'symbolically speaking, God answers man's questions, and under the impact of God's answers man asks them.'[120] Theology, insofar as it is apologetic, has to organize the materials provided in the human situation, in a given cultural context, in relation to the answers provided by the Christian message.

A fifth theologian who is in some ways related to the dialectical movement is Reinhold Niebuhr (1892–   ). As Alan Richardson says, Niebuhr is too critical of the presuppositions of this age to be a conventional apologist. More the prophet, he prefers to criticize and even repudiate the prevailing ideas and values in terms of which nonbelievers might be inclined to judge the worth of the Gospel.[121] But, as Richardson goes on to show, Niebuhr in his capacity as prophet seeks to arouse thoughtful people to the realization that the insights of the Bible have existential relevance for the problems of man and society today. In his Gifford Lectures, *The Nature and Destiny of Man*,[122] Niebuhr engages in a profound critique of modern culture from the point of view of the Christian vision of man and society. In this and other works he succeeds in showing how traditional Christian doctrines, notably the Pauline-Lutheran doctrine of salvation by faith, are capable of illuminating the issues of the 20th century. The central thrust of Niebuhr's apologetic is indicated by the following remarks on the validation of the Gospel:

> The Christian Gospel is negatively validated by the evidence that both forms of worldly wisdom, leading to optimism and to pessimism, give an inadequate view of the total human situation. This evidence is partly derived from the testimony which the optimists and the pessimists bear against each other.
> . . . There is nevertheless a positive apologetic task. It consists in correlating the truth, apprehended by faith and repentance, to truths about life and history, gained generally in experience. Such a correlation validates the truth of faith insofar as it proves it to be a source and center of an interpretation of life, more

adequate than alternative interpretations, because it comprehends all of life's antinomies and contradictions into a system of meaning and is conducive to a renewal of life.[123]

Reinhold's brother, H. Richard Niebuhr (1894–1962), in his book *The Meaning of Revelation*, was strongly critical of Schleiermacher and Ritschl on the ground that they wanted to justify Christianity before the bar of reason as the best religion. In the place of apologetical self-defensiveness, Niebuhr called for a 'resolutely confessional theology' that would renounce any claim to superior knowledge or virtue.[124] But Richard Niebuhr does not seem to have totally avoided apologetics. As several critics have pointed out, much of his own theology may be characterized as a rational defense of 'radical monotheism,'[125] a stance that in his view liberates man from subservience to any creature and makes him objectively critical of himself.

The six theologians here treated under the heading of dialectical theology do not constitute a single school. They have sharply disagreed with one another; but within their disagreements they have reciprocally influenced one another, and by their joint labors they were largely responsible for the revitalization of the Protestant churches in the 1940s and 1950s.

From the present standpoint, the most striking common trait of these authors is their refusal to erect any system of criteria that would permit the Christian message to be adequately evaluated from a position outside of faith. They tend to soft-pedal miracles—whether physical or intellectual or moral—if these are taken to be extrinsic signs validating Christianity in the eyes of unaided reason. They stress the demand for an inner conversion or repentance—in the Biblical sense of *metanoia*—as the prerequisite for judging the credibility of the gospel. This conversion takes place through a prophetic proclamation of the Christian message; and the proclamation finds a point of impact in man thanks to his God-given restlessness toward the divine. Apologetics in this view is not adequately distinct from preaching. It is the adaptation of Christian preaching to the existential needs of man in a particular sociocultural situation. Thanks to its meaningfulness and illuminative power, the gospel properly proclaimed is its own apologetic.

Germany since 1930

Notwithstanding the influence of the dialectical school some Protestant theologians in Germany continued to ply a rather traditional type of apologetics in the tradition of Sack and Tholuck. The most prolific was Karl Heim (1874–1958),[126] who taught at Tübingen from 1920 until his retirement and who wrote in answer to his Catholic colleague Karl Adam a work on *The Nature of Protestantism*.[127] His principal life work was to mediate to the modern secular mind the fruits of the Swabian pietistic faith in which he had been reared, and to this end he composed a six-volume *summa*, *The Evangelical Faith and the Thought of the Present*, which has been translated into English.[128]

Unlike Barth, Heim was convinced that God-talk had to be made meaningful to the modern secular mind; unlike Bultmann he believed that this could be done without radically changing the traditional content of Christian doctrine. Faithful to the Lutheran tradition, he avoids founding his apologetics on any kind of natural theology or seeking to reason from some common premises acceptable both to believers and nonbelievers. Instead he seeks to establish the incapacity of autonomous reason to achieve ultimate answers and in this way to make the secular thinker receptive to the word of God.

Heim is at his best in unmasking the idols of secular man. He makes deft use of Einstein's relativity and Heisenberg's indeterminism in order to show that modern physics has eliminated the very conception of an absolute object. If there is anything on which man can rely unconditionally and to which he can cleave with his whole heart, Heim reasons, this must be sought in the realm of the nonobjective. Then he proceeds to explain the notion of the transcendent in a manner that could make sense to modern secular man. In one's moral decisions, Heim believes, he encounters a dimension of depth that lies hidden to objective thinking. In this hidden dimension Heim finds the divine transcendence.

Finally Heim commends the Christian idea of Jesus as Lord and Savior to a generation all too inclined to worship human leaders. In the notion of Jesus as sole redeemer Heim sees the divine remedy not only for the guilt of sin but also for the despair of skepticism. Thus, as Althaus points out, Heim concocts a kind of natural theology out of modern skepticism and relativism.[129] The greatest weakness in his system is perhaps his unwillingness to rethink the traditional Christian doctrines in the light of a modern understanding of the universe. 'The latest insights of natural science are used by Heim to justify traditional views of creation, miracle, and eschatology—views which many exegetes and theologians are no longer able to purvey as either mandatory or meaningful.'[130]

Dietrich Bonhoeffer (1906–45), who studied briefly under Heim

I

at Tübingen, may have been partly indebted to his old teacher for his preoccupation with making Christianity meaningful to modern secular man. Like Heim, Bonhoeffer criticized Barth for his demand that modern man should be expected to submit to the gospel without first seeing it as a meaningful and credible message. But Bonhoeffer took a far more favorable view of the mature, serene secularist than Heim and other theologians of that day. Secularism, he believed, was correct in holding that man was himself responsible for the future of the world and in refusing to appeal to any *deus ex machina*. The whole effort of modern apologetics to keep man in dependence on religious forces Bonhoeffer considered illegitimate:

> The attack by Christian apologetic on the adulthood of the world I consider to be in the first place pointless, in the second place ignoble, and in the third place unchristian. Pointless, because it seems to me like an attempt to put a grown-up man back into adolescence, i.e. to make him dependent, and thrusting him into problems that are, in fact, no longer problems to him. Ignoble, because it amounts to an attempt to exploit man's weakness for purposes that are alien to him and to which he has not freely assented. Unchristian, because it confuses Christ with one particular stage in man's religiousness, i.e. with a human law.[131]

This triple indictment is directed particularly at the apologetics of Heim and Tillich. 'Heim sought, along pietist and methodist lines, to convince the individual man that he was faced with the alternative, "either despair or Jesus." He gained "hearts."' Tillich, in Bonhoeffer's opinion, set out to drive modern man into a kind of existential despair, so that he would be impelled to look for God in the threatening 'border situations' of life. 'That was very brave of him, but the world unseated him and went on by itself.'[132]

While Bonhoeffer rejected any apologetics based on the religious premise, his theology left room for a type of secular apologetic based on the capacity of Christianity to lead man to responsible maturity. Elements of such an apologetic may be most clearly glimpsed in the work of Friedrich Gogarten (1887–1967), who argued that Christian faith sustains the process of secularization.[133] It liberates man from the world, considered as an enclosed and enclosing entity; in Pauline language, it delivers man from subjection to the elemental powers (cf. Gal 4.9–10). Once the world is desacralized by monotheistic faith, man becomes lord of the visible universe, responsible for it and for his own history. For Gogarten secularization is the working out in history of the Pauline-Lutheran doctrine of justification by faith.

Faith is necessary not only to de-divinize the world but also to interpret the secularized world and to prevent it from falling prey to its own ideologies.

The theology of secularization launched by Bonhoeffer and Gogarten has made a powerful impact outside Germany. The Dutch missiologist Arend van Leeuwen has presented a total panorama of world history as a process of progressive secularization taking place under the aegis of Biblical faith.[134] Western technology, according to van Leeuwen, is a form of preevangelization of the non-Christian world—a necessary preconditioning for its conversion to the Christian faith.

In a more popular vein, best sellers such as Bishop J. A. T. Robinson's *Honest to God* and Harvey Cox's *The Secular City* have promoted the apologetics of Christian secularity. The most recent trend in Protestant apologetics thus mirrors in some respects the secular concern already noted in Catholic authors such as Teilhard de Chardin and J. B. Metz.

It is doubtful whether a convincing apologetic can be erected on the sole ground that Christianity contributes to secularization. The sacred has always occupied too prominent a place in Christianity for anyone to be drawn to Christianity in order to escape from the sacred. Besides, it could easily be objected that secularization was imposed upon Christianity reluctantly by the forces of the Enlightenment and that the success of secularity in no way depends upon Christian influences. At best the apologist might be able to show that for those who live by faith secularity does not constitute the threat to moral and spiritual values that it might otherwise entail.

Another very active area of apologetics in the past two decades in Germany has been the question of the historical Jesus. The efforts of the liberal theologians of the 19th century to reconstruct a historical Jesus according to their own predilections had been effectively demolished by Johannes Weiss and Albert Schweitzer at the turn of the century. This left the field open for Bultmann to deny the religious importance of the history of Jesus and to base his faith entirely on the faith and preaching of the post-Easter community. For this position Bultmann claimed the apologetical advantage that it made faith invulnerable to the assaults of historical criticism and left the historian free to follow the demands of his discipline without extrinsic pressure from the Church to reach some results rather than others. Many theologians, however, rebelled against Bultmann's separation of Christological faith from scientific history.

Paul Althaus, one of the most outstanding Lutheran confessional theologians of the mid-20th century, holds that one has no right to dismiss historical criticism as irrelevant on the ground that its supposed results are always subject to further questioning. To neglect the history of Jesus would be, in effect, to surrender His true humanity. Theology, according to Althaus, must accept the tension between the essentially inconclusive results of scientific historical knowledge and the assurance of the faith encounter that it mediates. 'The revelatory character of the history of Jesus is not known by means of historical reflection or historical reasoning. But on the other hand it is not known *without these*. For the gospel deals with facts which, it is claimed, happened in this history of ours; it has "historical facts" as content, and its foundation in history is a part of its credibility.'[135] Implicitly, then, Althaus seems to affirm that a historical apologetic can bring the unbeliever part way toward being in a position to make the assent of faith and can prevent the conscientious believer from being put in a position of having to renounce his faith in the flesh-and-blood Jesus.

A number of Bultmann's disciples—including Gerhard Ebeling, Ernst Käsemann, Günther Bornkamm, and Ernst Fuchs—all of whom hold important chairs in German universities, reject his dissolution of the bonds between faith and scientific history on the ground that it makes Christian faith indistinguishable from commitment to a mythical Lord. While eschewing the liberal effort to reconstruct the outward aspect of Jesus' career—His works, His deeds, and the chronology of His life—they believe that existential history, utilizing the earliest traditions of the NT, can reconstruct Jesus' existential self-understanding and thus unveil the true intention and meaning of His life. In this way, according to James M. Robinson, an American admirer of the post-Bultmannian school, the new quest can establish 'not that the *kerygma* is true but that the existential decision with regard to the *kerygma* is an existential decision with regard to Jesus.'[136] This identity would seem to pertain to apologetics insofar as it would be hard to accept a kerygma that rested on a misinterpretation of Jesus' true intention.

The new quest represents a real advance over the positivistic historiography of the old quest, with its ironclad presuppositions and rules of evidence. But Robinson's effort to point out the novelty of the post-Bultmannian quest betrays him into some exaggerations. He makes it appear almost as though Jesus' self-understanding could be known without careful scrutinizing of the evidences regarding His words and deeds. As Van A. Harvey remarks, the new quest 'puts the heaviest weight on just those kinds of historical judgments which, from a logical point of view, are the least capable of bearing it. By regarding historical inquiry as culminating in claims about a person's existential selfhood, it defines historical knowledge in terms of the weakest of its epistemological links.'[137]

In the 1960s a new development in apologetical theology has been promoted through the efforts of Wolfhart Pannenberg (1928–) and his circle.[138] They are seeking to establish the case for Christianity not on the credibility of an authoritative word but on the 'language of facts.' The Christian revelation, as Pannenberg understands it, coincides with a rational interpretation of the total course of world history. In the Resurrection of Jesus, he maintains, the total meaning of history is disclosed insofar as the end of history is proleptically made present. The Easter event, according to Pannenberg, is as reliably attested as any event in the ancient world.

Pannenberg's position is as yet too new to have an assured place in the history of apologetics. He has been accused of owing more to Hegel than to the Bible, and some of his statements are indeed reminiscent of the 19th-century semirationalists. But as he continues to write he has been introducing distinctions that seemed to be lacking in his original programmatical declarations. For example, he now admits and even insists that historical fact includes the 'transmission of traditions,' and by this device reintroduces much of the authoritative word-theology that he previously seemed to repudiate. It may be that Pannenberg's position when fully developed will come closer to that of Barth and the more moderate members of the Bultmann school, although it is the fideism of the kerygmatic school that he primarily set out to attack.

England since 1930

Anglican apologetics in the past generation has followed a middle way, sometimes inclining more toward Barthian kerygmatic theology, sometimes more toward Thomistic natural theology, but always avoiding the extremes of fideism and rationalism.

One of the Anglicans who came closest to dialectical theology was Sir Edwyn Clement Hoskyns (1884–1937), who after adhering for some time to the 'liberal Catholicism' of Gore was deeply affected by reading (about 1924 or 1925) Barth's *Epistle to the Romans*, which he later translated into admirable English. While he came to look upon the kingdom of God as a sudden and unexpected in-breaking of divine righteousness that brings man's highest idealism under judgment, Hoskyns did not believe that this position precluded a rational approach to the decision of faith making full use of the techniques of exact historical research. *The Riddle of the New Testament,* a work written by Hoskyns in collaboration with Noel Davey, is a fascinating piece of historicoliterary detective work. It argues on the basis of the independent and converging testimony of all the NT traditions that the Christological interpretation of Jesus' career could not possibly have been superimposed at a later date on an originally unchristological history and hence that Jesus Himself must have regarded His ministry as that of the Messiah inaugurating the kingdom of God.[139] Historical analysis thus confronts the reader with the challenge of Jesus Himself, whose claims were no less foreign to His own age than to the present one. 'The gospel was as much a scandal to the first century as it is to the twentieth.'[140] With an eloquence approaching Barth's Hoskyns brought out in the Bible those sharp, scandalous, and challenging notes that had been muted by the liberal theologians of the preceding generation.[141]

During the next decade the most vigorous apologetics among Protestants and Anglicans in Britain was conducted by NT scholars. The Congregationalist NT professor Charles H. Dodd (1884–) defended the authenticity of the apostolic preaching as summarized in the sermons attributed to Peter and Paul in the early chapters of Acts. This primitive kerygma, according to Dodd, was historically accurate and constitutes the very heart of the NT message.[142] Thus British Biblical scholarship in the hands of experts such as Dodd gave impressive support to Barth's kerygmatic theology and was generally unfavorable to Bultmann's dehistoricized reinterpretation of the kerygma.

In the 1930s and 1940s the Church of England was blessed by a number of talented authors such as T. S. Eliot, Charles Williams, and Dorothy Sayers who ventured into the realm of apologetics. The most influential lay apologist of this group was C. S. Lewis (1898–1963), who without profoundly investigating theological questions showed the plausibility of the traditional understanding of the Christian message. In *The Problem of Pain* (1940), *The Case for Christianity* (1943), and *Miracles* (1947) he proved himself a master of popularizing the Christian idea of a transcendent, personal, and provident God and of exposing the fallacies behind many of the common objections. In his allegorical novels and satires Lewis reached a vast number of readers who would not have found time for technical theological works.[143]

Several of the Anglican apologists of this period shared the enthusiasm of their Roman Catholic brethren for Thomas Aquinas.

Austin Farrer (1904–) in his *Finite and Infinite* (1943) composed a careful defense of natural theology, as did Eric L. Mascall (1905–) in his *He Who Is*, published the same year. Mascall's Bampton Lectures, *Christian Theology and Natural Science* (1943), explored many disputed border areas where there might be question of inter-disciplinary conflict between theology and the physical sciences. More recently, in *The Secularization of Christianity* (1965), Mascall has criticized some of the philosophical weaknesses and incon-sistencies in the new secular theology as propounded by J. A. T. Robinson and Paul van Buren.

The most prominent Anglican specialist in apologetics since World War II is probably Alan Richardson (1905–). Rejecting what he takes to be the Thomistic view—that autonomous reason can even in theory bring men to a natural knowledge of God and of grounds of credibility—he holds, with the Augustinian theologians, that reason must be assisted by the light of grace in order to rise from its fallen state. In his apologetics Richardson seeks to show that the Christian affirmations measure up to the exigencies of reason enlightened by faith.

The central argument in Richardson's principal apologetical works is, in effect, that Christianity offers an interpretation of history more coherent and adequate to the totality of the evidence than do the various rival views, including scientific rationalism. For one thing, Christian faith can make sense of Biblical testimonies that others have to explain away with considerable embarrassment. Furthermore, 'the events of our own contemporary history are best understood in the light of Christian faith in God's judgment and mercy in history.'[144] 'There is a universality and finality about the Christian faith which makes it relevant to the whole human race in every age and place, and which . . . has no parallel in the history of the world.' Christ is confessed by men of every nation as 'the Light of the world and the desire of all nations.'[145]

In order to ground these sweeping generalizations Richardson has given considerable attention to the nature of historical thinking. Following Dilthey, Collingwood, and Becker he holds that history should not aim at strictly scientific objectivity but should make liberal allowance for personal interpretation and evaluation. Under-stood in this way the category of history is wide enough to include miracles and even the Resurrection of Jesus. Richardson therefore rejects Bornkamm's statement that the faith of the Easter faith of the disciples is the 'last fact' accessible to the historian.[146]

Richardson shows, moreover, that the Resurrection of Jesus is not a totally anomalous event.[147] It has intelligibility insofar as it brings to a climax a whole series of revelatory events beginning with the Exodus cycle. While the reality of these revelatory events cannot be strictly demonstrated from a position outside faith, they can be discerned as credible by those to whom it is given to participate in analogous 'disclosure situations.'

This summary of Richardson has been too brief to do justice to the complexity of his positions or to afford a sufficient basis for criticism. But it may be proper to point out some questions commonly put to Richardson by his critics.[148] They ask if he admits a valid distinction between fact and interpretation. Are there some 'facts' that impose themselves on all men of judgment and good will by virtue of undeniable evidences? Is there a nonconfessional historical method that can be used by believers and unbelievers to establish an agreed corpus of facts of this character? If there are further facts that are admitted only by believers, is there some way of showing non-believers that believers have the better position? If so, why should Richardson have to appeal to the subjective point of view established by the grace of faith? If not, must the apologist renounce any effort to shield the believer from the charge of arbitrariness?

However these questions may ultimately be answered, it seems clear that in raising them Richardson has focused on issues of vital concern. He makes a good case for Christianity as a coherent interpretation of the total course of human history.

CONCLUSION

From the point of view of apologetical productivity, the 20th century has seen both progress and decline. Among Protestants, apart from conservative Evangelical groups, there have not been numerous authors primarily engaged in formally apologetical work. Karl Heim is one of the few major theologians commonly characterized as an apologist. The Anglicans, especially in the 1940s, have had a good number of apologists, many of whom have written in a light and popular vein. Catholic apologetics was particularly prolific especially in France during the 1st third of the century. The era of Gardeil, Garrigou-Lagrange, Grandmaison, and the *Apologetical Dictionary of the Catholic Faith* marks one of the high points in the history of Catholic apologetics. About the same time England experienced a Renaissance of Catholic literary activity led by apologists such as G. K. Chesterton.

In the 3d and 4th decades of the century, however, the legitimacy of apologetics was widely questioned. On the Protestant side theologians such as Bultmann attacked rationalistic, defensive apologetics in the name of the Protestant principle of faith alone. Tillich pointed out a temptation to which the apologist is particularly subject, namely, that of 'sacred dishonesty'; and H. Richard Niebuhr showed that apologetical defensiveness often results from vanity, insecurity, and lack of confidence in God. While Sperry rejected the 'accommodating' type of apologetics as unsatisfactory to the scientist, Barth was telling the world that apologetic compromise is a serious threat to the distinctiveness of the Christian message.

Among Catholics, authors such as Karl Adam, Henri de Lubac, and Jean Levie severely criticized the presuppositions of the neoscholastic apologetics of the previous century, which Garrigou-Lagrange and Gardeil were attempting to perpetuate with only minor adjustments. These critics noted the implicit rationalism in the efforts of apologists to prove the truth of Christianity without regard to the specific nature of religious knowledge and the indispensable role of grace in the decision of faith.

These challenges to apologetics on both the Protestant and Catholic sides did not, however, result in a qualitative decline. The 2d quarter of the century registered important gains in relating the Christian faith to advances in philosophy and in the other human sciences. In Maritain and Gilson Thomistic philosophy became almost a form of apologetics. Adam capitalized on the phenomenology of Scheler; Heim and Balthasar utilized the personalism of Buber; Bultmann and Rahner were influenced by the existentialism of the early Heidegger; Karl Heim drew on the results of modern physics; Alan Richardson profited from recent developments in historiography; and Teilhard de Chardin participated in new breakthroughs in physical anthropology. Thanks to their intimate involvement in nontheological disciplines, these 20th-century apologists have been able to speak with real credibility to many contemporary 'secular' men.

Some 20th-century apologists in their efforts to bridge the gap between the Church and the modern world have put forward daring hypotheses. The Catholic Modernists found themselves rejected by the Church of their day; Blondel and, in the next generation, Teilhard de Chardin narrowly escaped succumbing to the same fate. Protestants such as Tillich and Bultmann have been a scandal to many of their coreligionists.

While regretting what one judges to be aberrations, one must be grateful that there are theologians with the courage to launch out into the deep and seek radically new solutions for problems that are in many respects new. In more than one case the heresies of the fathers have foreshadowed the orthodoxy of the children and grandchildren.

Since the 1930s there have been few major apologetical syntheses of the sort associated with the names of Luthardt and Hettinger, Kaftan and Schanz. Some may see in this a failure of courage. From another point of view, however, it may appear that the growth of apologetics in the latter part of the 19th century was excessive. An overanxious defensiveness tended to penetrate all the theological tracts so that disinterested speculation was almost suffocated. The gigantic apologetical *summae* of that era rested upon too many uncriticized postulates. Because they failed to see the questionableness of their own enterprise, the apologists of the turn of the century have had no lasting influence. Their massive tomes gather dust on the shelves of theological libraries and are only rarely disturbed by the rummagings of the curious scholar.

The 20th century has seen more clearly than previous periods that apologetics stands or falls with the question of method. In the past few decades apologetical science has merged to an increasing degree with the epistemology of religious knowledge. It is in this difficult area that the most important work remains to be done.

Notes

1. Schubert M. Ogden, *The Reality of God and Other Essays* (New York, 1966), p. 120. See also Langdon Gilkey, 'Trends in Protestant Apologetics,' *Concilium*, vol. 46 (New York: Paulist Press, 1969), pp. 126–157.
2. Cf. Gregory Baum, *The Credibility of the Church Today: A Reply to Charles Davis* (New York, 1968); also his *Faith and Doctrine: A Contemporary View* (New York, 1969).

1. C. H. Dodd, 'The Primitive Preaching,' *The Apostolic Preaching and Its Developments* (London, 1936).
2. See J. Jeremias, *The Servant of God*, Studies in Biblical Theology, Vol. 20 (London, 1957), pp. 98–104.
3. It is also true, as C. H. Dodd remarks, that Is 6.10 'was clearly regarded as, constructively, providing documentation for the thesis that the Gospel is to be preached to the Gentiles, and in that sense obviously had great importance for primitive Christian apologetic'; *According to the Scriptures: The Substructure of New Testament Theology* (London, 1952), p. 39.
4. These observations on the Passion apologetic are indebted to X. Léon-Dufour, 'Passion, Récits de la,' DBSuppl 6:1419–92, esp. 1433–34.
5. For a discussion of the possible meanings of this term, and the OT references that Matthew might have had in mind, see B. Lindars, *New Testament Apologetic: The Doctrinal Significance of the Old Testament Quotations* (London and Philadelphia, 1961), pp. 194–199.
6. *Ibid.*, ch. 4.

7. For one point of view on the vexed problem of the term *Son of Man* and its relationship to the apocalyptic literature then current, see P. Benoit, 'The Divinity of Jesus in the Synoptic Gospels,' *Son and Saviour*, ed. A. Gelin, rev. ed. (Baltimore and Dublin, 1962), pp. 86–88.

8. See Raymond E. Brown, 'The Gospel Miracles,' *New Testament Essays* (Milwaukee, 1965), pp. 168–191.

9. E. D. O'Connor, *Faith in the Synoptic Gospels* (Notre Dame, 1961), esp. pp. 121–122.

10. See A. Lefèvre, 'Miracle,' DBSuppl 5:1299–1308.

11. The apologetical features of Acts are well treated in F. F. Bruce, *The Apostolic Defence of the Gospel: Christian Apologetic in the New Testament* (London, 1959), *passim*. For greater detail see J. Dupont, *Études sur les Actes des Apôtres* (Paris, 1967).

12. See P. Vielhauer, 'On the "Paulinism" of Acts,' *Studies in Luke-Acts*, ed. L. E. Keck and J. L. Martyn (Nashville, 1966), pp. 33–50.

13. B. Gärtner, *The Areopagus Speech and Natural Revelation*, Acta Seminarii Neotestamentici Upsaliensis, vol. 21 (Uppsala, 1955).

14. *The Epistle to the Hebrews* (Edinburgh, 1899).

15. A. E. J. Rawlinson, *St. Mark*, Westminster Commentaries (London, 1925), p. xxii.

16. C. F. D. Moule, 'The Intention of the Evangelists,' *New Testament Essays in Memory of T. W. Manson*, ed. A. J. B. Higgins (Manchester, Eng., 1959), p. 168.

17. *The Birth of the New Testament* (New York, 1962), pp. 87–88.

18. See J. A. Fitzmyer, 'Anti-Semitism and Matthew 27:15,' *ThSt* 26 (1965): 670.

19. The presence of legendary features in these incidents has been remarked by various commentators. See, for instance, the remarks of John L. McKenzie, *Jerome Biblical Commentary* (Englewood Cliffs, N.J., 1968), 2:111–113; he calls attention also to the apologetical motivation of the story about the guards at the tomb.

20. B. H. Streeter, *The Four Gospels: A Study of Origins* (London, 1924), pp. 535–539.

21. *The Theology of St. Luke* (London, 1960).

22. See 2 Pt 3.3–9 for evidence that the problem was a troublesome one.

23. R. E. Brown, *The Gospel According to John, I–XII*, Anchor Bible, vol. 29 (Garden City, N.Y., 1966), p. lxxv.

24. C. K. Barrett, *The Gospel According to St. John* (New York, 1955), p. 115.

NOTES TO CHAPTER TWO

1. *Dialogue with Trypho* 82; trans. T. B. Falls, FathCh 6:279.

2. On these literary forms see the following articles in ReallexAntChr: 'Apologetik' (by G. Bardy, 1:533–543), 'Dialog' (by A. Hermann

and G. Bardy, 3:928–955), and 'Diatribe' (by W. Capelle and H. I. Marrou 3:990–1009). On the more general problem of the relationship of early Christian apologetics to the classical background see Henry Chadwick, *Early Christian Thought and the Classical Tradition* (New York, 1966); C. N. Cochrane, *Christianity and Classical Culture* (New York, 1944); and W. W. Jaeger, *Early Christianity and Greek Paideia* (Cambridge, Mass., 1961).

3. H. A. Wolfson, *Philo: Foundations of Religious Philosophy in Judaism, Christianity, and Islam*, 2 vols. (Cambridge, Mass., 1947), 1:138–163; cf. Bardy, 'Apologetik,' 536–537.

4. Wolfson, *Philo*, 1:142.

5. *Ibid.*, quoting *Spec* 3.34.185.

6. Eng. trans in E. Hennecke, *New Testament Apocrypha*, trans. R. McL. Wilson (Philadelphia, 1964), 2:99–101.

7. *Hist. eccl.* 4.3.1–2; Eng. trans. K. Lake (Cambridge, Mass., 1953), 1:307–309.

8. Eng. trans. D. M. Kay, ANF 10 (New York, 1896): 259–279.

9. Eng. trans. T. B. Falls, FathCh 6:23–111, 115–140.

10. 1 *Apol.* 46, FathCh 6:83–84; 2 *Apol.* 8–10, FathCh 6:127–130.

11. Eng. trans. T. B. Falls, FathCh 6:139–366.

12. Eng. trans. T. B. Falls, FathCh 6:369–423.

13. *Ibid.*, pp. 427–436.

14. *Address to the Greeks*, Eng. trans. J. E. Ryland, ANF 2:65–83.

15. Quasten Patr 1:229.

16. Eng. trans. J. H. Crehan, AncChrWr 23:29–78.

17. Eng. trans. J. H. Crehan, AncChrWr 23:79–116.

18. *To Autolycus*, Eng. trans. Marcus Dods, ANF 2 (Buffalo, 1887): 87–121.

19. Eng. trans. J. A. Kleist, AncChrWr 6:127–147.

20. See Andriessen's articles in VigChr 1 (1947):129–147 and in LexThK² 6:366.

21. SourcesChr 33:266–268.

22. On Clement see especially Claude Mondésert, *Clément d'Alexandrie: Introduction à l'étude de sa pensée religieuse* (Paris, 1944).

23. *Exhortation to the Greeks*, Eng. trans. G. W. Butterworth, Loeb ClLib, vol. 92. See also the French translation with introduction and notes by Mondésert in SourcesChr, vol. 2.

24. LoebClLib. ed., p. 195.

25. *Ibid.*, p. 253.

26. On Celsus see Carl Andresen, *Logos und Nomos: Die Polemik des Kelsos wider das Christentum* (Berlin, 1955). In English see John Patrick, *The Apology of Origen in Reply to Celsus* (Edinburgh, 1892).

27. Eng. trans. with introd. and notes by Henry Chadwick, *Origen, Contra Celsum* (Cambridge, Eng., 1953; reprinted with corrections, 1965).

28. Eng. trans. Rudolf Arbesmann, FathCh, vol. 10.

29. In a famous tribute Ernest Renan called it, 'la perle de cette littérature apologétique des dernières années de Marc-Aurèle,' *Marc-Aurèle et la fin du monde antique*, 4th ed. (Paris, 1882), p. 389.
30. For a balanced judgment and references to the literature on this debate see Quasten Patr 2:159, 161–162.
31. Still valuable is Joseph Lortz, *Tertullian als Apologet*, 2 vols., Münsterische Beiträge zur Theologie (Münster, 1927–28).
32. Eng. trans. Sister Emily Joseph Daly, FathCh, vol. 10.
33. Eng. trans. S. L. Greenslade, LCC 5:25–64.
34. *Ibid.*, no. 7, p. 36. In spite of such disclaimers Tertullian continued to use pagan learning in his work, and on a large scale. For substantiation see Jan Waszink's great commentary on *De anima* (Amsterdam, 1947).
35. *On the Flesh of Christ*, Eng. trans. Dr. Holmes, ANF 3 (Grand Rapids, 1951):525.
36. Epistle no. 1, Eng. trans. E. Wallis, ANF 5 (Buffalo, 1886):275–280.
37. Treatise no. 6, ANF 5:465–469.
38. Treatise no. 5, ANF 5:457–465.
39. Eng. trans. Maurice Bévenot, AncChrWr, vol. 25. On the textual problems relating to the famous primacy text, see Maurice Bévenot, *St. Cyprian's De Unitate, ch. 4, in the Light of the Manuscripts*, Bellarmine Series, vol. 4 (London, 1938); *idem, The Tradition of Manuscripts: A Study in the Transmission of St. Cyprian's Treatises* (Oxford, 1961).
40. Eng. trans. E. Wallis, ANF 5 (Buffalo, 1886):507–557.
41. *Ibid.*, p. 507.
42. *Ibid.*
43. Cf. J. Rendel Harris, *Testimonies*, 2 vols. (Cambridge, Eng., 1916–20).
44. Eng. trans. George E. McCracken, AncChrWr, vols 7–8.
45. Bk. I, ch. 62; AncChrWr 7:108–109.
46. Bk II, ch. 5; AncChrWr 7:116–117.
47. B. Pascal, *Pensées*, ed. L. Brunschvicg (Paris, 1942), no. 233; see below, pp. 123–127.
48. Eng. trans. Sister Mary Frances McDonald, FathCh, vol. 49.
49. Bk V, ch. 3; *ibid.*, pp. 335–336.
50. Eng. trans. Clarence A. Forbes, AncChrWr, vol. 37. In addition to Forbes's introduction see, on this work, J. R. Laurin, *Orientations maîtresses des apologistes chrétiens de 270 à 361*, AnalGreg 61, ch. 5.
51. As F. H. Dudden illustrates at length, Ambrose 'consistently depreciates the function of reason in relation to Divine things'; *The Life and Times of Ambrose*, 2 vols (Oxford, 1935), 2:558.
52. *De fide* 1:78; CSEL 78:34.
53. *De Abraham* 1.21; PL 14:450.
54. *Expos. ps.* 118.9.12; PL 15:1394.

55. Symmachus' memorial to the Emperor and Ambrose's reply may be found in Eng. trans. H. de Romestin, NicPNicChFath 10 (2d series; London, 1896):411–422.
56. *The Poems of Prudentius*, vol. 2, Eng. trans. Sister M. Clement Eagan, FathCh 52 (Washington, D.C., 1965), pp. 113–176.
57. For some conjectures regarding the contents of this work see A. B. Hulen, *Porphyry's Work Against the Christians: An Interpretation* (Scottdale, Pa. 1933).
58. Eng. trans. E. H. Gifford, 2 vols. (Oxford, 1903).
59. Eng. trans. W. J. Ferrar, 2 vols. (London, 1920).
60. Eusebius of Caesarea, *On the Theophania, or Divine Manifestation*, Eng. trans. (Cambridge, Eng., 1843). For a summary of this work see D. S. Wallace-Hadrill, *Eusebius of Caesarea* (Westminster, Md., 1961), pp. 190–200. Eusebius's achievement as an apologist is capably evaluated by F. J. Foakes-Jackson, *Eusebius Pamphili* (Cambridge, Eng., 1933), pp. 118–141.
61. *Theophania* 2.76, p. 175.
62. Eng. trans. A. Robertson, NicPNicChFath, vol. 4 (2nd series; London, 1892), pp. 1–30.
63. *Ibid.*, 31–67; reprinted in LCC 3 (Philadelphia, 1954):55–110. There is a more modern but less literal version, *St. Athanasius on the Incarnation*, by a religious of C.S.M.V., with a perceptive introduction by C. S. Lewis (New York, 1946).
64. See Dan 9:24–27.
65. *St. Athanasius on the Incarnation*, no. 48, p. 85.
66. *Ibid.*, no. 55, p. 94.
67. PG 50:533–572.
68. PG 48:813–838.
69. PG 48:839–942.
70. Homily 1, no. 1. On Chrysostom's various writings against the Jews see A. Lukyn Williams, *Adversus Judaeos* (Cambridge, Eng., 1935), ch. 15; this quotation from p. 134.
71. PG 76:490–1058, and fragments, col. 1057–64.
72. For critique see J. Liébart, 'S. Cyrille d'Alexandrie et la culture antique,' MélSciReI 12 (1955):5–26, and P. Canivet, *Histoire d'une entreprise apologétique au Ve siècle* (Paris, 1957), pp. 112–113, 121–122. Canivet's work is a thorough study of Theodoret.
73. See Théodoret de Cyr, *Thérapeutique des maladies helléniques*, ed. and French trans. P. Canivet, SourcesChr 57, 2 vols. (Paris, 1958).
74. On Augustine as apologist see Eugène Portalié, *A Guide to the Thought of St. Augustine*, Eng. trans. R. J. Bastian (Chicago, 1960), and especially Ignace Stoszko, *L'apologétique de S. Augustin* (Strasbourg, 1932). The influence of Plotinus on Augustine has recently been studied by R. J. O'Connell, especially in his *St. Augustine's Early Theory of Man, A.D. 386–391* (Cambridge, Mass., 1968).

75. For Eng. trans. of these four works by various translators see FathCh 2 (New York, 1948).
76. Eng. trans. D. A. Gallagher and I. J. Gallagher, FathCh 56 (Washington, DC., 1966).
77. These two works are both given in Eng. trans. by J. H. S. Burleigh in LCC 6:218–283, 284–323.
78. Eng. trans. J. H. S. Burleigh, LCC 6:102–217.
79. Eng. trans. G. G. Walsh, Grace Monahan and Daniel J. Honan, FathCh, vols. 8 (New York, 1950), 17 (New York, 1952), and 24 (New York, 1954).
80. *On the Happy Life* 4.35; FathCh 2:83.
81. *On Free Will* 15.38; LCC 6:159.
82. *Of True Religion* 1.4; LCC 6:228.
83. *Ibid.*; cf. *Solil.* 6.12, FathCh 2:359; *Usefulness of Belief* 6.13, LCC 6:301.
84. *Of True Religion* 4.6; LCC 6:229.
85. *Of True Religion* 4.7; LCC 6:229.
86. *Solil.* 6.13; FathCh 2:358.
87. *Providence* 16.44; FathCh 2:320.
88. Cf. *Of True Religion* 1.1, LCC 6:225; *City of God* 18.41, FathCh 24:149.
89. *Answer to Skeptics* 3.20.43; FathCh 2:220.
90. *On Free Will* 2.1.6; LCC 6:137.
91. *On Free Will* 2.1.5; LCC 6:137.
92. 'Nullus quippe credit aliquid nisi prius cogitaverit esse credendum,' *De praedest. sanct.* 2.5; PL 44:963.
93. *Of True Religion* 24.45; LCC 6:247.
94. *Usefulness of Belief* 13.28; LCC 6:315.
95. *Usefulness of Belief* 14.31; LCC 6:316–317.
96. *Against the Epistle of Manichaeus Called Fundamental*, no. 6; Eng. trans. Richard Stothert, NicPNicChFath, vol. 4 (1st series; Buffalo, 1887):131.
97. *Usefulness of Belief* 8.20; LCC 6:307.
98. *Of True Religion* 3.5; LCC 6:228–229. In the third sentence I have substituted 'incontinence' for 'continence,' correcting what appears to be a slip in the translation.
99. *Way of Life* . . . 30.62 to 35.80; FathCh 56:47–61.
100. *Way of Life* . . . 34.75; FathCh 56:57.
101. *Usefulness of Belief* 17.35; LCC 6:321.
102. *City of God* 22.5; FathCh 24:424.
103. *Ibid.*, p. 425.
104. *City of God* 22.6; FathCh 24:428.
105. *City of God* 22.7; FathCh 24:431.
106. *Of True Religion* 35.47; LCC 6:248.
107. *City of God* 18.46; FathCh 24:163.
108. *City of God* 10.12; FathCh 14:140.

109. *City of God* 10.16; FathCh 14:147.
110. See for instance the criticisms of Stoszko, *L'apologétique de S. Augustin*, pp. 173, 183–184, 222.
111. *In Answer to the Jews*, ed. Roy J. Deferrari, FathCh 15 (New York, 1955), p. 414.
112. *Against the Epistle of Manichaeus Called Fundamental*, no. 5; NicPNicChFath 4:130.
113. *Retractations* 2.69; Eng. trans. Sister Mary Inez Bogan, FathCh 60 (Washington, D.C., 1968):209–210.
114. *City of God* 8.11; FathCh 14:40–42.
115. Eng. trans. Roy J. Deferrari, FathCh 50 (Washington, D.C., 1964).
116. *Seven Books of History* . . . 7.43; FathCh 50:363.
117. Salvian the Presbyter, *The Governance of God*, Eng. trans. Jeremiah O'Sullivan, FathCh 3 (New York, 1947).
118. *The Governance of God*, 7.1; FathCh 3:185.

NOTES TO CHAPTER THREE

1. *De fide orthodoxa* 1.1–3, PG 94:790–795.
2. PG 94:1201–06.
3. PG 96:1335–48. The major part of this dialogue is translated by J. Kritzeck in Anne Fremantle, ed., *A Treasury of Early Christianity* (New York, 1953), pp. 321–324.
4. 'Apologetics,' *Catholic Dictionary of Theology* (Edinburgh, 1962), 1:116. For a German translation of this treatise see Georg Graf, *Des Theodor Abu Kurra Traktat über den Schöpfer und die wahre Religion*, Beiträge zur Geschichte der Philosophie des Mittelalters, Bd. 14, Heft 1 (Münster, 1913). The circumstances of this dialogue are discussed in Alfred Guillaume, 'A Debate between a Christian and Muslim Doctors,' Centenary Supplement to *Journal of the Royal Asiatic Society* (London, 1924), pp. 233–244.
5. For a paraphrase with partial translation see William Muir, *The Apology of Al-Kindy* (London, 1882). A recent study, including a Latin translation, is José Muñoz Sendino, 'La apologia del cristianismo de al-Kindi,' *Miscelanea Comillas* 11–12 (1949):339–460. See also J. A. Devenny, 'Kindi,' NCE 8:183 and James Kritzeck, *Peter the Venerable and Islam* (Princeton, N.J., 1964), esp. pp. 101–107.
6. PL 83:449–538. For background and summary see A. Lukyn Williams, *Adversus Judaeos: A Bird's-Eye View of Christian Apologiae until the Renaissance* (Cambridge, Eng., 1935), pp. 216–217, 282–292.
7. PL 104:69–76, PL 104:77–100. Cf. Williams, *Adversus Judaeos*, pp. 350–357.
8. PL 116:141–184. Cf. Williams, *Adversus Judaeos*, pp. 358–365.
9. PL 141:305–318.

10. Jean Leclerq, *Saint Pierre Damien: Ermite et homme d'église* (Rome, 1960), pp. 218–219.

11. É. Gilson, 'La Servante de la théologie,' *Études de philosophie médiévale* (Strasbourg, 1921), pp. 30–50; cf. remarks in his *Reason and Revelation in the Middle Ages* (New York, 1938), p. 13.

12. *Antilogus contra judaeos*; PL 145:41–57.

13. *Dialogus inter judaeum requirentem et christianum e contrario respondentem*; PL 145:57–68.

14. See C. H. Haskins, *The Renaissance of the Twelfth Century* (Cambridge, Mass., 1927), pp. 341–367.

15. See S. W. Baron, *A Social and Religious History of the Jews*, 2d ed., rev. (New York, 1957), 4:89–106.

16. PL 160:1105–12.

17. PL 159:1005–36.

18. Latin text with introduction by C. C. J. Webb in MedRenSt 3 (1954):55–57.

19. Eng. trans. of these and other works in S. W. Deane, *Saint Anselm, Basic Writings*, 2d ed. (La Salle, Ill., 1962); hereafter cited as Deane.

20. G. v. d. Plaas, 'Des hl. Anselm "Cur Deus Homo" auf dem Boden der jüdisch-christlichen Polemik des Mittelalters,' DiThomF 7 (1929):446–467; 8 (1930):18–32.

21. See R. W. Southern, *St. Anselm and His Biographers* (Cambridge, Eng., 1963), pp. 88–91.

22. *Prosl.* 1; Deane, pp. 6–7.

23. *CDh* 1.2; Deane, p. 179.

24. *Ibid.*

25. 'Exemplum meditandi de ratione fidei,' Preface to *Prosl.*; Deane, p. 2.

26. *Prosl.* 1; Deane, p. 6.

27. *Monol.* 1.1; Deane, p. 38.

28. Preface to *Monol.*; Deane, p. 35.

29. Preface to *CDh*; Deane, p. 177.

30. *CDh* 1.1; Deane, p. 178.

31. PL 158:260.

32. *CDh* 1.2; Deane, p. 179.

33. *CDh* 1.1; Deane, p. 178.

34. *CDh* 1.3; Deane, p. 182.

35. *CDh* 1.2; Deane, p. 182.

36. *Prosl.* 4; Deane, p. 10.

37. *In Behalf of the Fool* 8; Deane, p. 168.

38. *CDh* 2.22; Deane, pp. 287–288. Whom did Anselm have in mind when in this text he referred to the *Pagans*? M. J. Charlesworth, *St. Anselm's Proslogion* (Oxford, 1965), p. 32, holds that he means unbelievers in a more radical sense than the Jews, for they accept neither the Old nor the New Testament and must be persuaded *sola ratione*. René Rogues, in the SourcesChr edition of *CDh* (vol. 91, 1963, pp. 72–74) surmises that Anselm may have envisaged the

Moslems. At least it is clear that the pagans must be monotheists other than Jews; for Anselm in this dialogue does not prove the existence or unicity of God, which he takes rather for granted.

39. This solution corresponds closely with the thought of Anselm himself as interpreted by A. M. Jacquin, 'Les "rationes necessariae" de S. Anselme,' *Mélanges Mandonnet* 2 (Paris, 1930), pp. 67–78.

40. Charlesworth, *St. Anselm's Proslogion*, p. 42, holds that a development of Anselm's thought in Aquinas's direction would do less violence to his intentions than Barth's fideist interpretation.

41. PL 157:535–672.

42. *De sua conversione opusculum*; PL 170:805–836.

43. *Annulus sive dialogus inter christianum et judaeum*; PL 170:561–610. Taking some satisfaction in this stress on miracles, which play so slight a role in earlier medieval apologetics, A. Gardeil holds that in Rupert of Deutz the scholastic notion of extrinsic credibility becomes complete, with all its essential elements (Scripture, prophecy, miracles) held in balance; 'Crédibilité,' DTC 3:2261.

44. *Adversus judaeorum inveteratam duritiem*; PL 189:507–650. See the sympathetic summary in Jean Leclerq, *Pierre le Vénérable* (Abbaye saint-Wandrill, 1946), pp. 233–241.

45. PL 189:587–602. Leclerq, *Pierre le Vénérable,* p. 239, refers to P. C. Grössbolting, *De miraculo in scriptis Petri Venerabilis* (Limbourg, 1937).

46. This point is made by Aloïs van Hove, *La Doctrine du miracle chez s. Thomas* (Paris, 1927), pp. 235–236.

47. Kritzeck, *Peter the Venerable and Islam.*

48. *Summa totius haeresis saracenorum*; text in Kritzeck, *Peter the Venerable and Islam*, pp. 204–211.

49. *Liber contra sectam sive haeresim saracenorum*; text in Kritzeck, *Peter the Venerable and Islam*, pp. 220–291.

50. *Contra perfidiam judaeorum*; PL 207:825–870.

51. See H. Ligeard, 'Le Rationalisme de Pierre Abélard,' RevScRel 2 (1911):384–396.

52. Several times in his writings Abelard discusses the assertion of Gregory the Great, 'Fides non habet meritum, cui ratio humana praebet experimentum' (*Homily on the Gospels* 2.26), quoted by Abelard in his *Intro. ad theologiam*, Bk. 2, PL 178:1050; *Theol. christiana* 3.1226; *Sic et non* 1.1349–50; *Dialogus*, col. 1638; cf. *Epitome* 2.1696. While agreeing that to assent simply on the basis of what one sees is not meritorious, Abelard argues that the *primordia fidei* achieved by reason are not to be despised since they may prepare the way for a meritorious act of faith, informed by grace and charity.

53. PL 178:1611–84.

54. Cf. Augustine, *supra*, p. 62.

55. *Theol. christiana*; PL 178:1126.

56. PG 178:1164.
57. PG 178:1314.
58. *De Trinitate* 1.2; SourcesChr 63:66; PL 196:891.
59. *De fide catholica contra haereticos sui temporis*; PL 210:305–430.
60. *Ars fidei catholicae*; PL 210:595–610. See comments on this work in Étienne Gilson, *History of Christian Philosophy in the Middle Ages* (New York, 1955), pp. 176–178.
61. The well-known warning of Gregory IX to the Parisian faculty of theology in his bull of 1228, *Ab aegyptiis*, is reproduced in part in Denz 824.
62. The constructive and nonpolemical character of St. Thomas's apologetic is well brought out by Léonce de Grandmaison, 'Sur l'apologétique de s. Thomas,' NouvRevTh 39 (1907):65–74, 121–130.
63. Leonine ed. of *Opera* of St. Thomas (Rome, 1918) 12.vi; quoted by A. C. Pegis in his introduction to the Image Books edition of Thomas Aquinas, *On The Truth of the Catholic Faith*, 4 vols. (Garden City, N.Y., 1955–56), 1:20–21. For recent opinion regarding the chronology see T. J. Murphy, 'The Date and Purpose of the *Contra Gentiles,*' *Heythrop Journal* 10 (1969): 405–415.
64. M. D. Chenu, *Toward Understanding St. Thomas,* Eng. trans. A. M. Landry and D. Hughes (Chicago, 1964), p. 291.
65. *C. gent.* 4.54; Eng. trans. C. J. O'Neil, *On the Truth of the Catholic Faith*, 4:228–233.
66. *C. gent.* 1.9; *On the Truth of the Catholic Faith*, 1:77–78.
67. ST 2a2ae.177.1.
68. ST 3a.43.1.
69. *C. gent.* 3.154.
70. ST 2a2ae.1.4 ad 2.
71. *De ver.* 14.11.
72. Van Hove, *La Doctrine du miracle chez s. Thomas,* pp. 249–252. Cf. A. Lang, *Die Entfaltung des apologetischen Problems in der Scholastik des Mittelalters* (Freiburg i.B., 1962), pp. 114–119, hereafter cited Lang, *Die Entfaltung.*
73. See, e.g., *C. gent.* 3.101.
74. *C. gent.* 1.6; *On the Truth of the Catholic Faith*, 1:72.
75. *Ibid.,* pp. 72–73.
76. Van Hove, *La Doctrine du miracle chez s. Thomas,* esp. pp. 310–315.
77. Cf. *C. gent.* 3.154, par. 21, on the charism of the discernment of spirits.
78. On Martini's life and work see André Berthier, 'Un maître orientaliste du XIIIᵉ siècle: Raymond Martin, O.P.,' ArchFrPraed 6 (1936):267–311. His work as an apologist against the Jews is discussed in Williams, *Adversus Judaeos,* pp. 248–255.
79. Frances A. Yates, *The Art of Memory* (Chicago, 1966), p. 176.
80. É. Gilson, *History of Christian Philosophy*, pp. 350–353; Frederick

Copleston, *A History of Philosophy* (Westminster, Md., 1952), 2:456–459.

81. See E. A. Peers, *Ramon Lull: A Biography* (London, 1929), pp. 312, 317, 338–339.
82. *Ibid.*, pp. 403–405.
83. *Impugnatio alchorani*; PG 154:1035–1152.
84. J. T. Addison, *The Christian Approach to the Moslem* (New York, 1942), p. 39.
85. *Prooemium in 1 sent.* q. 2; *S. Bonaventurae Opera Omnia*, 10 vols. (Quarrachi, 1882–1902), 1:11.
86. *In 3 sent.* 24:2.3; *Opera Omnia* 3:523.
87. Gilson, *History of Christian Philosophy*, pp. 411–413; R. Aubert, 'Le caractère raisonnable de l'acte de foi d'après les théologiens de la fin du XIIIe siècle,' RHE 39 (1943): 35–36.
88. Aubert, 'Le caractère raisonnable . . . ,' pp. 31–34.
89. *Ibid.*, pp. 62–70.
90. *Ord. prol.* 2:1.100–119; quoted by Josef Finkenzeller, *Offenbarung und Theologie nach der Lehre des Johannes Duns Scotus*, Beiträge zur Geschichte der Philosophie und Theologie des Mittelalters, Bd. 38, Heft 5 (Münster, 1961), pp. 39–42.
91. On these writings see F. Vernet, 'Nicole de Lyre,' DTC 9:1410–22; Williams, *Adversus Judaeos,* pp. 408–415; A. Lang, *Die Wege der Glaubensbegründung in den Scholastikern des 14. Jahrhunderts*, Beiträge der Geschichte des Philosophie und Theologie des Mittelalters, Bd. 3, Heft 1/2 (Münster 1930), pp. 117–121, hereafter cited as Lang, *Die Wege.*
92. See Lang, *Die Wege*, esp. pp. 218–240.
93. *Ibid.*, p. 232.
94. Latin text in Lang, *Die Entfaltung*, p. 209.
95. Tit. 67; Sulzbach ed., 1852 (reprinted with improvements, Stuttgart 1966), pp. 90–91.
96. Tit. 68, p. 93.
97. Tit. 206, p. 293.
98. Tit. 207, p. 299.
99. Tit. 211, p. 311.
100. Dionysii Cartusani, *Opera omnia* (Monstrolii [Montreuil-sur-Mer], 1899), 18:277–530.
101. In *Opera omnia*, 36:233–442.
102. Eng. trans. in J. P. Dolan, ed., *Unity and Reform* (Notre Dame, Ind., 1962).
103. See Edmond Vansteenberghe, *Le cardinal Nicolas de Cues 1401–64* (Lille, 1920), pp. 232–234.
104. See esp. the Preface to his *Theologia platonica*, in *Opera omnia* (Basel, 1576; fascimile ed., Turin, 1962), 1:78.
105. *The Philosophy of Marsilio Ficino* (New York, 1943), pp. 346–350. On Ficino as apologist see Raymond Marcel, 'L'apologétique de

Marcel Ficin,' *Pensée humaniste et tradition chrétienne aux XVᵉ et XVIᵉ siècles* (Paris, 1950), pp. 159–168.

106. Denz 1440–41.
107. *De religione christiana* in *Opera omnia,* 1:1–77.
108. *Ibid.,* ch. 4.
109. *Ibid.,* ch. 16.
110. *Ibid.,* cf. *Theol. plat.* 3.2.
111. *De rel. chr.,* ch. 27–34.
112. *Ibid.,* ch. 9.
113. *Ibid.,* ch. 10.
114. *Ibid.,* ch. 26.
115. *Ibid.,* ch. 22.
116. *The Triumph of the Cross* 2.11, Eng. trans. O. H. Hill (London, 1868), p. 88.
117. *Ibid.* 4.3, p. 215.
118. Quoted by O. T. Hill in his biographical sketch introducing *The Triumph of the Cross,* p. xiv.

NOTES TO CHAPTER FOUR

1. On this theme in Luther see B. A. Gerrish, *Grace and Reason: A Study in the Theology of Luther* (Oxford, 1962); also Bernard Lohse, *Ratio und Fides: eine Untersuchung über die Ratio in der Theologie Luthers* (Göttingen, 1958); idem, 'Reason and Revelation in Luther,' *Scottish Journal of Theology* 13 (1960): 337–365.
2. 'Deus est mens aeterna, sapiens, verax, iusta, casta, benefica, conditrix mundi, servans ordinem rerum, et puniens scelera,' *Erotemata dialectices* (1547 ed.), CorpRef 13:647; cited by Lohse, 'Reason and Revelation in Luther,' p. 361.
3. A. C. McGiffert, *Protestant Thought Before Kant* (New York, 1931), p. 76.
4. Jaroslav Pelikan, *From Luther to Kierkegaard* (St. Louis, 1950), p. 77.
5. Robert Preus, *The Inspiration of Scripture: A Study of the Theology of the Seventeenth Century Lutheran Dogmaticians* (Mankato, Minn., 1955), pp. 106–107.
6. On the uses of reason according to Calvin see E. A. Dowey, Jr., *The Knowledge of God in Calvin's Theology* (New York, 1952).
7. *De vera philosophia ex quattuor doctoribus ecclesiae* (Bologna, 1507, rev. ed., 1514). On Adrian of Corneto see P. Paschini, *Tre illustri prelati del rinascimento* (Rome, 1957).
8. *Examen vanitatis doctrinae gentium et veritatis christianae disciplinae* (Mirandola, 1520).
9. *De perenni philosophia* (Lyons, 1540).
10. *Disputationes de controversiis christianae fidei adversus huius temporis haereticos,* 3 vols. (Ingolstadt, 1586, 1588, 1593).

11. *Annales ecclesiasticae* (Rome, 1588–1607).

12. *De veritate christianae fidei* (Valencia, 1790; facsimile ed., London, 1964).

13. See Pablo Graf, *Luis Vives como Apologeta* (Madrid, 1943), pp. 99–114. This is a Spanish translation by J. M. Millas Vallicrosa of the original German, *Ludwig Vives als Apologet* (Freiburg i.Br., 1932).

14. F. Alfonsi de Castro Zamorensi, *Adversus omnes haereses*, rev. ed. (Cologne, 1559).

15. Published 1563; reprinted Louvain, 1564.

16. The following paragraphs depend principally on F. de Vizmanos, 'La apologetica de los escolasticos postridentinos,' *Estudios eclesiasticos* 13 (1934): 418–446.

17. *In 2–2* 1.1.4.7, 13, 18 (Venice ed., 1608), col. 91B, 97B, and 101D.

18. *De fide* 4.3.5 (Paris, 1588), 12:121.

19. *Ibid.*, 10, p. 124.

20. *Tract. de fide, spe, et charitate* 3.4 (Madrid, 1632), p. 54.

21. *De virt. fidei divinae* 5.4.57 (Paris, 1868), 1:263.

22. *In 2–2* 1.4.3, 4 (Venice, 1586), col. 55D and 57E.

23. *In 2–2* 1.2.3 (Paris, 1883), 8:45.

24. 'Hoc argumentum maximi ponderis est,' *Clypeus theol. thomisticae* 4.10.1 a. 8.251 (Venice, 1772), p. 158.

25. *Forma verae religionis quaerendae et inveniendae* (Naples, 1662). See observations of S. Harent, 'Foi,' DTC 6:491–495, and Guy de Broglie, 'La vraie notion thomiste des "praeambula fidei,"' Greg 34 (1953): 352–357.

26. *Manuductio ad conversionem mahumetanorum*, 2 vols. (Madrid, 1687).

27. 1593; reprinted Paris, 1914.

28. On Montaigne's fideism see R. H. Popkin, *The History of Scepticism from Erasmus to Descartes* (Assen [Netherlands], 1960), pp. 44–56, hereafter cited Popkin, *History of Scepticism*.

29. *Traité de l'Église* (London, 1578).

30. *La Vérité de la religion chrétienne* (Paris, 1581); Eng. trans. partly by Sir Philip Sidney, *A Work Concerning the Trueness of the Christian Religion Against Atheists, Epicures, Paynims, Iewes, Mahumetists, and Other Infidels*, 4th ed., corrected (London, 1617).

31. *Traité des religions contre ceux qui les estiment indifférentes* (Saumur, 1631); Eng. trans. Moyses Amyraldus, *A Treatise Concerning Religions . . .* (London, 1660).

32. *Les trois véritez* (Paris, 1595). On Charron see the views of Popkin, *History of Scepticism*, 56–63.

33. Popkin, *History of Scepticism*, 63–83.

34. *Les Triomphes de la religion chrestienne* (Paris, 1628). Cf. Julien-Eymard d'Angers, 'Le fidéisme de J. Boucher, cordelier,' *Études franciscaines* 50 (1938): 579–593.

35. Sister Mary Louis Hubert, *Pascal's Unfinished Apology: A Study of*

His Plan (New Haven, 1952), p. 97. The background of Pascal's apologetic is particularly well presented in Julien-Eymard d'Angers, *Pascal et ses précurseurs* (Paris, 1954).

36. *Pensées,* ed. Léon Brunschvicg (Paris, 1942), no. 693. On Pascal's apologetics see, in addition to the works already cited, R. E. Lacombe, *L'apologétique de Pascal* (Paris, 1958) and Jean Mesnard, *Pascal: His Life and Works,* Eng. trans. G. S. Fraser (London. 1952).

37. See above, p. 53.

38. *Discours sur l'histoire universelle,* 2.1 (Paris, 1836), p. 121.

39. *Ibid.,* 2.4, p. 169.

40. *Ibid.,* 2.30, p. 338.

41. *Ibid.,* 2.19, p. 210–211.

42. *Ibid.,* 2.21, p. 253.

43. *Ibid.,* 2.25, p. 284.

44. *Ibid.,* 2.27, p. 309.

45. Eng. trans. in 2 vols. (New York, 1945), 2:335.

46. *Histoire critique du vieux testament* (Paris, 1678).

47. *Discours sur l'histoire universelle,* 2.28, p. 333.

48. Most importantly in Huet's *Censura philosophiae cartesianae* (Paris, 1689).

49. *Demonstratio evangelica ad serenissimum delphinum* (Paris, 1679).

50. *Traité de la verité de la religion chrétienne* (Rotterdam, 1684); Eng. trans. Henry Lussan, *A Vindication of the Truth of the Christian Religion,* 2 vols. (London, 1694–98).

51. *Traité de la divinité de Notre Seigneur, Jésus-Christ* (Rotterdam, 1689); Eng. trans. Abraham Booth, *A Treatise on the Divinity of Our Lord Jesus Christ* (Charlestown, 1817).

52. Eng. trans. John Clarke, new ed. (London, 1829).

53. *De veritate religionis christianae: amica collatio cum erudito judaeo* (Gouda [Netherlands], 1687).

54. *Traité de l'incrédulité, où on examine les motifs et les raisons qui portent les incrédules à rejetter la religion chrétienne* (Amsterdam, 1696, 1714).

55. *De veritate,* Eng. trans. M. H. Carré (Bristol, 1937). See Basil Willey, *The Seventeenth Century Background* (New York, 1942), ch. 7.

56. See for example his *Discourse of Things above Reason* (London, 1681). On Boyle's religious thought see H. R. McAdoo, *The Spirit of Anglicanism* (New York, 1965), esp. pp. 260–285.

57. 5th ed. (London, 1724), p. 351.

58. Quoted in R. C. Jebb, *Bentley* (London, 1889), p. 26.

59. 'For this religion,' he adds, 'is founded upon his prophecy concerning the Messiah,' *Observations* . . . (London, 1733), p. 25.

60. *A Demonstration of the Being and Attributes of God . . . and the Truth and Certainty of the Christian Revelation,* 10th ed., corrected (London, 1749).

61. *Ibid.,* p. 445.

62. *Ibid.*, p. 440.
63. *Essay Concerning Human Understanding*, 1.3.17; 1.4.8.
64. *Ibid.*, 1.4.16.
65. *Ibid.*, 4.19.4.
66. 'Discourse on Miracles,' *Works*, rev. ed., 10 vols. (London, 1823), 9:262.
67. Gateway ed., Chicago, 1965.
67a. For fuller treatment of Locke's place in the history of British apologetics see, in addition to McGiffert's *Protestant Thought* (already cited), S. G. Hefelbower, *The Relation of John Locke to English Deism* (Chicago, 1918) and Richard Ashcraft, 'Faith and Knowledge in Locke's Philosophy,' in *John Locke: Problems and Perspectives,* ed. J. W. Yolten (Cambridge, Eng., 1969).
68. See Paul Hazard, *European Thought in the Eighteenth Century*, Eng. trans. J. Lewis May (London, 1954); John Hunt, *Religious Thought in England from the Reformation to the End of the Last Century*, vol. 3 (London, 1873); Leslie Stephen, *English Thought in the Eighteenth Century*, vol. 1 (London, 1876).
69. On Butler and his relationship to the English apologetical tradition see E. C. Mossner, *Bishop Butler and the Age of Reason* (New York, 1936).
70. *The Analogy of Religion* (New York, 1961), p. 121.
71. *Ibid.*, p. 142.
72. *Ibid.*, p. 213.
73. *Ibid.*, p. 220.
74. *Ibid.*, p. 238.
75. *Ibid.*, p. 244.
76. *Ibid.*, p. 204.
77. *Dialogues on Natural Religion*, ed. H. D. Aiken (New York, 1959), p. 79.
78. For a general sketch of Paley's life and work see L. Stephen, 'Paley, William,' *Dictionary of National Biography* 15: 101–107.
79. *Evidences*, 2.2, in *Works* (London, 1830), 2:13–14.
80. *Evidences*, 1.2, in *Works* 1:182.
81. *Works* 4:23.
82. *Works* 4:29.
83. Cf. G. W. Leibniz, *Philosophical Papers and Letters*, ed. L. E. Loemker (Chicago, 1955), 1:167–168; cf. pp. 86–87.
84. *Ibid.* 1:160.
85. *Methodus demonstrandae veritatis religionis christianae;* German trans., *Von der Art und Weise wie man die Wahrheit der christlichen Religion zu erweisen hat* in *Kleine philosophische Schriften* (Magdeburg, 1737), 2:200–225.
86. *Theologia naturalis,* 2 vols. (Frankfurt), 1736–37.
87. See H. E. Allison, *Lessing and the Enlightenment: His Philosophy and Its Revelation to Eighteenth Century Thought* (Ann Arbor, Mich.,

1966); also the fine introduction by Henry Chadwick to his selections, *Lessing's Theological Writings* (London, 1956).

88. 'On the Proof of the Spirit and of Power,' *Lessing's Theological Writings,* pp. 53–55. On the possible confusions in Lessing's argument see Chadwick's introduction, pp. 30–36.

89. Lessing, *Gesammelte Werke* (Berlin, 1956), 8.36; cf. Allison, *Lessing and the Enlightenment,* p. 106.

90. *Rettung der göttlichen Offenbarung gegen die Einwürfe der Freigeister* (Berlin, 1747).

91. *Briefe über einige Einwürfe noch lebender Freigeister wider die Offenbarung,* 3 vols. (Berne, 1774–75).

92. *Die gute Sache der in der hl. Schrift des A. u. N.T. enthaltenen göttlichen Offenbarung wider die Feinde derselben erwiesen und gerettet,* 16 vols. (1750–82).

93. Eng. trans. Roger Kingdon (London, 1804).

94. On the apologists of this period in France see, in addition to the work of P. Hazard already cited, Albert Monod, *De Pascal à Chateaubriand: Les défenseurs français du christianisme de 1670 à 1802* (Paris, 1916) and Robert R. Palmer, *Catholics and Unbelievers in Eighteenth Century France* (Princeton, N.J., 1939).

95. *Le Nouvel athéisme renversé, ou réfutation du système de Spinosa* (Paris, 1696).

96. *Vérité évidente de la religion chrétienne* (Paris, 1694).

97. *L'Incrédule amené à la religion par la raison* (Paris, 1710); reproduced in J. P. Migne, *Démonstrations évangéliques* (Paris, 1843–62), 4:509–618.

98. *La Vérité de la religion chrétienne prouvée par les faits* (Paris, 1722). For a good analysis of this work see Monod, *De Pascal à Chateaubriand,* pp. 219–228.

99. *Le Déisme réfuté par lui-même* (Paris, 1765).

100. Letter no. 3 in Migne ed., *Oeuvres complètes* 1: 440.

101. *La Certitude des preuves du christianisme* (Paris, 1767).

102. *Examen du matérialisme ou réfutation du Système de la Nature,* 2 vols. (Paris, 1771).

103. *Les Erreurs de Voltaire,* 1762; 3rd. ed., 2 vols. (Lyon, 1767).

104. *Lettres de quelques juifs portugais, allemands et polonais à M. de Voltaire* (Paris, 1769, 1771, 1772, 1776, 1781, and many later editions; Eng. trans. Dublin, 1777; Philadelphia, 1795 and 1848).

105. *L'incredulo senza scusa* (Florence, 1690). The self-confidence of the author's approach is indicated by his subtitle: 'Che non può non conoscere quale sia la vera religione, chi vuol conoscerla.'

106. *La vera Chiesa di Gesù Cristo dimostrata dai segni e dai dogmi contro i due libri di Giacomo Picenino* (Bologna, 1719).

107. *La Verità della fede fatta evidente per li contrasegni della sua credibilità* (Naples, 1767). Cf. Franz Meffert, *Der heilige Alfons von*

Liguori der Kirchenlehrer und Apologet des XVIII. Jahrhunderts (Mainz, 1901).

108. Turin, 1755; reprinted in *Oeuvres du Cardinal Gerdil*, ed. J. P. Migne (Paris, 1863), col. 191–899.

NOTES TO CHAPTER FIVE

1. *Reden über die Religion an die Gebildeten unter ihrer Verächtern* (Berlin, 1799); Eng. trans. John Oman, *On Religion* (New York, 1958).
2. *On Religion*, p. 1.
3. *Ibid.*, p. 124.
4. *Ibid.*, p. 3.
5. Quoted by Karl Barth, *Protestant Theology from Rousseau to Ritschl*, Eng. trans. Brian Cozens, rev. by H. H. Hartwell (New York, 1959), p. 321. Barth in this book has an excellent chapter on Schleiermacher as an apologist.
6. *On Religion*, p. 9.
7. *Ibid.*, p. 18.
8. *Ibid.*, pp. 26–101.
9. *Der christliche Glaube*, 2 vols. (Berlin, 1821–22); Eng. trans. H. R. Mackintosh and J. S. Stewart, *The Christian Faith* (New York, 1963), 1:70–76.
10. *The Christian Faith*, 1:5.
11. *On Religion*, p. 148.
12. *The Christian Faith*, 1:37.
13. *Ibid.*, 1:62–76.
14. *Kurze Darstellung des theologischen Studiums zum Behuf einleitender Vorlesung* rev. ed. (Berlin, 1830); Eng. trans. Terrence N. Tice, *Brief Outline* (Richmond, 1966), p. 25.
15. *Brief Outline*, p. 31.
16. *Christliche Apologetik* (Hamburg, 1829, rev. ed., 1841).
17. *Theologische Vorlesungen*, vol. 2, *System der chr. Dogmatik* (Berlin, 1847).
18. *Leben Jesu, kritisch bearbeitet*, 2 vols. (Tübingen, 1835–36); Eng. trans. George Eliot (pseud.) from 4th Ger. ed., *Life of Jesus* (London, 1846).
19. *Ueber die Sündlosigkeit Jesu: eine apologetische Betrachtung* (Hamburg, 1828); Eng. trans. Sophia Taylor from 7th Ger. ed. (Edinburgh, 1870), p. 64.
20. *Ibid.*, p. 106.
21. *Historisch oder mythisch?* (Hamburg, 1838).
22. *Der Cultus des Genius* (Hamburg, 1839); Eng. trans. Lucy Sanford (London, 1846).
23. *Ueber die unterscheidenden Charakter oder das Wesen des Christentums* (Hamburg, 1845); Eng. trans. Lucy Sanford (London, 1866).

24. *Theodor; oder, des Zweiflers Weihe*, 2 vols. (Berlin, 1822); Eng. trans. James F. Clarke (Boston, 1856).
25. *Die Lehre von der Sünde und vom Versöhner, oder die Weihe des Zweiflers* (Hamburg, 1823); Eng. trans. J. E. Ryland (Boston, 1854).
26. *Die Glaubwürdigkeit der evangelischen Geschichte* (1837); Eng. trans. G. V. Smith (London, 1844).
27. *Dogmatics*, vol. 1, Eng. trans. Olive Wyon (London, 1949), p. 100.
28. *On Authority and Revelation*, Eng. trans. Walter Lowrie (Princeton, 1955), p. 59.
29. *Concluding Unscientific Postscript*, Eng. trans. David F. Swenson and Walter Lowrie (Princeton, 1941), p. 31; hereafter cited as *Postscript*.
30. *Sickness Unto Death*, Eng. trans. Walter Lowrie (Princeton, 1941; reprinted Garden City, N.Y., 1954), p. 218; hereafter cited as *Sickness*.
31. *Philosophical Fragments*, Eng. trans. David F. Swenson (Princeton, 1936), pp. 31–36; hereafter cited as *Fragments*.
32. *Postscript*, p. 485.
33. *Ibid.*, p. 46.
34. *Fragments*, p. 77.
35. *Ibid.*, p. 78.
36. *Postscript*, p. 90.
37. *Fragments*, p. 53.
38. *Ibid.*, p. 87.
39. *Ibid.*, p. 92.
40. See Walter Lowrie, *A Short Life of Kierkegaard* (Garden City, N.Y., 1961), pp. 88–89.
41. *Sickness*, pp. 146–175.
42. Cf. Malcolm L. Diamond, 'Kierkegaard and Apologetics,' JRelig 44 (1964): 122–132.
43. *Ibid.*, p. 130; *Sickness*, pp. 215–216.
44. *Fragments*, p. 29.
45. See J. Robert Barth, *Coleridge and Christian Doctrine* (Cambridge, Mass., 1969), pp. 5–6.
46. *Aids to Reflection*, 4th ed. with author's last corrections, ed H. N. Coleridge (London, 1839), pp. 308–309.
47. *Confessions of an Inquiring Spirit*, ed. H. St.J. Hart (Stanford, Cal., 1957), letter 4, p. 64.
48. Barth, *Coleridge and Christian Doctrine*, p. 41 (quoting from Notebook 38, 1829).
49. *Ibid.*, p. 42 (quoting letter of Sept. 1807).
50. *What Is Revelation?* (London, 1859), pp. 55–56.
51. Alec R. Vidler, *The Theology of F. D. Maurice* (London, 1948), p. 35.
52. *Evidences*, in *Works*, vols. 3 and 4 (Edinburgh, 1848), 4:178.
53. Third Amer. ed. (Andover, Mass., 1860), pp. 12–13.

54. *Instruction pastorale sur l'excellence de la religion* (Langres, 1786), p. 5.
55. *Pensées sur la philosophie de l'incrédulité* (Paris, 1785), p. 143.
56. *Mémoires philosophiques du B^{on} de * * * , grand chambellan de sa majesté l'impératrice reine*, 2 vols. (Paris, 1777–78).
57. *Fragments de l'apologie de la religion*, in *Oeuvres*, vol. 16 (Paris, 1821), ch. 4.
58. *L'homme de désir* (Lyon, 1790); *Le ministère de l'homme-esprit* (Paris, 1802).
59. *Le génie du christianisme; ou, beautés de la religion chrétienne*, 5 vols. (Paris, 1802), p. viii.
60. 5th ed., 5 vols. (Lyon, 1809), 1:9.
61. *Ibid.*, 3:65.
62. *Défense du christianisme*, 3rd ed., 3 vols. (Paris, 1825–26); Eng. trans. J. B. Jones, 2 vols. (London, 1836).
63. L. P. Mahoney, 'Frayssinous,' NCE 6:83.
64. W. M. Horton, *The Philosophy of the Abbé Bautain* (New York, 1926), p. 7.
65. *Soirées de Saint-Petersbourg*, 2 vols. (Paris, 1821).
66. *Du pape* (1819); 2nd ed., enlarged (Lyon, 1821).
67. *Ibid.*, Bk 3, ch. 2; in *The Works of Joseph de Maistre*, ed. Jack Lively (New York, 1965), pp. 145–146.
68. See evaluation of Bonald by Edgar Hocedez, *Histoire de la théologie au XIXe siècle* (Paris, 1948), 2:82–83.
69. A thorough study is Louis Le Guillou's *L'Évolution de la pensée religieuse de Félicité Lamennais* (Paris, 1965).
70. Quoted by Alec R. Vidler, *Prophecy and Papacy: A Study of Lamennais* (London, 1954), p. 100.
71. *Essai sur l'indifférence en matière de religion*, 4 vols. (Paris, 1817–23); partial Eng. trans. Lord Stanley of Alderley (London, 1895).
72. Quoted in Jean-Dominique Folghera, *L'Apologétique de Lacordaire* (Paris, 1911), p. 46.
73. Quoted by Paul Poupard, *L'Abbé Louis Bautain* (Tournai, 1961), p. 286.
74. *La Philosophie du christianisme: correspondence religieuse de L. Bautain*, 2 vols. (Paris, 1835).
75. Poupard, *L'Abbé Louis Bautain*, p. 283.
76. Cf. Denz 2751–56, 2765–69.
77. *Einleitung in die christkatholische Theologie*, 2 vols. (Münster, 1819, 1829).
78. *Die Apologetik als wissenschaftliche Nachweisung der Göttlichkeit des Christentums*, 3 vols. (Mainz, 1843–47; enlarged ed., 3 vols., 1847).
79. *Die Einheit der Kirche; oder, das Prinzip des Katholicizmus* (Tübingen, 1825).
80. *Symbolik, oder Darstellung der dogmatischen Gegensätze der*

Katholiken und Protestanten nach ihrer öffentlichen Bekennt-nisschriften (Mainz, 1832); Eng. trans. J. B. Robertson (New York, 1843).

81. Cf. Y. M. J. Congar, 'The Encounter between Christian Confessions: Yesterday and Today,' *Dialogue Between Christians*, Eng. trans. Philip Loretz (Westminster, Md., 1966), pp. 135–159.

82. *El Criterio* (Barcelona, 1845); Eng. trans. a Catholic priest, *Criterion: or, How to Detect Error and Arrive at Truth* (New York, 1875); new partial trans. David Thomson, *Scientific Investigation of Religion* (Kyoto, 1959).

83. *Cartas á un escéptico en materia de religión* (Barcelona, 1846); Eng. trans. William McDonald (Dublin, 1875).

84. *Filosofía fundamental* (Barcelona, 1846); Eng. trans. Henry F. Brownson (New York, 1858).

85. *El protestantismo comparado con el catolicismo en sus relaciones con la civilización europea*, 4 vols. (Barcelona, 1842–44); Eng. trans. C. J. Hanford and R. Kershaw, *Protestantism and Catholicity Compared*, 2d ed. (Baltimore, 1851).

86. *Ibid.*, p. 38.

87. *Ensayo sobre el catolicismo, el liberalismo y el socialismo, considerados en sus principios fundamentales* (Madrid, 1851); Eng. trans. Mrs. M. V. Goddard (New York, 1925), p. 22.

88. *Osservazioni sulla morale cattolica* (1819, Paris, 1834); Eng. trans. anon. (London, 1836).

89. *Le bellezze della Fede nei misteri dell'epifania*, 2 vols. (Naples, 1854); new ed., 3 vols. (Milan, 1867), 1:7.

90. *L'ermesianismo* [offprints from *Annali delle scienze religiose*] (Rome, 1838–39); also 'Riflessioni sul metodo introdotto da Giorgio Hermes nella teologia cattolica,' *Annali* 16 (1843): 251–299, 374–440; Fr. trans. in Migne, *Démonstrations évangeliques* (Paris, 1854), 14:945–1024.

91. *Praelectiones dogmaticae*, 9 vols. (Rome, 1835–41).

92. *De vera religione adversus incredulos et heterodoxos*, ed. J. P. Migne, 2 vols. (Paris, 1852; from Roman ed. of 1840).

93. *Il protestantesimo e la regola di fede*, 3 vols. (Rome, 1853).

94. *De D. N. Jesu Christo divinitate, adversus hujus aetatis incredulos, rationalistas et mythicos*, 3 vols. (Turin, 1870).

95. 2d ed., London, 1842.

96. *Ibid.*, p. 3.

97. London, 1836; only the two vol. ed. of that date was authorized by the author; the one vol. ed. 1836 is unauthorized.

98. *Two Essays on Scripture Miracles and on Ecclesiastical* (1826, 1843), reissued in single volume (London, 1870).

98a. *Fifteen Sermons Preached Before the University of Oxford* (London, 1843; rev. ed., 1871).

99. London, 1845; reprinted Garden City, N.Y., 1960.

100. 17th impression, London, 1911.
101. London, 1864; new impression, London, 1924.
102. London, 1870; reprinted Garden City, N.Y., 1955; hereafter cited as *Grammar*.
103. Louis Bouyer, *Newman: His Life and Spirituality*, Eng. trans. J. L. May (New York, 1960), p. 293, quoting letter of Dec. 8, 1849.
104. *Grammar*, pp. 328–333.
105. *Lectures on Certain Difficulties Felt by Anglicans in Submitting to the Catholic Church*, 2 vols. (London, 1850; new impression, 1888), 2:312.
106. Cf. *Grammar*, pp. 331–332.
107. *Grammar*, p. 300.
108. J. M. Walgrave, *Newman the Theologian*, Eng. trans. A. V. Littledale (New York, 1960), p. 229.
109. See Note 2 in Appendices to *Grammar*, with references to Newman's other works.
110. Cf. *Grammar*, pp. 95–109, 304.
111. *Ibid.*, pp. 308–311; cf. *Apologia*, pp. 241–244.
112. *Grammar*, pp. 328–329.
113. *Ibid.*, pp. 333–335.
114. *Ibid.*, p. 320; cf. Émile Amort, *Demonstratio critica religionis catholicae nova, moderata, facilis* (Venice, 1744).
115. *Grammar*, p. 353.
116. *Apologia*, ch. 5; pp. 243–244.
117. *Ibid.*, p. 250.
118. London, 1852; reprinted Baltimore, 1855, p. 90.
119. London, 1871.
120. See Robert Gorman, 'Catholic Apologetical Literature in the United States (1784–1858)' (dissertation, Catholic University of America, 1939).
121. *The Convert; or, Leaves from My Experience* (New York, 1857).
122. For an exposition and critique of this argument see George K. Malone, 'The True Church: A Study in the Apologetics of Orestes A. Brownson' (dissertation, St. Mary of the Lake Seminary, 1957). As Malone points out, this is only one of five separate arguments used by Brownson, but it is perhaps the most original and the most characteristic of the times.
123. New York, 1866.
124. New York, 1855.
125. New York, 1857.
126. Paris, 1897.
127. Text in AmEcclRev 20 (1899); 399–409.
128. *Philosophie: De la connaissance de Dieu* (Paris, 1854); Eng. trans. A. L. Alber, *Knowledge of God: A Study of the Chief Theodicies* (Boston, 1892). On Gratry's dependence on Bautain see Horton, *Philosophy of Abbé Bautain*, esp. pp. 287–288.

129. *Études philosophiques sur le christianisme,* 4 vols. (Bordeaux, 1843).
130. *La divinité de Jésus-Christ: démonstration nouvelle tirée des dernières attaques de l'incrédulité* (Paris, 1864).
131. *L'Art de croire; ou, preparation philosophique à la foi chrétienne,* 2 vols. (Paris, 1867).
132. *Entretiens sur la démonstration catholique de la révélation chrétienne,* 2d ed. (Tournai, 1857).
133. See Maurice Becqué, *L'Apologétique du cardinal Dechamps* (Bruges, 1949). On Dechamps' relationship to the immanence apologetic of Blondel, see ch. 6 here.
134. See Denz 3009 and the analysis of Roger Aubert, *Le Problème de l'acte de foi,* 2d ed. (Louvain, 1950), pp. 164–176.
135. This question has been examined by R. J. Cronin in his unpublished doctoral dissertation, 'The Defense of the Average Catholic's Faith in the Apologetic of Cardinal Dechamps' (Institut Catholique, 1961).
136. E. Hocedez refers to some 80 important Catholic apologetical works, mostly defensive in character, produced in France in the last quarter of the century; *Histoire de la théologie au XIXe siècle* (Paris, 1947), 3:197–221.
137. *Apologétique scientifique de la foi chrétienne* (Paris, 1885); new ed., J. B. Senderens (Paris, 1903).
138. *Le Positivisme et la science expérimentale,* 2 vols. (Paris, 1880–81).
139. *La Transcendance du Christianisme* (Paris, 1885).
140. *Problèmes et conclusions de l'histoire des religions* (Paris, 1885).
141. A valuable summary of Paul de Broglie's apologetic may be found in C. Piat's introduction to the former's posthumous *Religion et critique* (Paris, 1906). See also, more briefly, Léon Cristiani, *Why We Believe,* Twentieth Century Encyclopedia of Catholicism, vol. 106 (New York, 1959), pp. 98–100.
142. *La Bible et les découvertes modernes en Egypte et en Assyrie* (Paris, 1877; 3d ed., 4 vols., 1881–82).
143. *Dictionnaire de la Bible,* 5 vols. (Paris, 1895–1912).
144. *Apologie des Christenthums,* 2 vols. (Freiburg i.B., 1865–67). Parts translated by H. S. Bowden under titles *Natural Religion* and *Revealed Religion* (London, 1890 and 1895 respectively).
145. *Lehrbuch der Fundamentaltheologie, oder Apologetik* (1879; 2d ed., Freiburg i.Br., 1888).
146. *Apologie des Christentums,* 3 vols. (Freiburg i.Br., 1887–88); Eng. trans. M. F. Glancey and V. J. Schobel (New York, 1891–92).
147. *Apologie des Christentums vom Standpunkt der Sitte und Kultur,* 5 vols. (Freiburg i.Br., 1878–89).
148. Cf. Otto Zöckler, *Geschichte der Apologie des Christentums* (Gütersloh, 1907).
149. *Wissenschaftliche Kritik der evangelischen Geschichte* (Frankfurt a.M., 1842).
150. *Apologetik: Wissenschaftliche Rechtfertigung des Christentums,*

2 vols. (Gütersloh, 1874–75); Eng. trans. William Stuart and John Macpherson, 3 vols. (Edinburgh, 1886–87).

151. *Apologetische Vorträge*, 4 vols. (Leipzig, 1864–1880). The fourth volume, *Die moderne Weltanschauung und ihre praktischen Konsequenzen*, was apparently never translated into English.

152. *Ueber die Grundwahrheiten des Christentums*; Eng. trans. Sophia Taylor (Edinburgh, 1865).

153. *Ueber die Heilswahrheiten des Christentums*; Eng. trans. Sophia Taylor (Edinburgh, 1868).

154. *Ueber die Moral des Christentums*; Eng. trans. Sophia Taylor (Edinburgh, 1873).

155. *Der Verkehr des Christen mit Gott* (Stuttgart, 1886); Eng. trans. J. S. Stanyon, *The Communion of the Christian with God*, rev. ed. (New York, 1906).

156. See the criticism of D. C. Macintosh, *The Problem of Religious Knowledge* (New York, 1940), pp. 256–261.

157. *Die Wahrheit der christlichen Religion* (Basel, 1889); *Truth of the Christian Religion*, Eng. trans. George Ferries, 2 vols. (Edinburgh, 1894).

158. *The Truth of the Christian Religion*, 2:387.

159. *Grundriss der christlichen Apologetik* (Göttingen, 1894); Eng. trans. A. B. Nichols, *Outlines* (New York, 1905).

160. *Outlines*, pp. 299–300.

161. *Ibid.*, p. 315.

162. *Das Wesen des Christentums* (Leipzig, 1900); Eng. trans. B. T. Saunders, *What is Christianity?* (1901; reprint ed., New York, 1957).

163. For an English example see the Bampton Lectures of C. A. Row, *Christian Evidences Viewed in Relation to Modern Thought* (London, 1877). For American examples see the Lowell Lectures of J. G. Palfrey, *The Evidences of Christianity* (Boston, 1843) or those of Mark Hopkins, *Evidences of Christianity* (Boston, 1846; rev. ed., 1863).

164. New York, 1865; rev. ed., 1870.

165. London, 1880.

166. *What Is Darwinism?* (New York, 1874).

167. London, 1890.

168. *Christianity and Positivism: Lectures to the Times on Natural Theology and Apologetics* (New York, 1871).

169. London, 1883.

170. 5th ed. (New York, 1899), p. 157; cf. p. 502.

171. *Ibid.*, p. 173.

172. *Ibid.*, p. 297.

173. *Ibid.*, p. 514.

K

270 *Notes*

NOTES TO CHAPTER SIX

1. See Roger Aubert, *Le Problème de l'acte de foi,* 2d ed. (Louvain, 1950), pp. 267–277.
2. A. Sabatier, *Esquisse d'une philosophie chrétienne* (Paris, 1897).
3. A. J. Balfour, *The Foundations of Belief* (London, 1895; Fr. trans., Paris, 1896).
4. *The Will to Believe and Other Essays* (New York, 1897; Fr. trans., Paris, 1898); *The Varieties of Religious Experience* (London, 1902; Fr. trans., Paris, 1906).
5. *La Certitude morale* (Paris, 1880); applied especially to apologetics in his *Ce qu'on va chercher à Rome* (Paris, 1895).
6. *La Science et la religion* (Paris, 1895), p. 62.
7. *L'Action: essai d'une critique de la vie et d'une science de la pratique* (Paris, 1893; reprinted Paris, 1950).
8. *Ibid.,* pp. 400–403, 491–492.
9. 'Lettre sur les exigences de la pensée contemporaine en matière d'apologétique . . .' AnnalPhilChr 131 and 132 (January–July 1896); Eng. trans. A. Dru and I. Trethowan, *The Letter on Apologetics* (New York, 1964).
10. *Letter on Apologetics,* p. 152.
11. *Ibid.,* pp. 163–164.
12. In AnnalPhilChr October 1905 to March 1907. On the relationship between Blondel and Mallet the remarks in Aubert's *Problème* require some correction. See for instance J. M. Somerville, *Total Commitment* (Washington, D.C., 1968), pp. 29 and 373.
13. AnnalPhilChr 154 (March 1907): 573–574.
14. *Qu'est ce que la foi?* (Paris, 1907), pp. 36–40.
15. *History and Dogma,* Eng. trans. A. Dru and I. Trethowan (New York, 1964), p. 226.
16. Cf. M. Blondel, 'Miracle,' in A. Lalande, ed., *Vocabulaire de la philosophie,* 7th ed. (Paris, 1956), pp. 628–632.
17. *L'Action,* pp. 396–397.
18. Cf. François Rodé, *Le Miracle dans la controverse Moderniste* (Paris, 1965).
19. 'Les Preuves et l'économie de la révélation,' *Revue du clergé francais* 22 (Mar. 15, 1900): 128.
20. AnnalPhilChr 1906–07; Dec. 1906, p. 249 *et passim.*
21. *Ibid.,* July 1907, pp. 337–362.
22. 'Les Preuves et l'économie de la révélation,' p. 142.
23. *Lex orandi* (London, 1904), p. ix.
24. *Ibid.,* p. xxxi.
25. *Ibid.,* p. 209.
26. ActApS 40 (1907):627.
27. *Ibid.,* p. 630.
28. Denz 3539.

29. *La Crédibilité et l'apologétique* (Paris, 1908; 2d ed., 1912; the latter is followed here).
30. *L'Objet intégral de l'apologétique*, 3d ed. (Paris, 1912).
31. *Ibid.*, p. 464.
32. *L'Apologétique: ses problèmes, sa définition* (Paris, n.d.), p. 46; reprint of 'Bulletin d'apologétique,' RechScRel 4 (1913): 443–488, 486. The term credibility in neo-Scholasticism is the attribute of that which may prudently be believed; credentity (Latin *credentitas*, French *crédentité*) is the attribute of that which ought to be believed. In NCE 1:672–673 P. J. Cahill, apparently moved by an etymological scruple, coins the term credendity as a synonym for the more common term credentity. The latter term is used here out of respect for general usage.
33. *Comment réaliser l'apologétique intégrale* (Paris, 1913).
34. An excellent account of Rousselot's positions on these points may be found in Aubert, *Le problème de l'acte de foi*, pp. 452–470.
35. *Ibid.*, pp. 498–502.
36. *La Science mène-t-elle à Dieu?* (Paris, 1933).
37. *La grand'route apologétique* (Paris, 1939).
38. 'Apologétique,' DictApolFoiCath, 4th ed., 1:189–251, esp. col. 246.
39. *Ibid.*, cols. 246–247.
40. *De revelatione per ecclesiam catholicam proposita*, 2 vols., 4th ed. (Rome, 1945; 1st ed., Rome and Paris, 1918). On Garrigou-Lagrange as an apologist, see S. Giuliani, O.P., 'R. P. Garrigou-Lagrange Apologeta,' *Angelicum* 42 (1965): 117–136.
41. *Ibid.*, 1.49–62. Here Garrigou-Lagrange discusses whether the distinction between apologetics and sacred theology is a specific one—and decides in the negative.
42. *Jesus Christus: Apologie seiner Messianität und Gottheit gegenüber der neuesten ungläubigen Jesus-Forschung*, 2 vols. (Paderborn, 1911–14); Eng. trans. John L. Stoddard from 2d Ger. ed., *Christ and the Critics*, 2 vols. (New York, 1924).
43. *Christ and the Critics*, 1:116.
44. *Ibid.*, 2.444.
45. 'Jésus-Christ,' DictApolFoiCath, 4th ed., 2:1288–1538.
46. *Jésus Christ: sa personne, son message, ses preuves*, 3rd ed., 2 vols. (Paris, 1928); Eng. trans. Basil Whelan and Douglas Carter, 3 vols. (New York, 1935, 1935, 1937).
47. The rather positive evaluation of the 'method of immanence' by Albert Valensin in the first printing was replaced by a wholly condemnatory assessment by J. de Tonquédec in the later printings.
48. *Apologétique: nos raisons de croire, réponses aux objections* (Paris, 1937).
49. 'Un essai de synthèse apologétique,' EphemThLov 14 (1937): 447–466.
50. *Ibid.*, p. 453.

51. *Essai sur Dieu, l'homme, et l'univers* (Tournai and Paris, 1950); Eng. trans. anon., *God, Man and the Universe*, with some additional material, from the rev. ed. of 1953 (New York, 1953).

52. In addition to the work of Garrigou-Lagrange already mentioned, the following textbooks rank among the best: Hermann Dieckmann, *De revelatione christiana* (Freiburg i.Br., 1930); Anthony C. Cotter, *Theologia fundamentalis* (Weston, Mass., 1940); Michael Nicolau and Ioachim Salaverri, *Theologia fundamentalis*, in *Sacrae theologiae summa*, vol. 1, 2d ed. (Madrid, 1952).

53. 'Apologétique et théologie,' NouvRevTh 57 (1930): 361–378.

54. *Sous les yeux de l'incroyant* (Paris, 1944; 2d ed., 1946).

55. *The Problem of Jesus: A Free-Thinker's Diary*, Eng. trans. A. G. Smith (New York, 1955), from the author's abridgement of his two volumes, *Le Problème de Jésus et les fondements du témoignage chrétien* (Paris, 1950) and *Le problème de Jésus II: divinité et résurrection* (Paris, 1953).

56. See his *Les évangiles et l'histoire* (Paris, 1963); Eng. trans. John McHugh, *The Gospels and the Jesus of History* (New York, 1968).

57. *Du Protestantisme à l'église* (Paris, 1954); Eng. trans. A. V. Littledale (Westminster, Md., 1956).

58. *The Spirit of Mediaeval Philosophy*, Eng. trans. A. H. C. Downes (New York, 1936), p. 37.

59. New York, 1937.

60. *Medieval Universalism at Its Present Value* (New York, 1937), p. 1.

61. *Ibid.*, p. 15.

62. 'A Confession of Faith' (1941), reprinted in J. W. Evans and L. R. Ward, eds., *The Social and Political Philosophy of J. Maritain* (New York, 1955), p. 334.

63. *L'Humanisme intégral* (Paris, 1936); 2d Eng. trans. J. W. Evans, *Integral Humanism* (New York, 1968).

64. *The Range of Reason* (New York, 1952), p. 193.

65. *Lettres de voyage, 1923–55* (Paris, 1961); Eng. trans. René Hague et al., *Letters from a Traveller* (London, 1962), p. 127.

66. References to these letters are given in C. F. Mooney, *Teilhard de Chardin and the Mystery of Christ* (New York, 1966), pp. 191–193.

67. *Le Milieu divin* (Paris, 1957); Eng. trans. Bernard Wall, *The Divine Milieu* (New York, 1960), p. 39.

68. *Comment je crois* (Paris, 1969); Eng. trans. René Hague, *How I Believe* (New York, 1969), p. 52.

69. *Le phénomène humain* (Paris, 1955); Eng. trans. Bernard Wall, *The Phenomenon of Man* (New York, 1959).

70. *Ibid.*, pp. 225–228.

71. *L'Avenir de l'homme* (Paris, 1939); Eng. trans. Norman Denny, *The Future of Man* (New York, 1964), pp. 286–287.

72. Quoted by Jacques Maritain, *Le Paysan de la Garonne* (Paris, 1966);

Eng. trans. Michael Cuddihy and Elizabeth Hughes, *The Peasant of the Garonne* (New York, 1968), p. 123.

73. Gilson, quoted *ibid.*, pp. 119, 121.
74. *Ibid.*, 268.
75. *Die moderne Apologetik* (Frankfurt a.M., 1903). Cf. several articles on the 'new apologetic' by Schanz and W. Koch noted by Aubert, *Le problème de l'acte de foi*, pp. 513–514.
76. On Schell's apologetics see Josef Hasenfuss, *Herman Schell als existentieller Denker und Theologe* (Würzburg, 1956), pp. 103–109; Paulus Wacker, *Glaube und Wissen bei Herman Schell* (Paderborn, 1961), pp. 277–279.
77. *Der Katholicismus als Princip des Fortschritts* (Würzburg, 1897).
78. *Gott und Geist*, 2 vols. (Paderborn, 1895–96).
79. *Religion und Offenbarung*, 3d ed. (Paderborn, 1907).
80. *Apologie des Christentums*, 2 vols. (Paderborn, 1901–05).
81. On Scheler as an apologist see James J. Kavanaugh, *The Struggle of the Unbeliever* (New York, 1968), pp. 11–37.
82. *Vom Ewigen im Menschen* (Leipzig, 1921); Eng. trans. Bernard Noble, *On the Eternal in Man* (London, 1960), p. 266.
83. *Das Wesen des Katholizismus* (Düsseldorf, 1924); Eng. trans. Justin McCann from 3d Ger. ed., *The Spirit of Catholicism* (New York, 1936).
84. *The Spirit of Catholicism*, p. 59.
85. *Jesus Christus* (Augsburg. 1933); Eng. trans. Philip Hereford (New York, 1934), pp. 37–38.
86. *Hörer des Wortes* (Munich, 1941; rev. ed., 1963); Eng. trans. Michael Richards from rev. ed., *Hearers of the Word* (New York, 1969).
87. This polemical note, clearly audible in the first ed., pp. 36–38, 225–227, is considerably muted in the rev. ed.; see *Hearers of the Word*, pp. 25–26.
88. *Hearers of the Word*, p. 179.
89. See his article, 'The Way to Faith,' in *Sacramentum Mundi* (Eng. ed., New York, 1968), 2:310–313.
90. 'Thoughts on the Possibility of Belief Today,' in *Theological Investigations*, Eng. trans. Karl H. Kruger (Baltimore, 1966), 5:3–22.
91. 'Apologetics,' *The New Schaff-Herzog Encyclopedia of Religious Knowledge* (New York, 1908), 1:232–238; quotation from p. 233.
92. Preface, *Lux mundi*, 10th ed. (London, 1890), p. x.
93. 3 vols. (London, 1921, 1922, 1924; combined ed., 1926).
94. New York, 1926.
95. *'Yes, But—'* (New York, 1931), p. 2.
96. *Ibid.*, p. 12.
97. *Ibid.*, p. 183.
98. For other examples of this style of apologetic see Edward J. Carnell, *Christian Commitment: An Apologetic* (New York, 1957); Gordon

H. Clark, *Religion, Reason, and Revelation* (Philadelphia, 1961); John H. Gerstner, *Reasons for Faith* (New York, 1960); Floyd E. Hamilton, *The Basis of Christian Faith* (New York, 1963); and Bernard Ramm, *Protestant Christian Evidences* (Chicago, 1953).

99. *Die kirchliche Dogmatik* 1/1 (Munich, 1932); *Church Dogmatics* 1/1, ed. G. W. Bromiley and T. F. Torrance (New York, 1936), pp. 26–47.

100. *Ibid.*, p. 31.

101. For an exposition and critique of these views of Barth see Gordon H. Clark, *Karl Barth's Theological Method* (Philadelphia, 1963), pp. 76–108.

102. *Protestant Theology from Rousseau to Ritschl*, Eng. trans. Brian Cozens and H. H. Hartwell (London, 1959), pp. 320–325; cf. supra, p. 263 , n. 5

103. *Ibid.*, p. 323.

104. *Die kirchliche Dogmatik* 2/1 (Zollikon-Zurich, 1940); *Church Dogmatics* 2/1, ed. Bromiley and Torrance (Edinburgh and New York, 1957), p. 8.

105. *Anselm: Fides Quaerens Intellectum*, Eng. trans. Ian W. Robertson (Richmond, Va., 1960), p. 71.

106. Peter Vogelsanger, 'Brunner as Apologist,' in Charles W. Kegley, ed., *The Theology of Emil Brunner* (New York, 1962), pp. 289–304, esp. 289; for Brunner's approval of this estimate see *ibid.*, p. 339.

107. *Dogmatik* 1 (Zurich, 1946); Eng. trans. Olive Wyon *Dogmatics* 1, (London, 1949), p. 98.

108. In Kegley, *Theology of Emil Brunner*, p. 16.

109. *Jesus Christ and Mythology* (London, 1960), p. 53.

110. 'The Question of Natural Theology,' *Essays Philosophical and Theological*, Eng. trans. J. C. G. Greig (New York, 1955), p. 113.

111. *Jesus Christ and Mythology*, p. 72.

112. *Ibid.*, pp. 65–66.

113. In H. W. Bartsch ed., *Kerygma und Mythos*; Eng. trans. R. H. Fuller, *Kerygma and Myth* (New York, 1953, paperback reprint, 1961), p. 207.

114. *Kerygma and Myth*, p. 42.

115. *Jesus Christ and Mythology*, p. 36.

116. Karl Barth, 'Rudolph Bultmann: An Attempt to Understand Him,' in *Kerygma and Myth*, vol. 2, Eng. trans. R. H. Fuller (London, 1962), pp. 118–119.

117. *Systematic Theology* (Chicago, 1951), 1:6–7.

118. *Ibid.*, 1:31.

119. *Ibid.*, 1:60.

120. *Ibid.*, 1:61. For a full study of Tillich as an apologist from a Catholic point of view, see Joseph Schmitz, *Die apologetische Theologie Paul Tillichs* (Mainz, 1966).

121. 'Reinhold Niebuhr as Apologist' in C. W. Kegley and R. W. Bretall,

eds., *Reinhold Niebuhr* (New York, 1956), pp. 215–217. For a critique from a conservative evangelical point of view see Jerry H. Gill, 'Reinhold Niebuhr and Apologetics,' *Theology Today* 17 (1960): 200–212.

122. 2 vols. (New York, 1941–43).

123. *Faith and History* (New York, 1955), pp. 164–165.

124. *The Meaning of Revelation* (New York, 1941), pp. 22–42.

125. L. A. Hoedemaker, *Faith in Total Life: Style and Direction of H. Richard Niebuhr's Theology* (Groningen, 1966), pp. 229–236, quotes several authors to this effect; notably J. B. Cobb, who refers to Richard Niebuhr's 'apologetic for radical monotheism'; see *Living Options in Protestant Theology* (Philadelphia, 1962), p. 288.

126. On Heim as an apologist see Carl Michalson, 'Karl Heim' in *A Handbook of Christian Theologians*, ed. D. G. Peerman and M. E. Marty (Cleveland, 1965); reprinted as chap. 4 of Michalson's *Worldly Theology* (New York, 1967), pp. 52–70. For a fuller discussion see the unpublished doctoral dissertation of John Pemberton III, 'Karl Heim's Conception of the Apologetic Task of the Christian Theologian' (Duke University, 1958).

127. K. Heim, *Das Wesen der evangelischen Christentums* (Leipzig, 1925), Eng. trans. John Schmidt from 4th rev. ed. (Philadelphia, 1963).

128. *Der evangelische Glaube und das Denken der Gegenwart* (Berlin, Tübingen, Hamburg, 1931–52). The six volumes are, in English: *God Transcendent*, trans. E. P. Dickie (London, 1935); *Jesus the Lord*, trans. D. H. van Daalen (Edinburgh, 1959); *Jesus the World's Perfecter*, trans. D. H. van Daalen (Edinburgh, 1959); *Christian Faith and Natural Science*, trans. N. H. Smith (New York, 1953); *The Transformation of the Scientific World View*, trans. W. A. Whitehouse (London, 1953); *The World: Its Creation and Consummation*, trans. Robert Smith (Edinburgh, 1962).

129. P. Althaus, *Die christliche Wahrheit*, 2d ed. (Gütersloh, 1949), 1:67–69.

130. Michalson, *Worldly Theology*, p. 69.

131. *Letters and Papers from Prison*, rev. and enlarged Eng. trans. R. H. Fuller et al. (London, 1967), p. 170.

132. *Ibid.*

133. Cf. F. Gogarten, *Verhängnis und Hoffnung der Neuzeit* (Stuttgart, 1953). For a good account, which here is followed in substance, see Ronald Gregor Smith, *Secular Christianity* (London, 1960), pp. 150–156, also Larry Shiner, *The Secularization of Christianity: An Introduction to the Theology of Friedrich Gogarten* (Nashville, 1966).

134. *Christianity in World History*, Eng. trans. H. H. Hoskins (London and New York, 1964).

135. *Der sogenannte Kerygma und der historische Jesus* (Gütersloh, 1958);

Eng. trans. David Cairns, *The So-Called Kerygma and the Historical Jesus* (London, 1959), p. 34.

136. *A New Quest of the Historical Jesus* (Naperville, Ill., 1959), p. 92.
137. *The Historian and the Believer* (New York, 1966), p. 188.
138. Pannenberg's views on faith, reason, and apologetics appear in his contributions to the symposium, *Offenbarung als Geschichte* (Göttingen, 1961), Eng. trans. David Granskou, *Revelation as History* (New York, 1968) and in his focal essay and response in J. M. Robinson and J. B. Cobb, Jr., eds., *Theology as History* (New York, 1967), pp. 101–133, 221–276. Robinson's introduction to this volume gives a good summary of the criticisms that have been directed at Pannenberg.
139. *The Riddle of the New Testament* (1931; paperback reprint, London, 1958), pp. 144–145.
140. *Ibid.,* p. 180.
141. Cf. A. M. Ramsey, *An Era in Anglican Theology: From Gore to Temple* (New York, 1960), p. 137.
142. *The Apostolic Preaching and Its Developments*, rev. ed. (London, 1944).
143. See R. B. Cunningham, *C. S. Lewis: Defender of the Faith* (Philadelphia, 1967) for an estimate of Lewis's accomplishments and limitations as an apologist.
144. *Christian Apologetics* (London, 1947; paperback reprint, 1960), p. 109.
145. *History Sacred and Profane* (Philadelphia, 1964), pp. 270–271.
146. *Ibid.,* pp. 196, 209.
147. *Ibid.,* pp. 213–241.
148. For critiques see John Navone, *History and Faith in the Thought of Alan Richardson* (London, 1966); C. H. Dodd, review of *History Sacred and Profane, Expository Times,* April, 1964, pp. 206–208; and V. A. Harvey, *The Historian and the Believer,* pp. 222–223, 231–235.

Bibliography

CLASSICS OF APOLOGETICS

Within each category, works are arranged in approximate order of authorship.

Anthology

Migne, Jacques Paul. *Démonstrations évangeliques*. 20 vols. Paris: Migne, 1843–62.
   An anthology of apologetical works from Tertullian to Gregory XVI (including some Protestants and Anglicans) in French translation.

Patristic Period

Aristides the Philosopher. *Apology*, translated by D. M. Kay (Ante-Nicene Fathers, vol. 10, pp. 259–279). New York, 1896.
Justin Martyr. *Works*, translated by Thomas B. Falls (Fathers of the Church, vol. 6). New York: Fathers of the Church, Inc., 1948.
   Contains *First* and *Second Apologies, Dialogue with Trypho*, and other works attributed to Justin.
Athenagoras. *Embassy for the Christians*, translated by Joseph H. Crehan (Ancient Christian Writers, vol. 23). Westminster, Md.: Newman Press, 1956.
Letter to Diognetus, translated by James A. Kleist (Ancient Christian Writers, vol. 6). Westminster, Md.: Newman Press, 1948.
Clement of Alexandria. *Exhortation to the Greeks*, translated by G. W. Butterworth (Loeb Classical Library, vol. 92). Cambridge: Harvard University Press, 1919.
Origen. *Contra Celsum*, translated by Henry Chadwick. 2d ed., rev. Cambridge, Eng.: University Press, 1965.
Marcus Minucius Felix, *Octavius*, translated by Rudolf Arbesmann

(Fathers of the Church, vol. 10). New York: Fathers of the Church, Inc., 1950.

Tertullian. *Apology,* translated by Sister Emily Joseph Daly (Fathers of the Church, vol. 10). New York: Fathers of the Church, Inc., 1950.

Arnobius Afer. *The Case Against the Pagans,* translated by George E. McCracken. 2 vols. (Ancient Christian Writers, vols. 7–8). Westminster, Md.: Newman Press, 1942.

Lactantius. *The Divine Institutes,* translated by Sister Mary Francis McDonald (Fathers of the Church, vol. 49). Washington, D.C.: The Catholic University of America Press, 1964.

Eusebius of Caesarea. *The Preparation of the Gospel,* translated by E. H. Gifford. 2 vols. New York: Oxford University Press, 1903.

——. *The Proof of the Gospel,* translated by W. J. Ferrar. 2 vols. London: S.P.C.K., 1920.

Athanasius, St. *The Incarnation of the Word of God,* translated by a Religious of C.S.M.V. New York: Macmillan, 1946. With an Introduction by C. S. Lewis.

Théodoret de Cyr. *Thérapeutique des maladies helléniques,* translated by Pierre Canivet. 2 vols. (Sources chrétiennes, vol. 57). Paris: Cerf, 1958.

Augustine, St. *Earlier Writings,* translation and introduction by J. H. S. Burleigh (Library of Christian Classics, vol. 6). Philadelphia: Westminster, 1953.

——. *The City of God,* translated by G. G. Walsh and Sister Grace Monahan. 3 vols. (Fathers of the Church, vols. 8, 14, 24). New York: Fathers of the Church, Inc., 1950, 1952, 1954.

Middle Ages (through Fifteenth Century)

Anselm, St. *Basic Writings,* translated by Sidney N. Deane. 2d ed. LaSalle, Ill. Open Ct., 1962.

Thomas Aquinas, St. *On the Truth of the Catholic Faith,* translated by A. C. Pegis et al. 4 vols. Garden City: Doubleday Image, 1955–56.

Sabundus, Raimundus. *Liber creaturarum.* Stuttgart: Fromann, 1966. Reproduces Sulzbach edition of 1852, adding Preface by F. Stegmüller and supplying a corrected edition of the Prologue and of Tit. 1.

Savonarola, Girolamo. *The Triumph of the Cross,* translated by O. T. Hill. London: Hodder & Stoughton, 1868.

Sixteenth through Eighteenth Century

Vives, Juan Luis. *De veritate fidei christianae* (Opera omnia, vol. 8). Valencia: Montford, 1790; facsimile ed., London: Gregg Int., 1964. 1st ed., Basel, 1543.

du Plessis-Mornay, Philip. *A Work Concerning the Trueness of the Christian Religion against Atheists, Epicures, Paynims, Iewes, Mahumetists, and*

Other Infidels, translated by Philip Sidney and Arthur Goldring. 4th ed., London, 1617; French original, 1581.

Grotius, Hugo. *The Truth of the Christian Religion in Six Books,* corrected and illustrated with notes by Le Clerc, translated by John Clarke. London, 1709; Latin original, 1627.

✓ Pascal, Blaise. *Pensées,* edited by Léon Brunschvicg. Paris: Nelson, 1942. For a conveniently accessible English translation see R. W. Gleason, ed., *The Essential Pascal.* New York: Mentor-Omega, 1966.

Bossuet, Jacques Bénigne. *Discours sur l'histoire universelle.* Paris: Lefèvre, 1836; translated by James Ephilstone as *An Universal History from the Beginning of the World to the Empire of Charlemagne.* London: T. Evans, 1778; New York, 1821; French original, 1681.

Abbadie, Jacques. *A Vindication of the Truth of the Christian Religion,* translated by Henry Lusson. 2 vols. London 1694–98; French original, 1684.

———. *A Treatise on the Divinity of Our Lord Jesus Christ,* translated by Alexander Booth. Charlestown, Mass., 1817; French original, 1689.

Clarke, Samuel. *The Unchangeable Obligations of Natural Religion and the Truth of the Christian Revelation.* 10th ed. London: Knapton, 1749.

Butler, Joseph. *The Analogy of Religion, Natural and Revealed, to the Constitution and Course of Nature.* New York: Ungar paperback, 1961; 1st ed., 1736.

Paley, William. *A View of the Evidences of Christianity* (Works, vols. 1–2). London: Longmans, Ltd., 1830; 1st ed., 1794.

———. *Natural Theology* (Works, vol. 4). London: Longmans, Ltd., 1830; 1st ed., 1802.

Nineteenth-Century Catholic

Chateaubriand, François René de. *The Genius of Christianity,* translated by Charles I. White. 2d ed., rev. Baltimore: J. Murphy, 1856.

Lamennais, Félicité de. *Essai sur l'indifférence en matière de religion.* 4 vols. Paris, 1817–23; partially translated by Lord Stanley of Alderley as *Essay on Indifference in Matters of Religion,* London, 1895.

Perrone, Giovanni. *De vera religione adversus incredulos et heterodoxos* (Praelectiones dogmaticae, vol. 1). Rome: Propaganda Fide, 1835.

Drey, Johann Sebastian von. *Die Apologetik als wissenschaftliche Nachweisung der Göttlichkeit des Christentums.* 3 vols. Mainz: Kupferberg, 1843–47.

Balmes, Jaime. *Protestantism and Catholicity Compared in Their Effects on the Civilization of Europe,* translated by C. J. Hanford and R. Kershaw. 2d ed. Baltimore: J. Murphy, 1851.

Dechamps, Victor. *Entretiens sur la démonstration catholique de la révélation chrétienne.* 2d ed. Tournai, 1857.

Newman, John Henry. *Apologia pro vita sua.* London: Longmans, Ltd., 1864.

Newman, John Henry. *An Essay in Aid of a Grammar of Assent.* London: Burns, Oates, 1870.

Broglie, Paul de. *Problèmes et conclusions de l'histoire des religions.* Paris: Putois-Cretté, 1885.

Hettinger, Franz. *Apologie des Christenthums.* 2 vols. in 5. 7th ed. Freiburg i.Br.: Herder & Co., 1895; parts translated by H. S. Bowden under titles *Natural Religion* and *Revealed Religion,* London: Burns, 1890 and 1895.

von Schanz, Paul. *A Christian Apology,* translated by Michael F. Glancey and Victor J. Schobel. 3 vols. New York and Cincinnati: Pustet, 1891–92.

Nineteenth-Century Protestant and Anglican

Schleiermacher, Friedrich. *On Religion: Speeches to Its Cultured Despisers,* translated by John Oman. New York: Harper Torchbooks, 1958; 1st German ed., 1799.

Sack, Karl Heinrich. *Christliche Apologetik.* 2d ed., rev. Hamburg: Perthes, 1841.

Kierkegaard, Søren. *Concluding Unscientific Postscript,* translated by David F. Swenson and Walter Lowrie. Princeton: University Press, 1941; 1st Danish ed., Copenhagen, 1846.

Luthardt, Ernest. *On the Fundamental Truths of Christianity,* translated by S. Taylor. 3d ed. Edinburgh: T. and T. Clark, 1873; 1st German ed., 1864.

Kaftan, Julius. *The Truth of the Christian Religion,* translated by George Ferries. 2 vols. Edinburgh: T. and T. Clark, 1894; 1st German ed., 1889.

Bruce, Alexander. *Apologetics; or, Christianity Defensively Stated.* 5th ed. New York: Scribner, 1899; 1st ed., 1892.

Twentieth-Century Catholic

Blondel, Maurice. *The Letter on Apologetics; History and Dogma,* translated by A. Dru and I. Trethowan. New York: Holt, Rinehart and Winston, 1964.

Schell, Herman. *Apologie des Christentums.* 2 vols. Paderborn: Schöningh, 1901, 1905.

Felder, Hilarin. *Christ and the Critics,* translated by John L. Stoddard. 2 vols. London: Burns, Oates and Washbourne, 1924.

Gardeil, Ambroise. *La Crédibilité et l'apologétique.* 2d. ed., rev. Paris: Gabalda, 1912.

Garrigou-Lagrange, Réginald. *De revelatione per ecclesiam catholicam proposita.* 4th ed. Rome: F. Ferrari, 1945; 1st ed., 2 vols., Rome, 1918.

Chesterton, Gilbert Keith. *The Everlasting Man.* New York: Dodd, 1925.

Grandmaison, Léonce de. *Jesus Christ: His Person, His Message, His*

Credentials, translated by Dom Basil Whelan (vols. 1–2) and Douglas Carter (vol. 3). 3 vols. New York: Sheed & Ward, 1935–37.

Adam, Karl. *The Spirit of Catholicism*, translated by Justin McCann. New York: Macmillan, 1929.

Gilson, Étienne. *The Spirit of Mediaeval Philosophy*, translated by A. H. C. Downes. New York: Scribner, 1935.

Levie, Jean. *Sous les yeux de l'incroyant* (Museum Lessianum: Section théologique, vol. 40). 2d ed. Paris: Desclée, 1946.

Guitton, Jean. *The Problem of Jesus: A Free-Thinker's Diary*, translated by A. Gordon Smith. New York: Kenedy, 1955.

Author's abridgement of *Le Problème de Jésus et les fondements du témoignage chrétien* (1959) and *Le Problème de Jésus II: Divinité et résurrection* (1953).

Teilhard de Chardin, Pierre. *The Phenomenon of Man*, translated by Bernard Wall. New York: Harper, 1959.

Rahner, Karl. *Hearers of the Word*, translated by Michael Richards. New York: Herder & Herder, 1969.

Twentieth-Century Protestant and Anglican

Gore, Charles. *The Reconstruction of Belief*. 3 vols. in 1. New York: Scribner, 1926.

Hoskyns, Edwyn, and Davey, Noel. *The Riddle of the New Testament*. London: Faber and Faber paperback reprint, 1958.

Niebuhr, Reinhold. *Faith and History*. New York: Scribner, 1949.

Heim, Karl. *Christian Faith and Natural Science*, translated by N. H. Smith. New York: Harper, 1953.

Richardson, Alan. *Christian Apologetics*. London: S.C.M., 1947.

————. *History Sacred and Profane*. Philadelphia: Westminster Press, 1964.

HISTORICAL STUDIES OF APOLOGETICS

Within each category, works are arranged alphabetically.

General Surveys

Books

Aubert, Roger. *Le Problème de l'acte de foi*. 2d ed. Louvain: Warny, 1950.
Particularly valuable for treatment of Catholic controversies concerning faith and reason in the 19th and early 20th centuries.

Copleston, Frederick. *A History of Philosophy*. 8 vols. Westminster, Md.: Newman Press, 1946–66.
Perhaps the most useful of the histories of philosophy for material touching on apologetics.

Cristiani, Leon. *Why We Believe: The Meaning and Use of Apologetics*, translated by Dom Mark Pontifex (Twentieth Century Encyclopedia of Catholicism, vol. 106). New York: Hawthorn, 1959.

A brief, popular work useful for its sketches of Augustine, Pascal, Bossuet, Paul de Broglie, and Teilhard de Chardin.

Martin, Jules. *L'apologétique traditionnelle*, 3 vols. Paris: Lethielleux, 1905–06.

Vol. 1, The First Five Centuries; vol. 2, Seventh through Sixteenth Centuries; vol. 3, Seventeenth-Century Catholic Apologists. These three small volumes are intended to back up Blondel's thesis that apologetics must build on subjective and supernatural factors.

Murphy, John L. *With the Eyes of Faith*. Milwaukee: Bruce Pub., 1966.

Ramm, Bernard. *Varieties of Christian Apologetics*. Grand Rapids: Baker Book House, 1962.

A textbook outlining the approaches of nine representative Christian apologists. Orientation is Conservative Evangelical.

Reid, John K. S. *Christian Apologetics*. London: Hodder & Stoughton, 1969.

A well-written but somewhat cursory treatment of apologetics from the beginnings to the most recent days; gives little attention to Catholics since the Reformation.

Thils, Gustave. *Les Notes de l'église dans l'apologétique catholique depuis la réforme*. Gembloux: Duculot, 1937.

An in-depth study of the argument for Catholicism based on the four notes of the Church; detailed and critical.

Webb, Clement D. J. *Studies in the History of Natural Theology*. Oxford: Clarendon, 1915.

In the latter part, deals with Anselm, Abelard, Aquinas, Raymond of Sebonde, Pietro Pomponazzi, and Lord Herbert of Cherbury.

Werner, Karl. *Geschichte der apologetischen und polemischen Litteratur der christlichen Theologie*. 5 vols. Schaffhausen: Hurter, 1861–67.

A voluminous history of religious controversies, especially between the Catholic Church and other Christian groups. Vol. 5 is devoted to apologetics since the seventeenth century.

Williams, A. Lukyn. *Adversus Judaeos: A Bird's Eye View of Christian 'Apologiae' until the Renaissance*. Cambridge, Eng.: University Press, 1935.

Valuable summaries and background concerning anti-Jewish polemics through the centuries; has been criticized for some omissions and for lack of synthesis.

Zöckler, Otto. *Geschichte der Apologie des Christentums*. Gütersloh: Bertelsmann, 1907.

The final work of a distinguished Lutheran confessional theologian in the tradition of Luthardt. This very thorough and iudicious history is still the best complete survey.

Articles

Aigrain, René. 'Histoire de l'apologétique.' In *Apologétique*, edited by M. Brillant and M. Nédoncelle, pp. 950–1029, 1st ed. Paris: Bloud et Gay, 1937.

Probably the best complete survey of article length. In the 2d ed. (1948) this chapter was drastically abbreviated.

Crehan, Joseph H. 'Apologetics.' *A Catholic Dictionary of Theology*, 1 (1962): 113–122.

Gardeil, Ambroise. 'Crédibilité.' *Dictionnaire de théologie catholique* 3.2 (1908): 2201–2310.

A very complete historical survey; the historical background for Gardeil's book, *La Crédibilité et l'apologétique*.

Le Bachelet, Xavier M. 'Apologétique.' *Dictionnaire apologétique de la foi catholique* 1 (1911): 189–251.

Maisonneuve, L. 'Apologétique.' *Dictionnaire de théologie catholique* 1.2 (1903): 1511–80.

New Testament Studies

Bruce, Alexander B. *The Epistle to the Hebrews: The First Apology for Christianity*. Edinburgh: T. and T. Clark, 1899.

A representative work of a major apologist who was also an exegete.

Bruce, Frederick F. *The Apostolic Defence of the Gospel: Christian Apologetic in the New Testament*. London: Inter-Varsity Fellowship, 1959.

Five lectures very helpful for lining up the apologetical motifs in the NT. Reprinted paperback 1961, 1967.

Conzelmann, Hans. *The Theology of St. Luke*, translated by Geoffrey Buswell. London: Faber and Faber, 1960.

An important study by a creative theologian of the post-Bultmann school.

Dodd, Charles H. *The Apostolic Preaching and Its Developments*. 2d. ed., rev. London: Hodder & Stoughton, 1944.

Three lectures with an appendix on history and eschatology.

Gärtner, Bertil. *The Areopagus Speech and Natural Revelation* (Acta seminarii neotestementici upsaliensis, vol. 21). Uppsala: Gleerup, 1955.

Harris, J. Rendel. *Testimonies*. 2 vols. Cambridge, Eng.: University Press, 1916–20.

Argues for the existence of a *Testimony Book* earlier in date than some of the earliest books of the NT.

Lindars, Barnabas. *New Testament Apologetic: The Doctrinal Significance of the Old Testament Quotations*. Philadelphia: Westminster Press, 1961.

A very careful study of the apologetical use of OT quotations by early Christians in controversy with Jews.

Moule, C. F. D. *The Birth of the New Testament* (Black's New Testament Commentaries, vol. 1). New York: Harper, 1962.

Scott, Ernest F. *The Apologetic of the New Testament*. New York: Putnam, 1907.

Argues that NT apologetic rests upon a 'purely ethical and spiritual' conception of the 'absolute worth of the personality of Jesus.'

Patristic Period

Altaner, Berthold. *Patrology*, translated by Hilda Graef. New York: Herder & Herder, 1960.

For more recent scholarship consult the German ed. of Altaner's *Patrologie*, revised by Alfred Stuiber. Freiburg i.Br.: Herder & Co., 1966.

Andresen, Carl, *Logos und Nomos: Die Polemik des Kelsos wider das Christentum* (Arbeiten zur Kirchengeschichte, vol 30). Berlin: W. de Gruyter, 1955.

The most scholarly treatment of the points at issue between Celsus and Origen.

Bardy, Gustav. 'Apologetik.' *Reallexikon für Antike und Christentum* 1 (1950): 533–545.

Brief but scholarly treatment of Jewish and early Christian apologetics and of pagan critiques of popular religion.

Canivet, Pierre. *Histoire d'une entreprise apologétique au Ve siècle*. 2 vols. Paris: Bloud et Gay, 1957.

An excellent study of Theodoret of Cyrrhus.

Chadwick, Henry. *Early Christian Thought and the Classical Tradition*. New York: Oxford University Press, 1966.

Reflections on Justin, Clement, and Origen by an eminent patrologist.

Fridrichsen, Anton. *Le Problème du miracle dans le christianisme primitif*. Paris and Strasbourg: Istra, 1925.

A form-critical study on the role of miracles in the aplogetics of the NT and the earliest period of the Church.

Geffcken, Johannes. *Zwei griechische Apologeten*. Leipzig: B. G. Teubner, 1907.

An old but still useful study dealing primarily with Aristides and Athenagoras.

Grant, Robert M. *Miracle and Natural Law in Graeco-Roman and Early Christian Thought*. Amsterdam: North-Holland Pub. Co., 1952.

Laurin, Joseph-Rheal. *Orientations maîtresses des apologistes chrétiens de 270 à 361* (Analecta gregoriana, vol. 61). Rome: Univ. Gregoriana, 1954.

Lortz, Joseph. *Tertullian als Apologet* (Münsterische Beiträge zur Theologie 9–10). 2 vols. Münster: Aschendorff, 1927–28.

Patrick, John. *The Apology of Origen in Reply to Celsus*. Edinburgh: W. Blackwood, 1892.

Pellegrino, Michele. *Studi su l'antica apologetica*. Rome: Ed. di Storia e Letteratura, 1947.

Puech, Aimé. *Les Apologistes grecs du 2e siècle de notre ère*. Paris: Hachette, 1912.

Quasten, Johannes. *Patrology*. Westminster: Newman Press, 1950–.

Stoszko, Ignace. *L'apologétique de S. Augustin*. Strasbourg: Université de Strasbourg, 1932.

Wolfson, Harry A. *Philo: Foundations of Religious Philosophy in Judaism, Christianity, and Islam*. Cambridge, Mass.: Belknap Press of Harvard University Press, 1961.

Middle Ages (through Fifteenth Century)

Aubert, Roger. 'Le Caractère raisonnable de l'acte de foi d'après les théologiens de la fin du XIIIe siècle.' *Revue d'histoire ecclésiastique* 39 (1943): 22–99.

Baron, Salo W. *A Social and Religious History of the Jews*. 12 vols. 2d ed., rev. New York: Columbia University Press, 1952–67.

Barth, Karl. *Anselm: Fides Quaerens Intellectum*, translated by Ian W. Robertson. Richmond: John Knox, 1960.
   An interesting interpretation of Anselm by a creative theologian.

Chenu, Marie-Dominique. *Toward Understanding St. Thomas*, translated by A. M. Landry and D. Hughes. Chicago: Regnery, 1964.

Finkenzeller, Josef. *Offenbarung und Theologie nach der Lehre des Johannes Duns Skotus* (Beiträge zur Geschichte der Philosophie des Mittelalters, Bd. 38, Heft 5). Münster: Aschendorff, 1961.

Gilson, Étienne. *History of Christian Philosophy in the Middle Ages*. New York: Random House, 1955.
   A comprehensive work by a leading expert.

———. *Reason and Revelation in the Middle Ages*. New York: Scribner, 1938.

Grandmaison, Léonce de. 'Sur l'apologétique de s. Thomas.' *Nouvelle revue théologique* 39 (1907): 65–74; 121–130.

Kristeller, Paul O. *The Philosophy of Marsilio Ficino*. New York: Columbia University Press, 1943.

Kritzeck, James. *Peter the Venerable and Islam*. Princeton: University Press, 1964.
   Informative on Christian apologetic to Islam through the 12th century.

Lang, Albert. *Die Entfaltung des apologetischen Problems in der Scholastik des Mittelalters*. Freiburg i.Br.: Herder, 1962.
   Concentrates on the relations between faith and reason in the assent of faith.

———. *Die Wege der Glaubensbegründung bei den Scholastikern des 14. Jarhhunderts* (Beiträge zur Geschichte der Philosophie des Mittelalters, Bd. 30, Heft 1–2). Münster: Aschendorff, 1930.

Marcel, Raymond, 'Les Perspectives de l'apologétique de Lorenzo Valla
à Savonarole.' *Courants religieux et humanisme à la fin du XVᵉ et au
début du XVIᵉ siècle.* Paris: Presses universitaires de France, 1959.
Colloque de Strasbourg, 9–11, mai, 1957.

Van Hove, Aloïs. *La Doctrine du miracle chez s. Thomas* (Universitas
Catholica Lovaniensis: dissertationes ad gradum magistri in facultate
theologica, Series 2, tomus 19).
   Examines St. Thomas against the background of the earlier scholastic
tradition.

Sixteenth through Eighteenth Centuries

Allison, Henry E. *Lessing and the Enlightenment: His Philosophy and Its
Relation to Eighteenth Century Thought.* Ann Arbor: University of
Michigan Press, 1966.

Dowey, Edward A., Jr. *The Knowledge of God in Calvin's Theology.* New
York: Columbia University Press, 1952.

Gerrish, Brian A. *Grace and Reason: A Study in the Theology of Luther.*
Oxford: Clarendon Press, 1962.

Hazard, Paul. *European Thought in the Eighteenth Century,* translated by
J. Lewis May. London: Hollis and Carter, 1954.

Hubert, Sister Marie Louise. *Pascal's Unfinished Apology: A Study of
His Plan.* New Haven: Yale University Press, 1952.

Julien-Eymard d'Angers. *Pascal et ses précurseurs.* Paris: Nouvelles
éditions latines, 1954.

Lacombe, Roger E. *L'apologétique de Pascal: étude critique.* Paris:
Presses universitaires de France, 1958.

Lohse, Bernhard. *Ratio und Fides: Eine Untersuchung über die Ratio in der
Theologie Luthers.* Göttingen: Vanderhoeck & Ruprecht, 1958.

McAdoo, Henry R. *The Spirit of Anglicanism: A Survey of Anglican
Theological Method in the Seventeenth Century.* New York: Scribner,
1965.

McDonald, Hugh D. *Ideas of Revelation: An Historical Study, A.D. 1700
to A.D. 1860.* London: Macmillan, 1959.
   A somewhat disorderly treatment with much good information on
lesser-known English theologians of the period.

McGiffert, Arthur C. *Protestant Thought before Kant.* New York: Scribner,
1931.
   From a Liberal point of view, unfavorable to Orthodoxy.

Meffert, Franz. *Der heilige Alfons von Liguori der Kirchenlehrer und
Apologet des XVIII. Jahrhunderts.* Mainz: Kirchheim, 1901.

Monod, Albert, *De Pascal à Chateaubriand: Les défenseurs français du
christianisme de 1670 à 1802.* Paris: Alcan, 1916.
   Very complete, sometimes severe in criticisms.

Mossner, Ernest. *Bishop Butler and the Age of Reason.* New York: Macmillan, 1936.

Treats of Butler's predecessors and successors, as well as of Butler and his times.

Palmer, Robert R. *Catholics and Unbelievers in Eighteenth Century France.* Princeton: University Press, 1939.

Popkin, Richard H. *The History of Scepticism from Erasmus to Descartes.* Assen, The Netherlands: Van Gorcum and Co., 1960.
A very interesting book on some lesser-known figures.

Vizmanos, F. de B. 'La apologetica de los escolasticos postridentinos.' *Estudios eclesiasticos* 13 (1934): 418–446.
Concise and richly informative.

Willey, Basil. *The Seventeenth Century Background.* New York: Columbia University Press, 1942.
Splendidly written essays, especially good on early Deism.

Nineteenth Century

At, Jean Antoine. *Les Apologistes françaises au XIXe siècle.* Paris: Bloud & Barral, 1898.

Barth, J. Robert. *Coleridge and Christian Doctrine.* Cambridge, Mass.: Harvard University Press, 1969.

Barth, Karl. *Protestant Thought: From Rousseau to Ritschl,* translated by Brian Cozens and H. H. Hartwell. New York: Harper and Bros., 1959.

Becqué, Maurice. *L'apologétique du Cardinal Dechamps.* Bruges: Desclée de Brouwer, 1949.

Bouyer, Louis. *Newman: His Life and Spirituality,* translated by J. Lewis May. New York: Meridian, 1960.

Diamond, Malcolm, L. 'Kierkegaard and Apologetics.' *Journal of Religion* 44 (1964): 122–132.

Folghera, Jean-Dominique. *L'Apologétique de Lacordaire.* Paris: Bloud, 1905.
This brochure is an expansion of an article in *Revue thomiste* 12 (1904): 77–89.

Gorman, Robert. *Catholic Apologetical Literature in the United States (1784–1858).* Washington, D.C.: The Catholic University of America Press, 1939.

Gunderson, Borghild. *Cardinal Newman on Apologetics.* Oslo: Dybwad, 1952.

Hocedez, Edgar. *Histoire de la théologie au XIXe siècle.* 3 vols. Paris: Desclée de Brouwer, 1948 (vol. 1), 1952 (vol. 2), 1947 (vol. 3).
Richly informative regarding Catholic publications, with balanced criticisms.

Horton, Walter M. *The Philosophy of the Abbé Bautain.* New York: New York University Press, 1926.
Good view of Catholic apologetical currents in France and Germany in the first half of the 19th century.

Le Guillou, Louis. *L'Évolution de la pensée religieuse de Félicité Lamennais.* Paris: Colin, 1966.
　A recent and thorough investigation.

McDonald, Hugh D. *Theories of Revelation: An Historical Study, 1860–1960.* London: Allen and Unwin, 1963.

Macran, Frederick W. *English Apologetical Theology.* London: Hodder & Stoughton, 1905.

Malone, George K. 'The True Church: A Study in the Apologetics of Orestes A. Brownson.' Dissertation, Mundelein, Ill.: St. Mary of the Lake Seminary, 1957.

Poupard, Paul. *L'Abbé Louis Bautain.* Tournai: Desclée, 1961.

Vidler, Alec R. *Prophecy and Papacy: A Study of Lamennais.* London: S.C.M., 1954; New York: Scribner, 1954.

Walgrave, J. M. *Newman the Theologian,* translated by A. V. Littledale. New York: Sheed & Ward, 1960.

Twentieth Century

Anderson, Hugh. *Jesus and Christian Origins: A Commentary on Modern Viewpoints.* New York: Oxford University Press, 1964.
　An informative study of the Bultmannians, post-Bultmannians, and others, mostly German and British.

Armagnac, Chrétien d'. 'La Pensée de Père Teilhard de Chardin comme apologétique moderne.' *Nouvelle revue théologique* 84 (1962): 598–621.

Bouillard, Henri. *Blondel et le christianisme.* Paris: Editions du Seuil, 1961; translated by James M. Somerville as *Blondel and Christianity,* Washington, D.C.: Corpus Books, 1970.
　A careful study by an able fundamental theologian.

Cunningham, Richard B. *C. S. Lewis: Defender of the Faith.* Philadelphia: Westminster Press, 1967.

Dulles, Avery. *Apologetics and the Biblical Christ.* Westminster, Md.: Newman Press, 1963.

Holstein, Henri. 'Le Traité apologétique de Christo legato.' *Bulletin du Comité des Etudes* no. 35 (October–December 1961).

Kavanaugh, James J. *The Struggle of the Unbeliever.* New York: Trident, 1968.
　A Catholic University of America dissertation on the apologetics of Max Scheler, Maurice Blondel, and John Henry Newman.

Lubac, Henri de. *Teilhard de Chardin: The Man and His Meaning,* translated by René Hague. New York: Hawthorn, 1960.

Macquarrie, John. *Twentieth Century Religious Thought: The Frontiers of Philosophy and Theology, 1900–60.* New York: Harper & Row, 1963.

Macintosh, Douglas C. *The Problem of Religious Knowledge.* New York: Harper, 1940.
　A thorough study of modern Protestant philosophers of religion by a distinguished Liberal theologian.

Page, Robert J. *New Directions in Anglican Theology: A Survey from Temple to Robinson.* New York: Seabury, 1965.

Ramsey, Arthur Michael. *An Era in Anglican Theology: From Gore to Temple.* New York: Scribner, 1960.

Roberts, Tom A. *History and Christian Apologetic.* London: S.P.C.K., 1960.

Criticizes Burkitt, Dodd, and Farrar on the basis of the theory that historical method is 'essentially a secular tool' and is useless to validate affirmations of faith.

Rodé, François. *Le Miracle dans la controverse moderniste.* Paris: Beauchesne, 1965.

Saint-Jean, Raymond. *L'Apologétique philosophique: Blondel 1893–1913.* Paris: Aubier, 1966.

Sperry, Willard L. *'Yes, But'—The Bankruptcy of Apologetics.* New York: Harper, 1931.

Valensin, Auguste, and Valensin, Albert. 'Immanence (méthode d').' *Dictionnaire apologétique de la foi catholique* 2 (1911): 579–612.

The section entitled 'Examen' was dropped in later printings to make room for a more hostile evaluation by Joseph de Tonquédec.

Vidler, Alec R. *Twentieth Century Defenders of the Faith.* London: S.C.M., 1965.

Subject Index

291

Name Index